GESTALT
THERAPY
NOW

GESTALT THERAPY NOW

THEORY
TECHNIQUES
APPLICATIONS

Edited by JOEN FAGAN and IRMA LEE SHEPHERD

SCIENCE AND BEHAVIOR BOOKS, INC.
Palo Alto, California

To Fritz . . .

a profound and disturbing teacher.

Second printing, May 1970

Library of Congress Card Number 69-20468
Standard Book Number 0-8314-0023-4

CONTENTS

PREFACE

This collection grew from the awareness of the editors of the increased interest in Gestalt therapy among psychotherapists throughout the country. The most extensive influence has been the lectures and demonstrations by Dr. Frederick Perls, Dr. Laura Perls, Dr. James Simkin, and others, presented before national and regional meetings of psychiatrists, psychologists, and psychotherapists. Further intensive involvement came from Gestalt workshops and training institutes held regularly at Esalen Institute at Big Sur, California; at the Gestalt Therapy Institutes in Los Angeles, New York, and Cleveland; and workshops in other cities. About a thousand therapists participated in these workshops, and more than two hundred therapists across the country identify themselves as being Gestalt or Gestalt-oriented.[1] The *Directory* of the American Academy of Psychotherapists lists Gestalt therapy as the sixth most common affiliation, with more members than better known or more extensively published schools such as Jungian or Rational-Emotive. Despite the increasing involvement of psychotherapists who find the concepts and techniques of Gestalt therapy exciting, intriguing, and effective, little written material is available, the major exceptions being Dr. Perls's two early and still basic books, *Ego, Hunger and Aggression,* (1949, 1969) and *Gestalt Therapy* (1951).

There are several reasons for the scarcity of published material on Gestalt therapy. Dr. Perls, who, with the assistance of his wife Laura, is responsible for the beginning and early development of Gestalt therapy, initially worked in relative professional isolation in South Africa and has shown little interest in creating a "school" of therapy as such. Also, Gestalt therapy, with its emphasis on the here and now, the immediacy of experience, and nonverbal expressiveness, and its avoidance of "aboutisms" or overuse of the mental "computer," tends to correct our tendencies toward wordiness and abstractions rather than to encourage the manipulation of words necessary for the writing of books. Thus, most Gestalt therapists tend to be doers rather than sayers.

---

[1] *Directory of Gestalt Therapists.* Beverly Hills, Calif.: Robert Resnick, 1969.

Finally, in Gestalt therapy, much importance is attached to tone of voice, posture, gestures, facial expression, etc., with much of the import and excitement coming from work with changes in these nonverbal communications. Transcribing these into type is difficult and loses much of the meaning and immediacy. Fortunately the increasing availability of Gestalt films and tapes helps in making the nonverbal communications more accessible.

In spite of the above problems, the need for available material on Gestalt therapy is marked. The present collection attempts to bring Dr. Perls's work into historical focus and to present his most recent thinking. A wide (though not exhaustive) sampling of techniques and applications from a number of therapists and teachers is offered.

The book is intended for the Gestalt therapist; for the psychotherapist of some other orientation who wishes to explore new ideas that may be stimulating and applicable in his own practice; for the therapist-in-training who wishes to become acquainted with recent developments in therapy; and for the sophisticated layman who is interested in ways of feeling, relating, and behaving other than those offered by our work-ridden, past-oriented, computer-programmed and game-laden modern life. This book will, of course, not give any complete or final answers, nor is it any replacement for actual training in or experience with Gestalt techniques. However, it should serve at least to point toward some of the exciting developments occurring in psychotherapy, and to suggest the increased capacity for living that they offer.

PART I

THEORY OF GESTALT THERAPY

Explicit and implicit in the work of any psychotherapist with patients is an underlying theory of personality. The therapist brings to the treatment situation ideas about personality—especially what constitutes good, healthy, satisfying, and valued behavior, and what is inadequate, maladaptive, problem-causing, or self-defeating—as well as ideas about what kinds of experiences and behaviors produce or continue to keep the negatively valued aspects ascendant. The therapist will then utilize procedures or techniques derived from his theory of therapy in order to effect change and to move the person toward more adequate functioning.

Historically, theories of personality have focused on the negative aspects of personality. In part this has been due to the use of the "medical model," which labeled problems in living as "sick" or "pathological"— like illnesses. But medicine has never been interested in health, which is considered only the absence of illness. One of the many costs of using the medical analogy is that we focus mainly on that which we would rather not see. (For example, the early textbooks of personality adjustment devoted most of their emphasis to defense mechanisms and emotional disorders.)

With the development of the "third force" in psychology, which concerns itself with man in his humanness rather than as defined in psychoanalytic or behavioristic terms, and with the beginning of models that view problems in living as difficulties in relating and communicating, there has been a marked shift in interest toward positive aspects of personality and living. Freud's famous statement, "Much has been accomplished if we can change neurotic misery into common unhappiness," is no longer sufficient for most therapists or for the persons requesting their help. Now we use words such as enhancement, intimacy, actualization, creativity, ecstasy, and transcendence to describe what we wish for ourselves and others. The theories of Maslow, Rogers, Jourard, Berne, and others offer as the alternative to misery, not unhappiness, but joy.

Gestalt therapy is strongly allied with this developing position, emphasizing positive directions and goals of living, and using techniques directly and immediately designed to produce them. The implicit message of Gestalt theory as translated into treatment is that there are values in living that persons know from their own experiences or from their observations of others to be valuable and enhancing: spontaneity, sensory awareness, freedom of movement, emotional responsiveness and espressiveness, enjoyment, ease, flexibility in relating, direct contact and emotional closeness with others, intimacy, competency, immediacy and presence, self-support, and creativity. The patient who comes for help, seeking to relate more adequately with other people and to be able to express his feelings more directly is instructed to express what he is feeling at that moment to another person. The ways in which he stops, blocks, and frustrates himself quickly become apparent, and he can then be assisted in exploring and experiencing the blockings and encouraged to attempt other ways of expressing himself and of relating.

Thus the general approach of Gestalt theory and therapy requires the patient to specify the changes in himself that he desires, assists him in increasing his awareness of how he defeats himself, and aids him in experimenting and changing. Blocks in awareness and behavior emerge in the same way that they manifest themselves in the person's life; his increased awareness of his avoidances and his relief as he becomes able to expand his experience and behavior are felt immediately in increases in capacity for living.

Even though a major contribution of Gestalt therapy has been the close relationship between theory and treatment, this book will initially effect a degree of separation, describing the historical ancestry of Gestalt therapy and presenting theoretical developments in order to provide a basis or "ground" from which techniques and applications can emerge.

The basic principles of Gestalt therapy are largely the work of one man, Frederick S. Perls. After his medical training, Perls was attracted to psychoanalysis; he underwent training analysis and received analytic supervision from several of the well-known "pioneers," including Wilhelm Reich. His education and early professional experiences brought him in contact with Kurt Goldstein and with the ideas of Gestalt psychology and existentialism. He was further influenced by exposure to the brutalizing conditions of World War I, the rejection by other psychoanalysts of his early efforts at contributing to psychoanalytic theory because he challenged the accepted tenets of libido theory, his emigration from Nazi Germany to South Africa, his need there as an army psychiatrist to develop more efficient modes of treatment, and the influences and contributions of his wife, Laura. (Dr. Perls's training and experiences are described in more detail in Esalen Recordings Tape S215-1 and AAP Tape 31 in his forthcoming autobiography, all listed in the Appendix of this book.) The interrelationship of Perls's ideas as developed from many of these sources will be described in more detail in several of the following chapters.

"Gestalt Therapy and Gestalt Psychology"(Wallen) identifies some of the ideas and concepts of Gestalt psychology that were adopted by Perls and serve as a cornerstone in his thinking. Gestalt psychology originated as a theory of perception that included the interrelationships between the form of the object and the processes of the perceiver. It was, in part, a reaction to earlier atomistic approaches that attempted to study perception and mental processes by reducing them to elements or mental contents. In contrast, Gestalt thinking emphasized "leaps" of insight, closure, figure-and-ground characteristics, fluidity of perceptual processes, and the perceiver as an active participant in his perceptions rather than a passive recipient of the qualities of form. Wallen describes the normal process of Gestalt formation and destruction, and the processes that interfere with closure or change. He indicates the contributions that Gestalt therapy has made to the theories of Gestalt psychology by extending its concepts to include self-perception, motivation, and the motoric aspects of behavior. Finally, Wallen demonstrates the relevance of Gestalt theory to the operations of the Gestalt therapist.

"Four Lectures" (Perls), which follow, constitute the most extensive statement of Perls's thinking about a number of issues since his basic writings in *Ego, Hunger and Aggression* and *Gestalt Therapy*. His first lecture begins by noting the split in psychology between the phenomenological approach, with its emphasis on sensation, perception, thinking, and awareness, that is, private behavior, and the behavioristic approach that focuses on observable or public behavior. He then describes four philosophical approaches to the study of behavior: the scientific, which talks *about* behavior with a lack of involvement; the religious and philosophical positions, which emphasize how behavior *should be*—with dissatisfactions; the existential, which focuses on what *is*, but still needs a causal framework; and the Gestalt, which attempts to discover the *how* and *now* of behavior. Freud's contributions to Gestalt therapy include his idea of the unconscious, which Perls translates as describing those aspects of behavior that are unavailable or potential rather than actual, and the concept of thinking as trial work or rehearsing, leading to the Gestalt therapy formulation of anxiety as stage fright.

In contrast to psychoanalysis, Gestalt therapy emphasizes the here and now, with the awareness of experience and varying behaviors. Many people, especially neurotics, avoid experiencing in awareness their self-critical "computing," projecting, or adapting of a variety of other procedures to maintain their usual behaviors. The usual, or status quo, involves holding onto past behavior and roles, or attempting to obtain environmental support by manipulation rather than utilizing self-support. Only by directly experiencing boredom or fear in the present will we find what we attempt to avoid and begin to utilize more of our potentiality.

Perls's second lecture is largely concerned with the five layers of neurosis. Many people spend much of their time on the first, or *phony*, layer, where we play games, live roles, try to be what we are not, and in the process create voids and disown much of ourselves. We constantly harass ourselves with what Perls calls the "top-dog/under-dog" game where part of ourselves attempts to lecture, urge, and threaten the other part into "good" behavior. The second neurotic layer he calls the *phobic* layer. As we become aware of phony behaviors and manipulations, we begin to get in touch with the fears that maintain them; we experience the wish to avoid new behavior or have fantasies about what the consequences might be if we behaved in a genuine way. The third layer is the *impasse*, where we are caught, not knowing what to do or where to move. We experience the loss of environmental support but do not have the support of belief in our own resources. The fourth stage is the *implosive*, where we may with grief, despair, or self-loathing come to a fuller realization of how we have limited and constricted ourselves; or with fear and doubt we may begin to experiment with new behavior. Following this, the fifth layer, or *explosive*, emerges as the previously unused energies are freed in an impactful way.

Lecture III describes the neurotic as holding onto his guilt and resentment toward his parents, who were not exactly what he needed and whom he can continue to blame for his problems instead of becoming self-supporting in developing his own resources. One of the most effective ways of finding what parts of the person are disowned or projected is by exploring his dreams. Gestalt therapy approaches dreams by having the person play all parts of the dream, both persons and objects, and then helping him to assimilate what has been projected. The person is also instructed to examine his dream for avoidances.

Lecture IV discusses exercises that can be used for self-growth. By following procedures of meditation, by listening to ourselves, by remaining with boredom, unpleasantness, or frustration, we may be able to resolve impasses and contribute to our own development. One technique is to fantasy the presence of a therapist who is giving us help or directions. Perls also makes several suggestions for therapists, including taking their own boredom seriously and withdrawing into fantasy instead of forcing attentiveness.

The lectures are followed by four papers which discuss more fully the theoretical aspects of Gestalt therapy. Kepner and Brien attempt to reconcile the phenomenological and behavioristic positions, keeping the strengths of each. Behaviorism, by dealing with observable events, can more easily experiment with, measure, and demonstrate change. Phenomenology, with its emphasis on internal experience, includes much of what is warm, personal, important, and rich in personality. However, the internal is private and difficult to communicate. Gestalt techniques help to unite these positions, both by bringing certain behaviors into awareness and by changing internal processes and fantasies into overt behavior.

"Present-centeredness in Gestalt Therapy" (Naranjo) undertakes an extensive exploration of the meaning of *now* in Gestalt theory and practice. Naranjo summarizes the underlying principles of Gestalt therapy and condenses them into three general processes: living in the present, awareness, and responsibility. In focusing on the implications of living in the present, he turns first to the Gestalt techniques of translating fantasies and memories into the present and of experimenting with the awareness continuum. He parallels the patient's attempt to focus and report on his present awarenesses with the Eastern process of meditation; this attempt is shared with the therapist whose presence sharpens awareness, enhances attention and meaning, adds interpersonal content, and points up difficulties. The therapist is also able to monitor errors and wanderings of attention. The Gestalt emphasis on present-centeredness is also a prescription for the good life. Many therapy techniques, such as expressing aggression and being honest, can be applied only with caution to living in the broader community. However, the prescription to live in the present is applicable to living in general, resulting in a humanistic hedonism in which an awareness of transitoriness and death sharpens the experience of living. Presentness is shown as an ideal, a sign of optimal living, akin to that described by Oriental sages, Western philosophers, and poets. It represents an acceptance of one's experiences, of the goodness of the world, and of the impossibility of living other than in the here and now.

"Sensory Functioning in Psychotherapy" (Polster) emphasizes the union or conjunction between sensory and motor functioning, or awareness and expression. Experiences may be described as *cumulative*, that is, as a total or unified event, or as *ingredient*, in which one aspect of an event is focused on. Often, when the ingredient experiences are explored by a process of analysis and resynthesis, the cumulative experience may be heightened. To reexperience and recover sensation requires effort and concentration. Polster describes ways of identifying and activating sensation and relevance of these procedures to therapy.

"The Paradoxical Theory of Change" (Beisser) deals with the finding in Gestalt therapy that change occurs when one becomes what he is, not when he tries to become what he is not. It is by not struggling against one's resistance and wish to be something else, and by recognizing oneself to be as one is, that the underlying need or wish may be recognized, the Gestalt completed, and new needs and behaviors can emerge. Beisser notes that since society continues to change in an accelerating pattern, therapy cannot prepare man to deal with a static or constant world, hence the ability to produce change becomes increasingly important.

CHAPTER 1

GESTALT THERAPY AND GESTALT PSYCHOLOGY*

Richard Wallen

Gestalt therapy has been nourished from all the main lines of theoretical development that have branched from the original psychoanalytic movement. It is not oriented exclusively to Gestalt psychology. Although it has important roots there, it also has roots with the Freudian psychoanalytic movement, with Otto Rank, and with Wilhelm Reich. The concept that unifies these varied approaches, which gives a rationale to the techniques employed in Gestalt therapy, is the conception of the need-fulfillment pattern in the individual as a process of Gestalt formation and destruction. I shall talk about this first. Then I shall show the ways this process is interfered with and the implications of the interference for neurotic behavior and for therapeutic technique.

The academic Gestalt psychologist dealt largely with external figures, notably visual and auditory. Interestingly enough, the academic Gestalt psychologist never attempted to employ the various principles of gestalt formation (proximity, the law of good continuation, *pregnanz,* similarity, and so on) to organic perceptions, to the perception of one's own feelings, emotions, and bodily sensations. He never really managed to integrate the facts of motivation with the facts of perception. It is this additional importation into Gestalt psychology that Frederick Perls made. Thus we can now conceptualize the process by which the organism finds its satisfactions in the environment as essentially that of a gestalt formation, in which there are a number of subwholes—certain subsidiary formations. To the external perceptions that the Gestalt psychologists Wertheimer and Kohler studied, the Gestalt therapist adds the figural perception of the *Gestalten* that form in the body and in the relationship of the individual to the environment.

---

*Paper presented at the Ohio Psychological Association Meeting, 1957. It is reprinted here through the courtesy of the Gestalt Institute of Cleveland, which has distributed copies upon request.

Consider a person sitting alone reading. The book holds the center of his interest: All the rest of the room has become background; in fact his body also has become background. It is not even correct to say that he is conscious or aware of this particular reading process: he is just engaged, in contact with the ideas. Suppose that in the midst of this reading, he gets progressively thirstier. What happens is that the mouth and the inside of the mouth become figural and soon dominate the field. The book moves into the background, and the person feels something akin to "I am thirsty!" He becomes aware, in other words, of a change in himself that has implications for his relationship to the external environment. His need tends to organize both the perceptual qualities of his own experience and his motor behavior. He may have a visual image of a faucet or a glass of water or a can of beer in the icebox. He gets up, walks, satisfies the thirst, and comes back to the reading. Once more, the ideas become figural; thirst has been destroyed.

In this simple model we have the prototype of gestalt formation and destruction. The phenomenal world is organized by the needs of the individual. Needs energize behavior and organize it on the subjective-perceptual level and on the objective-motor level. The individual then carries out the necessary activities in order to satisfy the needs. After satisfaction, the mouth recedes into the background, the concern with the particular figure of water or beer disappears, and something new emerges. We have a hierarchy of needs continually developing, organizing the figures of experience, and disappearing. We describe this process in Gestalt therapy as progressive formation and destruction of perceptual and motor gestalts.

When this process is going well, when it is well integrated—when the *Gestalten* are what the academic psychologist would call firm, or strong, or well formed—certain kinds of conditions can be reported by the individual himself or can be observed by an outside observer. For one thing, figure and ground become sharply differentiated. There is no longer a cluttered field, but rather one thing that draws the individual's attention. His perceptual activity becomes selective as he becomes concerned with this particular thing. The motor behavior too becomes well organized, unified, coherent, and directed toward the satisfaction of this particular need. Similarly, the figures that the individual experiences are unitary, they cohere, and they dominate his phenomenal field.

The interesting thing about this experience from the standpoint of adjustment is that this process of gestalt formation and destruction can provide an autonomous criterion for adjustment. In other words it is immaterial whether the individual is "mature" or "immature" by some cultural standard, or whether he conforms to society or not. The important thing from the Gestalt viewpoint is that the integrated individual is a person in whom this process is going on constantly without interruption. New figures are continually being formed. When the needs are satisfied, these figures are destroyed and replaced by others, permitting the needs next highest in the dominance hierarchy to organize behavior and perceptual experience. This process is of considerable interest because it never stops, and the Gestalt therapist can determine how well the process is going at each moment in the work he does. In the therapeutic session, the therapist can see the individual experiencing certain needs, trying to fulfill them but failing because the process is interrupted somehow or is cluttered up. This is not something that you have to talk about in the past tense. The individual's typical methods of gestalt formation and destruction are immediately apparent in the therapeutic session.

The importance of this process for biological survival should be evident, for only as the individual is able to extract from the environment those things that he needs in order to survive, in order to feel comfortable and interested in the world around him, will he actually be able to live on both a biological and psychological level. We cannot feed off ourselves; we cannot breathe without breathing in the environment; we cannot do anything to take into our bodies those necessary things that we require, whether it is affection, knowledge, or air, without interacting with the environment. Consequently, the clarity of this relationship that I have tried to describe, gestalt formation and destruction, becomes of the utmost importance for the individual's living.

What is it that causes this process to fail? Why is it that the process of progressive formation and destruction of strong *Gestalten* actually does not run its appropriate course for the individual? First, let me point out the signs that can be observed when this process is interfered with. There are subjective signs that can be reported by the patient and there are signs the therapist can see. An example of a subjective sign would be confusion: the patient feels confused and nothing stands out clearly to him. He doesn't know what he wants. He doesn't know what is important. Or, he may say that he is undecided; he doesn't know which of various alternatives to take—nothing draws him more than anything else. On the objective side, the therapist can see fixed and repetitive behavior. For example, we see a patient ask for advice again and again or ask for instructions when told to explore and find his own answers. The whole self-regulation of the environment-organism relationship is destroyed. Also noticeable is the patient's lack of interest in what he himself is doing, and consequently the feeling of great effort in connection with some simple task. Patients report: "I have to force myself to go to work"; "I have to force myself to study"; and so on. Speech is usually poorly organized, and there will be actual confusion in what the patient says. Sometimes these things may be only momentary; at other times they may last for a substantial period of time.

It is important, however, to remember that a field that is poorly organized is still organized. The principle of *pregnanz* points out that any psychological field is as well organized as the global conditions will permit at that particular time. So it is possible, as was recognized by Koffka and Kohler years ago, that certain circumstances can prevent a figure from forming itself into the strongest and most coherent possible figure. In neurotic self-regulation certain forces are impeded from exerting their full effect on organismic contact with the environment. These interferences are of three kinds:

First, there is poor perceptual contact with the external world and with the body itself. We notice, for example, that patients will often not look at us when they are trying to tell us something about how we impressed them; or they will not look at objects that they are trying to describe. They may be unable to notice what they themselves are doing with their hands; or they do not hear the sound of their own voices, and so on. Their perceptual contact with large parts of their environment and of their bodies is either poor or blocked completely.

Second, the open expression of needs is blocked. For example, the patient may feel some warmth but not be able to do anything about it. One can see why this would result in a failure of the destructive process. Since the patient does not express his needs, he actually never gets the satisfaction for them; a perceptual figure that could have been bright, unified, and meaningful becomes dull and uninteresting, and the need thus actually never gets discharged. For example, consider somebody with a need for affection that is only half expressed. Half satisfaction results because the need is never thoroughly discharged. This particular need then serves to energize parts of the perceptual field: the person is looking for affection but not really wholeheartedly. The end result is that the need continues interfering with other kinds of needs that might organize the field in a clear-cut and coherent way.

Third, repression can prevent the formation of good *Gestalten*. The Gestalt therapist's view of repression as essentially a motor process is rather surprising from a historical point of view because the academic Gestalt psychologist was not concerned with what the musculature was doing, what the total gestalt formation would be like in, for example, walking. Largely because of the influence of Wilhelm Reich, Gestalt therapists consider repression as essentially a muscular phenomenon. Thus when needs and impulses arise, there tends to be a muscular response. The response tends to play itself out on the motor level, and the only way that one can inhibit the response is by contracting antagonistic muscles that prevent this impulse from expressing itself fully. The simplest example would be an impulse to swear at somebody. Let us suppose that you are very angry and yet you have to hold the impulse back. Now this "holding back" process can be seen as a strictly muscular process.

There are contractions in the jaws; there are tensions in the arm that prevent, for example, shaking the fist. In the case of sadness, the normal postural responses if the need played itself out thoroughly would be dejected posture, drawn mouth, and empty face. In holding sadness back, the simplest alteration would be to push the lips upward into a smile, destroying the pattern associated with sadness and thus not expressing and discharging the emotion. In repression all sorts of impulse unawareness are maintained by chronic muscular contractions which are forgotten by the individual. They become habitual; the individual adapts to them and does not know that he is blocking something or what it is that he is blocking.

What are some of the implications for therapy? It seems to me that one of the most distinctive things about the Gestalt therapist is that he works almost exclusively in the present. He is not primarily concerned with the recovery of past memories. The past has some importance in certain special circumstances, but, by and large, the Gestalt therapist sees that the only thing he has to work with is that which is immediately in front of him. In the therapeutic session itself the process of gestalt formation and destruction goes on as it does anywhere. The therapist has an opportunity to see the confusions that arise. He can see how the patient blocks out portions of his environment or portions of himself. Thus, the therapist begins to work with this particular problem.

At this point it is only fair to say that this approach to the therapy process represents one of the great streams of psychotherapeutic thought that stems from Otto Rank, who influenced Carl Rogers' client-centered therapy in a somewhat different way. Rogers' followers were interested in the present situation, too. They also focused on what the client was doing, but they never did get to the problem of the real *awareness* of what was happening to the patient *at this instant*. There is a great tendency, it seems to me, for words to get in the way of experience, and the Gestalt psychologists have tried to remedy this. This is not to say that there are not very strong Gestalt implications in Rogers' client-centered therapy, as he himself has pointed out, but the Gestalt therapist is basically much more active than the Rogerian therapist.

What is the therapist's activity directed toward? First, to break up the patient's chronically poorly organized field. The patient has certain standard ways of perceiving or acting in relationship to a need. The Gestalt therapist isolates portions of this field so that the self-regulating tendency of the neurotic can be broken up into smaller subunits. This eventually will permit the reorganization of both the motor field and the perceptual field. Also the Gestalt therapist works to heighten each emerging figure. If the patient seems ready to cry, for example, if there is an emerging activity the therapist can see "on the surface," if he notices squeezing and contractions in the face and perhaps a glistening of the eyes, he knows that the figure of crying is emerging. Suppose, however, that the impulse is being held back by the patient. The therapist works to unblock the impulse so that it can organize the field. He may do this by taking the resistance, the muscular resistance to crying, as the figure of the patient's attention. In other words, instead of emphasizing "You want to cry," he emphasizes *"How* are you preventing yourself from crying?" He goes back over and over again to the problem of "What are you doing that prevents you from getting what you want at this moment, in this immediate situation?" This means, of course, that there must be a great deal of bodily sensitivity, so a large part of the therapist's activity is devoted to body awareness. Until the patient can *feel* how he contracts his muscles or how he manipulates his head or his eyes or his body in order to prevent himself from seeing or doing certain things, he cannot make the repressive mechanism a matter of choice. It is not that we want to destroy his ability to control himself, but rather that we want to make it a matter of intentional choice.

These then are the major theoretical issues which form the broad base on which the Gestalt therapist works. This approach represents an extension of academic Gestalt psychology by adding needs and bodily awareness to the gestalt-forming process and then utilizing these insights in therapy to help unblock the need-fulfillment pattern.

CHAPTER 2

FOUR LECTURES *
Frederick S. Perls

I

In my lectures in Gestalt therapy, I have one aim only: to impart a fraction of the meaning of the word *now*. To me, nothing exists except the now. Now = experience = awareness = reality. The past is no more and the future not yet. Only the *now* exists.

The plight of the psychology of our time is that we are basically divided into two classes: the one interested in behavior and the other interested in awareness, or lack of awareness—be it called consciousness, experience, or whatever. This is the phenomenological approach which emphasizes the messages that are self-evident—existential in the pure sense—that we receive through the organs of our senses. We know through seeing, hearing, feeling; from these come the primary information we get about ourselves and our relation to life. The behaviorist, on the other hand, is not interested in the phenomenon of awareness and the subjective approach. He does, however, have the great advantage over most other methods in that he works in the here and now. He sees *this* animal, looks at *this* person, and investigates how *this* person is behaving. If you put these two together—the phenomenological approach, the awareness of what is, and the behavioral approach with its emphasis on behavior in the now—then you have in a nutshell what we are trying to do in Gestalt therapy.

When we look at behavior, we see essentially two kinds: public behavior and private behavior. Public behavior is overt observable behavior of which observers and we ourselves may be aware, and private behavior includes those things of which we may be aware, but an observer is not. This private behavior is usually called thinking, or speculating, or rehearsing, or computing.

---

*Transcribed from talks given at the Atlanta Workshop in Gestalt Therapy, 1966.

Before I go any further, I would like to discuss briefly four basic philosophical approaches, as I see them. The first approach is *science,* or as I call it, "aboutism," which lets us talk *about* things, gossip *about* ourselves or others, broadcast *about* what's going on in ourselves, talk *about* our cases. Talking about things, or ourselves and others as though we were things, keeps out any emotional responses or other genuine involvement. In therapy, aboutism is found in rationalization and intellectualization, and in the "interpretation game" where the therapist says, "This is what your difficulties are *about.*" This approach is based on noninvolvement.

The second philosophy I call "shouldism." The "should" mentality is found overtly or covertly in every philosophy and definitely in every religion. Even in Buddhism there is an implied shouldism, in that you *should* experience Nirvana, you *should* achieve the state of freedom from suffering; at least it is praised as something worth achieving. Religions are full of taboos, of *shoulds* and *should nots.* I'm sure you all realize that you grow up completely surrounded by what you should and should not do, and that you spend much of your time playing this game within yourself—the game I call the "top-dog/under-dog game," or the self-improvement game," or the "self-torture game." I'm certain that you are very familiar with this game. One part of you talks to the other part and says, "You should be better, you should not be this way, you should not do that, you shouldn't be what you are, you should be what you are not." Shouldism is based on the phenomenon of dissatisfaction.

Lately a third kind of thinking has come about: ontological thinking, or the existential approach, or "is-ism." This looks at and perceives the world as it *is,* as we *are,* making irrelevant and bracketing off what we *should* be. You might call this the eternal attempt to achieve truth. But what is truth? Truth is one of what I call the "fitting games."

Here I will wander off a minute and talk about some of the important games. One of the main games we play is the "one-upmanship game": "I'm better than you are," "I can trump you," "I can depress you." A second main game is the "fitting game": "Does this concept *fit* reality?" "Is this correct?" "If I see this and this, can I fit them together so that I can see a comprehensive picture?" "Does the behavior of this person fit into my concept of how a person should behave?" These are some of the fitting games. Now in existentialism the fitting game is truth. By "truth" I mean nothing but the assertion that a statement we make fits the observable reality. If a person says, "I'm angry with you," in a soft, polite tone of voice, it doesn't fit. His tone of voice is inconsistent with the anger he claims to feel. If he says, "Damn you! I'm angry with you!" then his anger and voice fit.

But none of the existentialists, with the possible exception of Heidegger, can really carry through their existential idea to ontological behavior—that a thing is explained through its very existence. They keep asking "Why?" and so have to keep going back and getting support: Sartre from Communism, Buber from Judiasm, Tillich from Protestantism, Heidegger to a small extent from Nazism, Binswanger from psychoanalysis. Binswanger in particular is always trying to go back to the causal—to that semantic mistake—trying to explain the event by its precedent, by its history, and therefore making the usual mistake of mixing up memories and history.

Finally, there is the Gestalt approach, which attempts to understand the existence of any event through the way it comes about, which tries to understand becoming by the *how,* not the *why*; through the all pervasive gestalt formation; through the tension of the unfinished situation, which is the biological factor. In other words, in Gestalt therapy we try to be consistent with every other event, especially with nature because we are a part of nature. That our life is not consistent with the demands of society is not because nature is at fault or we are at fault, but because society has undergone a process that has moved it so far from healthy functioning, natural functioning, that our needs and the needs of society and the needs of nature do not fit together any more. Again and again we come into such conflict until it becomes doubtful whether a healthy and fully sane and honest person can exist in our insane society.

Now, I would like to discuss what I think are the two most important discoveries of Freud. Freud said (this is not his formulation, but my understanding of what he meant) that in a neurosis a part of our personality or of our potential is not available. But he said this in an odd way; he said, "it is *in* the unconscious," as if there were such a thing as *the* unconscious rather than simply behavior or emotions that are unknown or not available. Freud also saw the basis of the gestalt formation in what he called the "preconscious." We call it the "background" out of which the figure emerges. We can go further and point up the fact that only a small portion of our potential—of what we could be—is available.

The other important discovery of Freud, which he never followed up and which seems to have gotten lost, is his remark, *"Denken ist Probearbeit"* ("Thinking is trial work"). I have reformulated it this way, "Thinking is rehearsing." Thinking is rehearsing in fantasy for the role you have to play in society. And when it comes to the moment of performance, and you're not sure whether your performance will be well received, then you get stage fright. This stage fright has been given by psychiatry the name *"anxiety."* "What will I have to say on the examination?" "What will I say in my lecture?" You meet a girl and think "What will I have to wear to impress her?" and so on. All of this is rehearsing for the role you play. I think Freud's sentence *"Denken ist Probearbeit"* is one of his great ideas.

Part of the reason why Freud could not follow up this idea was because rehearsing is relating to the future, and Freud was concerned only with the past. So this concept did not fit into his general theory and he had to drop it. But I would like you to consider for a moment how much time and how much of your potential you invest in thinking or rehearsing for the future in comparison with how much time you invest in thinking about the past.

Now, I can again talk about the *now*.

I maintain that all therapy that has to be done can only be done in the now. Anything else is interfering. And the technique that lets us understand and stay with the now is the "awareness continuum," discovering and becoming fully aware of each actual experience. If you can stay with this, you will soon come across some experience which is unpleasant. For instance, you get bored, or feel uncomfortable, or feel like crying. At that moment, something happens which Freud did not see clearly enough; at that point we become phobic. Freud saw the active blocking out of experience and called it "repression." He also saw the alienation of our experience and called it "projection." What I want to point out is that the critical moment is the frequent interruption of whatever we experience in the now. We interrupt by various means: we start to explain, we suddenly discover that we have taken up too much of the group's time, we remember that we have something important to do, or we get into the schizophrenic flight of ideas which is called by psychoanalysis "free association" (even though it is compulsive dis-association). This interruption of the awareness continuum prevents maturation, prevents therapy from becoming successful, prevents marriage from becoming richer and deeper, prevents inner conflicts from being solved. The whole purpose of this avoidance tendency is to maintain the status quo.

And what is the status quo? The status quo is *holding onto the concept that we are children.* This is opposite to the psychoanalytic viewpoint. Freud thought we are infantile because of prior trauma, but this is backward rationalization. We are infantile because we are afraid to take responsibility in the now. To take our place in history, to be mature, means giving up the concept that we have parents, that we have to be submissive or defiant, or the other variations on the child's role that we play.

In order to extend this, I need to talk about maturing. Maturation is the development from environmental support to self-support. The baby is entirely dependent on environmental support. As the child grows up, it learns more and more to stand on its own feet, create its own world, earn its own money, become emotionally independent. But in the neurotic this process does not adequately take place. The child—or the childish neurotic—will use his potential not for self-support but to act out phony roles. These phony roles are meant to mobilize the environment for support instead of mobilizing one's own potential. We manipulate the environment by being helpless, by playing stupid, asking questions, wheedling, flattering.

The result is that in life, and especially in therapy, we come to the "sick point" (as Russian psychiatry calls it), to the point where we are stuck, to the impasse. The impasse occurs where we cannot produce our own support and where environmental support is not forthcoming. In Gestalt therapy we see this happening again and again and again. Psychoanalysis unfortunately tends to foster childishness and dependency, first by its fantasies that the patient is a child and that everything should be related to a "father image" or "childhood trauma" or "transference"; and then by giving environmental support again and again in the form of intellectual interpretation which says, "I know you are stupid and immature. I know what you are doing. I know more than you. I will explain everything." But this prevents the person from truly understanding himself.

This is why I am absolutely dogmatic in regard to the fact that nothing exists except in the now, and that in the now you are behaving in a certain way that will or will not facilitate your development, your acquisition of a better ability to cope with life, to make available what was unavailable before, to begin to fill in the voids in your existence. Everyone has to some extent the kind of voids that are so apparent in the neurotic and schizophrenic. One person has no eyes, another no ears, another no legs to stand on, another no perspective, another no emotion. In order to fill these voids, which are usually experienced as boredom with life, emptiness, loneliness, we have to get through the impasse and through the frustrations of the impasse, which usually lead us to shortcut the frustrations and with them the whole learning process.

Now there are two ways of learning. In the first, you get information; you get someone to tell you what your dreams mean, what concepts will be useful, what the world is like. Then you feed this into your computer and you play the fitting game. Does this concept fit in with these other concepts? However, the best way of learning is not the computation of information. Learning is discovering, uncovering what is there. When we discover, we are uncovering our own ability, our own eyes, in order to find our potential, to see what is going on, to discover how we can enlarge our lives, to find means at our disposal that will let us cope with a difficult situation. And all this, I maintain, is taking place in the here and now. Any speculation about things, any attempt at getting information and assistance from outside help will not produce maturation. So anyone who works with me has to do it with a continuous account of the now. "I am experiencing this; now I feel this; now I don't want to work anymore; now I am bored." From here we can go on to differentiate what of the now experience is acceptable to you, when you want to run away, when you are willing to suffer yourself, when you feel yourself being suffered, and so on. All of this is explored in reality, in our encounter here with each other.

Said in another way, most psychotherapies are trying to get to the deepest depth. We are trying to get to the outermost surface. As every need, every unfinished situation emerges, we are being controlled by this emergent need and have to get in touch with the world to satisfy this need. We use our senses to observe, to see what is going on. The world is opening up. This ability to see is health. Conversely, the neurotic can be defined as a person who can't see the obvious, as in Anderson's fairy tale where only the child points to the obvious—that the king is naked. This is why, when I start working with a group, I often play schoolteacher and ask them to discover and verbalize the obvious.

II

In addition to the now, I also emphasize the process of *centering,* the reconciliation of opposites so that they no longer waste energy in useless struggle with each other, but can join in productive combination and interplay. For example, let us look at one of the main problems that people think they have—the problem of their own existence.

What is the opposite of existence? The immediate answer would be nonexistence, but this is incorrect. The opposite would be antiexistence, just as the opposite of matter is antimatter. As you know, scientists have managed to create matter out of energy. What has this to do with us in psychology? Mainly that in science we have finally come back to the pre-Socratic philosopher, Heraclitus, who said that everything is flow, flux, process. There are no "things." *Nothingness* in the Eastern languages is *no-thingness.* We in the West think of nothingness as a void, an emptiness, a nonexistence. In Eastern philosophy and modern physical science, nothingness—no-thingness—is a form of process, ever moving.

In science we try to find ultimate matter, but the more we split up matter, the more we find other matter. We find movement, and movement equals energy: movement, impact, energy, but no things. Things came about, more or less, by man's need for security. You can manipulate a thing, you can play fitting games with it. These concepts, these somethings can be put together into something else. "Something" is a thing, so even an abstract noun becomes a thing.

When we work in therapy, we always come across the nothingness, and we see that this no-thingness is some very alive process. I hope you understand the meaning of dealing with things—that in order to bring things back to life, we have to change them into process again. Reification, the making a thing out of a process, is the functioning of what I call the implosive or catatonic or death layer. If you *have* a body, if you *have* a mind, these *things* are apparently objects that belong to some instance called "I." "I" am the proud possessor—or the despising possessor—of a mind, of a body, of a world. So in effect I say, "I *have* some body" (*some* body) rather than realize that I *am* somebody.

In Gestalt therapy we look at the way a person manipulates his language, and we see that the more alienated he is from himself, the more he will use nouns instead of verbs, and most especially, the word *it*. *It* is a "thing" that is convenient to use to avoid being alive. When I'm alive, I talk, I am "voicing." When I'm dead, I "have" a *voice* with *words*; this *language* will have an *expression*; etc. You notice that this description is mostly a string of nouns, and that all that remains of life is to put them together.

To help you understand the importance of the implosive layer and its role in neuroses, I will describe more completely what I consider the five layers of neurosis. The first layer we encounter is what I call the Eric Berne layer, or the Sigmund Freud layer, or the phony layer, where we play games, play roles. It is identical with Helene Deutsch's description of the "as if" person. We behave *as if* we are big shots, *as if* we are nincompoops, *as if* we are pupils, *as if* we are ladies, *as if* we are bitches, etc. It is always the "as if" attitudes that require that we live up to a concept, live up to a fantasy that we or others have created whether it comes out as a curse or as an ideal. What you call an ideal, I call a curse. It's an attempt to get away from oneself. The result is that the neurotic person has given up living for his self in a way that would actualize himself. He wants to live instead for a concept, for the actualization of this concept—like an elephant who had rather be a rose bush, and a rose bush that tries to be a kangaroo. We don't want to be ourselves; we don't want to be what we are. We want to be something else, and the existential basis of this being something else is the experience of dissatisfaction. We are dissatisfied with what we do, or parents are dissatisfied with what their child is doing. He should be different, he shouldn't be what he is; he should be something else.

Then comes religion, philosophy, the violin and strings—we should be wonderful and beautiful, and if you are a Christian, you should be unsubstantial. In the New Testament nature doesn't count: only the supernatural, miraculous counts. So there should be no substance. And if you are dead, you should not be dead. Everything is regarded as if it should not exist as it is. In other words, the constitution with which we are born—our inheritance—is despised. We are not allowed to be at home in ourselves, so we alienate those frowned-upon properties and create the holes I spoke of in my first talk, the voids, the nothingness where something should exist. And where there is something missing, we build up a phony artifact. We behave as if we actually have this property that is demanded by society and which finally comes to be demanded by what Freud called the superego, the conscience. This we encounter as the top-dog in those games that torture the under-dog, the other part of the self, by demanding the impossible—"Come on now, live up to that ideal!"

It would be nice if we could be such wonderful people, but Freud neglected an important element which we have to add. The superego is not opposed, as Freud thought, to an ego or to an id, or to a cluster of our impulses and memories and energies. The top-dog is opposed to another personality, which I call the under-dog. Both have their characteristics and both fight for control. The top-dog is characterized mainly by righteousness. Whether he is right or wrong, he always knows what the under-dog should do. But the top-dog has very few means by which to reinforce his demands. He is really just a bully and tries to get his way by making threats. If you don't do as he says, then you will be punished, or something terrible will happen. The under-dog who receives these orders is not righteous; on the contrary, he is very unsure of himself. He does not fight back or try to control by being a bully or by being aggressive. He fights back with other means. "Tomorrow." "I promise." "Yes, but . . ." "I do my best." So these two, the top-dog and the under-dog, live a life of mutual frustration and continued attempts to control each other.

This, then, is what I call the first, or phony, layer, which includes these roles, the top-dog/under-dog games, the controlling games. If we once become aware of the phoniness of game-playing and try to become more honest or genuine, then we encounter pain, unpleasantness, despair, etc. We especially don't like experiencing cruelty. "We shouldn't hurt our neighbors or anyone else." We completely forget that a basic law of nature is to kill in order to live. There is no creature, no organic substance that can sustain its life without killing other animals or plants. Of all the species, only the human being refuses to accept the need for killing and turns killing against himself: only the human being kills not for necessity but for greed and power. Especially now, as the individual is superseded by the superorganisms called states or nations, he is deprived of his need to kill and has surrendered his needs to kill to the state.

Killing and destroying get all mixed up. Actually, we can't even eat an apple without destroying the substance of the apple. We destructure the apple as a single unit, cutting it to pieces with our front teeth, grinding it down with our back teeth, dissolving it chemically until nothing of the apple is left except substances we can't assimilate, and so eliminate.

Once we are capable of understanding our reluctance to accept unpleasant experiences, we can get to the next layer, the phobic layer, the resistance, the objection to being what we are. This is where all the *should nots* that I have already discussed occur.

If we get behind the phobic layer, the objections, we find at that moment the impasse occurs. And within the impasse there is the feeling of being not alive, of deadness. We feel that we are nothing, we are things. In every bit of therapy we have to go through this implosive layer in order to get to the authentic self. This is where most schools of therapy and therapists shrink away, because they also fear deadness. Of course, it is not being dead, but the fear and feeling of being dead, of disappearing. The fantasy is taken for reality. Once we get through the implosive layer, we see something very peculiar happening. This can be seen most dramatically in the catatonic state, when the patient who has appeared as a corpse explodes to life. And this is what happens when the implosive state is dissolved—explosions happen.

The explosion is the final neurotic layer that occurs when we get through the implosive state. As I see it, this progression is necessary to become authentic. There are essentially four types of explosion: explosion into joy, into grief, into orgasm, into anger. Sometimes the explosions are very mild—it depends on the amount of energy that has been invested in the implosive layer.

Perhaps I can make clearer where the catatonic state, the implosive state, comes about by talking about physiology. You know that in order to move a muscle, you send an electric shock into the muscle, and the muscle jerks. If you interrupt the shock, again the muscle jerks. In order to keep the muscle contracted you must constantly repeat the electric shocks. So you can imagine in a catonic state, or anytime you get tense, how much energy is invested in keeping tense, keeping rigid. And if this energy is not invested in keeping yourself rigid, the energy is freed for all kinds of activities—thinking, moving about, being alive. If suddenly freed, the pent-up energy will explode. Implosion becomes explosion, compression becomes expression.

I think I will give the group now a few minutes for questions and remarks about this lecture.

> *Question:* You mentioned that getting through the implosive layer to the explosion may be perceived by both the patient and therapist as dangerous, and probably that's the reason for the implosive layer. How do the therapist and the

patient get beyond this? I have a patient that has exploded from a catatonic state into orgasm, and it looks like he may go back to the implosive layer or to catatonia because he can't adjust either way.

Perls: One thing you have to remember is that a person, in order to function well, has to have all four abilities for explosion available. The person who can explode into orgasm, but not anger or grief or joy is incomplete. What you're talking about is what I mentioned as the phobic layer avoiding the experience of the tension because of catastrophic fantasies, the fear of the risk. When so much energy is held back, so much life energy or *elan vital* is accumulated that the person can't hold it back any longer and the explosion may occur in a very violent way.

Comment: It reminds me of the explosion when atoms are separated—fission.

Perls: Fusion or fission. There is one way where the explosion and the danger of explosion is often diminished. This is the process of melting. Often you will find that at a certain point you are moved, you are involved, and you begin to melt, you feel soft, or you begin to cry. This is one of the buffers against a dangerous explosion. But basically one has to be willing to take risks.

Question: Is melting tenderness?

Perls: Tenderness is a form of melting. You will find that after a good explosion you will feel tender in the meaning of being subtle. But when you talk about tenderness, I am suspicious. It sounds like the undercore of toughness, and playing the toughy is a very important part of role-playing for the American youth.

Question: Would you say a bit about that—about youth playing the role of toughness?

Perls: Where does the American child get a great part of his information? From the comic strips. And what do the comic strips say? Do they talk about a man and a woman? No. They deal with the he-man and the glamour girl. This concept of a man is more like a cave man than a genuine man—and this is difficult to define—a man in the sense of living for his convictions. But the comic-strip message is that a man has to be a toughy because otherwise he's a sissy. He has no other choice except to become a baseball hero or a homosexual. Only as a homosexual is he allowed to be tender, to be soft. The same is true for the female. A rough estimate is that the American female is divided into 90 percent bitches and 10 percent women. Women have to become bitches because they have to become glamour girls. As glamour girls they have to spend most of their time being photogenic and being looked at instead of having eyes, having genitals, having relationships. This results in a permanent kind of irritation, a permanent hostility. The man is seen as the enemy, and the only way to keep the enemy under control is to become a bitch. So the he-man and the bitch fit together as the main characters on the American stage.

Question: I only heard you mention four of the layers of neurosis.

Perls: The phony layer, the phobic, the impasse, the implosive, the explosive. If I categorize in this way and make a thing out of a process, please be tolerant and see that this is just an approximation of what the process is like.

Question: The phony level is where the games go on?

Perls: Yes.

Question: And the implosive layer is where the reasons for the games are. Is this right?

Perls: No. There are no reasons for the games.

Comment: Then I don't understand the implosive layer.

Perls: The implosive level is where the energies that are needed for living are frozen and invested unused. In order to free them for living we have to go through the process of exploding. If I'm thirsty, I do not have to go into the woods and find a spring with water. This would be the biological, primitive way. In our culture, I have to use a number of manipulations. For example, at this conference I ring a bell, and give the waiter orders, and go through all kinds of processes so that I can get water to balance out the minus in my organism. In the culture in which we live, we have to play roles in order to satisfy our needs. Now I could conceivably go into the corridor and explode. *"Hello, hello! I want something to drink!"* But I don't do this. I play the prescribed roles. I'm polite and considerate.

Question: Will you say some more about the phobic layer?

Perls: The main phobic attitude I can think of is being phobic about discovering life. In order to avoid living a life of discovering the world and ourselves, we often take the short-cut of getting information. This is what you did right now—you asked me for information. But you could have set out and discovered what you are phobic about or what somebody else is phobic about—what you or they avoid. But instead you ask me to feed your computer, your thinking system. The basic phobic attitude is to be afraid to be what you are. And you will find relief immediately if you dare to investigate what you are like. You'll find that immediately you run into catastrophic fantasies. "If I am as I am, what will happen to me? Society will ostracize me. If I tell my boss to go to hell, I'll lose my job. If I tell my wife she's a bitch, she won't sleep with me." And so on and so on. So you become phobic, you start to manipulate, to play roles. Instead of saying, "You're a bitch," you compress your lips and don't talk to her. But you contract yourself and signal indirectly that you don't like what she's doing or the way she is. You *im*plode yourself, because you are afraid to *ex*plode.

Question: When one is at the impasse level, is one afraid to see the world for what it is?

Perls: No, there is more to it. The impasse occurs every time you are not ready or willing to use your own resources (including your eyes) and when enviromental support is not forthcoming. The extreme example of the impasse is the blue baby. The blue baby cannot provide its own oxygen, and the mother doesn't provide oxygen any more. The blue baby is at an impasse of breathing, and he has to find a way to breathe or die. Another good example of impasse is the average marriage, where the two partners are not in love with each other but with a concept of what the other should be. Each has almost no idea of what the other is like, and as soon as the behavior of one doesn't fit with what the partner expects, he becomes dissatisfied and starts playing the blaming game. He blames her: she should change; he blames himself: he should change—

all this rather than realize that they are in an impasse because they are in love with an image, a fantasy. They are stuck. But they don't know *how* they are stuck, and that's the impasse. The result of the impasse is to keep the status quo. They may want to change, but they don't: they keep the status quo because they are too frightened of going through the impasse.

Question: What breaks the impasse?

Perls: The impasse cannot be broken.

Question: It has to be accepted?

Perls: You might say that. The incredible thing which is so difficult to understand is that experience, awareness of the now, is sufficient to solve all difficulties of this nature, that is, neurotic difficulties. If you are fully aware of the impasse, the impasse will collapse, and you will find yourself suddenly through it. I know this sounds rather mystical, so I will give you an example. There are two items on the menu and you cannot decide which to order. But nature does not work by decisions but by preferences. If you prefer one food more than the other, you are through the impasse.

III

There are three themes I would like to touch on now. The first is the matter of answering patients' questions. You may have wondered about the fact that I almost never answer questions during therapy. Instead I usually ask the patient to change the question into a statement. The question mark has a hook the patient may use for many purposes, such as to embarrass the other person or, more often, to prevent himself from discovering what is really going on. This asking for environmental support keeps one in the infantile state. You will find that nothing develops your intelligence better than to take any question and turn it into a genuine statement. Suddenly the background will start to open up, and the ground from which the question grows will become visible.

A second theme concerns guilt feelings. According to psychoanalytic theory, the patient is cured if he is free from anxiety and guilt. Anxiety we have already dealt with as stage fright. The problem of guilt is even simpler: *guilt is projected resentment.* Any time you feel guilty, you will find a nucleus of resentment. But resentment in itself is still an incomplete emotion. Resentment is an effort at maintaining the status quo, a hanging-on; in resentment you can neither let go and be done by giving up, nor can you be aggressive and angry and clear up the situation. Resentment is the bite that hangs on.

Possibly the most difficult mental feat for any patient is to forgive his parents. Parents are never right. They are either too stern or too soft, too strong or too weak. There is always something wrong with parents. And the balance between guilt feelings (that he owes them something) and resentment (that they owe him something) is achieved by a very peculiar phenomenon—gratefulness. Gratefulness leads to closure. Neither party owes the other anything.

My third theme is the importance of dreams. The dream is an existential message. It is more than an unfinished situation; it is more than an unfulfilled wish; it is more than a prophecy. It is a message of yourself to yourself, to whatever part of you is listening. The dream is possibly the most spontaneous expression of the human being, a piece of art that we chisel out of our lives. And every part, every situation in the dream is a creation of the dreamer himself. Of course, some of the pieces come from memory or reality, but the important question is what makes the dreamer pick out this specific piece? No choice in the dream is coincidental. As in paranoia, the person who is projecting looks for a peg on which to hang his hat. Every aspect of it is a part of the dreamer, but a part that to some extent is disowned and projected onto other objects. What does projection mean? That we have disowned, alienated, certain parts of ourselves and put them out into the world rather than having them available as our own potential. We have emptied a part of ourselves into the world; therefore we must be left with holes, with emptiness. If we want to own these parts of ourselves again we have to use special techniques by which we can reassimilate those experiences.

In working with a dream, I avoid any interpretation. I leave this to the patient since I believe he knows more about himself than I can possibly know. I used to go through the whole dream and work through every part; but many patients have difficulty in reidentification, and the difficulty is absolutely identical with the amount of self-alienation. Lately I take more of a short cut. I look mainly for the holes, the emptiness, the avoidances.

The first problem, then, is to find out what the dream is avoiding. Often we are immediately able to find what the patient is avoiding by finding out at what moment he interrupts the dream and wakes up rather than continue it. Very often the dreamer is avoiding death, being killed, or sex. Actually, I find that the whole question of survival, of killing and destroying, is at least as important as the sexual question.

Question: You say when the dream is interrupted by waking, we are avoiding something, but what if it is not interrupted by waking?

Perls: Then it is not always as easy to find out what is being avoided. Usually when you allow yourself to go on dreaming, you are not trying to avoid some terrible shock, as in a dream of falling in which you have to wake before you are smashed. Evasion is the usual base of neurosis, based on a misunderstanding of fantasy and reality. I can fall a thousand times in fantasy. I can kill a hundred people in my dreams—it is only fantasy and they are still alive. It is tragic that we are so unwilling even to imagine certain situations, so this fear of imagination, this mixing up of reality and fantasy persists. We stop ourselves from doing many things because we imagine the bad things that will happen, or we feel disappointed because all the rosy things we expect and wish just do not happen. All those wonderful things—we go to Las Vegas with five dollars and come back with a hundred thousand; or we dream of being a wonderful, perfect human being. This doesn't happen, so we are disappointed. We prevent ourselves from using what we have or from reassimilating what we have disowned.

Let me give you an example. A woman dreamed that she had three orphans and each of the orphans had an artificial hand or arm, all very beautifully carved, and she was looking for the best surgeon to make the best possible prosthesis substitute for the hands. Where is the avoidance, the emptiness here? Well, it is obvious. So, I became very cruel and brutal, and took the protheses away from the children. The children were left without hands. Where were the hands? Obviously in the person who made the protheses. I learned that this woman was very artistically inclined and had sculpted for many years, but had lost the ability. So the carvings, the artistic abilities came out as a projection. The minus, the avoidance of existence in this case is the lack of organic hands. By working through this dream, I could give her back the use and appreciation of her hands.

Let me warn you to be very careful about dreams and dreamers who have no living beings in their dreams. Where there is only death or desert or buildings, you are most likely to have a severe psychotic case on your hands.

It is also important to let patients play at being the objects in the dream as well as the persons. Two of my favorite examples of this are from the same man. In one dream, he leaves my office, crosses the street into Central Park, and walks over the bridle path. I ask him to play the bridle path, and he answers, "What! And let everybody tramp and shit on me?" In another dream, he left his attache case on the stairs. I asked him to be the attache case. He said, "Well, I've got a thick hide, in a thick skin. I've got secrets and nobody is supposed to get to my secrets. I keep them absolutely safe." See how much he tells us about himself by playing, identifying with the objects in his dreams? Also, you will learn a lot by paying attention to the locale, where the dream is staged. If a person dreams that he is in court, you know he is concerned with guilt, being accused, etc. If the dream takes place in a motel, you can guess what his existence is like.

The more you refrain from interfering and telling the patient what he is like or what he feels like, the more chance you give him to discover himself and not to be misled by your concepts and projections. And believe me, it is never easy to be able to differentiate between what we project and what we see and hear. Probably the most dangerous thing for a therapist to do is to play the computer game. You find patients whose life exists of sentences and computing, and if you feed information into their computers, and they compute back to you, nothing will *ever* happen. The computer game can go on for years and years.

To recapitulate: The two main words I want to impress on you are *now* and *how*. The difficulties lie in getting again and again pulled away from the now and into all kinds of rationalizations and making cases as to who is right and who is wrong. "I have a better interpretation than you have." "I know all about you." There is also the great danger of the Freudian approach. "This happens *because* it has happened before." As if one railroad station could be explained because there was another one before it. And you must be very careful to teach your patients to differentiate between reality and their fantasies, especially the transference fantasy— where they see you as a father or someone who can give them the goodies. Make them look again and again to see the difference between this father and you until they wake up and come to their senses.

Even if you are compulsive about *now* and *how*, it can't do any harm, and the compulsion will dissolve into something alive and meaningful.

We don't know what the next step in history will be. We have come from the gods, to the causes of nature, to the process. Right now we live in the age of processes. I am sure that one day we will discover that awareness is a property of the universe—extension, duration, awareness. Right now the first experiments are being made. Flatworms have been cut up and fed to other worms, and experiments show that these know what the first generation had learned. Possibly this is the first step in demonstrating that awareness is a property of matter. But we cannot yet think in terms of billions and billions of parts of the quantum to measure awareness, and the idea that properties might exist that are not measurable is still beyond the concepts of today's psychologists.

Full identification with yourself can take place if you are willing to take full responsibility—*response-ability*—for yourself, for your actions, feelings, thoughts; and if you stop mixing up responsibility with obligation. This is another semantic confusion in psychology. Most people believe that responsibility means, "I put myself under obligation." But it does not. You are responsible only for yourself. *I* am responsible only for *my*self. This is what I tell a patient right away. If he wants to commit suicide, that's his business. If he wants to go crazy, that's his business. Jewish mothers have wonderful ways of manipulating people; they are experts on making one feel guilty, on pushing the buttons of conscience. But I am not in this world to live up to other people's expectations, nor do I feel that the world must live up to mine.

> *Question:* I've been putting together a number of things that you've said, and they're making me uncomfortable. If a law of nature is to kill to maintain life, then how do we decide when transgression is harmful to ourselves, or dangerous to others, or unacceptable to them?

> *Perls:* You want a prescription for behavior—for instance, how to make decisions. I cannot and will not provide you with that. Any decision has to be made by the situation in which an event occurs. Science has only recently proceeded from looking at pieces to recognizing the total approach, the Gestalt approach. Students have been taught that the organism consists of a number of reflex arcs, or that mind is over against matter, or that here is a person and there is the environment—not that here is a person who has accumulated some emotions that need to be relieved. I think that the Freudian "excremental" theory of emotions—that we have a certain quantum of aggression that should be discharged—is especially dangerous.

We are part of the universe, not separate. We and our environment are one. We cannot look without something to look at. We cannot breathe without air. We cannot live without being part of society. So we cannot possibly look on the organism as being able to function in isolation. So this organism here labeled "Fritz Perls" is a living sum of processes, of functions, and these functions are always related to something of the world he has, the world that we try to describe with the word *now*. The *now* is the world in which we live. And this organism is distinguished from this thing called "chair" by having an energy in itself which operates itself. Unlike a motor car, which has to take in gas and air to make the energy that explodes in the engine, we have to secure our own energy from the food and air we take in. We have no name for the energy we create. Bergson called it *elan vital;* Freud called it *libido* or *death instinct* (he had two energies); and Reich called it *orgone*. I call it *excitement*, because the word *excitement* coincides with the physiological aspect, *excitation*.

had two energies); and Reich called it *orgone*. I call it *excitement*, because the word *excitement* coincides with the physiological aspect, *excitation*.

Excitement is often experienced as rhythm, vibration, trembling, warmth. Again this excitement is not created for its own sake but in relation to the world. We take somebody's hand and we feel the hand is warm. This person is glowing toward the world. Here is another person's hand—he is cold. The frigid person always has cold hands. Of course, this person is implosive; the other explosive, outgoing. So some excitement is always being generated. Excitement = life = being. Now, excitement as such is not enough, because excitement has to energize the organism. Much of it will energize the motor system; some will mobilize the senses. These are the two systems with which we relate to the world: the motoric system of manipulation, acting, handling; and the sensory system, or system of orientation, how we see and feel.

Nature is not wasteful; nature does not just create emotions to be discharged as the excremental theory wants to have it. Nature creates emotions as a means of relating, for we were made to cope with the world in different intensities. We relate differently when we are angry than when we are loving. I believe that there is some intelligence or wisdom of the organism that differentiates these basic energies into the different tasks and functions. At present I call it the *hormonal differentiation.* Apparently excitement becomes tinged with some other substance— adrenalin for anger, or sexual hormones for libidinous emotions. Thus excitement varies according to the situation. When we are asleep, we need less excitement, and our metabolism goes down. In emergency situations, we can produce peaks of excitement. You know how much energy, how much violence a person can produce under a state of attack. We speak about the superhuman strength a person can have *if* he is involved, *if* he is investing his whole personality in his experience. Excitement, then, goes especially into the motoric outlet because the muscles link us with the environment. You find that in most emotional events, emotion is transformed into movement. We cannot have sex without sexual rhythm and movement; we can't grieve without our diaphragm shaking and tears being produced; we can't be joyous without dancing. So whatever excitement is necessary to create and to cope with the situation is forthcoming from the organism, and there is no unnecessary excitement. When you speak about actions that might not be acceptable by society, there is the impasse. What do you choose—to be hostile to that society or to be part of society, identified with it and willing to subdue yourself?

   Comment: That's my hang-up.

     Perls: This is the existential problem for most of us. And the more insane the society, the more it is a problem. The

American society dehumanizes people, making them into zombies without emotions, and the person without emotions will become like the machine. We don't live for the human being. I'm sure that at least 70 percent of the American people are employed in the production and service of machines. So if you violate the law of the machines, the machines will hit back through those in the service of the machines. The impasse can only be solved by finding a way that is acceptable to you *and* society. For instance, I am doing something against the society I described. I toss a Trojan horse—the human soul—into that society, yet I'm being paid for it. I don't do it because I'm a reformer or a dogooder, but because I enjoy it; I'm alive doing it.

I hope you don't expect me to give you a prescription for living. All I can say is that the neurotic way of living is a very uneconomical way. It's such a waste of time, waste of energy, waste of your existence.

Comment: I can accept my actions and the consequences of them for me, but I don't live alone. My life is tied up with others, especially my family. I have no right to accept the consequences for them. Only they can do that.

Perls: I object to that phrase, "no right." This is not a legal issue. "No right" is the top-dog speaking. You see what I mean about the excitement. As such, the excitement involved with our way of living has nothing to do with society itself. It is how we regulate our lives. If you decide that you like the society and identify with it by being a well-adjusted citizen, that is your existential choice. On the other hand, if you choose to be outside society, you are not necessarily being destructive.

Comment: You're making my greed show, because I want it both ways.

Perls: So you want it both ways. And you reproach me as if you are a bad man because you want it both ways. This is how you are. Eat *and* have. Everybody plays the role he plays; everybody is what he is. Nobody can at any given moment be different from what he is *at that moment*. If somebody comes to me and complains that his role is being depressed and he doesn't like it, then I can show this person that he is playing the depression game. He has a choice: he can play top-dog with another person and depress that person or depress himself. If this is the game he wishes to play, fine. If he wants to play this game the other way round by being nasty and depressing other people, fine. Or he may dislike certain people and go around depressing them, and so feel fine. In other words, all I can do is possibly to help people to reorganize themselves, to function better, to enjoy life more, to feel —and this is very important—to feel more real. What more do you want? Life is not violins and roses.

IV

I will conclude by discussing some ways you can continue your own growth, so you can help yourself to become aware. Now as long as we are aware, we are always aware *of something*. Sometimes the awareness is so dim that we are in a kind of trance, but basically we are always experiencing something. Even when the antiawareness forces are at work, as in sleep or fainting, very often some message is coming through, such as a dream. What we are aware of is always the message of the unfinished situation. Usually an unfinished situation is very pressing if you allow nature to take its course. If you have a letter to answer, then this letter is on your conscience not just on your desk. The situation demands to be finished.

We can use this demand for self-therapy in the form of meditation. There are many forms of meditation, and people do not understand how they differ. Many people think that meditation takes place in the realm of thoughts and ideas. When I talk of meditation, I do not mean this kind of game. To use the kind of meditation I mean is very difficult—it may take years to accomplish, especially if you are a talker. Usually people are either talkers or listeners; very few are both. People often say, "I told myself . . . " or "I said to myself . . . ," but they seldom say, "I listened to myself." The kind of meditation I suggest is learning to listen to your thinking. You can hear yourself thinking, and listen until you can hear whether *you* are talking or *somebody else* is talking.

You will find it very difficult to get the basic energy into your ears instead of your fantasy throat. But when you can do this, you will realize a very peculiar phenomenon—that is, in spite of being alone, all this thinking is essentially a substitute for encounters. It is an inner world or stage that replaces the external world or stage. But if you do not listen, you will not realize that you are always talking to somebody, even if it is as vague as talking to the world. You may be telling people what they should do or defending yourself, or manipulating somebody or impressing someone.

This is nothing especially new, but it is in this process that we come across the unpleasant experience, the block, the status quo that prevents us from becoming truly substantial and growing up. And this is where we can accomplish a great deal deliberately. It's very peculiar that we can become spontaneous only by utmost discipline. It is an absolute paradox. And absolute discipline is required in getting the antidote for our phobic attitude. The antidote is to become interested in your negative emotions. If you develop a kind of scientific objectivity, or a willingness to suffer yourself and focus on whatever unpleasant situation that might come up, then you come across the blocks for further development. I would say that one of the most important kinds of unpleasantness is boredom, so much so that I think that one of the hell gates that leads to maturity, to *satori*—the great awakening—is the ability to stay with boredom, not to try to jump out of it, do something interesting, or use it for complaining.

But boredom is not the only unpleasantness we encounter. There is also the feeling of frustration. It is true that in a final sense, we cannot possibly be frustrated. Either our self-esteem or the organism will always find some way out. If a girl rejects us, we will try to get a substitute satisfaction by becoming vindictive or violent. Whatever frustration we encounter, there is always some alternate attempt to get satisfaction. The only trouble is that if the key doesn't fit the lock, the door doesn't open— the substitute does not lead to the completion of the situation. But staying with frustration, staying with boredom, will evoke organismic self-regulation. It is like a cut. *You* cannot do anything to heal the cut. The organism takes over. You might prevent further complications by sterilizing the cut, but if you leave it alone, nature will take care of it. If you want a better understanding of the simplicity of life and environment, I recommend a pocketbook entitled *The Top of the World*,* which says much about the beauty and the meaningfulness of life. At one point an Eskimo says, "The white people are peculiar people. They bring their laws along but leave their wives at home."

You see, we clog up our lives with so many thousands of unnecessary unfinished situations. If you want to play the role of a lady, you must have a beautiful costume for this role. So you go out and buy it, or cut up pieces of cloth, and sew them together just so, in a fashionable way. But then, this costume is not finished in time, so you get angry, and so on. And think of all the other props—all for what is an unnecessary role!

If you can stay with your feelings of unpleasantness, you will find that situations tend more and more, quicker and quicker, to be finished or discarded as events that merely clog up your life. Therapists quickly become aware of how people clog up their lives by dragging unpleasant parents

---

*Hans Ruesch, *Top of the world*. New York: Pocket Books, Inc., #50198.

around with them. Well of course we are not Eskimos; we do not just put parents on sleds and let them freeze to death. But we can say, "I'm a big boy now. I don't need you."

Begin meditation by closing your eyes and just listening to your own thinking, whatever you are saying to yourself. Then, when you learn to listen, the next step is to produce a therapist. If you like me, take me, and have encounters with Fritz; take whomever you choose, it does not matter. By choosing your therapist and having him respond to you in what you are saying, you will be amazed at how much you know, at how much you can actually help yourself, at how much self-support you will discover. You will also be amazed to realize how much you have played stupid and helpless and phony rather than finding your self-support. You see, the psychoanalytic idea of transference is this: transference is the historical repetition of what has been. I look upon it as resentment of what it has not been.

Usually, the patient expects the therapist to give him what he is missing, to fill his holes. By playing therapist to himself, he is capable of filling his own holes. I am sure you know only too well the projection mechanism, what patients imagine, and project onto you. If you make them play at giving what you are supposed to give them, then they can reown what they have disowned—for instance, the power they hand over to others.

You can save yourself much strain and stress while doing therapy by withdrawing as often as possible. Most therapists think that they have to stay in contact with the patient all the time. But the two extremes of contact and withdrawal are both pathological. If you always hang on and cannot let go, you are fixated. If you are completely withdrawn and out of touch, then you are isolated. I can give you a simple example: A clenched fist is not a hand. A flat palm with rigidly outstretched fingers is not a hand. *This* is a hand—moving, changing, doing many things, and varying its position and movement. Similarly the heart is not a heart in its extension or in its contraction, but rather in its rhythm of contraction and relaxation. So contact with the world is a rhythm. At times it is a confluence, a oneness; at other times, isolation. As an example, sometimes you want to say something but a word is missing. You withdraw to your fantasy dictionary, find the right word, then you come back. Or perhaps you see someone and don't know what to say, so you withdraw and rehearse, then come back into contact.

As for the fixation, the deliberate energy that is called attention is very short-lived. The organism has inexhaustible awareness but it does not produce much deliberate energy. For example, if you try to concentrate on a red object, you immediately start to produce antiawareness in the form of a neutralizing color. When you look away or close your eyes you see green instead of red, indicating that you should have withdrawn from the red sooner and looked at something else. So, if you feel compelled to listen to all the garbage your patients say, especially if they are trying to bore you, hypnotize you, put you to sleep, you will be exhausted by the end of the session or of the day. But if you allow yourself to withdraw when there is no interest, you will find yourself immediately involved again when something of interest occurs. Again, if you trust the wisdom of the organism, you will be amazed at how much working capacity you have. Many times, when a group or an individual is bored or withdrawn, I will ask everyone to withdraw in fantasy.

Question: Is it possible to use some of the techniques you have talked about in a group situation?

Perls: Of course. In fact, I think that individual therapy is obsolete, that it should be the exception rather than the rule. There are certain situations when somebody in the group is not ready to be open with the group. In that case individual therapy is indicated. But workshops are, both financially and in regard to personal development, much more feasible. Consider how much you learn in a group from indirect participation.

Question: Do you have any suggestions that would help a group to function? Can a group function without a leader?

Perls: I think a group can function well without a leader if the group will agree to some basic rules and everyone watches to insure that the rules are being followed. Here are some of the basic rules: (1) Be alert when you leave the *now*, and always go back to the *now* in the sense of both the open now and the hidden now of fantasies. (2) Forbid the use of the word *it*. (3) Encourage everyone to change nouns into verbs. (4) Never gossip about any person who is not present. Bring the absent one into an encounter by having the speaker play both roles; (5) Never force a confession. Never force anyone to say something that he does not want to say, or intrude into him. Merely deal with objections and have them expressed. (6) Give support by helping the person find his own support—by asking, "How do you. . .?" rather than saying, "Do this." These are some of the attitudes that will facilitate maturation.

Question: Will you say something about *why*?

Perls: The word *why* is the infantile approach of explanation. *Why* cannot lead to understanding. There may be one exception—when you use *why* to mean *for what purpose.* But when *why* is used for causality, it is covering up the issue with computing and rationalization. Explanation prevents understanding. The great danger you encounter as therapists is that you were trained to play the interpretation game, and the assumption of this game is that you know something about the other person and that it will help him if you tell him. Sometimes that is correct. Sometimes you do actually see what is going on. Then you might not do great harm, unless you are premature in telling him something that he is not ready for. But *anything* you can do to help the other person *discover himself* is always good. Only what we discover ourselves is truly learned.

Question: How can the therapist use himself in trying to help the patient come to terms with himself?

Perls: By being open and honest. Freud was not able to be open, and his problem got changed into a technique that took many years to correct. What happened was similar to a friend in South Africa who sent a very delicate cup to Japan to have a copy made, since the Japanese are very good at copying things. He ordered many dozens of these cups. When they arrived, all the cups arrived with handles—not attached. What had happened was that the handle of the original cup had broken off in the mail, and the Japanese copied the cup exactly as it was, in two pieces. This is similar to what happened in psychotherapy. Freud had a deep phobia. He was embarrassed to look into anybody's face or to be stared at, so he avoided the situation by putting the patient on a couch and sitting behind him. Soon this symptom became standard procedure, like the broken handle. Now we have to do the opposite. We have to make a big fuss and discover the obvious—a new type of therapy called "encounter therapy." We have finally remembered that it seems only natural that we have eyes to see the other person, that we can talk directly to him, etc.

    In an encounter we must be aware of the polarities because everything, every energy is differentiated into opposites. We have many opposites: right and left, top-dog and under-dog, sadist and masochist. We try to integrate the opposed events and see how they fit until we find the center. We can be alert and have perspective only if we have a center. If we lose the center, we are out of balance.

Question: Will you talk about right and left as opposites?

Perls: The right hand is usually the motoric, male, aggressive side that wants to control, to determine what is, to decide what is "right." The left side is the female side; it is usually poorly coordinated. *Left* means *awkward* in many languages: *gauche* in French, *linkich* in German. When there is a conflict between emotional life and active life, there is neurosis. When the male and female side fight with each other, this uses up energy in inner conflict and frustration and games and so on. But when both power and sensitivity are working in coordination, there is genius. Every genius in literature has this female component integrated with the male, and every female genius has a strong male component. An important aspect of training in Zen is training for alertness, which involves really having a center so that one can always be alert to what is going on. Ultimate awareness can only take place if the computer is gone, if the intuition, the awareness is so bright that one really comes to his senses. The empty mind in Eastern philosophy is worthy of highest praise. So lose your mind and come to your senses.

CHAPTER 3

GESTALT THERAPY: A BEHAVIORISTIC PHENOMENOLOGY

Elaine Kepner and Lois Brien

It seems generally agreed now that human problem behavior is learned, and that psychotherapy is essentially a reeducational or learning process. Usually the use of such terms as *learning* and *behaviorism* implies that man is simply a collection of conditioned responses to environmental stimuli. We believe with Anderson (1968) that

> The behavior of human beings . . . is adequately accounted for only in terms of a radically different conception of the nature of man. Man is a creature, the only creature, with a sense of self. Given this sense of self, he is able to carry on internal dialogues with himself, and he does so during practically every waking moment [p.1].

In this article, we shall be translating Gestalt therapy into a behavioristic-phenomenological framework. That is, we propose to consider phenomenological events as actual behaviors.

Since our only access to experience is through some form of behavior, be it verbal or nonverbal, the Gestalt therapist considers *all* that is going on in a person—what he is thinking, feeling, doing, remembering, and sensing—as the data of behavior. This does not imply that Gestalt therapy is a form of behavioristic therapy (via the model of Wolpe, Goldiamond, etc.). We use the language of behavioristic learning theory because it allows us to refer to experiential events in operational terms and provides principles that account for changes in a subject's feelings, perceptions, and actions. Whether this translation will serve its function remains to be seen. As Scriven (1964) says, "The test as to whether a vocabulary imparts a new and genuine understanding is its capacity to predict new relationships, to retrodict old ones and to show a unity where there was a previous diversity [p. 183]."

BEHAVIORISM AND PHENOMENOLOGY:
TWO APPROACHES TO LEARNING

A brief description of learning theory seems in order to set a background for this analysis. Learning theory is used here as a generic term designating a number of different systems developed by psychologists to account for the acquisition of knowledge and/or the emergence of new responses. Historically, psychology has approached this subject from two different views:, the tradition of associationism, which today can be referred to as *behaviorism*, and the schools of introspection, functionalism, and Gestalt psychology, which may be grouped under the heading of *phenomenology* or *existentialism*.

Neither behaviorism nor phenomenology are in themselves psychological systems. Rather, they are approaches or methods in psychology for describing and studying the crucial variables which relate to and account for behavior. All learning theories take as their major function the specification of stimulus conditions that determine behavior. Both the behaviorist and the phenomenologist consider learning to be a lawful phenomenon whose laws can be discovered. Since learning is an internal state and not directly observable, the behaviorist studies a response or performance as an indicator of learning. The phenomenologist, on the other hand, studies learning as well as other behaviors through the individual's report of sensory, perceptual, or cognitive data.

There are a number of different theories. What they share in common is a language that emphasizes operational definitions of specifiable behaviors and a concern with the role of reinforcement or reward as a determinant of behavior. The behavioristic psychologist further believes that observable behavior is the only legitimate subject matter of psychology, and the only criterion against which the outcome of any experimental procedure, including psychotherapy, can be evaluated.

The phenomenologist, on the other hand, considers all that goes on inside a person—that is, his sensations, perceptions, cognitions— in a word, his experiencing—as valid psychological data, even though these events cannot be verified but must be inferred and labeled as hypothetical constructs by another person. Thus changes in such constructs as self-concept, or self-awareness, or ego-control are acknowledged as valid psychological data and valid criteria against which the outcome of therapy can be appraised.

Contemporary behaviorism and phenomenology are showing evidences of convergent thinking. For example, several learning theorists, notably, Miller, Tolman, and Skinner, have moved away from an almost exclusive concern with the environment (that is, with objective, observable, publicly verifiable behavior) to include internal psychological events as stimuli governing or shaping behavior. Osgood proposes a two-stage model of behavior utilizing an implicit stimulus-producing response assumed to mediate between observable S and observable R, yielding: S-r-s-R. The r-s refers to a covert process and might represent, for example, a listener's meaningful reaction to something just said (r) and the self-stimulation or thinking that the reaction triggers (s), both of which might lead to some overt responding.

This model is an attempt to overcome some of the limitations of the single-stage S-R behavioral model, chiefly its failure to handle symbolic processes such as ideation, cognition, and meaning. In this type of paradigm, phenomenological events can be regarded as intervening variables or internal mediating responses. Skinner (1964), in a discussion of public and private events in psychology, stated: "It is particularly important that a science of behavior face the problem of privacy. An adequate science of behavior must consider events taking place within the skin of the organism, not as physiological mediators of behavior, but as part of the behavior itself [p. 84]."

Concerning this same issue of private events in psychology, Homme (1965) coined the word *coverant* as a contraction of *covert-operant*. In Homme's words, "Coverants are events the laymen call mental. These include thinking, imagining, reflecting, ruminating, relaxing, day-dreaming, fantasying, etc. Difficulties in the control of one or the other of the coverant class undoubtedly underlie a good many behavioral or personality disorders [p. 502]."

To summarize, what seems to characterize the present scene is an increasingly fruitful dialogue between behaviorism and phenomenology. What seems to be developing is a view that "Man is at once both a whole being and a collection of habits and behaviors: that man's total being can be seen as a product of the interplay between molar self and the specific acts and habits that fill in the mosaic of daily living [Truax, 1967, p. 150]."

EXPERIENCE AS BEHAVIOR

Liverant (1965) has pointed out that:

> At its most primitive level, experience (as is usually understood) is involved whenever any organism reacts to any stimulus. As a consequence of learning (i.e., as a result of an organism's inter-actions with his environment), these experiences are undergoing continuous alteration which in some deterministic fashion affects an arbitrarily selected (by the observer) end-state called a response. Viewed in this manner, all learning formulations deal with experience [p. 4].

Verbal reports then are the direct tie to this experience.

In Gestalt therapy we treat the phenomenology of the person—that is, his sensations, perceptions, thoughts, visualizations, etc.—as behaviors.

In Skinnerian terms these could be called *internal mediating responses* or in Hommeian terms, *coverants*. We could then translate self-awareness as used in Gestalt therapy as a process by which these coverants are made observable to the subject and observer; that is, the therapist. In other words, in Gestalt therapy we make observable or visible the phenomenal world of the subject. As Perls (1951) has pointed out:

> We emphasize that in all types of activity, whether it be sensing, remembering, or moving, our blind-spots and rigidities are in some aspect aware and not completely buried in an inaccessible unconscious. What is necessary is to give whatever aspect *is* aware more attention and interest so that the dim figure will sharpen and become clear against its ground. We can, at least, be aware that there *is* a blind-spot, and, by working alternately on what we can see or remember and on the muscular manipulations by which we *make* ourselves blind, we can gradually dissolve the blocks to full awareness [p. 117].

In the Gestalt approach, then, work in the present, in the here and now, is designed to produce observable behavior rather than merely to lead the person to talk about what he is thinking. The questions which guide the therapist are *not*, "Why are you behaving this way," but "What are you doing?" "How are you doing it?" "What is it doing for you to behave this way?"

LEARNING, PERSONALITY THEORIES, AND PERSONALITY CHANGE STRATEGIES

As we have seen from the discussion of learning theory, learning is considered to be a relatively stable change in behavior, through practice, over time. Or, to put it more simply, learning is a change in behavior as a result of experience. As such, learning has a place in personality theory and in psychotherapy.

Personality theories have two major functions: meaningfully to describe a person as he is, and to explain how and why he has become this way. These explanatory concepts, as Gendlin (1964) pointed out, tell us what prevents an individual from changing or being changed by experience. In other words, people somehow learn to be the way they are, and personality theories tell us something about how they got to be that way. Psychotherapy is essentially a process designed to change the individual in a meaningful way. The strategies employed in psychotherapy to effect change are usually based on a theory of personality, but the overall aim is to enable the individual to learn new ways of thinking, feeling, and behaving. To put this into a learning framework, we could say that the psychotherapy strategies differ depending on what the particular personality theory sees as the crucial determinants of behavior.

For example, psychoanalytic personality theory explains behavior, particularly maladaptive or neurotic behavior, on the basis of past learnings. Psychoanalytic therapy then deals with the past, with the stimulus history of the client. Through the techniques of free association and dream interpretation, he learns to understand better how he came to be the way he is. The analysis of the transference relations with the therapist enables the client to discover how he still continues to behave as if the past existed. The discovery of reality comes about through new learning in his relationship with the nonpunitive person of the analyst.

The behavior therapists, on the other hand, focus on the actual behavior or symptom that is causing the chief problem for the client. If the therapy is based on operant principles, new and appropriate behavior is rewarded when it occurs. Old and inappropriate responses are extinguished either through punishment or nonreward.

The existential therapists consider the important determinants of behavior to lie inside the person, and thus they focus on the client's phenomenology, that is, the internal events, or his inner world of experience.

GESTALT THERAPY AND PHENOMENOLOGICAL LEARNING

The aim of Gestalt therapy is to develop more "intelligent" behavior; that is, to enable the individual to act on the basis of all possible information and to apprehend not only the relevant factors in the external field, but also relevant information from within. The individual is directed to pay attention at any given moment to what he is feeling, what he wants, and what he is doing. The goal of such direction is noninterrupted awareness. The process of increasing awareness enables the individual to discover how he interrupts his own functioning. These interruptions can be thought of as the resistances, or the evidence of resistances. What is being resisted is the awareness of the needs that organize his behavior. Awareness in the present then becomes a tool for uncovering those needs and for discovering the ways in which the individual prevents himself from experiencing the needs.

Because of the centrality of the concept of "awareness," Gestalt therapists call attention to the manner in which a person blocks or interrupts his communications, either with his internal self-system or with the interpersonal system. Awareness of the block can be facilitated by directing attention to what his body is doing, what his mind is doing, and what is or is not going on between people (*motoric, symbolic, and interpersonal* behaviors).

Motoric behavior refers to the language of the body and may be seen in how the client looks, how his voice sounds, how he is sitting, what parts of his body are moving. This is directly observable behavior, and the client's attention is directed to what he is doing. For instance, the therapist might initiate body work by saying, "Close your eyes and pay attention to your bodily sensations. Concentrate on them. What do you feel in your body? Can you stay with that?" Or the therapist might observe some movement in the client and begin there.

Focusing on a client's motoric behavior may, for example, call attention to the manner in which he is blocking his anger from awareness and from overt expression. In learning terms, the coverant, anger, is then labeled and identified as belonging to the self. Such identification makes possible a congruent and appropriate expression of the feeling.

Symbolic behavior refers to "mental events" such as thinking, imagining, daydreaming, etc. Such behavior is not directly observable by the therapist, but the client's attention may be directed toward his own phenomenology, that is, toward what he is *feeling*, chiefly by way of fantasy or actual visualization. Gestalt therapists are especially interested in the client's symbolic representations as these are the coverants that determine his overt behavior. Visualization may involve imagining a dialogue with another person or with a whole cast of characters. In working with visualization, the client is instructed to stay with the imagined situation and to let it change as it will. The therapist then deals with the client's feelings, movements, etc., in relation to the visualization as it is emerging. For example, one client, in visualizing an encounter with his father-in-law, has a fantasy about being pursued by Indians. As the fantasy develops, he is able to turn around and shoot back, thereby saving himself. The visualization was a symbolic representation of a problem; it showed his initial avoidance of it by running away, and his possible solution, namely, confronting the pursuer and asserting himself. By making these coverants overt, the client was able to discover an alternative response to avoidance.

Interpersonal behavior refers to those behaviors which bridge the psychological contact boundaries between separate organisms. The person has certain functions by means of which he contacts others, for example, seeing, hearing, touching, vocalizing, etc. If we see one of the basic purposes of therapy as being a return to contact with others, then it becomes especially important that the client become aware of how he is blocking contact and that he experiment with interpersonal behaviors that increase contact.

By experimenting, a client can discover how he keeps himself apart from others. For example, a woman who believed herself to be inferior was able to test the reality of this concept with other group members. She discovered that although she may have felt inferior to others in the group in some ways, she also felt adequate in relation to them in other ways.

Experiments in the here and now permit the client to observe, cognize and specify his coverants. Much of our behavior is under the control of these coverants. What is learned by experiencing is what governs behavior. In other words, the individual learns what it is he is doing, or not doing, that prevents him from being in contact with himself and with others. Such awareness means that he can choose to continue the behavior or to change it.

Thus we may view human problem behavior, that is, "pathology," as learned behavior and psychotherapy as essentially a reeducational process. All psychological learning theories attempt to specify the variables that determine behavior. The behaviorist is primarily concerned with and attempts to account for external events, that is, for stimuli and responses. The phenomenologist, on the other hand, assumes certain "givens" about the nature of man and is concerned with what goes on inside the person, that is, with the rich, variegated, and elusive internal world of the individual. The behavioristic phenomenologist deals with this world of personal experiencing in such a way as to make it external, overt, specifiable, and communicable.

REFERENCES

Anderson, Henry. Toward a sociology of being. *Manas,* 1968, *21* (3).

Brien, Lois. The behaviorist's approach to learning. *Ohio Journal of Speech and Hearing,* 1966, *2,* 74-79.

Deese, James. *The psychology of learning.* New York: McGraw-Hill, 1958.

Gendlin, Eugene T. A theory of personality change. In P. Worchel and D. Byrne (Eds.), *Personality change.* New York: John Wiley & Sons, 1964.

Hill, Winifred F. *Learning.* San Francisco: Chandler Publishers, 1963.

Homme, Lloyd E. Perspectives in psychology: XXIV, Control of coverants, the operants of the mind. *Psychological Record,* 1965, *15,* 501-511.

Kepner, Elaine. Application of learning theory to the etiology and treatment of alcoholism. *Quarterly Journal of Studies on Alcohol,* 1964, *25,* 279-291.

Koch, Sigmund. Psychology and emerging conceptions of knowledge as unitary. In T. W. Wann, (Ed.), *Behaviorism and phenomenology.* Chicago: University of Chicago Press, 1964. Pp. 1-45.

Liverant, Shephard. *Learning theory and clinical psychology.* Washington, D.C.: Clearing house for Federal Scientific and Technical Information, Defense Documentation Center, AD 612 – 126, 1965.

May, Angel E., and Ellenberger, H. F. (Eds.), *Existence.* New York: Basic Books, 1958.

Mednick, Sarnoff A. *Learning.* Englewood Cliffs, N.J.: Prentice-Hall, 1964.

Michael, Jack, and Meyerson, Lee. A behavioral approach to counseling and guidance. In R. L. Mosher, et al. *Guidance: An examination.* New York: Harcourt, Brace, and World, 1965.

Osgood, C.E., and Miron, M.S. (Eds.), *Approaches to the study of aphasia.* Urbana: University of Illinois Press, 1963.

Perls, Frederick, Hefferline, R. F., and Goodman, Paul. *Gestalt therapy,* New York: Dell, 1951.

Scriven, M. Views of human nature. In T. W. Wann (Ed.), *Behaviorism and phenomenology.* Chicago: University of Chicago Press, 1964.

Skinner, B.F. Behaviorism at fifty. In T. W. Wann (Ed.), *Behaviorism and phenomenology.* Chicago: University of Chicago Press, 1964.

Spence, Kenneth W. Behavior theory and conditioning. New Haven, Conn.: Yale University Press, 1956.

Truax, Charles B., and Carkhuff, Robert R. *Toward effective counseling and psychotherapy: Training and practice.* Chicago: Aldine, 1967.

CHAPTER 4

PRESENT-CENTEREDNESS:
Technique, Prescription, and Ideal

Claudio Naranjo

Psychoanalysis borrowed a haughty axiological neutrality from that complex cultural entity of our times called science. Like science, it prided itself on being "unbiased" by values, this being an aspect of what is generally understood as its "objectivity." Yet, the valuation of aloofness or noncommitment is in itself a value orientation, after all, and in the light of this the objectivity of science entails a built-in self-deception. As Laing (1960) put it:

> It may be maintained that one cannot be scientific without retaining one's "objectivity." A genuine science of personal existence must attempt to be as unbiased as possible. Physics and the other sciences of things must accord the science of persons the right to be unbiased in a way that is true to its own field of study. If it is held that to be unbiased one should be "objective" in the sense of depersonalizing the person who is the "object" of our study, any temptation to do this under the impression that one is thereby being scientific must be rigorously resisted. Depersonalization in a theory that is intended to be a theory of persons is as false as schizoid depersonalization of others and is no less ultimately an intentional act. Although conducted in the name of science, such reification yields false "knowledge." It is just as pathetic a fallacy as the false personalization of things [p. 24].

That psychoanalysis entails an underground of values amounting to a tacit philosophy may be revealed by any inquiry into the language, themes, and statements in a standard psychoanalytic publication, especially if this is carried out with an anthropological eye. Yet a characteristic of such an underground of beliefs is to be informal and claim nonexistence. Explicitly, psychoanalysis is a science, and its application an art; it is a theory of the mind and, particularly, a theory of the psychoneuroses.

Gestalt therapy, in contrast to psychoanalysis, has little to add to a dynamic interpretation of psychopathological phenomena. It is a "therapy" more than a theory, an art more than a psychological system. Yet, like psychoanalysis, Gestalt therapy involves a philosophical underground. More than that, it rests on an implicit philosophical posture which is transmitted from therapist to patient or trainee by means of its procedures without need of explication. In addition, I would like to suggest that the experiential assimilation of such implicit *Weltanschauung* is a hidden key to the therapeutic process. This amounts to the claim that a specific *philosophy* of life provides the background for Gestalt therapy just as a specific *psychology* provides that for psychoanalytic therapy.

The transmission of certain attitudes through the use of the tools characteristic of this approach may be likened to the process whereby a sculptor creates a form with the tools of his art. In both instances the content transcends the instruments, although the instruments have been conceived for its expression. Unfortunately, it is one of our human weaknesses to trust that formulas and techniques will do everything for us, as is shown by the history of every cult, where truth petrifies into rigid forms.

In calling the philosophy of Gestalt therapy "implicit" I am not saying that it is, as in psychoanalysis, covert. It is *simply* implicit, for the Gestalt therapist places more value in action than in words, in experience than in thoughts, in the living process of therapeutic interaction and the inner change resulting thereby than in influencing beliefs. Action engenders substance or touches substance. Ideas can easily float by, cover up, or even substitute for reality. So nothing could be more remote from the style of Gestalt therapy than preaching. Yet it involves a kind of preaching without injunctions or statements of belief, just as an artist preaches his world-view and orientation to existence through his style.

Morality beyond Good and Evil

"Good" and "evil" are suspicious to the Gestalt therapist, who is used to perceiving most of human advice as subtle manipulation, discussion on moral issues as self-justification and rationalization of needs, and statements of worth or worthlessness as overgeneralizations and as projections of personal experience onto the environment—all done to avoid responsibility for the person's feelings and reactions. As Perls (1953, 1954) put it:

> Good and bad are responses of the organism. We say, "You make me mad." "You make me feel happy." Less frequently, "You make me feel good." "You make me feel bad." Among primitive people such phrases occur with extreme frequency. Again we use expressions like "I feel good," "I feel lousy," without considering the stimulus. But what is happening is that

an ardent pupil makes his teacher feel good, an obedient child makes his parents feel good. The victorious boxer makes his fan feel good, as does the efficient lover his mistress. A book or a picture does the same when it meets your aesthetic needs. And *vice versa*: if people or objects fail to meet needs and produce satisfaction, we feel bad about them.

The next step is that instead of owning up to our experiences as ours, we project them and throw the responsibility for our own responses onto the stimulus. (This might be because we are afraid of our excitement, feel that we are failing in excitement, want to shirk responsibility, etc., etc.) We say the pupil, the child, the boxer, the lover, the book, the picture "is" good or bad. At that moment, labeling the stimulus good or bad, we cut off good and bad from our own experience. They become abstractions, and the stimulus-objects are correspondingly pigeon-holed. This does not happen without consequences. Once we isolate thinking from feeling, judgment from intuition, morality from self-awareness, deliberateness from spontaneity, the verbal from the non-verbal, we lose the Self, the essence of existence, and we become either frigid human robots or confused neurotics.

In spite of such views on good and bad, Gestalt therapy abounds in injunctions as to the desirability of certain attitudes toward life and experience. These are *moral* injunctions in the sense that they refer to the pursuit of the good life. Even though the notion of morality in common parlance has come to indicate a concern about living up to standards extrinsic to man, it is possible that all the great issues in morality once originated in a humanistic ethic where good and evil were not divorced from man's condition. Thus the concept of *righteousness* in Judaism, that eminently law-giving religion, once indicated the condition of being in tune with God's law or will, which we may understand as similar to that alluded to by the nontheistic Chinese as living in the Tao—following one's proper *Way*. So it would seem that what in a living vision of life is seen as right, just, adequate, or good, after being expressed in laws, turns against man and enslaves him by claiming some authority greater than himself.

If we want to list the implicit moral injunctions of Gestalt therapy, the list may be longer or shorter according to the level of generality or particularity of our analysis. Without claiming to be systematic or thorough, here are some that may give an impressionistic notion of the style of life entailed:

1.   Live now. Be concerned with the present rather than with past or future.

2.   Live here. Deal with what is present rather than with what is absent.

3.   Stop imagining. Experience the real.

4. Stop unnecessary thinking. Rather, taste and see.
5. Express rather than manipulate, explain, justify, or judge.
6. Give in to unpleasantness and pain just as to pleasure. Do not restrict your awareness.
7. Accept no *should* or *ought* other than your own. Adore no graven image.
8. Take full responsibility for your actions, feelings, and thoughts.
9. Surrender to being as you are.

The paradox that such injunctions may be part of a moral philosophy that precisely recommends giving up injunctions may be resolved if we look at them as statements of truth rather than duty. Responsibility, for instance, is not a *must*, but an unavoidable fact: we *are* the responsible doers of whatever we do. Our only alternatives are to acknowledge such responsibility or deny it. All that Gestalt therapy is saying is that by accepting the truth (which amounts to a non-undoing rather than a doing) we are better off—awareness cures. Of course, it cures us of our lies.

I think that the specific injunctions of Gestalt therapy may in turn be subsumed under more general principles. I would propose the following three:

1. Valuation of actuality: temporal (present versus past or future), spatial (present versus absent), and substantial (act versus symbol).
2. Valuation of awareness and the acceptance of experience.
3. Valuation of wholeness, or responsibility.

None of the three broad life-prescriptions of Gestalt therapy listed above is the direct opposite of any world philosophy that I am aware of, although the emphasis on personal responsibility runs counter to the authoritarian streak in most mass religions. Instead, the value-orientation of Gestalt therapy is the opposite of many people's implicit philosophy of life—a philosophy that falls into familiar cultural concepts. Thus an opposite to the valuation of actuality can be found in traditionalism with its emphasis on subordinating present actions to the past, whether in the form of dead ancestors, cultural heritage, or the opinion of the aged. Also opposite to it is the future-orientation of technological societies, such as the United States. Kluckhohn (1959) has proposed time orientation as a basic issue for the understanding of values in a culture.

An opposite to the valuation of awareness and experience is the common trait that the authors of *The Authoritarian Personality* (1950) call *anti-intraception*, which they find typical of the fascist mind. This is an opposition, dislike, and rejection of the tendency to be interested in what we call "the inner life," whether in oneself or others. A typical statement endorsed by such people is, for instance, that "when a person has a problem or worry, it is best for him not to think about it, but to keep busy with more cheerful things."

The tenet of responsibility in Gestalt therapy also finds more support than challenge in the world of philosophy, but it contradicts the prevalent assumption of a divine authority *outside* the individual—in kings, priests, parents, or scientists—which is responsible for the choice of the individual's course of action or orientation. It also contradicts our common perception of ourselves as helpless playthings of accident and circumstances rather than creators of our destiny.

In the following pages I will consider in some detail one of the aspects of actuality, in itself one aspect of the philosophy of life of Gestalt therapy. In choosing *living-in-the-moment* as a theme, I am not implying that this is more important than the issues of consciousness or responsibility, but only limiting the scope of this paper to the subject on which I feel most inclined to write at the moment. I think, too, that whatever the point of departure, the content will be somewhat similar, for the three issues are only superficially distinct. On close examination we may discover, for instance, that the question of actuality is not only related to the valuation of present tense and present locus, but also to the valuing of concrete reality, sensing and feeling rather than thinking and imagining, to awareness, and to self-determination. More specifically, I hope that the following pages will show that the willingness to live in the moment is inseparable from the question of openness to experience, trust in the workings of reality, discrimination between reality and fantasy, surrender of control and acceptance of potential frustration, a hedonistic outlook, and awareness of potential death. All these issues are facets of a single experience of being-in-the-world, and looking at such an experience from the perspective of present-centeredness rather than other conceptual vantage points amounts to an arbitrary choice.

PRESENT-CENTEREDNESS AS TECHNIQUE

Although the *hic et nunc* formula recurs in scholastic literature, the relationship of the here and now to contemporary psychotherapy has been the outcome of a gradual evolution.

Psychoanalysis began with a past-oriented approach. Freud's discovery of free association had its origin in his experience with hypnosis, and his first explorations into the method were in the nature of an attempt to do away with the trance state and yet elicit the same clues for the understanding of his patient's past. He would, in those days, pose a question to the patient and ask him to report the first thought that came to his mind at the moment of touching his forehead. With increasing experience, he found that he could omit the touch on the forehead and also the question, and regard instead every utterance as an association to the preceding one in the spontaneous flow of thoughts, memories, and fantasies. At the time, this was to him no more than the raw material for an interpretive endeavor, the most precious associations being those related to the patient's childhood. His assumption then was that only by understanding the past could the patient be free from it in the present.

The first step toward an interest in the present in psychoanalysis was Freud's observation of "transference." Insofar as the patient's feelings toward the analyst were understood as the replica of his earlier feelings toward parents or siblings, the understanding of the therapeutic relationship became at once significant to the understanding of the still basic issue of the patient's past.

At the beginning, the analysis of transference was still subservient to retrospective interpretation, but we may assume that it became increasingly valued in its own right, for the next step was a gradual shift in stress from past to present, not only with respect to the material being examined but as the very goal of understanding. So although at first the analysis of the present was a tool or a means for the interpretation of the past, many today regard the analysis of childhood events as a means toward the understanding of *present* dynamics.

The lines of development have been multiple. Melanie Klein, for instance, retains an interpretational language based on assumptions about early childhood experience, but the trend of her school, in actual practice, is to focus almost exclusively on the understanding of the transference relationship. A similar focus on the present was carried by Bion into the group situation.

Wilhelm Reich's shift toward the present was the outcome of his shift of interest from words to action, the goal in his character analysis becoming that of understanding the patient's *form* of expression rather than the content of his speech. There can be no better way of doing so than by observing his conduct in the ongoing situation.

A third contribution to the valuing of the present in the therapeutic process was made by Karen Horney, touching on the very foundation of the interpretation of neuroses. In her view, emotional disturbances that originated in the past are sustained *now* by a false identity. The neurotic once sold his soul to the devil in exchange for a shining self-image, but he is still choosing to respect the pact. If a person can understand how he is burying his true self in this very moment, he can be free.

The growing emphasis on present-orientation in contemporary psychotherapy can be traced to the impact of two other sources aside from psychoanalysis: encounter groups, which are becoming increasingly widespread: and the Eastern spiritual disciplines, with Zen in particular having contributed to the shaping of Gestalt therapy into its present form.

There are at least two ways in which present-centeredness is reflected in the technical repertoire of Gestalt therapy. One is the outspoken request to the patient to attend to and express what enters his present field of awareness. This will most often be coupled with the instruction to suspend reasoning in favor of pure self-observation. The second is the *presentification* of the past or future (or fantasy in general). This may take the form of an inward attempt to identify with or relive past events or, most often, a reenacting of the scenes with gestural and postural participation as well as verbal exchanges, as in psychodrama.

Both techniques have antecedents in spiritual disciplines older than psychotherapy, and it could not be otherwise, given their importance. Presentification is found in the history of drama, magic, and ritual, and in the enacting of dreams among some primitive people. Dwelling in the present is the cornerstone of some forms of meditation. Yet both presentification and dwelling in the present find in Gestalt therapy a distinctive embodiment and form of utilization that deserve discussion at length. In the following pages I will concentrate on the approach called *the exercise of the continuum of awareness*. Since it is very much like a meditation translated into words, and its role in Gestalt therapy is comparable to that of free-association in psychoanalysis, I will deal with it mostly in comparative terms.

Gestalt Therapy and Meditation

The practice of attention to present experience has had a place in several traditions of spiritual discipline. In Buddhism it is a corollary of "right-mindfulness," one of the factors in the "Noble Eightfold Path." An aspect of right-mindfulness is the practice of "bare attention":

> Bare Attention is concerned only with the *present*. It teaches what so many have forgotten: to live with full awareness in the Here and Now. It teaches us to *face* the present without trying to escape into thoughts about the past or the future. Past and future are, for average consciousness, not objects of observation, but of reflection. And, in ordinary life, the past and the future are taken but rarely as objects of truly *wise* reflection, but are mostly just objects of day-dreaming and vain imaginings which are the main foes of Right Mindfulness, Right Understanding and Right Action as well. Bare Attention, keeping faithfully to its post of observation, watches calmly and without attachment the unceasing march of time; it waits quietly for the things of the future to appear before its eyes, thus to turn into present objects and to vanish again into the past. How much energy has been wasted by useless thoughts of the past: by longing idly for bygone days, by vain regrets and repentance, and by the senseless and garrulous repetition, in word or thought, of all the

banalities of the past! Of equal futility is much of the thought
given to the future: vain hopes, fantastic plans and empty
dreams, ungrounded fears and useless worries. All this is again
a cause of avoidable sorrow and disappointment which can be
eliminated by Bare Attention [Nyaponika Thera, 1962, p.41].

Past and future do not qualify as "bare objects" in that they are in
the nature of imagining, but are also to be avoided because dwelling in
them entails a loss of freedom: illusion ensnares us in its recurrence. As
Nyaponika Thera (1962) says:

> Right Mindfulness recovers for man the lost pearl of his free-
> dom, snatching it from the jaws of the dragon Time. Right
> Mindfulness cuts man loose from the fetters of the past which
> he foolishly tries even to re-inforce by looking back to it too
> frequently, with eyes of longing, resentment or regret. Right
> Mindfulness stops man from chaining himself even now, through
> the imaginations of his fears and hopes, to anticipated events
> of the future. Thus Right Mindfulness restores to man a free-
> dom that is to be found only in the present [p. 41].

The most important practice related to the view in the quotation
above is that form of meditation the Chinese call *we-hsin* (or
idealessness), which consists, as Watts (1950) puts it, in the ability to retain one's normal and everyday consciousness and at the same time let go
of it.

> That is to say, one begins to take an objective view of the stream
> of thoughts, impressions, feelings and experiences which con-
> stantly flows through the mind. Instead of trying to control and
> interfere with it, one simply lets it flow as it pleases. But whereas
> consciousness normally lets itself be carried away by the flow,
> in this case the important thing is to *watch* the flow without
> being carried away . . . one simply accepts experiences as they
> come without interfering with them on the one hand or identify-
> ing oneself with them on the other. One does not judge them,
> form theories about them, try to control them, or attempt to
> change their nature in any way; one lets them be free to be just
> exactly what they are. "The perfect man," said Chuang-tzu,
> "employs his mind as a mirror; it grasps nothing, it refuses
> nothing, it receives but does not keep." This must be quite
> clearly distinguished from mere empty-mindedness on the one
> hand, and from ordinary undisciplined mind-wandering on the
> other [p. 176].

The practice of attention to the present in the context of Gestalt
therapy is very much like verbalized meditation. Moreover it is a meditation carried into the interpersonal situation as an act of self-disclosure.
This permits a monitoring of the exercise by the therapist (which may be

indispensable to the inexperienced) and may also add significance to the contents of awareness.

I would not doubt that the search for words and the act of reporting can interfere with certain states of mind; yet the act of expression also adds to the exercise in awareness, beyond its being merely a means of information for the therapist's intervention. At least the following advantages of communicated awareness over silent meditation may be listed:

1. The act of expression is a challenge to the sharpness of awareness. It is not quite true to say that we know something but cannot put it into words. Of course, words are mere words and we can never *put* anything into words; yet, within limits, clarity of perception goes together with the ability to express, an artist being a master in awareness rather than a skilled patternmaker. And in art, as in psychotherapy, the task of having to communicate something involves having to really look at it rather than dreaming about looking.

2. The presence of a witness usually entails an enhancement both of attention and of the meaningfulness of that which is observed. I think too that the more aware an observer is, the more our own attention is sharpened by his mere presence, as if consciousness were contagious or one person could not as easily avoid seeing what is exposed to the gaze of another.

3. The contents of consciousness in an interpersonal setting will naturally tend to be that of the interpersonal relationship, whereas the solitary meditator focused on the here and now will systematically fail to find such contents in his field of awareness. Since it is mainly the patterns of relating and the self-image in the process of relating that are disturbed in psychopathological conditions, this factor looms large in making the here-and-now exercise a therapy when in the I-thou setting.

4. The interpersonal situation makes present-centeredness more difficult, for it elicits projection, avoidances, and self-delusion in general. For instance, what for the solitary meditator may be a series of observations of physical states may, in the context of communication, become embedded in a feeling of anxiety about the therapist's eventual boredom, or in an assumption that such observations are trivial, or that they show the patient's essential barrenness. The elicitation of such feelings and fantasies is important.

   a. If present-centeredness is a desirable way of living which is usually marred by the vicissitudes of interpersonal relationships, the challenge of contact entails the ideal *training* situation. I would like to invite the thought that the practice of living in the moment is truly an *exercise* and not merely an occasion for self-insight. Just as in behavior therapy, this is a process of desensitization in the course of which a person becomes free of the central conditioning of avoiding experience, and he learns that there is nothing to fear.

b. Related to the above is the fact that it is precisely the awareness of the difficulties in present-centeredness that can provide the first step toward overcoming them. Experiencing the compulsive quality of brooding or planning may be inseparable from an appreciation of the alternative to them, and of a true understanding of the distinction between these states of mind and present-centeredness.

5. The therapeutic context allows for a monitoring of the process of self-observation, whereby the therapist brings the patient back to the present when he has been distracted from it (that is, from himself). There are two main ways of doing this. The simplest (aside from merely reminding him of the task) is to call his attention to what he is doing unawares, by directing his attention to aspects of his behavior that seem to be automatic response patterns or to clash with his intentional actions. Simply being mirror to him may serve to bring into focus his relationship to himself and his actions in general:

P.: I don't know what to say now. . . .

T.: I notice that you are looking away from me.

P.: (Giggle.)

T.: And now you cover up your face.

P.: You make me feel so awful!

T.: And now you cover up your face with both hands.

P.: Stop! This is unbearable!

T.: What do you feel now?

P.: I feel so embarrassed! Don't look at me!

T.: Please stay with that embarrassment.

P.: I have been living with it all my life! I am ashamed of everything I do! It is as if I don't even feel that I have the right to exist!

An alternative to this process of simply reflecting the patient's behavior is that of regarding the occasions of failure in present-centeredness as cues to the patient's difficulties (or rather, living samples thereof), just as in psychoanalysis the failure to free-associate is the target of interpretation. Instead of interpretation, in Gestalt therapy we have explicitation: the request that the patient himself become aware of and express the experience underlying his present-avoiding behavior. One of the assumptions in Gestalt therapy is that *present-centeredness is natural*: at depth, living in the moment is what we want most, and therefore deviations from the present are in the nature of an avoidance or a compulsive sacrifice rather than random alternatives. Even if this assumption were not true of human communication in general, it is made true in Gestalt therapy by the request that the patient stay in the present. Under such a structure, deviations may be understood as failures, as a sabotaging of the intent, or as distrust in the whole approach and/or the psychotherapist.

In practice, therefore, the therapist will not only coach the patient into persistent attention to his ongoing experience, but will especially encourage him to become aware and to express his experience at the point of failing at the task. This amounts to stopping in order to fill in the gaps of awareness:

P.:   My heart is pounding. My hands are sweating. I am scared. I remember the time when I worked with you last time and . . .

T.:   What do you want to tell me by going back to last week?

P.:   I was afraid of exposing myself, and then I felt relieved again, but I think that I didn't come out with the real thing.

T.:   Why do you want to tell me that now?

P.:   I would like to face this fear and bring out whatever it is that I am avoiding.

T.:   O.K. That is what you want now. Please go on with your experiences in the moment.

P.:   I would like to make a parenthesis to tell you that I have felt much better this week.

T.:   Could you tell me anything of your experience while making this parenthesis?

P.:   I feel grateful to you, and I want you to know it.

T.:   I get the message. Now please compare these two statements: "I feel grateful," and the account of your well-being this week. Can you tell me what it is you felt that makes you prefer the story to the direct statement of your feeling?

P.: If I were to say, "I feel grateful to you," I would feel that
     I still have to explain . . . Oh! Now I know. Speaking of my
     gratefulness strikes me as too direct. I feel more comfortable
     in letting you guess, or just making you feel good without
     letting you know my feeling.

In this particular instance we can see that the patient has avoided expressing and taking responsibility for his feeling of gratitude (because of
his ambivalence, it later became apparent) and has acted out his feeling
instead of disclosing it in an attempt to please the therapist rather than
becoming aware of *his* desire for the therapist to be pleased.

When the patient deviates from the present, exploration of his motivation often fills gaps in awareness and leads to direct and effective
expression.

T.: Now see what it feels like to tell me of your gratefulness as
     directly as possible.

P.: I want to thank you very much for what you have done for
     me. I feel that I would like to recompense you for your
     attention in some way . . . Wow! I feel so uncomfortable
     saying this. I feel that you may think that I am being a hypo-
     crite and a boot-licker. I guess that *I* feel that this was a
     hypocritical statement. I don't feel *that* grateful. I want *you*
     to believe that I feel grateful.

T.: Stay with that. How do you feel when you want me to believe
     that?

P.: I feel small, unprotected. I am afraid that you may attack me,
     so I want to have you on my side.

We can look at the foregoing illustration in terms of the patient's initially not wanting to take responsibility for his alleged gratefulness.
Finally, when he did take responsibility for *wanting the therapist to
perceive him as grateful*, it became clear this was because of his ambivalence and his reluctance to tell an explicit lie (or, at least, a half-truth)
and he could acknowledge his fear at the root of the whole event. It is
true that his first statement referred to the pounding of his heart and his
fear, but now in speaking of the expectation that the doctor might attack
him, he has gone more into the substance of his fear. Looking back at the
excerpt, it seems reasonable to assume that he deviated from present-
centeredness when he implicitly chose to manipulate rather than experience. Mere insistence on returning to the present could have possibly
told more of the contents of his surface consciousness, but it would have
failed to reveal the out-of-awareness operation of his avoidance.

The Continuum of Awareness and Free Association

Reporting the experience-at-the-moment not only holds a place in Gestalt therapy comparable to that of free association in psychoanalysis, but the difference between the two in practice is not as clear-cut as it would seem from their definitions.

In principle, "free association of *thought*" emphasizes what Gestalt therapy avoids the most: memories, reasoning, and explanations. In actual practice, however, the psychoanalytic patient may be primarily experience-centered in his communication, while a Gestalt-therapy patient may frequently deviate from the field of present sensing, feeling, and doing. Aside from the instructions given to the patient in Gestalt therapy to limit his communication to actuality and the field of immediate experience, there is a difference brought about by the therapist's approach to the patient's communication in both instances.

Let us take the case of a patient reminiscing about a pleasant event. An analyst might lead the patient to become engaged with the significance of the event remembered. The Gestalt therapist, on the contrary, will most probably attend to the missing report on *what is happening with the patient now, while he chooses to remember rather than dwell in the present.* Rather than focusing on the content of the memory, the therapist is concerned with the patient's present *action* of bringing the event to mind or reporting it.

The analyst, too, may choose to focus on the patient's present. In such a case he will most probably *interpret* the reminiscing as either a compensation and defense in face of the patient's feelings at the moment, or as a cue or indirect indication of his actual pleasurable feelings. The Gestalt therapist, on the other hand, will consider interpretations as messages to the patient's analytical mind, which must step out of reality in order to "think about" it. His efforts are in precisely the opposite direction—to minimize the current estrangement from experience involved in abstraction and interpretation. Therefore he will recruit the patient's efforts as a co-phenomenologist to the end of *observing*, rather than theorizing about or labeling this act of remembering. The awareness of "I am remembering something pleasant" is already a step beyond the act of remembering in itself, and may open up an avenue to the understanding of the actual motive or intent in the process. For instance, it might lead to the realization that "I want to make you feel that I have lots of good friends so you think that I am a great guy." Or, "I wish that I could feel as happy as I did in those days. Please help me." Or, "I am feeling very well-cared-for right now—just as on that occasion," and so on.

In fact, if the patient knew what he was doing in his actions of remembering, anticipating, and interpreting, there would be nothing "wrong" with them. The usual trouble is that such actions replace, cover up, and amount to an acting-out of an ongoing experience rather than its acknowledgement and acceptance. What is wrong is that they stem from the assumption that something is wrong, and the consciousness tends to be entrapped in them to the point of self-forgetfulness. Watts (1950) has commented that, after practicing for some time the exercise of living-in-the-moment, it will become apparent

> that in actual reality it is impossible to live outside this moment. Obviously our thoughts of past and future transpire in the present, and in this sense it is impossible to concentrate on anything except what is happening now. However, by *trying* to live simply in the present, by trying to cultivate the pure "momentary" awareness of the Self, we discover in experience as well as theory that the attempt is unnecessary. We learn that never for an instant has the time-thinking of the ego actually interfered with the eternal and momentary consciousness of the Self. Underlying memory, anticipation, anxiety and greed there has always been this centre of pure and unmoved awareness, which never at any time departed from present reality, and was therefore never actually bound by the chain of dreams [p. 179].

As soon as this is realized, he notes,

> it becomes possible once more to entertain memory and anticipation, and yet be free from their binding power. For as soon as one is able to look upon memory and anticipation as present, one has made them (and the ego which they constitute) objective. Formerly they were subjective, because they consisted in *identifying oneself* with past or future events, that is, with the temporal chain constituting the ego. But when one is able, for instance, to regard anticipation as present, one is no longer identifying oneself with the future, and is therefore taking the viewpoint of the Self as distinct from the ego. To put it in another way: as soon as the ego's act of identifying itself with the future can be seen as something present, one is seeing it from a standpoint superior to the ego, from the standpoint of the Self.
>
> It follows that when our centre of consciousness has shifted to the strictly present and momentary outlook of the Self, memory and anticipation guide peripheral and objective actions of the mind, and our being is no more dominated by and identified with the egoistic mode of thought. We have all the serenity, all the keen awareness, all the freedom from temporality, of one who lives wholly in the present, and yet without the absurd limitation of not being able to remember the past or to provide for the future [p. 179-186].

The Continuum of Awareness and Asceticism

In spite of the last statement, it may be a psychological truth that a person can hardly attain present-centeredness while remembering, before having known the taste of it in the easier situation of reminiscence-deprivation. The same may be parenthetically said on the matter of contacting one's experience while thinking. Ordinarily, thinking dispels the awareness of the self-in-the-activity-as-thinker and the feelings constituting the ground of the thinking-motivation , just as the sun during the daytime prevents our seeing the stars. The experience of thinking and not being lost in thought, (that is, caught up in the exclusive awareness of the figure in the totality of figure-ground) is a condition that can be brought about most easily by contacting such experience-ground in moments of thoughtlessness. In this the Gestalt therapy techniques of suspending reminiscence, anticipation, and thinking fall in with the implicit philosophy of asceticism in general: certain deprivations are undergone in order to contact what is currently hidden by the psychological activity involved in the renounced situations. Thus deprivation of sleep, talking, social communication, comfort, food, or sex is supposed to facilitate the access to unusual states of consciousness but is not an end or ideal in itself.

The practice of attention to the stream of life relates to asceticism in that it not only entails a voluntary suspension of ego-gratification, but also presents the person with the difficulty of functioning in a way that runs counter to habit. Since the only action allowed by the exercise is that of communicating the contents of awareness, this precludes the operation of "character" (that is, the organization of coping mechanisms) and even *doing* as such. The practice of the now is one of ego-loss, as emphasized by Buddhism and discussed in the quotation from Watts.

PRESENT-CENTEREDNESS AS PRESCRIPTION

Not all that is of value as a psychological exercise need automatically be a good prescription for living. Free association may be a useful exercise, but not necessarily the best approach to conversation, just as the headstand in Hatha Yoga need not be the best posture to be in most of the time. To a greater or lesser extent, techniques have a potential for being carried into ordinary life, thus making of life the occasion for a growth endeavor. Yet it is not only the specific value of a certain approach that makes it appropriate as a prescription, but its compatibility with other desirable purposes in life; the degree of clash that it will bring about with the existing social structure and, especially, its compatibility with a conception of the good society. Thus the abreaction of hostility in a situation of no constraints can be of value in psychotherapy, but is this approach the one that would maximize sanity and well-being in a community? I think that opinions on the matter would be divided. They would be divided even on the question of truth. Whereas aggression tends to be socially reproved and the commandment states, "Thou shalt not kill," truth is commonly regarded as virtue, and lying a sin. One might therefore expect that the technique of self-disclosure, valuable in the context of psychotherapy, would be immediately applicable to life. Given the ordinary condition of humanity, though, truth has been and may continue to be not only uncomfortable or inconvenient but dangerous. The examples of Socrates, Jesus Christ, or the heretics at the time of the Inquisition, point out that an unconditional embracing of truth may mean the acceptance of martyrdom, for which I am sure the average human being is not ready. The desire to turn feelings into prescriptions in cases where society did not make such a project feasible has been one of the implicit or explicit rationales in the creation of special communities among those who share the goal of living for the inner quest. In such groups, sometimes veiled by secrecy, man has sought to live according to principles not compatible with other than a monastic, therapeutic, or otherwise special setting.

Humanistic Hedonism

Living in the moment, in contrast to other techniques, seems a perfectly appropriate prescription for life. Moreover, it appears to be more in the nature of a technicalization of a life formula than the prescribing of a technique. The idea of prescription may evoke images such as that of the bad-smelling tonic that children were frequently compelled to take "for their own good," before the time of gelatin capsules and flavor chemistry. This is part of a dualistic frame of mind in which "the good things" seem different from the "things for our good," and the goal of self-perfecting seems something other than "merely living."

This is not what the classic injunctions of present-centeredness convey. Take, for instance, King Solomon's "A man hath no better thing under the sun, than to eat, and to drink, and to be merry [Eccles. 15]." The character of this quotation, like that of most statements that stress the value of actuality, is hedonistic. And it could not be otherwise, for if the value of the present is *not* going to be for a future, it must be *intrinsic*: the present must contain its own reward.

In our times the hedonistic outlook seems to be divorced from and to run counter to religious feeling (just as to "prescription orientation" in general). Insofar as "body" and "mind" are regarded as incompatible sources of value, idealism and spirituality tend to be associated with a grim asceticism, while the defense of pleasure is most often undertaken by the cynically practical, tough-minded, and hard-nosed "realists." This does not seem to have always been so, and we know that there was a time when religious feasts were real festivals. So, when we read Solomon's words in the Old Testament, we should not superimpose on them our present body-mind split, or the tough-mindedness with which those words are often repeated. Behind them was an outlook according to which living life and living it now was a holy action, a way in accordance with God's will.

Rarely do we find this balance of transcendence and immanence in Western thought, with the exception of remarkable individuals that seem to be marginal to the spirit of the times—heretics to the religious, or madmen to the common folk. William Blake, for instance, was such a man in claiming that "eternity is in love with the productions of time."

Even in psychoanalysis, which in practice has done much for mankind's *id*, the "pleasure principle" is looked upon as a childishness and a nuisance that the "mature," reality-oriented ego must hold in check.

Contrariwise, Gestalt therapy sees a much stronger link between pleasure and goodness, so that its philosophy may be called hedonistic in the same sense as the good old hedonisms before the Christian era. I would like to suggest the notion of humanistic hedonism, which does not necessarily entail a theistic outlook and yet seems to distinguish this approach from the egoistic hedonism of Hobbes, the utilitarian hedonism of J. S. Mill, and that of the ordinary pleasure seeker. (If at this point the reader wonders how Gestalt therapy can be called ascetic and hedonistic at the same time, let him remember that in Epicurus's view the most pleasurable life was one devoted to philosophical reflection while on a simple diet of bread, milk, and cheese.)

"Carpe Diem"

The hedonistic vein is inseparable from an intense appreciation of the present, not only in Gestalt therapy, but in the thinking of many (mostly poets and mystics) who have voiced a similar prescription. Perhaps the most insistent on this subject was Horace, whose *carpe diem* ("seize the day") has become a technical label to designate a motif that runs throughout the history of literature. Here it is in its original context:

> *Dom loquimur fuerbit invide aetas:*
> *carpe diem, quam minimum credula postero.*

> In the moment of our talking, envious time has ebbed away,
> Seize the present, trust tomorrow e'en as little as you may.

Horace's present-centeredness runs parallel to his awareness of the running away of "envious time": the irreparable loss of life that is the alternative to living in the moment. In the biblical injunction to eat, drink, and be merry, death is both the argument and the teacher. The same is true of many other statements, such as the saying, "Gather ye rosebuds while you may," or Ovid's passage in the *Art of Love*:

> *Corpite florem*
> *Qui nisi corptas erit turpiter ipse cadet.*

> Seize the flower,
> for if you pluck it not 'twill fade and fall.

Ovid, in particular, shares with Horace not only his hedonism and present-centeredness but his allusions to the cruelty of time: *"tempus edax rerum"* ("time devours things"). It would seem, therefore, that the prescription of living in the present goes hand in hand with the *awareness of death*—either the ultimate death or the chronic death of the moment as it becomes mere memory. In this sense it is a perception of the past as nothingness or unreality.

Awareness of potential death is also part of the spirit of Gestalt therapy, for such awareness is inseparable from human consciousness when freed from the avoidance of unpleasantness and from the veil of illusory satisfactions in unreality: wishful thinking and regressive reminiscence.

I would like to suggest that the triad of (1) present-centeredness, (2) the view of the present as a gift of pleasure, and (3) awareness of potential death or decay, amounts to an archetype: an experience for which the potentiality lies in human nature, so it need not be explained by tradition alone as is the custom among literary critics. Were it not for its archetypal substratum, the recurrent rewordings of the experience would impress us as mere plagiarism. Compare, for instance, King Solomon's and Ovid's injunctions with the following:

> Catch then, oh *catch the transient hour,*
> Improve each moment as it flies!
> Life's a short summer, *man a flower;*
> *He dies*—alas! how soon he flies!
> > Johnson

> Gather therefore the rose whilest yet is prime,
> For soon comes the age that will her pride deflowre:
> Gather the rose of love whilest yet is time,
> Whilest loving thou mayst loved be with equall crime.
> > Spenser, *The Faerie Queene*

Make use of time, let not advantage slip;
Beauty within itself should not be wasted:
Fair flowers that are not gathered in their prime,
Rot and consume themselves in little time.
Shakespeare, *Venus and Adonis*

If you let slip time, like a neglected rose
It withers on the stock with languished head.
Milton, *Comus*

As mentioned above, the focus of Gestalt therapy on the present is inseparable from its valuation of consciousness itself, expressed in its pursuit of relinquishing the avoidances with which our life is plagued. Not to avoid the present is not to avoid living in it, as we all too often do as a way of avoiding the consequence of our actions. Inasmuch as confronting the present is a commitment to living, it is freedom: the freedom to be ourselves, to choose according to our being's preference, to choose *our way*. Exposure to Gestalt therapy can demonstrate experientially that when the present is met in the spirit of nonavoidance—that is, with *presence*—it becomes what Dryden saw in it:

This hour's the very crisis of your fate,
Your good and ill, your infamy or fame,
And the whole colour of your life depends
On this important now.
The Spanish Friar

The issue is *now*, but we do not acknowledge it in our half-hearted way of living, thereby turning life into a deadly substitution of itself. We "kill" time or incur that "loss of time" at which "the wisest are most annoyed," according to Dante. Another way in which this particular aspect of living fully turns up in Gestalt therapy is in the *concept of closure*. In Gestalt psychology closure is applied to perception; in Gestalt therapy it is applied to action. We are always seeking to finish the unfinished, to complete the incomplete Gestalt, and yet always avoiding doing so. By failing to act in the present, we increase "unfinishedness" and our servitude to the load of the past. Moreover, as Horace puts it in one of his *Epistles*. "He who postpones the hour of living as he ought is like the rustic who waits for the river to pass along before he crosses; but it glides on and will glide on forever."

Perhaps we would not suspend life in the present if it were not for the dream of *future* action or satisfaction. In this connection the present-centeredness of Gestalt therapy bespeaks its realism in placing tangible existence and actual experience ahead of conceptual, symbolical, or imagined existence. Both the future and the past can only be alive in the present as thought forms—memories or fantasies—and Gestalt therapy aims at the subordination of these thought forms to *life*. Its attitude is the same as in J. Beattie: "The present moment is our ain,/The neist we never saw." Or Longfellow:

> Trust no future, howe'er pleasant,
> Let the dead Past bury its dead!
> Act, act in the living Present!
> Heart within and God o'erhead.

Or in a Persian proverb versified by Trench: "Oh, seize the instant time; you never will/With waters once passed by impel the mill." Or in another, "He that hath time and looketh for a better time, loseth time."

All these statements are inspired by the apprehension of a contrast between the *livingness* of the present and the nonexperiential (therefore relatively unreal) nature of past and future:

> Nothing is there to come, and nothing past,
> But an eternal now does always last.
>   Abraham Cawley

More often than not, our life is impoverished by the process of *substitution*, replacing substance with symbol, experience with mental construct, reality with the mere reflection of reality in the mirror of the intellect. Relinquishing past and future to come to the enduring present is one aspect of the prescription, "Lose your mind and come to your senses."

PRESENT-CENTEREDNESS AS IDEAL

> *Der den Augenblick ergreift / Das ist der rechte Mann.*
>
> He who seizes the moment is the right man.
>   Goethe

The word *ideal* needs clarification. Ideals are frequently understood with a connotation of duty and/or intrinsic goodness that is foreign to the philosophy of Gestalt therapy. If we deprive an ideal of its quality of *should* or *ought*, it remains as either a statement of the desirable way to an end—that is, a prescription—or else a "rightness." By this I mean an *expression* of goodness rather than a means or an injunction: a sign or symptom of an optimal condition of life. This is the sense in which we may speak of ideals in Taoism, for instance, in spite of its being a philosophy of nonseeking. In spite of its noninjunctional style, the Tao Te

Ching is always elaborating on the qualities of the sage: "For this reason the sage is concerned with the belly and not the eyes. . . . The sage is free from the disease because he recognizes the disease to be disease. . . . The sage knows without going about. . . accomplishes without any action," and so on. In the same sense, present-centeredness is regarded as an ideal in statements such as: "*Now* is the watchword of the wise."

Some recipes for better living are means to an end that differ from such an end in quality, but this is not true of present-centeredness. Here, as in Gestalt therapy in general, *the means to an end is a shifting to the end state right away*: the way to happiness is that of starting to be happy right away; the way to wisdom that of relinquishing foolishness at this very moment—just as the way to swim is the practice of swimming. The prescription of living in the now is the consequence of the fact that we *are* living in the now; this is something that the sane person *knows*, but the neurotic does not realize while enmeshed in a dreamlike pseudo-existence.

In Buddhism the now is not merely a spiritual exercise but the condition of the wise. In a passage of the *Pali Canon*, Buddha first utters the prescription:

> Do not hark back to things that passed,
> And for the future cherish no fond hopes:
> The past was left behind by thee,
> The future state has not yet come.

and then the ideal:

> But who with vision clear can see
> The present which is here and now
> Such wise one should aspire to win
> What never can be lost nor shaken.

Whereas the Buddist version of the now injunction stresses the illusoriness of the alternatives, the Christian view stresses the trust and surrender entailed by present-centeredness. When Jesus says, "Take, therefore, no thought of the morrow, for the morrow shall take thought for the things of itself," giving the example of the lilies of the fields [Matt. 6], he is not only saying, "Don't act upon catastrophic expectations," but more positively, "Trust!" While the Christian version is framed in a theistic map of the universe, and trust means trust in the heavenly Father, the attitude is the same as that regarded as the ideal in Gestalt therapy, which may be rendered as trust in one's own capacities for coping with the now as it comes. The ideal of present-centeredness is one of experiencing rather than manipulating, of being open to and accepting experience rather than dwelling in, and being defensive in the face of, possibility. Such attitudes bespeak two basic assumptions in the *Weltanschauung* of

Gestalt therapy: *things at this moment are the only way that they can be*; and *behold, the world is very good!*

If the present cannot be other than it is, the wise will surrender to it. Furthermore if the world is good, why not, as Seneca puts it, "gladly take the gifts of the present hour and leave vexing thoughts." To say of anything that *it* is good is, of course, a statement alien to Gestalt therapy, which hold that things can only be good to *us*. Whether they are depends on us and what we do with our circumstances.

Our current perception of existence is full of pain, helplessness, and victimization. As Edmund Burke remarked over two centuries ago: "To complain of the age we live in, to murmur of the present possessors of power, to lament the past, to conceive of extravagant hopes of the future are the common disposition of the greatest part of mankind." In the view of Gestalt therapy, however, such complaints and lamentations are no more than a bad game we play with ourselves—one more aspect of rejecting the potential bliss of now. At depth, we are where we want to be, we are doing what we want to do, even when it amounts to apparent tragedy. If we can discover our freedom within our slavery, we can also discover our essential joy under the cover of victimization.

The whole process of estrangement from reality, as reality is given in the eternal now, may be conceived as one of *not trusting* the goodness of the outcome, of *imagining* a catastrophic experience or, at best, an emptiness for which we compensate by creating a paradise of ideals, future expectations, or past glories. From such "idols" we keep looking down on present reality, which never quite matches our constructs and therefore never looks perfect enough. This is how the question of present-centeredness ties in with accepting experience rather than being judgmental.

As Emerson said,

> These roses under my window make no reference to former roses or to better ones; they are for what they are; they exist with God today. There is not time to them. There is simply the rose; it is perfect in every moment of its existence . . . but man postpones and remembers. He cannot be happy and strong until he, too, lives with nature in the present, above time.

Searching for the ideal rose, we don't see that each rose is the utmost perfection of itself. For fear of not finding the rose we seek, we hang on to the concept of "rose" and never learn that "a rose is a rose is a rose." Our greed and impatience do not permit us to let go of the substitute through which we enjoy the reflection of reality in the form of promise or possibility, and by which we are at the same time cut off from present enjoyment. The intuition of Paradise Lost and the Promised Land is better than total anesthesia, but short of the realization that they are right here. Omar Khayyám knew well:

Here with a loaf of bread beneath the bough,
A flask of wine, a book of verse—and thou
    Beside me singing in the wilderness—
And wilderness is Paradise enow.

"How sweet is mortal sovereignty!" think some,
Others, "How blest the Paradise to come!"
    Ah, take the cash in hand and waive the rest;
Nor heed the music of a *distant* drum!

Rubáiyát

REFERENCES

Adorno, T.W., Frenkel-Brunswik, E., Levinson, D.J., & Sanford, N. *The authoritarian personality*. New York: Harper & Row, 1950.

Blyth, R.H. *Zen and Zen classics*. Vol. 1. Japan: Hokuseido Press, 1960.

Kluckhohn, F.R. Dominant and variant value orientations. In C. Kluckhohn & H.A. Murray (Eds.), *Personality in nature, society, and culture*. (Rev. ed.) New York: Knopf, 1959. Pp. 342-357.

Laing, R.D. *The divided self*. Baltimore: Pelican Books, 1965.

Nyaponika Thera. *The heart of Buddhist meditation*. London: Rider, 1962.

Perls, F.S. Morality, ego-boundary and aggression. *Complex*, Winter issue, 1953-54.

Watts, Alan. *The supreme identity*. New York: Pantheon, 1950.

CHAPTER 5

SENSORY FUNCTIONING IN PSYCHOTHERAPY

Erving Polster

I would like to show how psychotherapy can help close the gap between a person's basic sensations and the higher experiences derived from these sensations. Identifying these basic sensations has become difficult for people because of the complexities of our society. A person may eat not only because he is hungry but also because certain tastes delight him, because it is mealtime, because he likes the company, or because he doesn't want to feel depressed or angry. His sensations are often only obscurely related to each other. What he does about the resulting muddle contributes to our current, frequently described crisis of identity because in order to know who we are, we must at least know what we feel. For example, knowing the difference between being hungry, angry, or sexually aroused surely is a lengthy step toward knowing what to do. In this interplay between feeling and doing lies the crux of our search for good living.

As conceptual background for identifying and activating sensation, I would like to introduce the concept of *synaptic experience*. The synaptic experience is an experience of union between awareness and expression. You may feel this union if you become aware, for example, of breathing while talking, of the flexibility of your body while dancing, or your excitement while painting. At times of union between intensified awareness and expression, profound feelings of presence, clarity of perception, vibrancy of inner experience, and wholeness of personality are common.

The term *synapse* is derived from the Greek word meaning conjunction or union. Physiologically, the synapse is the area of conjunction between nerve fibers, where they form a union with one another. The synaptic arc facilitates union between sensory and motor nerves, bridging the gap between these neural structures by special, though not altogether understood, energy transmissions. The metaphoric use of the synapse focuses our attention on united sensori-motor function as represented by awareness and expression.

Various therapies differ as to their methods for bringing expression and awareness together, but most, if not all, do share in calling attention to the individual's inner processes, sometimes including sensation as well as expression. Some therapies do not acknowledge any concern with inner process (the operant-conditioning people are among them), yet they repeatedly inquire about how the patient experiences anxiety. Most therapists would agree that if a patient were, for example, to tell about his feelings of love when his mother sang him to sleep, his story would have a greater effect both for him and his listener if he were aware of his feeling. The patient, if given timely direction, may become aware of many sensory phenomena as he speaks. His body may be moist, warm, flexible, tingly, etc. The emergence of these sensations increases the restorative powers of the story because through the resulting unity of feelings and words it becomes a more nearly incontrovertible confirmation of a past love experience.

Exploring sensations is, of course, not new to psychology. Wilhelm Wundt foresaw sensory experience as the root support from which all higher feeling emerged, but his research and that of many others never had the humanistic flavor that attracts the psychotherapist. However, there are many recent humanistic views that do herald a new recognition of the power of sensation. Schachtel (1959) for one, has shown the commonality of the infant and the adult in their experience of primitive, primary, and raw sensation. He says, "If the adult does not make use of his capacity to distinguish . . . the pleasurable feeling of warmth . . . [from] perceiving that this is the warmth of air or the warmth of water . . . but instead gives himself over to the pure sensation itself, then he experiences a fusion of pleasure and sensory quality which probably approximates the infantile experience. . . . The emphasis is not on any object but entirely on feeling or sensation [p. 125]."

The child's sensation tone is the paradigm for the purity of sensory experience. Although sensations do become cluttered over the years, early experiences need not be merely infantile. In our quest for fulfillment, many of our energies are directed toward the recovery of early existential possibilities. The early innocence of sensation has been neutralized by social forces that dichotomize the child and the adult into altogether separate creatures. However, the adult is not merely a replacement for the child. Rather he is the result of accretions which need not make the character of childhood irrelevant. A child-like sense may orient and vitalize us even in the face of newly developing realities. As Perls, Hefferline, and Goodman (1951) have said about the recovery of past memories, "the content of the recovered scene is unimportant but the childish feeling and attitude that lived that scene are of the utmost importance. The childish feelings are important not as a past that must be undone, but as some of the most beautiful powers of adult life that must be recovered: spontaneity, imagination, directness of awareness, and manipulation [p. 297]."

Reports of LSD users also extoll the primacy of sensation. Alan Watts (1964) says that while on LSD he is aware of changes in his perception of such ordinary things as "sunlight on the floor, the grain in wood, the texture of linen, or the sound of voices across the street. My own experience," he adds, "has never been of a distortion of those perceptions as in looking at one's self in a concave mirror. It is rather that every perception becomes—to use a metaphor—more resonant. The chemical seems to provide consciousness with a sounding box . . . for all the senses, so that sight, touch, taste, smell, and imagination are intensified like the voice of someone singing in the bathtub [p. 120]." In our own way, we psychotherapists may also provide a sounding box for resonance, as I shall now describe.

We may start by dividing the whole range of human experience into *culminative experiences* and *ingredient experiences*. The culminative experience exists in a composite form. It is a total and united event of primary relevance to the individual. As I write these words, for example, the act of writing is the culmination of a lifetime of experiences leading to this moment and forming a part of the composite structure of writing. Furthermore, each movement of my finger, each breath I take, each tangential thought, each variation in attention, confidence, zest, and clarity join together to form the composite experience I-am-writing. As elements in the composite unit, however, each of these is an ingredient experience. These ingredient experiences frequently go unattended, but when one does explore their existence and discovers their relationship to the culminative event, one may develop a heightened experience. The gourmet does this as he tastes a sauce. Hopefully, he encounters the quality of that taste in totality, as an integrated experience. However, he also examines his experience more pointedly so that he may identify the ingredients that make up the sauce. He may identify certain herbs, a familiar wine, proportions of butter, etc. This awareness enriches him, leading him to a new dimension of taste experience. The analysis and resynthesis create a rhythm between destruction of the composite taste and re-creation of it. This reverberation between destruction and re-creation occurs over and over, helping to intensify the vibrant taste. So also, when we explore our inner sensations, we may identify the ingredients of the everyday experiences which form the substance of our lives. Enrichment occurs when there is maximal possibility for the emergence of underlying or component parts into the foreground of our knowledge. The adventure of unlimited accessibility of experience and the fluctuations between a synthesized experience and the elemental parts of our existence provides a dynamic and continually self-renewing excitement.

The recovery of this dynamic process frequently requires close attention, much as relearning to walk after a illness. Concentration is one technique for the recovery of sensation. It is well known that one must concentrate to do good work, but instructions to do so usually sound vague, moralistic, and general. Yet, concentration can be a specific mode of operation that involves giving close regard to the specific object of one's interest. It must be pointed and single-minded. When these conditions are satisfied and one's concentration is brought to bear on internal sensations, events may occur that are remarkably comparable to events arising out of hypnosis, drugs, sensory deprivation, heroic eruptions, and other conditions that take the individual out of his accustomed frame of reference. Although not usually as potent as these other conditions, a great advantage of concentration for heightening experience is that one may readily return to ordinary events and ordinary communications. Thus, one may move in and out of other modes of interaction such as talking, roleplaying, fantasy, dream work, etc., which makes it easier to accept the experience as relevant to everyday consciousness.

Moving now to the therapeutic situation itself, I shall describe the role of sensations with three therapeutic purposes in mind. They are: (1) the accentuation of fulfillment, (2) the facilitation of the working-through process, and (3) the recovery of old experiences.

First, with respect to fulfillment, there seem to be two kinds of people, the action-oriented and the awareness-oriented. Both can live rich lives if one orientation does not exclude the other. The action-oriented person who has no deep barrier to the awareness of experience will, through his actions, arouse his experience of self. The swimmer, for example, may discover many powerful inner sensations, as may the business executive who won leadership of a new company. The individual who is oriented toward awareness will find that so long as he does not exclude action, his awarenesses will direct him to action. The psychologist may write a book or create an organization, the restless person may move to another city, and the sexually aroused person may have intercourse. Psychological troubles result when the rhythm between awareness and expression is faulty.

To illustrate, an action-oriented person, a successful businessman, came to therapy because he was not experiencing fulfillment in life. Unusually vital and active, he needed to make every second count and became impatient with any moment of nonproductivity. He could not accept the accumulation of sensation, keeping always ahead of himself by prematurely discharging sensation either through action or through planning action. Consequently he was having great difficulty knowing "who I am." During the first ten sessions we talked a great deal and made some introductory explorations into his inner experience. These included certain awareness experiments and breathing exercises. Then, one day when I asked him to close his eyes and concentrate on his inner experience, he began to feel a quietness in himself and to experience a feeling of union with the birds singing outside the window. Many other sensations followed. He kept them to himself, as he told me later, because to describe them would have meant interrupting himself, a wise but atypical appreciation for feeling rather than productivity. At one point, seeing that his abdomen was not integrated into his breathing, I asked him to use his abdomen more fully, which he was readily able to do. When he did, he began to feel a new ease of breathing, accompanied by an easy strength as distinct from the impatient strength with which he was familiar. He could really tell the difference between the two kinds of strength. He said he felt like a car that had been perfectly tuned. He then left, saying he was recovering a missing link in his life. He felt as though he had *experienced* time rather than having *wasted* it.

We may illustrate our second therapeutic purpose, the facilitation of the working-through process, by the story of a woman who recently became an executive in a toy factory. Her secretary had been in her department for years, but was a disorganized and controlling person. My patient became aware that this secretary was the root of many of the previous departmental troubles and confronted her with certain departmental requirements. This was a great blow to the secretary, who suddenly looked "like a waif." My patient felt as though she were now sitting face-to-face with another part of herself. She and her brother had grown up in an impoverished section of New York and had indeed been waifs. However, since she had always nurtured her younger brother, she only saw him as a waif, not herself. In her life she had alternately supported waifs and played the waif herself.

In our talk, she realized she didn't want to be a waif any more and knew that in this confrontation with her secretary she had accepted the chance to get rid of the waif in herself and become a woman in her own right. As she told me about this, a new look came over her face, a mixture of absorption, alert introspection, and yielding to puzzlement. When I asked her what she felt, she said in surprise that she felt a tightness in her breathing and in her legs. She concentrated on these sensations and after a few moments of silence looked surprised again and said she felt a tightness in her vagina. I asked her to attend to this sensation, which she did. Again, after a few moments of concentration a brightness arose in her face, and she said the tightness was leaving. Then she seemed startled and suddenly had a deep sensation that she didn't describe but instead burst into paroxysms of crying, calling out the name of a man she loves and with whom she has for the first time had a relationship of mutuality and strength. When she looked up, there was great beauty and wholeness apparent in her. As we spoke further, she realized the importance of her confrontation with her secretary, whom she subsequently fired, and the rediscovery of her feelings about waifs. But she knew that her deepest breakthrough came with the discovery of the sensation in her vagina. The subsequent awakening of her palpable feelings of womanhood gave substance and therefore primal resolution to problems which might otherwise only be verbalized.

Finally, a third purpose served by the recovery of sensation is the recovery of old events. The unfinished situation moves naturally into completion when barriers are dissolved and when new inner stimulation propels one toward completing the unfinished business. Psychoanalysis, although differing from Gestalt therapy in many details of conceptualization and technique, has made the return of the old and forgotten a familiar expectation in psychotherapy. Although many words about the past have been spoken in therapy, these are frequently without the accompaniment of deep sensations. The next situation illustrates how sensations rather than mere words may lead the way to an old event.

A woman whose husband had died about ten years previously, had spoken about her relationship with him but had never gotten across a sense of the profundity of their experience together. In one session, a series of awarenesses evolved, including the experience of her tongue tingling, a burning feeling around her eyes, tenseness in her back and shoulders, and then dampness around her eyes. Following a lengthy sequence of these experiences, she caught a deep breath and realized that she felt like crying. There was a sense of tears in her eyes and a sensation in her throat that she could not describe. After a very long pause, she felt an itch, which she concentrated on at some length. It should be said that with each new sensation, the silence and inner concentration was lengthy, frequently lasting for minutes. Silence when joined with focused concentration has the effect of building up the intensity of feeling. Soon she began to feel itchy in many places. She found it difficult to stay with these sensations without scratching, but she did. She was feeling somewhat amused about the surprising spread of her itching sensation, but she also began to feel frustrated and sad again, as though she might cry. She talked about an irritating experience she had had the night before at the home of her parents where she had not been able to show her irritation. Then she felt a lump in her throat, and after a period of concentrating on the lump, a palpitation appeared in her chest. Her heart started beating rapidly and this made her quite anxious. She verbalized the *pump, pump, pump* sounds, then became aware of a sharp pain in her upper back. She paused at great length to concentrate on the pain in her back, then said under considerable stress, "Now I remember that horrible night that my first husband had a heart attack." Another lengthy pause followed where she appeared under great tension and absorption. Then she said in a hushed tone that she was aware again of the pain, the anxiety, and the whole experience of that night. At this point she gave in to deep, heartfelt crying, which lasted about a minute. When she finished she looked up and said, "I guess I still miss him." Now the vagueness was gone and I could experience the reality and wholeness of her relationship with her husband. The clear transformation from superficiality to depth was apparently brought on by the buildup in sensation through self-awareness and concentration, letting her own sensations lead the way rather than her ideas or explanations.

To summarize, the concept of synaptic experience provides a background for the relevance of sensation for good living and accentuates the importance of the rhythm between one's awareness and one's expression. Although it represents only part of the total therapeutic methodology, the individual's discovery of his sensations, where it becomes relevant, may lead him to an experience of fulfillment, may help complete the working-through process, and may stimulate the recovery of old events.

REFERENCES

Perls, F., Hefferline, R., and Goodman, P. *Gestalt therapy*. New York: Dell, 1951.

Schachtel, E. *Metamorphosis*. New York: Basic Books, 1959.

Watts, A., A psychedelic experience: Fact or fantasy. In D. Solomon (Ed.), *LSD, the consciousness expanding drug*. New York: Putnam, 1964.

CHAPTER 6

THE PARADOXICAL
THEORY OF CHANGE

Arnold R. Beisser

For nearly a half century, the major part of his professional life, Frederick Perls was in conflict with the psychiatric and psychological establishments. He worked uncompromisingly in his own direction, which often involved fights with representatives of more conventional views. In the past few years, however, Perls and his Gestalt therapy have come to find harmony with an increasingly large segment of mental health theory and professional practice. The change that has taken place is not because Perls has modified his position, although his work has undergone some transformation, but because the trends and concepts of the field have moved closer to him and his work.

Perls's own conflict with the existing order contains the seeds of his change theory. He did not explicitly delineate this change theory, but it underlies much of his work and is implied in the practice of Gestalt techniques. I will call it the *paradoxical theory of change*, for reasons that shall become obvious. Briefly stated, it is this: *that change occurs when one becomes what he is, not when he tries to become what he is not.* Change does not take place through a coercive attempt by the individual or by another person to change him, but it does take place if one takes the time and effort to be what he is — to be fully invested in his current positions. By rejecting the role of change agent, we make meaningful and orderly change possible.

The Gestalt therapist rejects the role of "changer," for his strategy is to encourage, even insist, that the patient *be* where and what he *is*. He believes change does not take place by "trying," coercion, or persuasion, or by insight, interpretation, or any other such means. Rather, change can occur when the patient abandons, at least for the moment, what he would like to become and attempts to be what he is. The premise is that one must stand in one place in order to have firm footing to move and that it is difficult or impossible to move without that footing.

The person seeking change by coming to therapy is in conflict with at least two warring intrapsychic factions. He is constantly moving between what he "should be" and what he thinks he "is," never fully identifying with either. The Gestalt therapist asks the person to invest himself fully in his roles, one at a time. Whichever role he begins with, the patient soon shifts to another. The Gestalt therapist asks simply that he be what he is at the moment.

The patient comes to the therapist because he wishes to be changed. Many therapies accept this as a legitimate objective and set out through various means to try to change him, establishing what Perls calls the "top-dog/under-dog" dichotomy. A therapist who seeks to help a patient has left the egalitarian position and become the knowing expert, with the patient playing the helpless person, yet his goal is that he and the patient should become equals. The Gestalt therapist believes that the top-dog/under-dog dichotomy already exists within the patient, with one part trying to change the other, and that the therapist must avoid becoming locked into one of these roles. He tries to avoid this trap by encouraging the patient to accept both of them, one at a time, as his own.

The analytic therapist, by contrast, uses devices such as dreams, free associations, transference, and interpretation to achieve insight that, in turn, may lead to change. The behaviorist therapist rewards or punishes behavior in order to modify it. The Gestalt therapist believes in encouraging the patient to enter and become whatever he is experiencing at the moment. He believes with Proust, "To heal a suffering one must experience it to the full."

The Gestalt therapist further believes that the natural state of man is as a single, whole being—not fragmented into two or more opposing parts. In the natural state, there is constant change based on the dynamic transaction between the self and the enviroment.

Kardiner has observed that in developing his structural theory of defense mechanisms, Freud changed processes into structures (for example, *denying* into *denial*). The Gestalt therapist views change as a possibility when the reverse occurs, that is, when structures are transformed into processes. When this occurs, one is open to participant interchange with his environment.

If alienated, fragmentary selves in an individual take on separate, compartmentalized roles, the Gestalt therapist encourages communication between the roles; he may actually ask them to talk to one another. If the patient objects to this or indicates a block, the therapist asks him simply to invest himself fully in the objection or the block. Experience has shown that when the patient identifies with the alienated fragments, integration does occur. Thus, by being what one is—fully—one can become something else.

The therapist, himself, is one who does not seek change, but seeks only to be who *he* is. The patient's efforts to fit the therapist into one of his own stereotypes of people, such as a helper or a top-dog, create conflict between them. The end point is reached when each can be himself while still maintaining intimate contact with the other. The therapist, too, is moved to change as he seeks to be himself with another person. This kind of mutual interaction leads to the possibility that a therapist may be most effective when he changes most, for when he is open to change, he will likely have his greatest impact on his patient.

What has happened in the past fifty years to make this change theory, implicit in Perls's work, acceptable, current, and valuable? Perls's assumptions have not changed, but society has. For the first time in the history of mankind, man finds himself in a position where, rather than needing to adapt himself to an existing order, he must be able to adapt himself to a series of changing orders. For the first time in the history of mankind, the length of the individual life span is greater than the length of time necessary for major social and cultural change to take place. Moreover, the rapidity with which this change occurs is accelerating.

Those therapies that direct themselves to the past and to individual history do so under the assumption that if an individual once resolves the issues around a traumatic personal event (usually in infancy or childhood), he will be prepared for all time to deal with the world; for the world is considered a stable order. Today, however, the problem becomes one of discerning where one stands in relationship to a shifting society. Confronted with a pluralistic, multifaceted, changing system, the individual is left to his own devices to find stability. He must do this through an approach that allows him to move dynamically and flexibly with the times while still maintaining some central gyroscope to guide him. He can no longer do this with ideologies, which become obsolete, but must do it with a change theory, whether explicit or implicit. The goal of therapy becomes not so much to develop a good, fixed character but to be able to move with the times while retaining some individual stability.

In addition to social change, which has brought contemporary needs into line with his change theory, Perls's own stubbornness and unwillingness to be what he was not allowed him to be ready for society when it was ready for him. Perls had to be what he was despite, or perhaps even because of, opposition from society. However, in his own lifetime he has become integrated with many of the professional forces in his field in the same way that the individual may become integrated with alienated parts of himself through effective therapy.

The field of concern in psychiatry has now expanded beyond the individual as it has become apparent that the most crucial issue before us is the development of a society that supports the individual in his individuality. I believe that the same change theory outlined here is also applicable to social systems, that orderly change within social systems is in the direction of integration and holism; further, that the social-change agent has as his major function to 'work with and in an organization so that it can change consistently with the changing dynamic equilibrium both within and outside the organization. This requires that the system become conscious of alienated fragments within and without so it can bring them into the main functional activities by processes similar to identification in the individual. First, there is an awareness within the system that an alienated fragment exists; next that fragment is accepted as a legitimate outgrowth of a functional need that is then explicitly and deliberately mobilized and given power to operate as an explicit force. This, in turn, leads to communication with other subsystems and facilitates an integrated, harmonious development of the whole system.

With change accelerating at an exponential pace, it is crucial for the survival of mankind that an orderly method of social change be found. The change theory proposed here has its roots in psychotherapy. It was developed as a result of dyadic therapeutic relationships. But it is proposed that the same principles are relevant to social change, that the individual change process is but a microcosm of the social change process. Disparate, unintegrated, warring elements present a major threat to society, just as they do to the individual. The compartmentalization of old people, young people, rich people, poor people, black people, white people, academic people, service people, etc., each separated from the others by generational, geographical, or social gaps, is a threat to the survival of mankind. We must find ways of relating these compartmentalized fragments to one another as levels of a participating, integrated system of systems.

The paradoxical social change theory proposed here is based on the strategies developed by Perls in his Gestalt therapy. They are applicable, in the judgment of this author, to community organization, community development and other change processes consistent with the democratic political framework.

PART II

TECHNIQUES OF GESTALT THERAPY

Techniques or therapeutic procedures are central to any therapy endeavor. Techniques arise from two sources, coming in part from the theoretical underpinnings of a specific "school" or approach and in part from the therapist's ongoing treatment interactions, where the requirement of "making something happen" exists. Out of his boredom, frustration, desperation, inspiration, and/or creativity, a therapist will periodically devise new procedures or approaches. When these work, he will extend them to other patients and begin developing a rationale or theory. Techniques therefore both feed into and out from theory. If the techniques can be taught and are useful to other therapists, then a specific approach develops. Both the techniques that a therapist devises and those that he adopts from others must have some degree of congruity with his own personality make-up before he can use them effectively. The therapist who is able to use Gestalt techniques effectively generally prefers activity to passivity, accepts power but does not need it for personal gratification, acts with firmness and assurance, enjoys improvising rather than following a fixed plan, is not unduly afraid of intense emotional explosions, and can utilize himself and his emotional reactions without great fear of exposure. Persons who have high investments in cognitive or "computer" processes, who prefer emotional distance, who tend to be conservative, who prefer to reflect or "follow" the patient's responses, or who lack awareness of their own experience have more difficulty with Gestalt techniques.

Gestalt techniques offer considerable flexibility in their usefulness. Perhaps their greatest contribution lies in their utilization in day, weekend, or month workshops where their variety, power, and immediacy quickly involve participants, foster rapid "knowing" of others, and produce vivid personality change. The techniques are also of considerable value for long-term individual therapy, and may be utilized, with appropriate caution, for a wide variety of people and problems. (For instance, the papers that follow describe therapy with children and adults, normal, neurotic, and psychotic, seen individually, in groups, or with the family.) Gestalt techniques can be used in productive combination with a variety of other approaches. Finally, they are adaptable to use with one's self and, if necessary, colleagues. However, they need to be approached with caution and full respect for their ability to have powerful effects. It is not intended nor expected that reading these papers can make even an experienced therapist into a "Gestaltist" without personal experience and training. Nor are the papers intended in any way as a "cookbook" for the inexperienced.

A number of problems have traditionally been associated with the general topic of techniques. Five of these will be explored briefly, with references to the papers that deal with some of the issues at more length. In general, the directness and immediacy of theory and practice in Gestalt therapy have contributed to the reduction of many dichotomies that have been persistent problems for psychotherapists.

Inconsistencies between theory and techniques. Beginning with Freud, many theories of therapy have seemed only remotely connected to the specific operations of the therapist. For example, if psychoanalysis views the core of maladjustment to be instinctual and sexual, with problems produced in part by man's basic nature and in part by impulses blocked and distorted by past experiences, then it does not follow directly that adjustment should come as a result of communicating verbally, in a situation with many limitations, to a relatively unresponsive therapist. Similarly, while Fromm was writing his most important books detailing the sources of men's problems as residing in the economic and political structure of society, he was attempting to treat these ills by individual therapy. However, in Gestalt therapy the theory that people's problems arise from their lack of awareness and from the ways in which they block awareness leads directly to the therapist's focusing attention on this area and offering suggestions, tasks, and exercises designed either to promote awareness in general or to assist an individual with his specific avoidances. Also, the patient's stated problems or concerns are translated directly into the therapy situation and in essence are demonstrated rather than simply described.

Discrepancy between artificial techniques and genuine response. This issue is discussed in several of the articles that follow, especially those by

Fagan, Cohn, and Kempler. Briefly, the Gestalt therapist follows the same directions that he gives to the patient, staying with his own awareness. His awareness will most often, without real effort on his part, be focused on the patient and his words, movements, tone of voice, etc. As he becomes aware of discrepancies, he will almost automatically translate these into suggestions and experiments for the patient. If the patient refuses or resists, or if the therapist responds with boredom, irritation, or perplexity, then his attention will switch from the patient to himself, and his own experiences will hold center stage in his awareness. He must then find ways of resolving these, by withdrawing, verbalizing them, etc., which is usually part of the same process as helping the patient to the next step in awareness. If the therapist continues to feel blocked, then he will utilize the same procedures for himself that he might suggest to a patient. If, during the process of therapy, a memory, joke, personal experience, or idea emerges strongly, then the therapist will probably choose to share it in a routine way. In short, the Gestalt therapist believes that he can be only what he is in the situation and that the procedures he suggests for the patient are the ones he follows himself. He experiences little dichotomy and views the problem of techniques versus authenticity, which has been subject to many heated debates in other therapeutic approaches, as practically a dead issue.

Emphasis on historical material versus present happenings. As described by Enright, and by Naranjo in Section I, the Gestalt emphasis on the *now* often leads to important and affect-laden memories. When this occurs, the past is made present by the use of the present tense and the enactment of interactions. It is generally taboo in Gestalt procedures to allow past history to be simply talked about.

Status difference and distance between therapist and patient. The Gestalt therapist is, and regards himself as, an expert. This does not imply, however, that he regards the patient as inferior or different. He realizes the potential interchangeability of patient and therapist roles, and indeed has found himself on many occasions wrestling with his own blocks and unfinished business. He is also more than willing to leave the patient and

therapist roles in the therapy situation and, once outside, respond and interact on a personal and social basis, avoiding as necessary, however, contact with the person who cannot leave behind the patient position. In
groups an artificial distinction may sometimes be enforced by the
therapist, who usually has specific directions or procedures in mind in
working with a patient; if a group member insists on "breaking in" and
being helpful, he may be put down gently or asked to explore his own projections.

Discrepancy between the therapeutic situation and "real life." While the
structure and limits of therapy do make distinctions between it and other
aspects of living, the experiencing is not artificial nor remote. Naranjo
discusses this issue at length in Section I.

Of the papers that follow, "The Tasks of the Therapist" (Fagan) attempts to spell out the skills and characteristics needed by the therapist,
dividing them into five categories: patterning, control, potency, humanness, and commitment. Fagan describes the contributions to and
difficulties with each of these in a number of therapeutic approaches, as
well as some of the contributions of Gestalt therapy.

"Techniques of Gestalt Therapy" (Enright) describes goals and
strategy, tactics and techniques. Enright begins by defining attention and
awareness, and suggests that an appropriate way to conceptualize maladjustment is to view it as blocks in the development of awareness. Therapy
basically consists of the reintegration of attending and awareness, with the
emphasis placed on helping the patient develop his own problem-solving
capacity rather than letting the therapist attempt to solve his problems for
him. The therapist's awareness of the patient's blocks and incongruencies
results in techniques to bring these obstacles to the patient's attention in
various ways. Enright gives a number of excellent examples and pro-
cedural strategies. There are four main ways in which patients block
awareness: retroflection, when the person opposes and holds back wishes,
impulses, and behaviors, resulting in unfinished business; desensitization
of sensory and physical messages; introjection of other's "shoulds"; and
projection of expectations, criticisms, etc., onto other persons. Finally,

Enright discusses six issues from the Gestalt point of view: the actual therapeutic agent or change-producer; who decides when to terminate; the range of applicability; work with dreams; the use of the therapist as a person; and utilization of the past. Turning specifically to Gestalt procedures, Laura Perls answers questions dealing with her approach to some of the typical problems presented by patients, including motivation, physical contact, and the personal involvement of the therapist. "Psychoanalytic, Experiential, and Gestalt Therapy in Groups" (Cohn) utilizes wide experience with group therapy in a comparative study of the theory, goals, procedures, and techniques of the three approaches. Cohn includes her own subjective reactions and her observations of student responses to Gestalt workshops and demonstrations.

"Rules and Games of Gestalt Therapy" (Levitsky and Perls) supplies a compendium of suggestions for increasing direct confrontation and awareness, and in assisting the patient to assume responsibility. These "rules" are applied generally, but not dogmatically, in Gestalt sessions, with the patient being reminded or corrected when he has broken their letter or spirit. Then a number of Gestalt games are described. These have several purposes, including warming up a group, involving the entire group, and assisting specific individuals.

"Experiential Psychotherapy with Families"(Kempler) describes the utilization of Gestalt techniques by a therapist who integrates them with his personal and emotional responses in a direct and immediate way. Kempler gives a rationale for his approach and several examples of his interaction with families.

Simkin, in "Mary," demonstrates, with considerable skill and subtlety, ways of responding to and assisting a passive woman who "ties up" herself and others by asking that they take responsibility for her. With increased self-support and a more vivid awareness of her blocking, she reexperiences an incident from the past that demonstrates her internal and interpersonal maneuvers. Now she is able to release herself and maintain her strength. "Gestalt Techniques with a Woman with Expressive Difficulties" (Fagan) reports on a set of exercises and experiments designed to assist a student who had major blocks in written and oral communication. The "Diary of a Girl with Blue Paint on Her Nose," which follows, contains the student's account of her experiences. While there are many accounts by therapists of their procedures and a number of first-hand reports by patients (usually written in retrospect rather than during the process), there are few that have reported the same experience from both sides as it was occurring. "Exaggeration with a Schizophrenic" (Close) offers an account of a brief interaction between a hospitalized psychotic and Close, in which he exaggerates and ridicules the patient's obsequiousness and self-effacement while fantasying his being assertive and disruptive. The patient enjoyed the exchange and showed some improvement in behavior. Close gives a rationale for this procedure from the standpoint of Gestalt theory and Bateson's theory of the "double-bind."

"A Child with a Stomachache" (Cohn) describes a combination of Gestalt and psychoanalytic approaches and demonstrates how Gestalt techniques can be used effectively with a young child. The article also raises the question of assisting friends therapeutically, a procedure which contains many hazards from the standpoint of other approaches but which can, at times, be utilized with caution with Gestalt procedures.

"Two Dream Seminars" (Perls) presents a brief description of Perls's ideas concerning the importance and use of dreams and then demonstrates his approach with four volunteers. The first dreamer, as she plays through some of the objects, persons, and animals in her dream, begins to come to grips with her conflict between power and passivity, or between masculine and feminine aspects of herself, and works toward a partial resolution. The second dream deals with a conflict between sterile artificiality and deeply buried creativity. The third dream opens up an important piece of unfinished business, with the dreamer becoming intensely involved in the struggle between being independent and being cared for by her mother at the cost of helplessness and lack of self-support. The rapid progression of emotional responses from helplessness, to the expression of anger toward her mother, to sadness at giving up the old pattern is a very typical one. The fourth dream vividly illustrates a patient's attempts to impress others by taking risks, and the importance to him of gaining others' liking and acceptance at the cost of suppressing his fear and anger.

He is encouraged to face his catastrophic expectations of death and/or rejection. Utilizing members of the group as projection screens is illustrated. It is interesting to note that while the first and second dreams share several types of content and include similar behaviors, as do the third and fourth, working out the dreams results in very different meanings to the dreamers.

Finally, Shepherd discusses "Limitations and Cautions in the Gestalt Approach." She describes a number of areas where the therapist using Gestalt techniques needs to be aware of possible difficulties or dangers and suggests ways of avoiding unfortunate outcomes in these areas.

CHAPTER 7

THE TASKS OF
THE THERAPIST

Joen Fagan

All professional persons are basically problem solvers who are employed to reduce discomfort or conflict and to increase the possibilities of certain valued outcomes for the persons who request their assistance.* Therapists, specifically, are engaged by persons who are dissatisfied with their own, or another's experiencing and behaving, which may include internal experiences of anxiety, discomfort, conflict, or dissatisfaction, and external behaviors that are either inadequate or insufficient for the tasks at hand or that result in difficulties with other people. The problems presented to the therapist may be central to the person and require extensive changes, or they may be peripheral and quickly solved. Not only the problems are varied, but also therapists differ widely, both in their procedures and in their effectiveness with different kinds of persons and problems. I believe that therapists and therapeutic techniques will become increasingly specialized and increasingly effective, partially as a function of research and partially as a function of rapidly growing willingness to experiment with a variety of new techniques. However, while many changes will occur, the basic tasks of the therapist will remain similar. The purpose of this chapter is to examine the tasks or requirements of the therapeutic endeavor under five headings: patterning, control, potency, humanness, and commitment; to indicate briefly the contributions of various approaches or "schools" to each of these; and to focus on contributions from Gestalt therapy.

PATTERNING

The therapist is first of all a perceiver and constructor of patterns. As soon as he is informed of a symptom or a request for change, and begins listening to and observing a patient and responding to him, he begins a

---

*While this article deals specifically with therapists, the tasks described can be modified and extrapolated to describe any professional group.

process that I refer to as *patterning*. While *diagnosis* is a more common term, it has the disadvantage of provoking the analogy of the medical model and implying that the purpose of the process is arriving at a specific label. A better analogy for the process of patterning is that of artistic creation, involving sometimes cognitive, sometimes perceptual and intuitive skills in interaction with the material and demands of the environment as, for example, in the creation of a mobile, in which a variety of pieces or systems are interconnected into an overall unity and balance.

As the therapist begins his contact with the patient requesting help, he has available a body of theory which is largely cognitive in nature, a background of past experience, and a number of awarenesses and personal responses derived from the ongoing interaction that have large emotional and intuitive components. From these, which may be given varying degrees of importance by a specific therapist, he begins to form an understanding of the interaction of events and systems that result in a given life style that supports a given symptom pattern. *Events* refers to the things that have happened or do happen to the patient; *systems* includes all those interlocking events that interact on a specific level of existence, such as biological systems, self-perception systems, family systems, etc. The patient is visualized as a focal point of many systems, including the cellular, historical, economic, etc. The more the therapist can specify the entire interaction, or be sensitive to the possible effects of systems he is not directly concerned with (such as the neurological), or intuit the connecting points between systems where the most strain exists, the more effective he can be in producing change. He can act on a level and at a point that promises the most positive change in symptoms or conflicts at the least cost of effort, and where the least disruptive change will occur to other systems.

An example may clarify some of the above description. A mother refers her son whose increasing stomach distress causes him frequently to stay home from school. The therapist shortly begins to accumulate information of various sorts. He learns that: the boy also has stomachaches that keep him from going to camp or from visiting relatives; the mother has few interests outside the home; the father does not like his job and also has frequent illnesses; the mother and father have intercourse very infrequently; the boy has average intelligence; the grandmother is very interested in his becoming a doctor; the other children tease him for being a sissy; his teacher is considered strict; the school system has a new superintendent who has made many changes, etc. The therapist observes that the boy waits for his mother to answer for him; that his voice is weak when he does answer; and so on through a long list of responses, observations, and experiments in which the therapist obtains some sort of assessment of the abilities of the boy and his family to respond to varying suggestions and pressures. Through these processes a picture emerges with increasing clarity. The boy, his stomach, his family, his peer group, the school, the school system, and the community come into focus with varying degrees of explicitness.

We first label our understanding of the crux of the problem and then move to intervene on one or possibly several levels, depending on our personal preference, style, and understanding. No matter how badly we do initially in spotting the interactions that are most important, there is a clear possibility that intervention on any level may sooner or later produce the changes we wish, since the systems are interlocking and a change in one system may produce changes in some or many of the other systems. (This may be paraphrased, "Everyone has a little bit of the truth.") We may start with a medical approach, choosing antispasmodics, antiemetics, or tranquilizers. We may attempt to produce primarily internal psychological changes by play therapy, hypnosis, rational-emotive procedures, or desensitization. We may attempt to set up environmental learning situations by academic coaching or by activity group therapy. We may use behavior modification by observing the ways in which the mother reinforces the boy's avoidance behavior and may work with her to change these. We may see the mother individually to help her change her perception of mothering, support her in developing outside interests, or involve her in sensitivity training. We may work with the father in exploring his frequent illnesses or in helping him to find more job satisfaction. We may select couple therapy to assist the parents in dealing with their sexual problems and developing a more satisfactory marriage. We may use family therapy to increase communication, clarify the parents' interactions with the boy, and find ways of modifying the grandmother's influence. It is also possible to arrange environmental changes, such as changing teachers or schools. We could work with the teacher or school counselor, and finally (but grandiosely) we could envision involving the school system, the community, or eventually, the country.

No matter what procedures are chosen, we will need to evaluate our results by three main criteria: how rapidly the symptom has been removed, what positive behavior has replaced it, and how little disturbance has been created in the interlocking systems. These areas of evaluation will be discussed at more length in the section on techniques that follows.

Each therapy system has its own rationale and its own ideas about personality and procedure. Techniques are designed to intervene at the place or places where the theory says the pattern can most easily be modified. All theories and techniques fail at times because no two patterns are exactly alike and the points of conflict may vary widely. However, all theories that are taken seriously have some successes since changes in any system can affect others.

The Gestalt contribution to patterning involves a de-emphasis on cognitive theory and provides extensive assistance with the therapist's own awareness. Enright, in chapters 8 and 21, describes this process in detail, emphasizing the clues to underlying events and life styles that can be uncovered by awareness of the person's movements, tones, expressions, word choice, etc., and suggesting some appropriate techniques for exploration. Much of Gestalt patterning is worked out in the therapy process itself rather than by history-taking or interviewing. The meanings that result, as in dream work, are very different from the more traditional analytic interpretive approaches where certain meanings are specified in advance by theory or predicted from the patient's previous history. Of course, past events of much importance do arise from the process of exploring posture, gestures, and dreams. However, the Gestalt therapist is not interested in the historical reconstruction of the patient's life, nor in weighing the effects of various environmental forces, nor in focusing upon one specific behavior such as communication style. Rather, he is interested in a global way in the point of contact between the various systems available for observation. The interactions between a person and his body, between his words and his tone of voice, between his posture and the person he is talking to, between himself and the group he is a member of are the focal points. The Gestalt therapist does not hypothesize nor make inferences about other systems that he cannot observe, though he may ask the patient to reenact *his* perceptions of them, as in a dialogue with his father, for example. Most Gestalt procedures are designed to bear upon the point of intersection, and the nature of the other system is viewed as less important than how the patient perceives or reacts to it.

In other words, the patterning emphasis in Gestalt therapy is on the process of interaction itself, including the patient's skills in fostering and risking interaction, or blocking awareness and change. Since these are skills of importance in the intersection of any systems from the biological through the social, the Gestalt therapist sees himself as preparing the individual to interact more effectively in all aspects of life. Perls's ideas concerning a therapeutic community, which he is presently formulating, represent a possible extension of Gestalt thinking to a more extensive system.

CONTROL

No matter how clear and adequate the therapist's patterning is, he must be able immediately to exercise control or nothing else can follow. Control is defined as the therapist's being able to persuade or coerce the patient into following the procedures he has set, which may include a variety of conditions. Control is not used here with cynicism or a Svengali attitude, nor is there any implication of ignoring the value of genuine concern and liking for the patient; it simply reflects the reality that unless patients do some of the things that therapists suggest, little will happen, and that which does happen will be mostly by accident.

Whitaker (1968) makes this idea very explicit: "Therapy has to begin with a fight . . . a fight over who controls the context of therapy. . . . I want it understood that I'm in charge of what happens. I see this as the administrative battle I have to win [in Haley and Hoffman, 1968, pp. 266, 267]." (A number of other therapists have written extensively about the importance of control: Haley, 1961 a, 1961 b, 1963; Rosen, 1953.) Haley and Erickson often use a paradoxical double-bind, a command so phrased that there is no way of disobeying it, or disobedience involves making admissions that are extremely damaging or revealing. These not only maintain control but often contribute to a very rapid reduction in symptoms. Rosen, Bach, and others often use group pressure as a means of control. A patient may be able to meet or defeat the therapist in a fight, but his chances against eight or ten people who are aware of what he is attempting are very slim.

Part of the importance of control is that all symptoms represent indirect ways of trying to control or force others into certain patterns of behavior. The therapist has to counter being controlled by the patient's symptom pattern and also establish the conditions he needs to work. Some of the conditions will be overt behavioral requirements, such as keeping appointments, paying, bringing other family members, etc. Other conditions will be more covert or implicit, such as the willingness to give information, attempt suggestions, or produce fantasies. While the required aspects of external behavior vary from therapist to therapist, it is essential that the conditions most important to him be met to his reasonable satisfaction. It is common knowledge that patients who initially ask for special favors or conditions, such as special appointment times or reduced fees, will be more difficult to work with; and the therapist often counters by setting up stronger-than-usual controls, such as payment at each interview or the use of a consultant.

Two of the major aspects of implicit control can be examined under the concepts of motivation and rapport. Motivation is often thought of as being related to the patient's discomfort or anxiety; the higher these are, the more the patient is willing to work. However, the degree of distress can be thought of with equal validity as the willingness of the patient to relinquish control to the therapist. Some persons who are experiencing marked distress are difficult to work with because they attribute their discomfort to others via blame. Their motivation for change is high but their willingness to surrender control is low.

Rapport is usually presented somewhat ideally as the "good feeling" and amount of positive relationship between patient and therapist; more accurately it is the therapist's ability to persuade the patient, or the patient's willingness to trust the therapist's control of the situation. While liking for the therapist is probably necessary somewhere along the therapeutic process, and of value even initially, it is probably more important in the early stages for the patient to believe that the therapist knows what he's doing.

The techniques the therapist uses to gain and maintain control are often, though not necessarily, different from the ones he uses to produce personality or behavioral change. (All techniques, of course, depend heavily on the style of the individual.) The therapist must recognize, manifest, and counter the patient's efforts at taking control by his usual means, some of which will be represented by his symptoms, others more deviously. He must manage to avoid being put off, frightened, or bored by the psychotic; to keep from being had by the psychopath or enjoying him too much; and to avoid being too sympathetic or agreeing with the neurotic's formulations. He must be able to remain his own man while also becoming enough involved with the patient's life style to experience its problems and difficulties.

A special problem is presented by the patient who comes because of external coercion, such as court order, divorce threat, or parent's commands. The situation is such that the external agent has the control, and the therapist runs the risk of becoming his hireling, ostensibly agreeing that he and the patient will work hard to please this outside person. The therapist has, however, at least three main ploys to regain control: he can involve the referring agent, thus indicating that both the agent and the patient need help; he can disavow the external payoff ("It's no concern of mine whether you flunk out of school"); or he can go along by an initial identification with the person's goals to contrast with the agent's as, for example, in Schwartz's (1967) and Greenwald's (1967) offering to make their patients into better psychopaths.

External compliance with a threatened punishment has an internal parallel—the pseudocompliance and "improvement" labeled by analysts as "intellectual insight" or "transference cure" and by transactional analysts as playing "Greenhouse" or "Psychiatry" or "Gee, You're a Wonderful Therapist" (Berne, 1964). Perls's label is "bear-trapper," which describes the patient who, having learned something about the expectations of the therapist, goes through the motions of cooperation, then at a crucial moment refuses to comply with suggestions, thus catching the therapist off balance. Often the bear-trapper is a person with considerable underlying pathology who has much invested in demonstrating that he cannot be helped or changed, and that those who try do not have the power to force him. In this situation, regaining control is difficult since the patient has made it clear that efforts on the part of the therapist to control only indicate an admission of his failure. Renouncing control and admitting failure is one way of regaining it.

Another problem of control can be anticipated with the patient whose presenting symptoms include psychosis or potential psychosis, suicide, and the more severe varieties of "acting out." These are persons who in the past have effectively utilized the threat, "If you don't do what I want, then I'll . . . (kill myself, go crazy, embarrass you, etc.)." These are potent threats and can invoke fear and self-doubts, or may even blackmail the therapist into acting in ways that jeopardize his purpose and position. Suicide or homicide are the ultimate threats, and each of these may force the therapist into assuming more control than he wishes—which, of course, admits that the patient is in control. One of the most effective ways of neutralizing such threats is to make a clear contract initially. Szasz (1965a) informs patients that they will need to make arrangements with someone else if they require hospitalization; Goulding (1967) requires signed contracts from potentially suicidal patients in which they agree without reservation to make no suicide attempts while they are seeing him.

Another type of control only now beginning to be explored systematically is that offered by total environments, such as prisons and mental hospitals. For many years we attempted to deny that external control, other than gross loss of liberty and bare conformity with institution procedures, was either important or desirable. The success of behavior-modification procedures, which make many of the bare amenities of living dependent on certain patient behaviors, is forcing a reevaluation of the position that external control is not appropriate for persons who are unwilling or unable to utilize internal control. The painfully sincere and extensive study by Rogers and his associates (1967) in which competent and dedicated men attempted to modify the behavior of chronic schizophrenics by ignoring external control and attempting to assist the recovery of internal control by nondirective therapy resulted in almost complete futility. It is becoming increasingly evident that in patterning and control, chronic schizophrenics have obliterated almost all of the usual systems and procedures, and can be approached initially most effectively by very specific controls related to the immediate environment. Evidence is also accumulating to suggest that treatment of acute schizophrenic episodes may be approached most effectively by treatment of the total family (Langsley et al., 1968). The major implication of environmental control as represented by behavior modification is that it is needed to the extent to which the individual is unable or unwilling to assume internal control; to the extent to which internal control is possible, external control is insulting, inefficient, or a violation of civil liberties.

Control is most important in the beginning of therapy. The need for control decreases as cooperative control by patient and therapist increases because of greater ability to communicate in each other's language and the development of trust. However, at important points of change, the struggle for control will reemerge, usually on a more intense level, and the therapist should be prepared to fight this battle periodically.

Even initially, the attempt to maintain complete control is impossible and the appearance needs to be periodically renounced, first as a paradoxical way of maintaining control and secondly as a way of encouraging the patient's own assumption of responsibility and growth. (An excellent example of this is found in Simkin's chapter "Mary," page 162. However, the abandoning of control should be viewed as an occasional technique and not as a complete system, as in the early days of nondirective therapy, or in group situations (see, for example, Bion, 1961) where the leader refuses to assume a leadership role. The inevitable outcome is that the group, in order to fill the vacuum, engages in a struggle for leadership accompanied by considerable expression of anger. Since this is a systems effect, the leader cannot claim credit for having produced any special results, and the value to the participants is dubious. While the person whose electric supply is disrupted may be able to get along with candles and a fireplace, this demonstration of self-sufficiency is not what he is paying the power company to produce.

The Gestalt contribution to problems of control includes a number of responses and procedures. Initially the therapist encourages patient autonomy and minimizes struggles by telling the patient that if he has strong objections to complying with suggestions he can (has the therapist's permission to) refuse, and his refusal will be honored. However, he is told that he has to state his reason for refusal. Often, as the reason is given, it can be explored for validity ("What's so terrible about being embarrassed?") and the patient will decide to continue.

Gestalt therapists ask for a clear statement from the patient concerning what he wishes to accomplish. Proceeding from this central theme keeps the emphasis on the patient's stated wishes, not the therapist's expectations. Procedures that keep in the present and make it clear that the therapist is in sensitive awareness with what is happening also decrease resistance. (When a patient begins meeting opposition from his conflicts and the discomfort that surrounds them, he may clearly resist, but this is on a very different order from resistance of control.) The patient is often asked if he would be willing to try an experiment: an acceptance carries a mild commitment to continue, while a refusal is honored if a reason is given. The patient who freezes, draws a blank, or has nothing come to mind can be asked to verbalize his refusal more specifically or to take responsibility for it by saying, "I am making my mind blank." Another procedure is to go with the resistance ("Tell me that it's no business of mine what you're thinking") and then have the fantasied therapist answer back. The value of resistance can also be approached ("What are all the good reasons for refusing me now; what does refusing do for you that is valuable for you?").

POTENCY

To justify his hire, the therapist must be able to assist the patient to move in the direction that he wishes, that is, to accelerate and provoke change in a positive direction. We are rapidly leaving the time when the therapist, in the absence of more specific knowledge, relies on "something" in the relationship that will result in "something" happening. We are approaching the time when the therapist can specify procedures that promote rapid change in a way that the patient can experience directly and others can observe clearly. For a given patient, many of the changes that do occur are a direct or by-product of the therapeutic relationships as described in the next section on humanness. (The therapeutic relationship is both a technique and a transcendence of techniques.) However, the therapist has need at many points of techniques, procedures, experiments, gimmicks, directions, and suggestions that can overcome inertia and promote movement. The patient who asks for specific assistance should expect to receive it.

Techniques are one of the more publicized aspects of psychotherapy; everyone knows that Freudians interpret and analyze dreams, and others hypnotize, analyze transactions, give tokens, etc. With increasing speed and accuracy, we are able to remove symptoms and change behaviors such as phobias, sexual deviations, inhibitions, etc., that only a few years ago were thought to require extended treatment. The increasing power of the therapist has resurrected two old topics that have a long history: the question of therapist authenticity versus techniques and the problem of symptom substitution.

The existentialists and neo-Rogerians (Rogers, 1951; Bugental, 1965; Carkhuff and Berenson, 1967) write powerfully of the human condition and the need for genuine relationships. However, techniques are often ignored or decried as being artificial, with the implication that authenticity cannot occur in their presence. I observed one of the most highly respected existential therapists in the country leading a group that was being observed by several hundred people and video-taped as a record of his way of working. The group, composed of student volunteers, spent over forty minutes continuing to be uncomfortably aware of the audience and verbalizing their discomfort at being observed and expected to produce. The therapist periodically shared with the group his own anxiety, selfconsciousness, and fears that nothing would happen. When, at the end of the hour, a group member finally volunteered a "problem"—that he was temporarily short of money— the group responded with great relief and vast amounts of concern and sympathy. However, neither the therapist nor the group would have had to remain "stuck" had he been willing to utilize any of a number of techniques.

Gestalt techniques appropriate to the situation would have had members of the group in turn play the part of the critical audience and the stupid, helpless child, externalize their projections, take the role of critic and criticize the audience, "ham up" their own discomfort, etc. These procedures would have allowed them to further their own growth by reducing the internalized demands of others' expectations and to reclaim and modify their disowned disapproval, while at the same time they would be reducing the audience to "ground" and then could continue with whatever needs emerged as "figure." Suffering with another when the reasons for his suffering are not genuine or allowing him to continue with discomfort when this can be reduced is hardly humane.

A second therapist on the program specialized in behavior modification in groups. His techniques invoked persons in the group into becoming involved in such obviously insincere and artificial interactions that it came as no surprise to discover that he had carefully rehearsed the group members the night before. However, there is no need to think of suffering-with or artificial techniques as representing an either-or choice; rather, they are two undesirable extremes, between which lie many combinations of the values of potency and humanness.

The problem of symptom substitution has reappeared with the advent of behavior modification, and it has apparently become important for behavior modifiers to defend their procedures and their potency against questions as to the possibility of substitution of other unwished-for behavior and lack of permanency in the behavioral changes (see, for example, Calhoon, 1968). Part of the problem concerns the rapidity of the change—the extent to which rapid change is permanent or will be replaced with equivalent symptoms. The speed with which behavior can be changed with a reasonable degree of permanence depends on whether it is central or peripheral to personality structure and to what extent it intersects with other systems that can reapply pressure to keep it in force. In other words, the combination of speed and potency of behavior change depend on the number and strength of the props that hold up a given bit of behavior. Props may be the reinforcements of other people, catastrophic expectations on the part of the patients, ignorance, unchecked assumptions, etc. Some of these may be removed easily, especially if they are discomfort-producing and if other systems are minimally affected. The question of symptom substitution must take into account three questions: whether the symptom is replaced by another on the same level, what positive goals have occurred, and to what extent other systems have been disrupted. Let us return to the example of the boy with the stomachache presented earlier and assume that he is given medical treatment of such potency that he ceases to have stomach complaints. However, he then develops acrophobia that just as effectively keeps him at home. The physician, concerned only with the physical system, states that there is no symptom substitution, that is, there are no other medical problems and therefore the problem is solved. However, the therapist, who views the boy's main problem as avoiding school, defines the phobia as symptom substitution and proceeds to treat him by behavior modification. As a result the boy attends school but cries all the time and fails his work. Another result might be that the boy's mother, finding that she can enjoy directly controlling passively resisting men, puts such pressure on her husband that a divorce occurs. While Freud apparently cured the phobia of Little Hans, his parents did divorce (Strean, 1967). Other therapists who define the problem as success at school or the mutual satisfaction of the entire family would see each of these attempts as evidences of inadequate, incomplete, or inept therapy. We can continue moving up the systems ladder by hypothesizing other possibilities: what if, because of the improvement in the entire family, they come into conflict with the authoritarian school system; or the father, by deciding to leave his job, contributes to the bankruptcy of the company he worked for?

There are no final nor even clear answers to this morass, but I can offer some suggestions:

1. It is not enough to specify the symptom to be removed; it is also necessary to describe what positive functioning is expected.

2. The most important interconnecting systems should be specified and attempts made to keep disruptions to a minimum.

3. If disruptions are inevitable, the therapist should specify his value choice.

The three points above need amplification and the detailing of underlying assumptions. One is that, with very few exceptions, symptoms represent a positive as well as a negative force. Most symptoms, be they medical, individual, or social, even though painful, disturbing, and time consuming, are indicative of intersections that need to be repaired lest greater damage occur. In trying to change symptoms, we must always look to the larger system to note whether the symptom is justified. (It is possible that the school system could become so destructive that to force children's attendance would be to contribute to much more serious problems than would arise from nonattendance.) Symptoms may also have positive value, such as holding a couple together.

With our powerful Western technology we change and redo large parts of our physical environment without any appreciation of the values that we are negating and without any provisions for replacing their loss. As a result we are constantly being faced with land erosion, floods, air pollution, drops in water-tables, etc. Similarly, in therapy we are creating a technology that lets us change personality faster than we know how to solidify it or provide for the fragments left behind. If we attempt to specify what is healthy in a symptom pattern, then we will know more clearly what to leave alone.

It is also important to specify the replacement behavior for symptomatic difficulties, even though this is presently somewhat utopian. Of what value is it to remove a snake phobia—what does this contribute to living in a positive sense? Or, if we remove overt homosexual behavior, is asexuality adequate, or ability to have intercourse with randomly chosen females? Or do we aim toward the formation of a sustained, personally satisfying heterosexual involvement? Most therapists would prefer to avoid the specification of positive goals, since this involves them in clear value choices and since achievement may be embarrassingly short of the goals. It is also true that most patients request the removal of symptoms rather than specifying replacement behavior, and their goals usually change during the treatment process as additional possibilities become available. However, the therapist who does not consider the question of goals in their broader aspect becomes a mere techician, or a flunky of the values of the culture and its institutional systems.

Finally, and also ideally, if we have done our jobs thoroughly, we have not markedly disrupted any other system. This is a complicated issue, and only some of the parameters can be suggested here. It is, of course, true that growth and change are both disruptive of systems. The child will leave home in the process of growing up; changes in other systems will make an institutional administrative arrangement inadequate, causing different and expanded procedures and organization, and perhaps another kind of discomfort. We therefore have to decide whether the disruption of a system is inevitable or whether it is destructive, that is, whether it creates wounds that require extensive energy to heal, energy that could be better used for expanded growth. This question is one for Solomon; however, the therapist, even with his much more limited resources, should still have at least an awareness of his role as a system disrupter. A denial of this effect ("The only thing I do is to change a person's specific behavior") can be regarded as gross myopia. For example, consider a therapist whose patients are primarily dissatisfied housewives. In his work with them, he fosters their becoming appropriately more demanding and assertive. However, the end result is frequent marital problems and divorces, as the husbands reject their wives' demands or use them as excuses for affairs, etc. Much of this could be avoided if the therapist were willing to see couples jointly (or could modify his strong rescue needs). If the goal is to make a person less dependent, then the immediate question can be raised, less dependent upon whom? It follows that the "whom" may have some responses of his own that will likely lead to strains in the family system. If the therapist is aware of these strains, he can take steps to anticipate and deal with them.

Sometimes disruption cannot be avoided. If we are able to "decraze" a late-adolescent schizophrenic whose family refuses to be changed, then one or both parents may show psychotic symptoms themselves. (At times, one measure of change is the disruption of interrelated systems or the extent of the pressures they employ to force return to earlier states.) There are times when systems may well need to be abandoned: when the student should drop out of school or the worker quit his job. The therapist no longer has the luxury of avoiding the problem by decreeing that no decisions be made during therapy (life moves too quickly for this), nor can he ignore the fact that changes resulting from therapy inevitably create decision situations. Helping the patient with deciding in a given situation whether to run, fight, or compromise requires a full measure of the therapist's humanness. In general, I would prefer to maintain rather than to disrupt systems. However, this implies degrees of wisdom and power that are not yet consistently available.

When leaving a system is inevitable, the therapist can assist the patient with the reduction of unfinished business by having him in the therapy session confront, in directly spoken fantasy, the person(s) with his resentments, appreciations, regrets, and good-bys.

Finally, the therapist can predict for the patient as early as possible that system disruption may occur, allowing him to anticipate and have increased choice in the outcome. While the choice of end goals is basically the patient's, the therapist has the responsibility of anticipating and reminding the patient of as many choices as possible. There are unfortunately many conditions that reduce the number of options, and with a given patient, quite limited goals are often inevitable, given limited resources and rigid systems. The therapist should be able to accept these while being aware of further possibilities.

One of the major contributions of Gestalt therapy is the power of its techniques, which make possible the very rapid reaching of deep emotional levels. Since the other papers in this section ably describe these, no effort will be made to include them here. It should be noted, however, that having access to potent techniques presents a temptation to overuse them, and the therapist needs to be aware that he has other tasks of importance.

HUMANNESS

The therapist's contribution to the therapeutic process as a person and the importance of the genuineness and depth of the therapeutic relationship have been emphasized by a large number of therapists. Humanness, as it is used here, includes a variety of involvements: the therapist's concern for and caring about his patient on a personal and emotional level; his willingness to share himself and bring to the patient his own direct emotional responses and/or pertinent accounts of his own experiences; his ability to recognize in the patient gropings toward deepened authenticity, which need support and recognition; and his continued openness to his own growth, which serves as a model for the patient.

Some patients' needs are peripheral and can be adequately attended to by therapists with only brief or minimal involvement. But many—if not most—people were raised by families who, even while doing the best they could, taught them less about being human than they need to know. If a patient's problems stem from inadequate rearing, then the teaching of more adequate behavior is basically a process of rearing. This requires adequate humanness in the therapist who assumes the parenting role, since he will serve extensively as a model and will have to make many value-laden decisions. This does not rule out briefer therapeutic contacts. There is a trend among some therapists who assume long-range responsibility to suggest or arrange for patients at certain stages such adjunct experiences as sensitivity training, art therapy, structural reintegration, or marathons. There is also an increasing emphasis among some behavior modifiers to consider their assignment unfinished until more adequate behavior is substituted for the symptom that is removed.

In raising children, it is the subtle learnings, attitudes, and non-verbal messages that are perhaps the most important. As the father teaches his son to fix the sled, or the mother shops for clothes with her daughter, they communicate perceptions of the child as stupid or bright, pleasant or unpleasant, likable or disgusting, and demonstrate attitudes such as interest, endurance, and enjoyment. Factual knowledge and routine bits of information are most efficiently taught by teaching machines or their equivalents, but not tolerance or curiosity, nor the value of "wasting" time.

Patients inevitably put therapists in a parental position, that is, they see them as having the secrets of living and test them in many ways to see if they will be adequate models. I tell patients, "Basically what we are doing here is seeing if I, as I am now, could have grown up in your family as you present it to me in your person, and remain sane." The patient in rapidly alternating ways involves me with his problems to see if I can respond more adequately than his parents could, and presents me with his parent's problems to see if I can find better ways of dealing with them than he was able to. For those patients for whom therapy is and becomes a central and intense experience, external living crises become relatively less important, and reenactments of growing-up crises occupy increasing attention. They progress backward through time and present their unsolved problems in a roughly reverse temporal order. Most often the final decision to accept me totally as parent comes as the result of a crisis, often following a minor mistake I made at the same time the patient is beginning to come to grips with core problems. (A somewhat limited example is given in Fagan, 1968.) The crisis is unexpected in that I can never anticipate its presentation; in retrospect it becomes apparent that the patient sets up a situation in which I am put to the test that his parents failed most badly. The crisis clearly measures my understanding of the patient's patterning, my ability to control, my potency, but most of all my humanness, since a response is unavoidable and usually must be immediate and genuine, drawing on resources that lie far below the level of techniques. I do not always pass the test. Sometimes when I do not, the patient tries again later; sometimes he gives up and adopts lesser goals; sometimes he turns to other sources of help. When I have passed, I know immediately since the patient in an unmistakable way becomes my infant and our feelings toward each other involve a kind of adoration (for example, Searles, 1965, Chap. 21). We work our way back up through developmental milestones of childhood and adolescence until the patient is as well regrown as my own resources as a parent allow. [Other descriptions of this process are given by Whitaker and Malone (1953) as the *core phase*, and by Carkhuff and Berenson (1967) as the *downward and upward stages* of therapy.] It is of course true that many therapists do not and/or cannot involve their patients to this extent, and many patients ask for assistance of a much more limited nature. However, deep personal regrowth is still experienced by those involved as either patients or therapists as the crux of therapy.

On a less intense and involved level, but still important, are those crises of living on which the therapist must respond to the patient more from this humanness than from his knowledge or techniques. These would include a severe illness, a child killed, an important goal having become unattainable, a deep rejection. Before or after dealing with those aspects that are correctable, there exists the need for bearing those parts that can only be borne. The therapist needs to know from inside himself when his presence is the most important contribution he can make to the healing process, and when his response as one human being to another is more important than any therapeutic busywork.

The events of the past few years—the civil rights struggles, student rebellions, experimental college movements, hippie communities, and the explosive growth of sensitivity training and group experiences—bespeak a level of hunger for new ways of experiencing, relating, learning, governing, etc., but they also are contributing to the development of a number of people whose experimentations are producing new levels and patterns of authenticity. If therapists fall too far behind in their own growth, they will be out of touch with an increasing proportion of the population.

The making of oneself into a whole and genuine person is probably the most difficult and painful aspect of becoming a therapist, but, for many, it is also the most valuable and important part. Many therapists who see authenticity as a primary task of the therapist fear those who, having stopped short in their own struggles with growing, substitute increased emphasis on control and potency, with a corresponding lack of regard for questions of value associated with the ability to produce personality change. The question of who controls the controllers becomes more acute as control over behavior becomes more possible. In the name of mental health, many horribly inhumane and degrading things have been done to people (Szasz, 1965b) and will no doubt continue to be done. Those who are certain of the good that they do are more to be feared than those who are more willing to admit and struggle with their own personal limitations, to share their doubts, and to express their values.

The contributions of Gestalt therapy to the humanness of the therapist come primarily in the workshop setting, which offers therapists direct experience with their own inauthenticities and avoidances. The emphasis on experiencing rather than computing, and the fostering of here-and-now awareness, pleasure, excitement, deep emotional involvement, and direct interaction seem especially designed for therapists, many of whom tend toward obsessive and depressive styles. Experiencing and observing ways in which authenticity can be distinguished from its many imitations is a valuable contribution.

Gestalt theory confronts therapists as directly as patients with reminders of the values and pleasures of living that can get pushed aside by our occupational hazards of overemphasis on work, responsibility, accomplishment, and study. Finally, in work with patients, Gestalt techniques offer a variety of ways of allowing them a rapid, deep, and authentic experience with themselves which provides an increased knowledge of what is possible as well as allowing a quick and direct "knowing" on the part of the therapist.

COMMITMENT

A number of major and minor commitments are necessary to the therapy process. The therapist commits himself to a vocation with its attendant demands for continued growth of his own understanding and ability. He also commits himself to individual patients in his work with them. Finally, he commits himself to contributing to the field as a whole by his research, writing, training of students, etc.

Commitment, or the continuing involvement and acceptance of assumed responsibilities, requires high levels of interest and energy.

Interests may be maintained in a variety of ways. There are many problems that have large cognitive components, including understanding patients and constructing patterns. There is the broader task of theory addition and construction, or the long-term satisfaction of a research program. Also involving are the deep satisfaction of seeing the growth of patients, the challenge and excitement of devising new procedures and techniques, and the steady increments of the therapist's person and powers. However, no therapist can avoid boredom, depression, and doubts related to the therapeutic process and his own procedures, either for brief moments or for extended periods. If the therapist's techniques are mechanical and boring, involving him only passively or superficially, or if the interaction required creates too much anxiety, then the therapist will either be spurred to less directly central areas such as research or, unfortunately, training.

Gestalt therapy places most emphasis on the therapist's commitment to himself in terms of enhancing his involvement and excitement in the day-to-day tasks. It also provides or suggests ways for the therapist to assist himself in exploring his own boredom and doubts when they occur. In these respects it enhances both therapist and patient interest and offers ways of getting both "unstuck" when faced with the inevitable impasses.

Some final thoughts: The five tasks described in this paper will vary in their relative importance in response to many factors; the context surrounding therapy, specific requirements and limitations, the types of problems presented, and the time sequence or stage of therapy. At times the therapist will experience conflicts between two of the tasks, for example, between control and humanness. As the emphasis shifts from task to task, to some extent the image of the therapist shifts, in a way that, with much magnification, parallels the popular stereotypes of the therapist as the mind reader who knows all, as the hypnotist who can control persons against their will, as the magician who has a collection of magic tricks, as the loving Big Daddy or Mommie, and as the faithful, patient family retainer.

In summary, many requirements are made of the therapist as he sets out to assist another person. These have been discussed under five headings: patterning, control, potency, humanness, and commitment. The therapist's response to these involves him as a complete person, including his intellectual knowledge and cognitive abilities, his interpersonal effectiveness, his emotional awareness and personal sensitivity, his values and interests, and his experience in living. Certainly one of the continued challenges and fascinations of therapy is the variety of demands that it places on the therapist and its ability to require and evoke from him an involvement and utilization of all his resources.

REFERENCES

Berne, E. *Games people play.* New York: Grove Press, 1964.

Bion, W. R. *Experience in groups, and other papers.* New York: Basic Books, 1961.

Bugental, J. F. T. *The search for authenticity: An existential-analytic approach to psychotherapy.* New York: Holt, Rinehart & Winston, 1965.

Calhoon, D. D. Symptom substitution and the behavioral therapies: A reappraisal. *Psychological Bulletin,* 1968, *69,* 149-156.

Carkhuff, R. R., & Berenson, B. G. *Beyond counseling and therapy.* New York: Holt, Rinehart & Winston, 1967.

Fagan, J. Message from mother. *Psychotherapy: Theory, Research and Practice,* 1968, *5,* 21-23.

Goulding, R. Introductory lectures in transactional analysis. Atlanta, Ga., 1967.

Greenwald, H. Treatment of the psychopath. *Voices,* 1967, *3* (1), 50-61.

Haley, J. The art of psychoanalysis. In S. I. Hayakawa (Ed.), *Our language and our world.* New York: Harper & Brothers, 1959.

Haley, J. Control in brief psychotherapy. *Archives of General Psychiatry,* 1961, *4,* 139-153. (a)

Haley, J. Control in psychotherapy with schizophrenics. *Archives of General Psychiatry,* 1961, *5,* 340-353. (b)

Haley, J. *Strategies of psychotherapy.* New York: Grune & Stratton. 1963.

Haley, J. & Hoffman, L. *Techniques of family therapy.* New York: Basic Books, 1968.

Langsley, D. G., Pittman, F. S., Machotka, P., & Flomenhaft, K. Family crisis therapy—results and implications. *Family Process,* 1968, *7,* 145-158.

Rogers, C.R. *Client-centered therapy.* Boston: Houghton-Mifflin, 1951.

Rogers, C. R. (Ed.) *The therapeutic relationship and its impact: A study of psychotherapy with schizophrenics.* Madison, Wisc.: University of Wisconsin Press, 1967.

Rosen, J. N. *Direct analysis: Selected papers.* New York: Grune & Stratton, 1953.

Schwartz, L. J. Treatment of the adolescent psychopath—theory and case report. *Psychotherapy: Theory, Research and Practice,* 1967, *4,* 133-137.

Searles, H. F. *Collected papers on schizophrenia and related subjects.* New York: International Universities Press, 1965.

Strean, H. S. A family therapist looks at "Little Hans." *Family Process,*
1967, *6,* 227-234.

Szasz, T. S. *The ethics of psychoanalysis: The theory and method of autonomous psychotherapy.* New York: Basic Books, 1965. (a)

Szasz, T. S. *Psychiatric justice.* New York: Macmillan, 1965. (b)

Truax, C. B., & Carkhuff, R. R. *Toward effective counseling and psychotherapy: Training and practice.* Chicago: Aldine, 1967.

Whitaker, C. A., & Malone, T. P. *The roots of psychotherapy.* New York:
Blakiston, 1953.

CHAPTER 8

AN INTRODUCTION TO GESTALT TECHNIQUES

John B. Enright

Gestalt therapy has been (and is still being) developed by Frederick S. Perls out of three quite distinct sources and influences: psychoanalysis, particularly as modified by the early Wilhelm Reich; European phenomenology-existentialism; and Gestalt psychology. Perls's *Gestalt Therapy* presents the theory of personality structure and growth from which the therapy can be derived, and a series of experiments in self-awareness to be directly used by the reader. However, the range, variety, and power of the techniques developed by Perls and his associates deserve more extensive description, both within a general framework of purpose and procedure and in terms of specific types of interventions. This paper will concentrate primarily on therapeutic goals and strategy, with occasional brief discussion of specific tactics and techniques.

In the Gestalt point of view, the healthy organism-in-its-environment is constantly attending to matters of importance to its maintenance or survival. These matters of importance are organism-environment *transactions* that keep or restore equilibrium or smooth functioning. "Attending" here does not refer to a conscious state but to a behavioral focusing of parts of the organism toward relevant parts of the environment, with muscular tonus, sensory tracking, etc. Most of this directed behavior takes place at the shifting boundary of organism and environment, where that which is novel and alien in the environment is contacted and made part of the organism (for example, food is ingested and assimilated or words are heard and understood).

In human beings, *awareness* develops where novelty and complexity of transaction are greatest, and the most possibilities (for good or ill) exist. Awareness seems to facilitate maximum efficiency by concentrating all the organism's abilities on the most complex, possibility-loaded situations.

In this oversimplified account, awareness is a state of consciousness that develops spontaneously when organismic attention becomes focused on some particular region of the organism-environment contact boundary at which an especially important and complex transaction is occurring. If this view is accepted, a disarmingly simple definition of psychological malfunctioning becomes possible. Something is going wrong when awareness does *not* develop at this region of complex interaction. A correspondingly simple theory of therapy follows, as a first approximation to a statement of the goal of Gestalt therapy: therapy consists of the *reintegration of attention and awareness.*

The task of the therapist is to help the patient overcome the barriers (of which more later) that block awareness, and to let nature take its course (that is, awareness develop) so he can function with all his abilities. Note that the therapist in this view does not help directly with the transaction—he does not help solve the problem—but helps reestablish the conditions under which the patient can best use his own problem-solving abilities.

From this simple formulation follows a considerable amount of what the Gestalt therapist does in practice. He watches for splits in attention and awareness, for evidence that focused organismic attention is developing outside of awareness. Though the patient may be talking about some problem, he is also from moment to moment sensorily registering and motorically doing much else. Though his awareness is generally concentrated on the verbal content, he also may be gazing into space, fiddling with his hands, shifting around, smiling—at times in congruence with verbal content, at times perhaps not. His voice also varies in quality, sometimes matching the shifts in verbal content, sometimes not. In addition to the "intended" content of his words, there is also the rich and subtle texture of imagery and metaphor, the selection of verb voice, mode, and tense, the shifts in pronouns, etc. These serve as the linguistic "ground" that modifies and enriches the lexical meaning of his words. All this bears relationship to the patient's difficulties in living an organismically satisfying life. He is showing us from moment to moment and in detail just how he avoids being in full contact with his current actuality—how he avoids awareness of ongoing matters of organismic importance to him.

When the patient is communicating well verbally, and his other ongoing activities are minimal or congruent, I listen. At those times I assume his awareness to be integrated with his organismic attention, and thus he is doing nothing that I as a psychotherapist can help him with; his problems are his, and he is working in them effectively at the moment. In a family or group, members are in good contact with each other at such times, communicating well and dealing with their interpersonal problems effectively. My task begins when these other "unconscious" activities begin to stand out in the total gestalt and vie with the verbal content. I then encourage the patient(s) to devote some attention to these other activities, asking him to describe what he is doing, seeing, feeling. I make no interpretations but simply draw awareness to these phenomena, and let him make of them what he will. Quite often, if my timing is good and my perception of increasing saliency accurate, the patient can make quite good sense of these and gain in awareness of what he is doing. Some brief clinical examples may be helpful here.

A woman in individual therapy is going over, in a very complaining voice, some examples of how she was recently mistreated by her mother-in-law. I am impressed in her account by her lack of awareness of how much she invited this, and how she underperceives her capacity to interrupt this behavior but said nothing. My attention is caught by a rapid repetitive movement of her hand against her other arm, though I can't make the movement out.

T.: What are you doing with your hand?

P.: (*slightly startled*) Uh, making a cross.

T.: A cross?

P.: Yes (*pause*).

T.: What might you do with a cross?

P.: Well, I certainly hung myself on one this weekend, didn't I?

She returns to her account, but with more awareness of her martyr attitude and its contribution to events.

A couple in marital therapy are going over their problems rather repetitiously and fruitlessly. The wife is staring past me quite fixedly.

T.: What are you looking at?

W.: The tape recorder.

T.: Can you describe what you are seeing?

W.: Yes. It's just going round and round and round.

T.: Round and round?

W.: Yes.

T.: Is anything else going round and round?

H. & W.: (*simultaneously and rather impatiently*) *We* certainly are.

They return to their discussion, but more fully aware of their sterile circularity, and they begin to take more productive steps to break out of it.

An intellectualizing male graduate student in group therapy announces blandly to no one in particular, "I have difficulty in relating to people." In the ensuing silence, he glances briefly at the attractive nurse who was cotherapist. The therapist immediately asked, "Who *here* do you have trouble relating to?" The student is able to name the nurse, and spends a fruitful five minutes exploring his mixed frustration, attraction, and anger focused on this desirable but inaccessible woman.

A paranoid woman in her first group therapy meeting on the ward begins by telling in a flat, affectless voice that her husband tried to poison her. She continues to enumerate her delusional complaints, but also mentions a severe pain in the back of her neck. Asked to describe this, she says that it is a though she had been struck a judo blow and also indicates that her husband knows judo. Able now to say that she feels as though her husband had actually struck her, she can, when questioned, soon begin to talk about ways in which her husband symbolically hurt her. Soon she is telling the group, with appropriate tears and anger, how her husband slights and ignores her, and flirts with other women. Temporarily she has abandoned the paranoid solution to her problems.

A constricted, overinhibited man is tapping his finger on the table while a woman in the group talks on and on. Asked if he has anything to comment about what the woman is saying, he denies much concern with it but continues the tapping. He is asked then to intensify the tapping, to tap louder and more vigorously, and to continue until he feels more fully what he is doing. His anger mounts quickly and in a minute or so he is pounding the table and expressing vehemently his disagreement with the woman. He declares that she is "just like my wife," but in addition to this historical perspective, he has had an experiential glimpse of his excessive control of strong assertive feelings and the possibilities of more immediate and hence less violent expression of them.

There are several important characteristics of the therapeutic interventions described above that attempt to help the patient integrate attention and awareness. (*a*) The intervention builds on actual present behavior—some *present* concern of the organism is involved, although neither patient nor therapist may have any idea what it is when the intervention is made, and it may turn out to be quite unrelated to the verbal material concurrently expressed. (*b*) Ideally, and usually, the intervention is noninterpretive. I ask what is going on or what he is doing; where we go from there depends on the patient's answer. If he makes connection with the verbal material or achieves some understanding of what he is doing, he has done it for himself in his own language. If he denies any connection or experiences nothing in his behavior, that is up to him; typically I let the matter drop. My timing was bad or he was not ready. If I push for a response or give my interpretation, he may only mobilize more defenses against me. If the behavior is important, it will happen again. (*c*) A third characteristic of this style of intervention is that it continually operates to enhance and expand the patient's sense of responsibility for his own behavior. Responsibility here means not the broad sense of "social responsibility," but rather the feeling that "I, here and now, am aware of doing thus and so." (However, I feel that true responsibility in the broader sense is rooted in this feeling of being the actual agent.) Thus, throughout the course of therapy, whatever the content, the patient is learning to do for himself, and to face indecision and make choices—on a small but increasing scale.

The questions that introduce these interventions are almost exclusively "what" and "how" questions, seldom "what for" or "why." Most people most of the time don't fully know *what* they are doing, and it is a considerable therapeutic contribution if the patient can achieve a vivid and ongoing awareness of his moment-to-moment behavior and surroundings. In a sense, the achievement of such full awareness is all that therapy need do; when a person feels fully and vividly what he is doing, his concern about why usually fades away. If he does remain interested, he is in a good position to work it out for himself.

In keeping with this bias of Gestalt therapy in favor of "what" and "how" questions, I will now consider in more detail some of the ways in which areas of self-functioning are kept out of awareness, and some of the consequences of this blocking. Four ways will be considered: retroflection, desensitization, introjection, and projection. All four can be seen functioning from moment to moment in the here and now to block awareness of current behavior, or as repetitive residuals of earlier attempts to avoid awareness. A brief discussion may leave the false impression that these only rephrase existing concepts, and certainly there is extensive overlap with related concepts from psychoanalysis and general psychiatry. The difference in emphasis is often quite subtle and would require a fairly extensive discussion to clarify.

Projection. The individual attributes disowned aspects of himself to others, becoming hypersensitive or critical of minor manifestations. There is perhaps more emphasis in Gestalt therapy than in psychiatry on the less pathological forms of projection in which the individual does not distort reality seriously but shows his overconcern only in his perceptual selectivity of certain phenomena from the whole range of his surroundings.

Retroflection. An impulse or idea is rooted in organismic sensorimotor tension, shaped partly by inner drives and focused on environmental events or objects. Retroflection describes the general process of negating, holding back, or balancing the impulse tension by additional, opposing sensorimotor tension. The concept includes most of what is often referred to as repression and inhibition, and emphasizes the *how* of the processes involved. Since the net result of all this canceled-out muscular tension is zero—no overt movement—there is no particular increase in activity at the contact boundary, and awareness does not develop. Later, perhaps, since there is increased activity at the points of muscular opposition, awareness may develop there as pain or discomfort. This process of retroflection can be transitory or chronic. The cry of distress begins with moistening of the eyes and a characteristic facial expression; the "stiff upper lip" and the literal holding (squeezing) back of tears constitute the retroflection. This can last a moment before the tears break through or (as Tomkins, 1963, describes so vividly) a lifetime.

Perls's debt to Wilhelm Reich is most clear in the development of this concept. Reich's "character armor" is chronic retroflection. It is important to note that the organism is expending energy in maintaining the tension of both the impulse and resistance, and both are quite typically alienated from the self and awareness. Both need to be "reclaimed" in therapy and made available for satisfying, constructive use.

Desensitization. This is the sensory analog to motoric retroflection. Scotomata, visual blurring, chronic "not hearing," sensory dullness, frigidity, etc., are equal in importance to retroflection in the blocking of awareness. They are, however, more dependent on verbal report and hence less accessible to direct observation and study than motoric phenomena.

Introjections. These consist of complex, integrated ways of behaving or being, adopted wholesale by the developing organism from significant others *without assimilation or integration with the self.* They correspond quite closely to Berne's (1961) "parent" or "exteropsychic" ego states. They can be detected by the repeated concurrence of a certain voice quality, type of verbal content, and gesture-posture style, and by the similarity with which others respond to this unified complex of behavior. The details of the process by which these introjects are taken in are complex and unnecessary for this discussion. Our interest here is primarily in the role they play in current life. There they are the chief actors in the endless self-nagging and inner argument between the "ideal" and "real" self in which so many people fritter away their lives. They also clutter up interpersonal relations, when the self plays out one of these roles with significant others or projects one of them onto another person. Introjects are one of the main transmitters of pathology across the generations. An individual who may have successfully minimized his use of introjects in other areas of his life still may activate them when he functions as a parent with his own children.

Insofar as the individual relies on any of these means for the transitory or chronic blocking of awareness, he leaves himself with vast areas alienated and inaccessible, interfering with rather than facilitating the flow of life. He feels—and in a sense is—weak and divided, pushed and pulled by forces outside himself. His behavior tends to be graceless and awkward; breathing and vocal expression are crippled. And with so little energy left over to live with, a great deal of "unfinished business" piles up.

Unfinished business is perhaps the major consequence of the blocking of awareness. Need cycles cannot be completed; tension is aroused but not reduced; affect mounts and is unexpressed. The flow of behavior is clogged with unexpressed action; little new can happen in the ensuing constriction and frustration. The individual becomes "hung up" on the unexpressed; life slows down into despair and boredom with lack of autonomy, spontaneity, and intimacy. The neurotic's life is not a happy one, even if he does not happen to develop one of the specialized symptoms such as phobias, obsessions, or anxiety; it remains merely gray and unfulfilled. Frequently his conscious ego is not in very good touch with what is wrong, and his verbal account of his "problems" is often quite wide of the mark. He has successfully distracted himself from even knowing where he hurts, and his "problem" or "presenting complaint" is not the meaningful place to start therapy. Quite often he would be only too happy to talk indefinitely and abstractly about The Problem, keeping "it" safely at a distance. If he is trained as a patient, he may come in ready to ruminate his current fantasies about his childhood, with the same distancing intent and result.

Fortunately, the general strategy of Gestalt therapy does not depend on the patient's accuracy in self-report. We simply tell him, in effect, to sit down and start living, then note where and how he fails. The therapeutic value we implicitly ask him to accept is that he will probably be more effective and comfortable in his life in the long run if he is more fully aware of what he is doing from moment to moment, and if he can accept responsibility for this behavior. He may have to accept this on faith for a short time, but we hope very soon to demonstrate the advantages of this orientation directly and concretely.

In this situation the organism will immediately turn in some way to whichever of its store of unfinished businesses is pressing and more or less relevant to the current situation. His techniques for blocking awareness will immediately come into play: he will begin to show in his projections, tension, and dissociated activity the portions of his self that are alienated and inaccessible. The therapist can choose the most salient of these with which to begin. I have become impressed with the importance and probable centrality of the *very first* opening gambit—verbal or not—of the patient. Where he sits, at whom he glances, the sigh, the smile, the posture, the idiosyncratic image in his opening remark—anything he says before he formally begins to talk about The Problem—all are rich leads to the most deeply involving material he is likely to be able to get to, if the way can be found to use this material nonthreateningly.

The beginning can be—indeed should be—some trivial surface event, such as a smile at the therapist. When this is expressed more fully and awarely, the patient is ready to go on to the next, slightly more involving fact that he is, now that he thinks about it, also a little angry at the nice therapist. And so on, through layers of resistance and impulse—each one dwelt on as long as necessary, and hopefully not left behind until the energy invested in it is available for use, and the patient is not too anxious about the next step into the unknown and unexpressed. Resistances are not "overcome," but identified with and made one's own. Affect or impulse are not balanced or blocked in expression, but encouraged into more intense and full expression, finishing the business, and leaving decks cleared for new action. No attempt is made to keep the patient on any "topic" as verbally presented; instead, a systematic and aggressive attempt is made to keep him in constant contact with *what he is doing*. He is then encouraged to do whatever this is as fully and completely as he can, with growing awareness of what he is doing. If he blocks himself from doing it, we then turn attention to how he is blocking himself and encourage fuller and more aware expression of this. The therapist spends as little time and energy as possible speculating on what is likely to emerge from each step the patient takes but instead concentrates on timing of the steps and listening as fully as possible to what the patient is doing. This is perhaps the most significant gain of noninterpretative therapy. The therapist is liberated from his endless fantasies about what is going to emerge from the patient in the next few minutes (with associated anxiety about whether he is right or wrong) and instead can simply listen and help the patient find his own way through the pauses and blocks.

The basic assumption of this therapeutic approach is that patients deal adequately with their own life problems—if they know what they are and can bring all their abilities into action to solve them. Our task is to unblock awareness by helping patients relax their retroflected energies, restore sensitivity, assimilate introjects, and change projection into direct expression. Once in good touch with their real concerns and their real environment, they are on their own.

GESTALT TECHNIQUES IN GROUP AND FAMILY THERAPY

So far, an effort has been made to present techniques of Gestalt therapy that are generally applicable to all modes of therapy: individual, group, and family. Some of the techniques and tactics presented can be more powerful when we ask the patient to sit down and start living in a group with new people he must learn to deal with; or to sit down with his family and become aware of interactions with these significant but frustrating others. In a group, abstract problems can more quickly and readily be brought to earth. A patient who complains that he can't speak up and criticize his wife might be asked to address a critical remark to each group member present, thus experiencing immediately his difficulty instead of talking *about* it. A patient who claims to have an "inferiority complex" might be greeted with the request to indicate to whom in the present group she feels inferior, and how. With many more people available, the range of unfinished business that can be quite readily contacted is much greater. More people provide more screens on which projections can be cast, and the work of reclaiming and expressing them can be more easily done. For example, a patient who comments that another patient is "looking contemptuously at the group" might be asked himself to "try out" looking contemptuously at the group to see if he can make contact with his own feelings of contempt, and express them directly instead of through projective oversensitivity.

In addition to the enhancing effects of getting several patients together, there are certain techniques that are specific to people in a group. In addition to the therapeutic value of awareness and responsibility already mentioned, we ask the group or family patient to accept another group-specific value: that in the long run he will probably deal more effectively and better with people around him if he is direct with them and listens to them with respect for them as individuals. Again, he must briefly accept this on faith, but we hope soon to demonstrate its validity concretely. In essence, the techniques about to be presented all follow from this value assumption and are simply ways of implementing this belief about human relations. The goal we set for the patients as they sit down together in a group or family is an "I-thou" relationship in which each person is aware, responsible, and direct in his own communications and listens as fully as possible to the other person as an equal.

The first technique implementing this point of view about human relations is to ask as quickly and fully as possible, in all interactions that take place in the group, that people speak directly to each other without use of the third person. A is discouraged from making some comment about B to the therapist and is asked rather to rephrase his comment in some form directly to B. This sounds simple, almost trivial, but in practice it is very powerful. Patients often respond to this request first by saying that it is too simple to bother with, or that it doesn't matter; but when they try, they go on rebelling strongly against it. The affect mobilized by such direct confrontation is very different from that which can be dissipated indirectly in the third-person comment. Typically, a patient has considerable difficulty in making very much of a direct statement to another. The most common result of an attempt at directness is that ambivalence immediately becomes apparent, usually nonverbally, and the "simple" statement immediately turns out to be very complicated indeed. This ambivalence and difficulty with directness then become the focus of therapy. For example, a patient may attempt a critical statement to another, and look away from the other in the middle of the statement or interrupt it with a smile. We might ask him then what he was looking away from, or to put the smile into words. If he says he was looking away from the other's angry expression, he can get immediate feedback, and perhaps go on to find out that the anger he saw was his own, projected. As he gropes to put his placating smile into words, he becomes more aware of how he blocks and weakens his own assertiveness. As he succeeds in expressing the placation in words, he is then open to the further possibility of becoming aware of how his placating is tinged with contempt toward the other for being fooled by it, and is itself complex and ambivalent. The advantages of directness—the more immediate and fuller feedback from the other and the expansion of one's own awareness—are experienced almost immediately in this approach. Since the individuals are engaged face to face with each other in this small-scale encounter, they learn these advantages in the most direct way possible, with the greatest likelihood of carry-over into their outside lives.

A second technique to encourage the patient's awareness of responsibility for his own position, is to discourage questions. A question from one patient to another usually serves either or both of two purposes. For one, it says in effect, "you speak, not me," and thus is a way of avoiding the questioner's participation. Second, almost all questions turn out to be implied statements, usually critical, about the other person. "Why did you do that?" almost always means "You shouldn't have done that," "I don't like it that you did that," or something to that effect. A question is almost never an uncomplicated request for information. As much as possible, depending on the level of the group, the Gestalt therapist will insist that a question be rephrased as a statement before the other person is asked to "answer" it. Then, since the statement is no longer masked as a question, B is released from the necessity of "answering" it (that is, defending or justifying himself) and can more easily give his total response to A.

The second therapeutic value of the group—listening to others—can be implemented in a variety of ways. I often question the intent of an interruption. If people seem to be drifting off, I will ask if it is becoming hard to listen, thus getting the group to consider simultaneously its obligation to listen and the speaker's obligation to be worth listening to. A game of hostile and unproductive "verbal ping-pong" might be interrupted by insisting that each participant paraphrase the other to the other's satisfaction before being permitted to give his own response.

The details of technique vary, but the strategy is always to keep a steady, gentle pressure toward the direct and responsible I-thou orientation, keeping the focus of awareness on the difficulties the patients experience in doing this, and helping them find their own ways through these difficulties.

This strategy of Gestalt therapy is most effective in family therapy. Family therapy differs from individual-focused therapy in that the patient's central presenting life problem is itself brought into the consulting room. The patient does not have to increase his awareness in relation to some stranger, then figure out later how to use this to modify his relations to significant others. His significant others are present with him. In a very real sense, the family is the patient and can work on its *joint* unfinished business. The unsaid accusations, the unexpressed guilt, love, and resentment that are clogging up the flow of interfamily feeling must be expressed by the family, in its own language, at its own pace. The therapist's task is again to keep turning the focus of awareness on the difficulties that stand in the way of maintaining the I-thou orientation.

KEY ISSUES IN THERAPY

There are a number of issues on which any theory of therapy must take some stand. The position of Gestalt therapy on some of these could be induced from the above account, but it might be helpful to make these stands explicit. Six issues will be discussed: (1) the actual therapeutic agent as seen by Gestalt therapy and the concept of the mentally healthy person that follows from this position; (2) the criteria for termination of Gestalt therapy; (3) the range of applicability of the therapy; (4) the use of dreams; (5) the place of the therapist as a person in the technique; and (6) the place of the past in a here-and-now therapy.

Awareness, Consciousness, Insight, and the Mentally Healthy Person

The theoretical and therapeutic core of Gestalt therapy is *awareness*. This is essentially an undefined term referring to a particular kind of immediate experience, but it is possible to attempt some verbal description and distinguish it from other states of consciousness. Awareness develops *with* and is integrally *part of* an organismic-environmental transaction. It includes thinking and feeling, but it is always based on current perception of the current situation.

Much of the usual "content" of consciousness for many people is a flow of fantasy-imagery and subvocal speech (thinking) that is *not* deeply rooted in ongoing behavior, but only partially and tangentially related to it. Occasionally this fantasy-thinking is focused, in necessary anticipatory problem-solving or working on some unfinished business that is important but not currently represented in the environment. More frequently this detached thinking-imagery is a more unfocused, pointless, dreamlike reverie, obsessing about, without particularly working on, unfinished business and serving mainly to distract and attenuate awareness of the actual.

The difference between awareness and this unfocused reverie is most clear in the process of eating. Awareness of eating would include the appearance, smell, and taste of the food; the kinesthetic sense of the destruction of the food though chewing and swallowing; and the associated affects of pleasure or disgust. In fact, of course, most people while eating are engaged primarily in some sort of reverie. They engage, perhaps, in revenge fantasies about some recent slight, a rerun of the latest Giants' game, or even fantasies about what they are going to eat for dessert in a few minutes—anything rather than the actual ongoing organismic activity. Many people clutter up their lives almost constantly with this internal noise of pointless and only shallowly gratifying fantasy. Since it is not substantially gratifying and does not successfully resolve any unfinished business, its consequences are to make the actual ongoing behavior (in this case, eating) less satisfying and to create more unfinished business. For example, consider an obsessive student who interrupts his studying with fantasies of the evening's date. When evening comes, and studying is not completed or well done, he ruins his date worrying about studying.

No implication is intended that in healthy life awareness is particularly big, grand, or ever-exciting. It is simply there, flowing along with behavior. In therapy, however, when awareness develops where it has been previously blocked, it does tend to be accompanied by a sense of release of tension and a feeling of increase in energy. The experience is in a sense pleasurable. Even when the developing awareness is of a painful affect such as mourning or anger, it is accompanied by a feeling of "I want this; I'm glad it's happening even though it is painful." This gratifying aspect of therapeutic awareness is crucial since it is the internal rewarding and motivating factor that permits and encourages the patient to press on even into very painful feelings.

Awareness needs particularly to be distinguished from introspection. In introspection, the self is split; part is "looking at" another part as object, self-consciously. Awareness is the whole self, conscious of that to which the organism is attending. Introspection is effortful, forced concentration; awareness is spontaneous concentration on that which is exciting and of interest. Introspection, being relatively detached from ongoing total organismic concern and being out of touch with the actual environment, can never discover anything very new, but only rearrange and rehash the verbally remembered and hence unnourishing past. Awareness, being in contact with the current environment and organism, always includes something refreshingly new. Genuine awareness is always a little bit of a surprise since neither the organism nor the environment is ever quite the same. (A person who claims that an experience is "the same" as a previous one is telling us that he is actually replaying a fantasy rather than attending with awareness to his actual experience.) Awareness as it develops in therapy almost always follows a sense of taking a chance or taking a step into the unknown—of groping to say the unsayable or beginning something without being sure of the ending. When this experience is not present, almost certainly the "insight" being presented is a sterile rehash rather than an expansion of awareness.

It would be impossible in the scope of this introduction fully to articulate this fundamental concept of awareness with its analog in psychoanalysis (*insight*), but a brief consideration of their relation might be helpful. Quite early in the history of psychoanalysis, its theoreticians and therapists became concerned that insight did *not* always produce the expected and desired therapeutic changes. One insight would seem to work; another remarkably similar-seeming one would lead nowhere. In the attempt to account for this difference a distinction was introduced between *intellectual* and *emotional* insight—the latter being the insight that "worked." The Gestalt therapist would say that the "emotional" insight (whatever its verbal form: past, present, or future) was based on an expansion of awareness of an ongoing organism-environment relationship with its associated positive affect and sense of discovery, while the "intellectual" insight lacked this crucial rootedness in the actual. This is an oversimplification of a very complex matter, but hints at the relationship of these two central concepts.

A complete theory of therapy should include some image of the healthy functioning it purports to help people achieve. Gestalt therapy considers the mentally healthy person as one in whom awareness can develop without blocking, wherever his organismic attention is drawn. Such a person can experience his own needs and the environmental possibilities fully and clearly from moment to moment, accepting both as given and working toward creative compromises. He still has his full share of inner conflicts of needs and environmental frustrations, but, being in close touch with these developing needs and the environment, he is capable of achieving reasonably adequate solutions quickly and does not magnify his real problems with fantasy elaborations.

Since he is carrying around much less of a filtering cloud of thought - fantasies to obscure the world, his sensual world is vivid and colorful, and his interpersonal world relatively uncontaminated with projections and unreal expectations. He can perceive and respond to others much more as they are and become from moment to moment, rather than as fixed stereotypes. He has a clear sense of the relative importance of things and can do what has to be done to finish situations. Since unfinished business does not pile up, he is free to do and be quite fully and intensely whatever he is doing or being, and people around him often report a sense of his being much more *with* them when he is with them. Seeing people reasonably clearly and without excessive fantasy, it is easy for him to be quite direct with others and appreciate them for what they are. Again, he has his share of conflicts with others, but he can resolve those conflicts that are resolvable, and let go of those that are not. (And he can usually tell the difference!) He is self-respecting in every sense, including an appreciation and enjoyment of his body with consequent physical grace.

Criteria for Termination of Therapy

A central characteristic of Gestalt therapy is that the patient as much as possible carries out his own therapy, with the therapist standing by as observer-commentator and occasional guide. The patient as much as possible makes his own interpretations, formulates his own direct statements to others, and achieves his own awareness. We see this not as thrusting the patient's responsibility for his own behavior onto him, but rather as refusing to permit him to thrust it onto us. It rightfully is his, and we do him a disservice if we do something for him, depriving him of the learning experience and enhancement of ego functions consequent on his doing it himself.

It is quite consistent with this general orientation to ask the patient as quickly as possible to take over the responsibility for deciding to continue therapy, for deciding what he is getting from it and whether he values this sufficiently to continue. We quickly show him what we have to offer; he experiences immediately some rewards of increased awareness and evaluates for himself if this is valuable and meaningful to him.

This can be implemented in many ways. I ask individuals and families almost from the first meeting if they would like another session, and end almost every group session by asking the members how they feel it went. Doubts about progress—verbally or nonverbally expressed— become the focus of discussion, and the patient is asked in effect what he intends to do about his discontents.

Not surprisingly, many patients find this request to make their own decision rather startling. It often brings quite precipitously into the foreground some otherwise quite well-concealed fantasies about magical cures and what the therapist is going to "do for" him. In the very process of exploring these, the patient can sometimes get glimmers of his own potential strength and capacity for self-direction. Issues of responsibility, choice, goals of therapy, and autonomy often then become the beginning foci of therapy.

The whole course of therapy goes differently when termination is a central issue from the beginning. The patient cannot reasonably terminate without evaluating his progress and cannot do this without being aware of his goals. Goals can—indeed, usually do—change, but the danger of both patient and therapist's losing sight of goals and drifting is minimized. Occasionally there are practical consequences of this approach in the form of quite irregular schedules as some patients, finding it very difficult to say directly, "I want an appointment next week," come more sporadically. Although these patients will have fewer contacts over a given time span, perhaps for them this is best.

Range of Applicability

It is clear from the above discussion that Gestalt therapy in pure culture is not for every patient. Basically it is designed for someone who is dissatisfied with some way he is, and is willing to expend some effort to be different—or to become more content the way he is. Many of the specific techniques and principles can be applied to less willing patients—children, some psychotics, and some character disorders—but it is beyond the scope of this introduction to discuss the modifications necessary for such applications.

Therapeutic Use of Dreams

Since Freud's brilliant work, any system of therapy must provide either a way of working with dreams or a justification for avoiding them. Gestalt therapy meets this challenge with a totally noninterpretive approach that permits the patient to progress at his own pace and find his own meaning in his dreams. Every image in the dream, whether human, animal, vegetable, or mineral, is taken to represent an alienated portion of the self. By reexperiencing and retelling the dream over and over again in the present tense, from the standpoint of each image, the patient can begin to reclaim these alienated fragments, accept them, live with them, and express them more appropriately.

For example, a restless, domineering, manipulative woman dreamed of walking down a crooked path in a forest of tall straight trees. Asking her *to become* one of these trees, makes her feel more serene and deeply rooted. By taking these feelings back into her current life, she then experienced both the lack of them and the possibilities of achieving them. *Becoming* the crooked path, her eyes filled with tears as she experienced more intensely the devious crookedness of her own life, and again, the possibilities of straightening out a little if she chose.

The role of the therapist is simply to suggest the order in which the images might be contacted, usually from the less to the more vivid ones. He also helps deal with the resistances—the tendencies to talk about and interpret instead of entering the experience of the image—and occasionally suggests when to carrry the dream images and feelings back into the context of the patient's current existence.

Place of the "Therapist-as-a-Person"

A major issue between current theories of therapy is: Is the therapist a technician or a person? Does he greet the patient's gambit with a professional technique, or with his own spontaneous human response? In the ranks of Gestalt therapists, I have encountered both extremes, for Gestalt therapy takes no stand on this. Anything goes, if it contributes to the patient's expansion of awareness. I have found myself moving slowly but steadily in the direction of more open revelation of my own feelings of boredom, pleasure, annoyance, embarrassment, etc. Strictly speaking, this is still technique. If the patient is talking in a monotone, staring at the floor, and I am getting a little bored, I might ask him if he is aware of his voice, or what he is looking at. I might also help him to the same awareness of his withdrawal by commenting that I am finding it hard to listen closely to him. Although this is indeed my human response, it is hardly spontaneous if I pause to decide between these approaches! In any case, I steer clear of the presumptuous interpretation, "You are trying to bore me." This may well be true, but I want him to discover it himself if it is so, and I want to set a model of responsibility by stating only what I know to be true—that I am finding it hard to listen.

Place of the Past in a Here-and-Now Therapy

Any here-and-now system of therapy must have some way of dealing, both in theory and practice, with the past. In theory, after all, the past "caused" the present. In practice, the patient often comes in fully expecting—in fact bound and determined—to deal with the past. This is especially true now that the popularization of psychoanalysis is pretty much complete.

Frequently a preference for talking about the past (either on the part of the patient or therapist) is a maneuver to maintain distance from potentially threatening current concerns. The patient would rather blame her mean daddy for past deprivations than upbraid the therapist here and now for withholding the here-and-now goodies (advice, cure, insight, or whatever). The therapist would far rather talk about the patient's "incestuous fantasies" than about her here-and-now coy flirtatiousness— and perhaps his own growing response to it. So a conspiracy of verbiage about the past is quite often purely defensive and distancing, and should be short-circuited as rapidly as possible.

At times, however, the patient presents some past events in a genuinely involved and concerned manner. At these times I respect his concern and listen. I still view this language of the past as a fable wherein the patient is telling me allegorically about some present concern, but at least the discourse is concernful rather than defensive. I treat the material very much as a dream, listening in it for the parallels to the patient's current existence, and trying to help make the transition when appropriate. Almost never do I find it fruitful to inquire into the details about "what really happened." The fable then turns into a "just-so" story that can be used to prove anything the patient wants to prove.

This tendency to limit the discourse to the present is feasible only because in Gestalt therapy we listen to the *total communication* rather than the strictly verbal. The relevant past *is* present here and now; if not in words, then in some bodily tension and attention that can hopefully be brought into awareness. It is impossible to overstress the importance of this point. For a purely verbal therapy to remain in the here and now would be irresponsible and disastrous. It is only the aggressive, systematic, and constant effort to bring the patient's total communication into his awareness that permits a radical concentration on the here and now.

This is an appropriate place to take up the fundamental psychoanalytic concepts of repetition-compulsion and transference, to articulate these with the concept of unfinished business, and to discuss the Gestalt therapy alternatives to the use of these concepts. This is again a complex and subtle task, and this presentation will only attempt to suggest the nature of the relationships of these concepts. Gestalt therapy does not deny that the hand of the past has, to a large extent, shaped the present, but in addition it points out two facts: one, that the past-shaped present nevertheless does exist in its own right, with all the relevant past actually present in some form; the other, that there is always something a little new in this current instance of the repeated compulsion or in this recurrence of the transference relationship. The organism may be rigid, but the environment at least is always a little different. This particular here-and-now relationship may be 99 percent determined by transference but nevertheless have a 1 percent leeway for creative variability, since the therapist *is not* the father and cannot be "exactly like " him.

Gestalt therapy attempts to expand the 1 percent and draw the patient's awareness to the discrepancy between his transference expectations and the reality sitting in front of him. This can be implemented sometimes very directly by asking the patient to describe physically the therapist or the group member involved in the transference, and by helping him see and experience in vivid concrete detail the discrepancies between transference fantasies and reality. In doing this, we are asking him simply *to come to his senses*; to cut for a moment through the filtering fog of fantasy which he maintains around himself and experience the reality of the person who sits across from him. Simple as it sounds, when this is done at the actual moment of distorted perception, it can be effective in jarring the patient into closer touch with the real world of his own senses.

REFERENCES

Berne, E. *Transactional analysis in psychotherapy.* New York: Grove, 1961.

Kempler, W. Experiential family therapy. *International Journal of Group Psychotherapy,* 1965, *15,* 57-71.

Perls, F. S. *Ego, hunger and aggression.* London: Unwin, 1947.

Perls, F. S., Hefferline, R. F., & Goodman, P. *Gestalt therapy: Excitement and growth in the human personality.* New York: Julian Press, 1951. (Republished: Dell, 1965.)

Tomkins, S. *Affect, imagery, consciousness.* Vol. 2. New York: Springer, 1963.

CHAPTER 9

ONE GESTALT THERAPIST'S APPROACH*

Laura Perls

(At the Fourth Annual Conference of the American Academy of Psychotherapists in New York in 1959, leading therapists of five different orientations were asked a series of questions about their theoretical views and therapeutic approaches. Representing Gestalt therapy, Dr. Laura Perls gave the following answers.)

What do you do with the reluctant patient—either poorly referred or poorly motivated?

All patients are reluctant about something or other, sometime or other. Almost all patients are poorly motivated in the sense that they come, or are made to come, for the wrong reasons. I am suspicious of the patient who shows a great deal of insight and wears his suffering on the tip of his tongue. And I am wary of the overeager, enthusiastically cooperative patient who agrees and confirms, picks up the jargon in a jiffy, and dreams to order. He is reluctant to experience and express his differences of opinion, his doubts and objections.

But altogether, I am not particularly interested in the questions of motivation and referral. I take the patient as he presents himself at the time of his session with me. He was motivated enough to come for that appointment, and we take it from there, making contact with one another strictly on the basis of our mutual awareness at the time. Focusing on *what is* rather than on *what is not* or *what should be* usually gives the patient sufficient support to come for the next session—not necessarily better motivation for "having therapy" but at least a willingness to continue contact with the therapist.

Have you ever made a home call, and why?

I have made home calls only in cases of immobilizing accidents and in two cases of agoraphobia. After a few weeks both of the latter patients were able to come to my office.

---

*Adapted by permission of the author and publisher from *Annals of Psychotherapy*, Special Combined Issue edited by J. Barron & R. A. Harper, Vols. 1 and 2, 1961.

How do you deal with a patient's reluctance to pay for therapy?

The patient who forgets or refuses to pay the therapist's fees will give indications of his reluctance right from the beginning in respect not only to money but to anything else you may ask of him: punctuality for appointments, information, expression of opinions and feelings, attempting an experiment, evaluation of his own or other peoples' attitudes and actions. He may be reluctant for many reasons: fear or spite, a confused sense of values, an infantile need to be cared for without having to do anything in return.

These are the problems that ultimately must be tackled.

In the meantime, of course, he can be coaxed and prodded into paying reluctantly, one way or another. You must make it clear that whatever you do for or with him cannot be evaluated and compensated for in money. What he pays for is your time and your attention. Everything that takes place during the session is in the service of his needs, even those demands we make of him that at the time make him anxious or uncomfortable. For his own needs the therapist asks only the regular payment. This explanation is usually intellectually accepted as fair, but you will find that the patient's reluctance changes into genuine willingness to pay only when he has developed an awareness of his own value. Only he who *has* and *is* can *give*.

On the other hand, the regularly paying patient is not necessarily the most genuinely promising one. He may get some secret satisfaction from his family's sacrifices for him or he may be buying you off.

There is also the window-shopping patient who precisely does *not* "buy," but pays the admission fee for a consultation as for a fashion show, tries out the analyst for size, and repeats the same stunt with another therapist during the next "season" of confusion or depression. I find that my awareness of the patient's "style," and the fact that I show him only what immediately "fits" him, usually makes him "buy." So I get stuck finally with the window-shopper, saddled not only with his "reluctance" but also with the particular problems accruing from his former abortive attempts at therapy. But this is another story!

Do you assume that you unconsciously want every one of your patients to get better?

This is a question that I cannot answer—I don't know what I unconsciously want. As far as I am aware, I want my patients to get better. If they don't, then I have to search for what I have failed to become aware of or to make them aware of in the ongoing relationship.

Do you assume that all your awareness and feelings, if shared with the patient, have therapeutic value?

I share *verbally* only as much of my awareness as will enable the patient to take the next step on his own, and lend him support for taking a risk in the context of his actual present malfunction. If I communicate too much, I may provoke a negative therapeutic reaction: intolerable anxiety, flight, resistance, paralysis, desensitization, projection. Of course, the patient learns to become aware of my reactions and expressions even if they are not verbalized.

Do you express your own problems or history at any time?

I will describe some problems and experiences from my own life or from other patients if I expect this to give support to the particular patient for a fuller realization of his own position and potentialities. In other words, only if it may help him to take the next step.

How do you control the acting-out patient?

This question seems to me to *create* a problem rather than to pinpoint one. Every patient, all the time, is acting in some way, and we call it "acting out" mainly when it is obviously undesirable, inadequate, exaggerated, overaggressive, perverted—that is, when it interrupts the patient's ongoing development and relationships. But the patient is or may be "acting out" when he behaves very correctly and even when he verbalizes most rationally and articulately. He will continue to "act out" as long as he has insufficient support for more appropriate behavior. So the task of therapy is not to interfere in or prevent his "acting out," which is at the time the only possible way for him to act, but to help him build up more adequate self-support for more continuously integrating and integrated behavior.

This time-consuming process is usually not aided by the imposition of restrictions, limitations, or threats, at least not as far as the patient's behavior outside the therapy situation is concerned. Within the therapy situation, some restrictions can be part of an experimental exploration of the patient's behavioral patterns and possibilities; but it is the *patient's* reaction that sets the limitations of tolerance of *therapist* behavior.

I am not punitive. I don't think that the attitude: "You better do what I am telling you, or else . . . !" goes with a genuine respect for the patient, whose resistances are his main support. To punish him for what he relies on most always provokes a negative reaction: fear, spite, resentment, vindictiveness, all of which interrupt the ongoing process of communication and understanding. The punitive therapist is himself "acting out" in the worst possible way; and he does so for the same reason as the "acting out" patient: because he does not know what else to do—because he himself has not enough support to give support where it is most needed.

What psychotherapeutic physical contact do you engage in with male or female patients, and is there a difference?

This question of *physical contact with the patient* I shall answer very briefly. I will use any sort of physical contact if I expect it to facilitate the patient's next step in his awareness of the actual situation and what he is doing (or not doing) in and with it. I have no special rules with regard to male or female patients. I will light a cigarette, feed someone with a spoon, fix a girl's hair, hold hands or hold a patient on my lap—if that appears to be the best means of establishing the nonexistent or interrupted communication. I also touch patients or let them touch me in experiments to increase body-awareness: to point out tensions, malcoordination, rhythm of breathing, jerkiness, or fluidity in motion, etc.

There seems to be great divergence of opinion and a lot of anxiety about the admissibility of physical contact in therapy. If we want to help our patients to realize themselves more fully as truly *human* beings, we ourselves must have the courage to risk the dangers of being human.

What does your school say about the basic nature of man, and how does it affect your treatment process?

I am sorry that this has been put as the last question, for I consider it the most important one, in the light of which all the others either make sense or are irrelevant. I believe that not only every therapeutic measure, but every single thought and act is informed by our basic conviction of what makes man "human," even if we never manifestly express this conviction and take it so much for granted that we are hardly aware of it ourselves. Speaking strictly for myself—the only way a Gestalt therapist can say anything at all—I am deeply convinced that the basic problem not only of therapy but of life is *how to make life livable for a being whose dominant characteristic is his awareness of himself as a unique individual on the one hand and of his mortality on the other.* The first gives him a feeling of overwhelming importance and the other a feeling of fear and frustration. Suspended between these poles, he vibrates in a state of inevitable tension and anxiety that, at least to modern Western man, seems unrelievable. This causes various neurotic solutions that are prevalent not only in our patients but to a greater or lesser degree in our total culture.

When awareness and the expression of uniqueness and individuality are repressed, we have uniformity, boredom, and ultimate meaninglessness of mass culture, in which the awareness of one's own dying becomes so intolerable that it has to be alienated at any price, by "having fun" with accumulated inanities or artificial excitements (alcohol, dope, delinquency). When uniqueness and individuality are overemphasized, we have a false "humanism" with man as the measure of all things, resulting in exaggerated expectations, frustration, and disappointment. As a reaction-formation, we find either a false detachment, a hopeless or blasé laissez faire, or a false commitment, a frantic pursuit of a pseudocreative-ness (the obsessional fiddling around with "hobbies" and "cultural activi-ties," from do-it-yourself painting of the kitchen shelves to "seeing my analyst" or going to church).

Real creativeness, in my experience, is inextricably linked with the awareness of mortality. The sharper this awareness, the greater the urge to bring forth something new, to participate in the infinitely continuing creativeness in nature. This is what makes out of sex, love; out of the herd, society; out of wheat and fruit, bread and wine; and out of sound, music. This is what makes life livable and—incidentally—makes therapy possible.

As long as the Judaeo-Christian orientation was the structural mainstay of his society and personality, Western man could accept the identity of living and dying without questioning. In the East, the aim of Zen Buddhism is precisely this realization of identity of living and dying, of commitment and detachment. In our Western world, the neurotic is the man who cannot face his own dying and therefore cannot live fully as a human being. Gestalt therapy, with its emphasis on immediate awareness and involvement, offers a method for developing the necessary support for a self-continuing creative adjustment—which is the only way of coping with the experience of dying and, therefore, of living.

CHAPTER 10

THERAPY IN GROUPS: PSYCHOANALYTIC, EXPERIENTIAL, AND GESTALT

Ruth C. Cohn

Within the past twenty years group therapy has found ever-enlarging circles of application, accelerated by the needs of large groups (military, educational, civic, and business), the desire to reduce the length and cost of treatment for the mentally ill, and the search by many individuals for a less painful and more meaningful existence. During this period psychotherapists have acquired more experience, knowledge, and skill, which has led to modifications of individual psychotherapy and new models of group therapy.

This paper will describe three models of group therapy. It does not claim scholarly precision; rather, it is based on my personal impressions and theoretical reflections about the three models of group therapy I have experienced as a participant and practiced as a coleader with pioneering group therapists in analytic, experiential, and Gestalt methods. Among those practitioners were the group analysts Alexander Wolf, Asya Kadis, the late Sandy Flowermann, and Hyman Spotnitz; the experiential therapists Carl Whitaker, John Warkentin, and many close friends in the American Academy of Psychotherapists; and Frederick Perls as a teacher in Gestalt therapy workshops. *

PSYCHOANALYTIC THERAPY IN GROUPS

The therapist creates a setting in which verbal exploration and interaction are facilitated. The interaction among group members helps the individual explore his behavior patterns, feelings, and thoughts, and helps him understand his historical and present psychodynamics. The group analyst's goal is to stimulate interaction, differentiate content in the group, and communicate interpretation of meanings of personal and interpersonal threads.

---

*James Simkin, from whom I have learned a great deal about Gestalt therapy, was not using group therapy at that time.

Psychoanalytic theory regards a person as sick as long as he is unable to perceive and make choices realistically. His ego—the central function of perceiving, integrating, and executing—is not sufficiently in charge. He is misled by faulty perceptual, emotional, and cognitive fixations stemming from distortions established in early childhood. These distortions have various causes, such as undeveloped abilities (spotty ego-development), infantile misperceptions, or identification with neurotic or psychotic adults. The persistence of such distortions is mainly due to their being rooted in early childhood. Such distortions are often not suspected by the neurotic who believes that his world image is realistic until he fails badly and repeatedly because of his illusion. (A person who has always worn purple glasses could hardly avoid perceiving a purple world; a more accurate perception could occur only if he were to remove the glasses and be confronted with his error.)

Analytic therapy aims at improving perception and reality adjustment. The neurotic may wish for such change, yet resistance to basic changes is as much a biological factor as is the drive for improvement and growth. The patient's resistances to recognizing reality are fortified by the (unconscious) wish to hold onto his early defenses, which have protected him from his archaic fears of isolation, mutilation, and destruction. While children establish pseudosecurity in their illusionary world (by such fantasies as imagining their parents to be omnipotent and to own magic powers), they simultaneously create a future set of transferences into which each newcomer in life can be fitted. The patient either fits people into his transference images or chooses partners (mates, friends, bosses, etc.) who are likely to play the assigned transference roles that, as a child, he attributed to the important figures in his limited universe.

In the therapeutic process the psychoanalyst must take into account the patient's defenses against any change threatening the foundation of his pseudosecurity. He will give up his defenses of helplessness and omnipotence only when he experiences his realistic potency evolving from greater ego-integration of liberated id and superego forces. The recovering patient learns to accept the realistic insecurity inherent in the lot of man.

Group therapy is a new analytic tool with the same aim. Whereas in individual analysis the patient meets with only one other person onto whom he transfers the various relationship patterns of his childhood, in the therapy group he has several people to endow with these qualities. A network of multiple transferences ensues. Also, in individual analysis the therapist uses skilled efforts not to reveal his personality traits and feelings unless they are directly induced by the patient, but in group analysis he has moved his chair from behind the couch into the circle of his patients. With this gesture he has lost his traditional invisibility but not his value as a transference object. Furthermore, the patient meets head-on the open reality of his peers. To the surprise of the analytic profession, the transference buds, which previously had been protected and nurtured (to bring them to full bloom before they would be analyzed), proved to be much hardier than had been suspected: transferences remained all-pervasive even in full view of the peer group's nonneutral, nonmirrorlike behavior.

The group analyst stimulates interaction with questions, silence, comments, and interpretations; he accepts expressions of the here-and-now events in the group as well as communications about the there and then of the patient's life.

He encourages group members to tell their dreams and fantasies and to relate their associations and feelings to each other. He may concentrate on one person at a time and use the group as assistant therapists, or he may address most of his interventions to the group as a whole. For instance, the interaction of one "monopolizing" member in a group could be approached in three analytically correct ways: (1) "Why does X talk so much? What does he want or fear to express?" (2) "Why is the group so silent? What does the group achieve, avoid, or use X for?" (3) X speaks: all others are silent." (Description.)

Psychoanalytic group therapy relies on verbalization as the only acceptable vehicle of communication and integration. All nonverbal expressions are regarded as "acting in" (when it occurs during the session) and "acting out" when the patient symbolizes his conflict in activity outside the group. Both are analyzed as resistance against analytic insight; for example, the patient may resent the analyst or a group member, yet instead of searching for the childhood facsimile of this resentment, he acts out against his boss and thereby keeps his transference world intact. He has shed the resentful emotion without therapeutic gain.

No physical touching is allowed in the session, and personal motor expressions are permitted only as small expressive gesticulations. Kicking or walking around would be interpreted as resistance against insight and integration. Some analysts even forbid smoking or drinking coffee in order to maintain a high level of frustration, which they believe to be the necessary driving force for inducing change. Most analytic group therapists forbid social contact of their group patients, although "alternate sessions" (therapeutic sessions without the analyst) are supported by many. Such alternate sessions provide a specific forum for the special family transference pattern: the feelings of children in the absence of their parents.

Cure in analysis is seen as the process by which disassociated parts of the patient's perceptual, emotional, and cognitive world are integrated. In group analysis this process is supported and furthered by various "corrective emotional experiences" among the patients and between the patients and therapist. Analysis does not promote any specific value in living other than that of free choice versus fixated unconscious bondage. As each patient reveals himself in verbalizing his past and present life story and conflicts, he also reenacts and reexperiences past feelings in the pseudo-family constellation of his therapy group.

The process of sorting out what has irrationally been carried over from the past into the present takes place through emotional and cognitive confrontation, analysis, and interpretation of what *is* rather than what has been fancied. Under the guidance of an unrevealing but accepting therapist, the triad of the curative process takes place: (1) the analysis and lowering of archaic defensiveness, (2) the experience and interpretation of transference illusions, and (3) the corrective emotional experience within a self-revealing group of fellow patients.

EXPERIENTIAL THERAPY IN GROUPS

Like his analytic colleague, the experiential therapist creates an atmosphere in which free communications and interaction are promoted. However, his primary interests are immediate behavior and feelings rather than psychodynamic connections and interpretations. He is connerned with the *how* of the patient's dealings within his family, his job situation, and the present group setting rather than with the *why*. The guiding concepts are not transference and resistance, but authenticity and directness. His main tool is exposing himself as an authentic and direct human being, and he affirms his unique identity in steady confrontation with the group.

The group members are encouraged to state whatever they feel and think. The therapeutic goal is the acceptance of being in the fluidity of life with its pleasures and pains, and in the ambiguity of existence in the face of death. The way is the goal, the "courage to be" and the honesty of communications. While the group analyst stimulates interaction by imposing the frustration of his relative silence and withholding of private communications, the experiential group therapist enters the group process as a partner. For him the group session is not a laboratory in which old family patterns are relived, explored, and replaced with a better set of relationships, but an important part of living that differs from other situations only by its greater authenticity, directness, and concentration on the essence of living. (An experientialist, whose name I don't recall, said that the end of formal therapy can be defined as the point in time when the patient is able to use any life situation as therapeutic.)

The experientialist, of course, does not indiscriminately act upon his feelings or reveal everything and anything to the group. The experientialist is not impulsive but states himself in the interest of the therapeutic process. He chooses from the multitude of his experiences those events, feelings, and thoughts that he judges or intuits to be relevant to the specific situation. I have labeled his choice of self-statements "selective authenticity." Such statements must feel right to him, must be in tune with his patient's needs and his own needs. His personal communications, however, are not limited by their content; they may include embarrassing and painful events as well as happy and proud experiences, or dreams and fantasies.

In experiential group therapy, words, although prevalent, are not the only form of interactional communication. All honest self-statements are permitted and cherished. These may include physical signs of affection and rejection (punching bags or throw pillows may be used). Excluded are sexual intercourse and damage to furnishings and people.

The experientialist, like the psychoanalyst, avoids social mingling with his patients although, generally speaking, he is less likely to request his patients to refrain from meeting socially. (Mingling with patients outside the therapy sessions became an overwhelming burden to most experientialists who tried this "more natural" structure in earlier years; difficulties in maintaining the necessary therapeutic honesty were greater than they could comfortably manage.)

Although there are different modalities of working as an analytic group therapist (determined by the therapist's personality and his various viewpoints of group analysis), the analytic group therapy model is more clearly defined than the experiential one. It is more likely that the student analyst would be told by his "control" analyst that he was right or wrong, correct or incorrect in his therapeutic work than that the student of the experiential school would be so evaluated by his supervisor. In an analytic group there are more factual data to be accounted for (establishing case histories, psychodynamic connections, exploration of transference and countertransference patterns and defense mechanisms) than there are in the experiential setting, where the therapeutic emphasis is placed on the individual's uniqueness and spontaneity in group interaction. The quality of experiential therapy depends on the therapist's mature and broad approach to life. He also needs knowledge of psychodynamics, trained intuition, and many interactional techniques (such as role-playing, encounter games, sensitivity training, etc.), but basically, the more he is in touch with himself and the world, the fuller is the reservoir of offerings with which he can intuitively and creatively react to his patients.

GESTALT THERAPY IN GROUPS

At this point, I feel drawn to a more subjective form of writing. Frederick Perls has in the past few years created a workshop model which represents a new way of using a group in psychotherapy. I will therefore present the Gestalt therapy model by discussing my experience with Perls.* The primary difference in Perls's approach is his making group interaction almost taboo. "Who wants to work with me now? I am available" is the extended invitation. The patient is always a volunteer with whom Perls will work for ten or a hundred minutes, as the situation requires, with the group mainly observing. In my opinion, Perls is a radical experientialist in his request for the *now* of experiencing. I also see him as an "instant detective" skilled in drawing a vertical line through the mud of details and the rocks of defenses straight to the core of the patient's emotional fixations, which he calls "unfinished business." Perls asks the patient for his *now*, which means to stay in the "stream of awareness" and "to lose his mind and find his senses." He stays with the patient in close perceptual contact, usually close enough to touch, often asking the patient what he sees or hears, rather than what he thinks.

Perls's attentiveness is to the obvious and subtle discrepancies in physical and verbal expressions, such as the sound of the voice giving a different message than the spoken words. An inappropriate smile or "canceling" manual gesture may express what the patient does not dare to think or hides behind flat "preachings." Perls also challenges the patient to engage in a role-playing dialogue between discrepant facets of his personality, or he will ask the patient to tell a dream and thereafter to let each part of the dream talk for itself (like objects in a fairy tale). The patient acts out every detail of the dream, be it a person, a chair, a body part, a house, or a country. It (he) talks. This resembles fiction-writing in reverse. The invented fictional parts talk to their author (dreamer), who had not been aware of inventing them. The patient now listens to his self-invented creatures, who rise from the status of rejected or unknown procreations to emotionally exciting and accepted parts of the personal self.

Perls, like Freud, treats the dream as the royal road to recovery and progress. However, his technique for using dreams is experiential rather than analytic. The patient experiences the explicitly verbal and play-acted statements of his dream parts and listens to their messages. Free associations, spiraling around the core of meaning toward the essence of the dream, are replaced by dream voices that form an orchestrated chorus. The music evolves in the process of singing and does not require interpretation. The "medium is the message."

The similarity and contrast of psychoanalysis and Gestalt therapy are most clearly evidenced in their regard for dreams. The analyst invites an abundance of images and thoughts into the dreamer's awareness, helping

---

*Many of his followers are using a combination of interactional techniques with Perls' workshop model. Among those I know are John Brinley, Joen Fagan, Erving Polster, Irma Shepherd, and myself.

him to integrate split-off events and feelings of his past and present life. In group analysis, this endeavor is supported by multiple transference projections onto the group members. Their reactions, associations, and interpretations help the patient (through the similarity of unconscious processes) to widen and deepen his understanding of the dream. (The Jungian concept of the "collective unconscious" helps clarify this process.)

The Gestalt therapist relates to the immediacy of the dreams' statements by moving in and focusing spotlights on each segment. This procedure connects emotional present and past into a telescopic multiexposure and leads towards the relevant "unfinished business."

Avoidance and *unfinished business* are, in my opinion, Perls's core concepts in Gestalt therapy. Unfinished business includes emotions, events, memories, which linger unexpressed in the organismic person; avoidance is the means by which one keeps away from the unfinished business. By avoidance the person tries to escape from feelings that must be felt in order to release him into his own custody.

These concepts and hypotheses certainly sound familiar to the psychoanalyst and appear to be almost identical with the concepts of integrating repressed unconscious material under the supremacy of the ego as guiding power. However, although the concepts of avoidance and unfinished business are closely related to the analytic concepts of resistance and fixation, the differences in wording signal essential differences between the two approaches. "Resistance and fixation express the deterministic philosophy of cause-and-effect-oriented thinking; the analyst "treats" the patient and "controls" the student. He takes responsibility for his interventions as carefully as the contractor plans his work with the demolition crew, the architect, and the builders. Avoidance and unfinished business belong to a philosophy that challenges the patient to take responsibility for whatever he is. The therapist or teacher helps him own up to himself by stimulating responses to areas of his blindness.

Correspondingly, Perls does not appear to be a therapist in the analytic or experiential sense of the word, but rather a Zen master who guides his apprentice on the paradoxic road to self-mastery, discipline, and freedom. He teaches the patient to do what he wants with every moment of his life rather than hiding behind "I can't" (which Perls patiently replaces over and over again with "Say: 'I don't want to' "), or behind "catastrophic expectations"—the fear of what will happen if he accepts whatever he really is and feels.

Unfinished business connotes the steadily nagging underground feelings that are not available to the patient in his daily living as long as he avoids confronting and fully experiencing his pain, anxiety, mourning, rage, etc. While the psychoanalyst times his interventions carefully, in order to reduce anxieties to a bearable level, Perls encourages the experience of the most intense emotions in the now of the therapeutic session. It is the catastrophic expectation of painful emotions and their psychophysical impact that magnifies anxiety, pain, and rage, and lets them linger on with their eroding and destructive power. Complete and unabashed acceptance of, and total abandonment to, feelings lead to "organismic change," which is an experience rather than an insight. *

Perls forbids *ifs*, *buts*, *I can'ts*, and *I feel guiltys* in the therapy session. *If* and *but* are replaced by *and*; *can't* by *I don't want to* ; and *I feel guilty* by *I resent*. "I want to write to my friend but I can't" is translated into "I want to write to my friend and I don't want to write to him." The two confused wants are then un-fused and talk for themselves or to each other, stating the emotional conflict in repeated and increasingly emotional forms, often taking on the pattern of the top-dog talking as the *should* ("You should write this letter") to the under-dog ("I don't want to write this letter"). As long as the pseudo conflict is repetitively reenacted, the under-dog always wins. (He makes sure that the letter is not being written. Guilt is the price the under-dog pays to the top-dog for winning—or the person to the friend for not writing.

The skillful separation of conflicts into their duality and their subsequent reenactment leads, after a series of dialogues, to feelings of blankness, confusion, helplessness, etc. This experience is the *impasse*: the ultimate expression of two strivings pulling in opposite directions. The therapist's guiding words are: "be blank," "be confused," "be empty." When the patient can endure and experience the extent of his feelings of confusion, blankness, impotence, etc., organismic change takes place. It is the theory of this impasse phenomenon which I regard as Perls's unique and most important contribution to psychotherapeutic practice. It has helped to improve the efficacy of psychotherapy, both in depth and in speed, in an exhilarating and fruitful way.

Like most experientialists, Perls keeps the controls of "selective authenticity." However, he rarely communicates feelings that do not seem to be responses to the patient's behavior. This choice of communications resembles the analyst's maxim to express feelings only if and when they seem to be "induced" by the patient's behavior.

While Perls works with a volunteer patient in the group (nobody is ever requested or told to take the "hot seat"), the group must remain silent. However, at some point Perls brings the group into play in a unique way which I call the "Greek chorus method." The "Greek

---

*Insight, however, in my experience, usually follows sometime later, as in any other form of therapy—a fact I call the "cementing" function of interpretation.

chorus" forecasts, underlines, and cements strivings and achievements of the working patient in a way that combines conditioning with a very limited but effective form of group interaction. For example, the patient has come to a therapeutic realization: "I don't have to live up to any-body's expectations." He is now asked to "make the rounds" and say to each participant this sentence, adding individual formulations such as "I am not here to live up to your expectations. I do not have to give you my chair when I don't want to," "I don't have to write a paper with you." The group members reply briefly with whatever their reactions are, such as, "You are right, you don't have to: Neither do I have to live up to yours." etc. Expressions of physical affections or rejection are permitted.

I have taught workshops on "Five Models of Group Interaction," which have included the experiential, analytic, and Gestalt therapy models together with the T-group and my own theme-centered interactional approach. In these workshops the students were led to experience each demonstrated model by participation. Invariably, the groups reacted with the greatest personal involvement in the Gestalt therapy workshop, in spite of the fact that they were spectators rather than interacting participants most of the time. Observing the dramatic therapeutic dialogue was of greater impact than personal interactional exchange. The patient's vertical plunge into previously avoided emotions seemed to touch the group of observers in the truest sense of identification and purification of a Greek drama. The members of the Greek chorus seem indeed to experience the tragic and joyful feelings of the patient's responses within themselves. *

In concluding, I want to describe an episode from one of Perls's workshops. He said, "Can you imagine that I, the Gestalt man, was ever a training analyst at an analytic institute?" And before I caught on to what I was saying, it popped out of my mouth, "That's why you are so good at it, Fritz." Since the phrase "*it* popped out of my mouth" is sacrilege for a Perls's student who is charged with owning her feelings and actions "per *I*" and not "per *it*," I will corroborate this statement with my credo. I am firmly convinced that Perls's skill in guiding patients to their unfinished business in a straight vertical line without overstepping their level of endurance is bound up with his rich background knowledge and experience.

---

*However, in Gestalt therapy groups I have led, I became impressed with the partici-pants' desire to work through the impact of the intense experiences they had had as observers. Therefore I either have combined the Gestalt workshop with post-sessions of interaction, or have used group-integrating techniques within the Gestalt therapy dialogue. The group has also occasionally taken over the role of the therapist.

These include theory and practice of psychoanalytic therapy, the acceptance of the experiential credo of the here-and-now values of authenticity and directness, acquaintance with Moreno's psychodrama and with Zen philosophy, and work with body awareness. In the same historical sequence, the three models of group therapy presented in this paper have developed from earlier procedures and each has, in important aspects, superseded what has gone before.

CHAPTER 11

THE RULES AND GAMES OF GESTALT THERAPY

Abraham Levitsky and Frederick S. Perls

The techniques of Gestalt therapy revolve largely around two sets of guidelines which we will call "rules" and "games." The rules are few in number and are usually introduced and described formally at the outset. The games, on the other hand, are numerous and no definitive list is possible since an ingenious therapist may well devise new ones from time to time.

If we are to do justice at all to the spirit and essence of Gestalt therapy, we must recognize clearly the distinction between rules and commandments. The philosophy of rules is to provide us with effective means of unifying thought with feeling. They are designed to help us dig out resistances, promote heightened awareness—to facilitate the maturation process. They are definitely *not* intended as a dogmatic list of *do*'s and *don't*s; rather, they are offered in the spirit of experiments that the patient may perform. They will often provide considerable shock value and thus demonstrate to the patient the many and subtle ways in which he prevents himself from fully experiencing himself and his environment.

When the intention of the rules is truly appreciated, they will be understood in their inner meaning and not in their literal sense. The "good boy" for instance, totally incapable of understanding the liberating intent of the rules, will frequently follow them exactly but to absurdity, thus endowing them with his own bloodlessness rather than with the vitality they seek to promote.

True to its heritage in Gestalt psychology, the essence of Gestalt therapy is in the perspective with which it views human life processes. Seen in this light, any particular set of techniques such as our presently used rules and games will be regarded merely as convenient means—useful tools for our purposes but without sacrosanct qualities.

THE RULES

The principle of the now. The idea of the now, of the immediate moment, of the content and structure of present experience is one of the most potent, most pregnant, and most elusive principles of Gestalt therapy. Speaking from my own experience [A.L.], I have been at various times intrigued, angered, baffled, and exhilarated by the implications of the seemingly simple idea "being in the now." And what a fascinating experience it is to help others become aware of the manifold ways in which they prevent themselves from having true immediate awareness.

In order to promote *now* awareness, we encourage communications in the present tense. "What is your present awareness?" "What is happening now?" "What do you feel at this moment?" The phrase "What is your *now*?" is an effective one from therapist to patient.

It would not be accurate to say that there is no interest in historical material and in the past. This material is dealt with actively when it is felt to be germane to important themes of the present personality structure. However, the most effective means of integrating past material into the personality is to bring it—as fully as possible—into the present. In this way we avoid the bland, intellectualized "aboutisms" and strive vigorously to give all material the impact of immediacy. When the patient refers to events of yesterday, last week, or last year, we quickly direct him to "be there" in fantasy and to enact the drama in present terms.

We are active in pointing out to the patient how easily he leaves the now. We identify his need to bring into the dialogue absent individuals, the nostalgic urge to reminisce, the tendency to get preoccupied with fears and fantasies of the future. For most of us, the exercise of remaining in present awareness is a taxing discipline that can be maintained only for short periods. It is a discipline to which we are not accustomed and which we are inclined to resist.

I and thou.   With this principle, we strive to drive home as concretely as possible the notion that true communication involves both sender and receiver. The patient often behaves as if his words are aimed at the blank wall or at thin air. When he is asked, "To whom are you saying this?" he is made to face his reluctance to send his message directly and unequivocally to the receiver, to the *other*.

Thus the patient if often directed to invoke the other's name—if necessary, at the beginning of each sentence. He is asked to be aware of the distinction between "talking to" and "talking at" the listener. He is led to discover whether his voice and words are truly reaching the other. Is he really touching the other with his words? How far is he willing to touch the other with his words? Can he begin to see that this phobic avoidance of relating to others, of making genuine contact with others is also manifested in his voice mechanisms and his verbal behavior? If he has slight or insufficient contact, can he begin to realize his serious doubts as to whether others actually exist for him in this world; as to whether he is truly *with* people or feeling alone and abandoned?

"It" language and "I" language. This rule deals with the semantics of responsibility and involvement. It is common for us to refer to our bodies and to our acts and behaviors in distantiated, third person, *it* language:

> What do you feel in your eye?
> *It is blinking.*

> What is your hand doing?
> *It is trembling.*

> What do you experience in your throat?
> *It is choked.*

> What do you hear in your voice?
> *It is sobbing.*

Through the simple—and seemingly mechanical—expedient of changing *it* language into *I* language we learn to identify more closely with the particular behavior in question and to assume responsibility for it.

Instead of "It is trembling," "*I* am trembling." Rather than "It is choked," "*I* am choked." Going one step further, rather than "I am choked," "I am choking myself." Here we can immediately see the different degree of responsibility and involvement that is experienced.

Changing *it* to *I* is an example in microcosm of many of the Gestalt game techniques. As the patient participates, he is far more likely to see himself as an active agent who does things rather than a passive creature to whom things somehow "happen."

A number of other semantic games are available. If the patient says, "I can't do that," the therapist will ask, "Can you say, I *won't* do that?" As the patient accepts and uses this formulation, the therapist will follow with "And what do you experience now?"

> T.: What do you hear in your voice?

> P.: My voice sounds like it is crying.

> T.: Can you take responsibility for that by saying, "I am crying"?

Other gambits in the semantics of responsibility are having the patient substitute verbs for nouns and frequently use the imperative mode of speech as the most direct means of communication.

Use of the awareness continuum. The use of the so-called awareness continuum—the *"how"* of experience—is absolutely basic to Gestalt therapy. With it we often achieve effects both striking and startling. The frequent return to and reliance on the awareness continuum is one of the major innovations in technique contributed by Gestalt therapy. The method is quite simple:

T.: What are you aware of now?

P.: Now I am aware of talking to you. I see the others in the room. I'm aware of John squirming. I can feel the tension in my shoulders. I'm aware that I get anxious as I say this.

T.: How do you experience the anxiety?

P.: I hear my voice quiver. My mouth feels dry. I talk in a very halting way.

T.: Are you aware of what your eyes are doing?

P.: Well, now I realize that my eyes keep looking away—

T.: Can you take responsibility for that?

P.: —that I keep looking away from you.

T.: Can you be your eyes now? Write the dialogue for them.

P.: I am Mary's eyes. I find it hard to gaze steadily. I keep jumping and darting about. . . .

The awareness continuum has inexhaustible applications. Primarily, however, it is an effective way of guiding the individual to the firm bedrock of his experiences and away from the endless verbalizations, explanations, interpretations. Awareness of body feelings and of sensations and perceptions constitutes our most certain—perhaps our only certain—knowledge. Relying on information provided in awareness is the best method of implementing Perls's dictum to "lose your mind and come to your senses."

The use of the awareness continuum is the Gestalt therapist's best means of leading the patient away from the emphasis on the *why* of behavior (psychoanalytic interpretation) and toward the *what* and the *how* of behavior (experiential psychotherapy):

P.: I feel afraid.

T.: How do you experience the fear?

P.: I can't see you clearly. My hands are perspiring. . . .

As we help the patient rely on his senses ("return to his senses"), we also help him distinguish between the reality *out there* and the frightening goblins he manufactures in his own fantasies:

P.:   I'm sure people will despise me for what I just said.

T.:   Go around the room and look at us carefully. Tell me what
      you *see*, what your eyes—not your imaginings—tell you.

P.:   (*after some moments of exploration and discovery*) Well, ac-
      tually people don't *look* so rejecting! Some of you even look
      warm and friendly!

T.:   What do you experience now?

P.:   I'm more relaxed now.

No gossiping.   As is the case with many Gestalt techniques, the no-
gossiping rule is designed to promote feelings and to prevent avoidance of
feelings. Gossiping is defined as talking about an individual when he is actually present and could just as well be addressed directly. For example,
let us say the therapist is dealing with Bill and Ann:

P.:   (*to therapist*) The trouble with Ann is she's always picking on
      me.

T.:   You're gossiping; say this to Ann.

P.:   (*turning to Ann*) You're always picking on me.

We often gossip about people when we have not been able to handle
directly the feelings they arouse in us. The no-gossiping rule is another
Gestalt technique that facilitates direct confrontation of feelings.

Asking questions.   Gestalt therapy gives a good deal of attention to
the patient's need to ask questions. The questioner is obviously saying,
"Give me, tell me . . ." Careful listening will often reveal that the questioner does not really need information, or that the question is not really
necessary, or that it represents laziness and passivity on the part of the patient. The therapist may then say, "Change that question into a statement." The frequency with which the patient can actually do this validates
the action of the therapist.

Genuine questions are to be distinguished from hypocritical questions. The latter are intended to manipulate or cajole the other into seeing
or doing things a particular way. On the other hand, questions in the form
of "How are you doing?" and "Are you aware that . . ." provide genuine
support.

THE GAMES

Following is a brief description of a number of "games" used in
Gestalt therapy. They are proposed by the therapist when the

moment—in terms of either the individual's or the group's needs—seems appropriate. Some of the games, such as the "I have a secret" game or the "I take responsibility" game are particularly useful as group warm-ups at the beginning of a session.

It is, of course, no accident that some of the major techniques of Gestalt therapy are couched in game form. This is evidently a basic metacommunication on the part of Perls, highlighting one of the many facets of his philosophy of personality functioning. The game language (itself a game) can be seen as a commentary on the nature of all or most of social behavior. The message is *not* to stop playing games, since every form of social organization can be seen as one or another game form. Rather the message is to be aware of the games we play and to be free to substitute satisfying for nonsatisfying games. Applying this view to any two-person relationship (love, marriage, friendship), we would not be inclined to seek out a partner who "does not play games" but rather one whose games fit comfortably with our own.

Games of dialogue.   In trying to effect integrated functioning, the Gestalt therapist seeks out whatever divisions or splits are manifested in the personality. Naturally, whatever "split" is found is a function of the therapist's frame of reference and his observational powers. One of the main divisions postulated is that between the so-called top-dog and under-dog. Top-dog is roughly the equivalent of the psychoanalytic superego. Top-dog moralizes, specializes in *shoulds*, and is generally bossy and condemning. Under-dog tends to be passively resistant, makes excuses, and finds reasons to delay.

When this division is encountered, the patient is asked to have an actual dialogue between these two components of himself. The same game of dialogue can, of course, be pursued for any significant split within the personality (aggressive versus passive, "nice guy" versus scoundrel, masculine versus feminine, etc.). At times the dialogue game can even be applied with various body parts such as right hand versus left, or upper body versus lower. The dialogue can also be developed between the patient and some significant person. The patient simply addresses the person as if he were there, imagines the response, replies to the response, etc.

Making the rounds.   The therapist may feel that a particular theme or feeling expressed by the patient should be faced vis-à-vis every other person in the group. The patient may have said, "I can't stand anyone in this room." The therapist will then say, "OK, make the rounds. Say that to each one of us, and add some other remark pertaining to your feelings about each person."

The "rounds" game is of course infinitely flexible and need not be confined to verbal interaction. It may involve touching, caressing, observing, frightening, etc.

Unfinished business.   Unfinished business is the Gestalt therapy analogue of the perceptual or cognitive incomplete task of Gestalt psychology. Whenever unfinished business (unresolved feelings) is identified, the patient is asked to complete it. Obviously all of us have endless lists of unfinished business in the realm of interpersonal relations, with, for instance, parents, siblings, friends. Perls contends that resentments are the most common and important kinds of unfinished business.

"I take responsibility."   In this game we build on some of the elements of the awareness continuum but we consider all perceptions to be acts. With each statement, we ask patients to use the phrase," . . . and I take responsibility for it." For example, "I am aware that I move my leg . . . and I take responsibility for it." "My voice is very quiet . . . and I take responsibility for it." "Now I don't know what to say . . . and I take responsibility for not knowing."

What seems at first blush a mechanical, even foolish procedure is soon seen as one heavily laden with meaning.

"I have a secret."   This game permits exploration of feelings of guilt and shame. Each person thinks of a well-guarded personal secret. He is instructed *not* to share the secret itself but to imagine (project) how he feels others would react to it. A further step can then be for each person to boast about what a terrible secret he nurses. The unconscious attachment to the secret as a precious achievement now begins to come to light.

Playing the projection.   Many seeming perceptions are projections. For instance, the patient who says, "I can't trust you," may be asked to play the role of an untrustworthy person in order to discover his own inner conflict in this area. Another patient may complain to therapist, "You're not really interested in me. You just do this for a living." He will be told to enact this attitude, after which he might be asked whether this is possibly a trait he himself possesses.

Reversals.   One way in which the Gestalt therapist approaches certain symptoms or difficulties is to help the patient realize that overt behavior commonly represents the reversal of underlying or latent impulses. We therefore use the reversal technique. For example, the patient claims to suffer from inhibition or excessive timidity. He will be asked to play an exhibitionist. In taking this plunge into an area fraught with anxiety, he makes contact with a part of himself that has long been submerged. Or, the patient may wish to work on his problem of extreme touchiness to criticism. He will be asked to play the role of listening very carefully to everything that is said to him—especially criticism—without the need to defend or counterattack. Or, the patient may be unassertive and overly sweet; he will be asked to play the part of an uncooperative and spiteful person.

The rhythm of contact and withdrawal. Following its interest in the totality of life processes, in the phenomena of figure and ground, Gestalt therapy emphasizes the polar nature of vital functioning. The capacity for love is impaired by the inability to sustain anger. Rest is needed to restore energy. A hand is neither open nor closed but capable of both functions.

The natural inclination toward withdrawal from contact, which the patient will experience from time to time, is not dealt with as a resistance to be overcome but as a rhythmic response to be respected. Consequently when the patient wishes to withdraw, he is asked to close his eyes and withdraw in fantasy to any place or situation in which he feels secure. He describes the scene and his feelings there. Soon he is asked to open his eyes and "come back to the group." The on-going work is then resumed, usually with new material provided by the patient who has now had some of his energies restored by his withdrawal.

The Gestalt approach suggests that we accept withdrawal needs in any situation where attention or interest has lagged but that we remain aware of where our attention goes.

"Rehearsal." According to Perls, a great deal of our thinking consists of internal rehearsal and preparation for playing our accustomed social roles. The experience of stage fright simply represents our fear that we will not conduct our roles well. The group therefore plays the game of sharing rehearsals with each other, thus becoming more aware of the preparatory means employed in bolstering our social roles.

"Exaggeration." This game is closely allied to the principle of the awareness continuum and provides us with another means of understanding body language. There are many times when the patient's unwitting movement or gesture appears to be a significant communication. However, the gestures may be abortive, undeveloped or incomplete—perhaps a wave of the arm or a tap of the leg. The patient will be asked to exaggerate the movement repeatedly, usually making the inner meaning more apparent. Sometimes the patient will be asked to develop the movement into a dance to get more of his self into integrative expression.

A similar technique is used for purely verbal behavior and can well be called the "repetition" game. A patient may make a statement of importance but has perhaps glossed over it or in some way indicated that he has not fully absorbed its impact. He will be asked to say it again—if necessary a great number of times—and, where necessary, louder and louder. Soon he is really hearing himself and not just forming words.

"May I feed you a sentence?" In listening to or observing the patient, the therapist may conclude that a particular attitude or message is implied. He will then say, "May I feed you a sentence? Say it and try it on for size. Say it to several people here." He then proposes his sentence, and the patient tests out his reaction to the sentence. Typically, the therapist does not simply interpret for or to the patient. Although there is obviously a strong interpretative element here, the patient must make the experience his own through active participation. If the proposed sentence is truly a key sentence, spontaneous development of the idea will be supplied by the patient.

Marriage counseling games. We will mention only a few of the great number of possible variations on these games.

The partners face each other and take turns saying sentences beginning with, "I resent you for . . . " The resentment theme can then be followed by the appreciation theme, "What I appreciate in you is . . ." Then the spite theme, "I spite you by . . ." Or, the compliance theme, "I am compliant by . . ."

Lastly, there is the discovery theme. The partners alternate describing each other in sentences beginning with "I see . . ." Many times this process of discovery involves actually seeing each other for the first time. Since, as Perls points out, the most difficult problem in marriage is that of being in love with a concept rather than an individual, we must learn to distinguish between our fantasied image and the flesh-and-blood person.

Finally, we should mention a particular approach that does not fall under the heading of either rules or games but which can well be included at this point. It is an important gambit in Gestalt therapy and symbolizes much of Perls's underlying philosophy. We might call it the principle of "Can you stay with this feeling?" This technique is invoked at key moments when the patient refers to a feeling or mood or state of mind that is unpleasant and that he has a great urge to dispel. Let us say he has arrived at a point where he feels empty or confused or frustrated or discouraged. The therapist says, "Can you stay with this feeling?"

This is almost always a dramatic moment and a frustrating one for the patient. He has referred to his experience with some sourness and an obviously impatient desire to get on with it, to leave this feeling well behind him. The therapist however asks him deliberately to remain with whatever psychic pain he has at the moment. The patient will be asked to elaborate the *what* and *how* of his feelings. "What are your sensations?" "What are your perceptions, fantasies, expectancies?" At these moments, it is frequently most appropriate and necessary to help the patient distinguish between what he imagines and what he perceives.

The stay-with-it technique illustrates par excellence Perls's emphasis on the role of phobic avoidance in all of neurotic behavor. In his view, the neurotic has habitually avoided vigorous contact with a variety of unpleasant and dysphoric experiences. As a result avoidance has become ingrained, a phobic anxiety has been routinized, and major dimensions of experience have never been adequately mastered.

It is interesting, in this connection, to be reminded of the title of Perls's first book, *Ego, Hunger and Aggression.* The title was chosen carefully to carry the message that we must adopt toward psychological and emotional experiences the same active, coping attitudes that we employ in healthy eating. In healthy eating we bite the food; then we effectively chew, grind, and liquefy it. It is then swallowed, digested, metabolized, and assimilated. In this way we have truly made the food a part of ourselves.

The Gestalt therapist—most especially with the stay-with-it technique—encourages the patient to undertake a similar "chewing up" and painstaking assimilation of emotional dimensions of life that have hitherto been unpleasant to the taste, difficult to swallow, and impossible to digest. In this way the patient gains improved self-confidence and a far greater capacity for autonomy and for dealing energetically with the inevitable frustrations of living.

CHAPTER 12

EXPERIENTIAL PSYCHOTHERAPY WITH FAMILIES*

Walter Kempler

Upon two commandments hangs all the law on which experiential psychotherapy with families stands: (1) attention to the current interaction as the pivotal point for all awareness and interventions, and (2) involvement of the total therapist-person, who brings overtly and richly his full personal impact on the families with whom he works—not merely a bag of tricks called therapeutic skills. While many therapists espouse such fundamentals, in actual practice there is a tendency to hedge on this biprincipled commitment. This paper is offered as a hedge-clipper.

The extant interaction—the current encounter—demands constant vigil. It means attention to the here and now, not to the exclusion of past and future but to the extent that any pertinent deviation from the here and now be considered a transient, although necessary, diversion, and that each detour be succinct and promptly integrated into the current interaction.

For example, a mother, father, and their eight-year-old daughter are embroiled in a discussion about the daughter's behavior. The father, clearly and firmly, contends that the daughter is quite able to express herself, while the mother contends that she never speaks up in her own behalf and needs help on this matter. The therapist, believing direct confrontation is preferable whenever possible, urges the mother to explore her concern with her daughter rather than gossip with the father about her.

M.: [*to daughter*] I wish you could speak freely with us about anything you want [*with obvious condescension*]. It's so important for you to be able to do that.

D.: [*readily*] I say what I want.

---

*Originally published in *Family Process*, 1968, 7, 88-99. Reprinted with the permission of the author, The Mental Research Institute, and The Family Institute.

M.: Oh no, you don't. You should be able to say anything you wish.

D.: [*again easily*] I do.

M.: [*ignoring her comment*] I wish you did.

T.: [*to mother*] You ignore her remarks.

M.: [*to therapist*] I do because I know I'm right.

T.: [*attempting to assist them to bridge their distance and negotiate anew*] Can you give her an example?

M.: I don't think she's saying here what she wants to.

T.: For instance? [*The therapist does not perceive or share the mother's concern but wishes to give her the opportunity to explore further.*]

M.: That she thinks we are bad parents. For instance, we don't let her speak about what she doesn't like about us . . . like my husband's yelling and maybe my crying bothers her.

T.: [*now that mother is more specific*] Check those out with her.

[*Mother inquires.*]

D.: I don't like Daddy's yelling, but it doesn't bother me too much except when it's to me. I've told him. And it doesn't bother me to see you cry. It used to, but you do so much of it I don't pay attention to it any more.

To this mother shakes her head sadly as if to say, "I know you're suffering, poor child—if I could only help you know how you are suffering."

The therapist, the father, and the daughter are now all convinced that the daughter isn't suffering—at least not in this area. The therapist offers this to the mother and urges her to consider this information. She ponders awhile and finally says, "I know what it's like to be constantly shut up. It's terrible."

She has left the here and now and returned to her own childhood. She is in the "there and then" so to speak; her current awareness has gone to another time. The therapist encourages her to stay there by saying, "Could you be the little girl now?" She already is. The therapist is merely permitting her to openly acknowledge it. "Close your eyes and speak to your parents about what it's like to be constantly shut up."

The mother closes her eyes and begins crying. The therapists says, "Talk to them."

After sobbing a while, the mother speaks with her eyes closed: "Oh Mother, if only you knew. I don't think you ever knew. [*Cries more heavily*] I could never tell you anything. And it wasn't even all bad. I just wanted you to listen to me—just once—just let me say what's on my mind." She continues speaking to her mother in fantasy (her reality of the moment), citing an instance that was particularly painful to her.

When she seemed finished, the therapist suggested she respond as though she were now her mother. This was a novel idea to her. As she began to explore, she found herself at first apologizing by pleading ignorance, and as she continued, now as her own mother, she began defending her right not to listen; then, in tears, explained how inadequate she felt as a mother so she dared not listen.

With this awareness, she at once became the child again, sobbing heavily, exclaiming, "I never knew. That never occurred to me. I never knew. I thought you didn't like me. That's what was so terrible. I never thought it was you—that you *couldn't* listen. I just thought you weren't interested. Oh, how horrible it must have been for you. I feel that way too so much of the time (*now she is becoming the parent-mother of today and the crying stops*). That's why I keep telling Cathy [*her daughter*] to speak up. She does, you know, better than I could."

During this work, the mother reunited parts of her own psyche that had become estranged during her own growing up. When she finished, she looked pensive and fell silent, staring at an empty chair. A meditative silence often follows important cognitions, as though the psychic apparatus needs to be allowed time for reorganization.

After several minutes of comfortable silence had passed, the mother began to move and look about. The therapist, wanting the experience integrated into her current world, urged her to speak to her daughter.

The mother, smiling now, says, "I'm not as bad a mother as you may think—I guess it's more accurate to say 'as I thought I was.' You know, you do speak up much better than I ever did."

The daughter smiles. Their encounter seems completed. The father is then invited to respond. To the therapist, he begins, "I knew I was right but I never thought . . . "

The therapist, interrupting, suggests that he speak to his wife. The father turns to her and continues, "I never thought about what was going on. It just made me angry to see the way you nagged at her. That feeling is all gone now. If you start nagging again, it will probably come back, but I sure feel different about you right now."

The mother replies, "I feel so relieved about all this. I'm sorry I've been such a pill."

The father, doing some work for himself, ignores her apology and says, "Well, maybe I can be more helpful to you in the future if you should get upset again about Cathy."

They fall silent. The therapist feels he has finished with father and daughter; to complete his business of the moment with the mother, he adds, "I didn't like your apology. You needn't be the perfect wife, either."

History-taking, ruminating about genetic derivatives to current behavior, discussion about the *why* of behavior are all antithetical to this approach. Attention to the subject matter of any encounter is considered necessary for launching an encounter. It is best jettisoned, however, as quickly as possible to make way for an experience that exposes to awareness what we do to each other and how we do it. Briefly, the *what* and *how* of behavior displaces the *why;* experiences displace discussion.

When a family arrives, the therapist observes how this family appears, how they impinge on him. Does anxiety prevail in one or more of them? What are they doing? How do they come in? Does the father usher his family in or is he one of the ducklings? What is their mood? Does the therapist like the looks of them? Are they friendly with each other?

The therapist's potential awareness about what he sees is infinite and, of course, colored by his own needs of the moment. He may greet the family much as a good host, smiling and offering his hand, and may begin by introducing himself if a family member has not already done so. Whatever his awareness, hopefully, the therapist approaches the family, curious about what they want from him, interested in how they go about seeking what they need, and ready to engage them with his feelings of the moment.

One family member may begin the verbal exchange. If not, the therapist is obliged to initiate it. Opening statements (like interventions in general) are considered best when they are an "I" statement that identifies the therapist in the here and now, such as an observation about himself: "I'm almost ready for you people. I'm still thinking about the previous session which was quite moving." And if that is not sufficient to complete his departure from the prior hour, a further comment of his current residual would be considered appropriate. The therapist is obliged, not merely urged, to clear himself so that he may be in the present more completely.

His awareness may now go to someone's restlessness, an unusual hair style, or an attractive article of clothing. An opening comment acknowledging such awareness is preferred to a studied silence or a trite question that is not self-disclosing such as "And how are you today?" or "What can I do to help you?" Trivial as this may seem, a self-disclosing atmosphere is best created by example, and the opening statement is an excellent place to begin. In these initial moments of therapy, the therapist serves primarily as a catalyst striving to encourage negotiations among family members. Later, the therapist becomes, at times, a principal in the fray.

"I'd like you to meet my family," a mother may begin, introducing her two sons, Daryl, 15, and Steve, 12, and then her husband, who trails in, unsmilingly offers his hand, grunts courteously, and heads for a chair, obviously a reluctant, dragged-in dragon.

Everyone sits, and during the initial moments of silent settling, the mother, smiling, visually checks out each member of her family and then looks at the therapist as if to say "I'm ready." The children watch the therapist or look about the office. The father visually alternates between therapist and wife, finally settling on his wife. In the brief silence, the mother speaks to the therapist, "Where would you like us to begin?"

Avoiding a question such as "Where would *you* like to begin?" he sets a good example: he says what he wants. "Since you seem most ready to engage, I would suggest you begin by telling each member of your family what you do not like about living with him." He could have intensified the encounter at the outset by directing attention to the dissimilarity of the mother and father in their readiness to lead and engage. Preferring a softer opening, the therapist accepts the mother's readiness to begin and moves to create an engagement within the family.

But the mother responds by turning to the father, asking him, "Do you want to start?" Ignoring the therapist's suggestion, she invites the father's leadership. Leading with a question is generally not engagement but rather an attempt to remain obscure, hoping someone else will initiate the interaction. By turning to her husband after the therapist's instruction, she confirms that, at least in part, this is her intention. The therapist now suspects she knows very well where she would like to begin.

The father replies, "You've started. Go ahead."

The therapist notes that an excuse has been given ("you've started") and a rather feeble one at that—a fact which both ignore—as the mother, now with the father's assertion and the therapist's direction, readily begins.

M.:   Our trouble has been mostly with Steve . . .

T.:   [*interrupting*] Tell him what you don't like about his behavior.

M.:   He knows very well what I don't like. It doesn't help to tell him.

T.:   Then I suggest you consult your husband. That's what husbands and wives are for.

M.:   I know. I've talked to him but he's not interested.

T.: Then I suggest you discuss *that* with your husband.

M.: I have but when I do he either ignores me or just gets mad at the kids and spanks them. And I don't think that's the way to handle it.

T.: Tell him.

M.: I do. He won't listen to me.

T.: Then discuss that with him.

Her mood suddenly changes from casual and conversational to sadness. She stares at the floor saying "It's no use," and falls silent, withdrawing from the encounter. Her casual conversational posture was acceptable to share with us but to her, obviously, her sadness was not. Since feelings are the cushions of encountering that keep us from crashing into others and breaking, by curbing her feelings of the moment, she has converted this most valuable coping equipment into a wall that inhibits rather than enhances further negotiation. Bringing her nonverbal behavior into the verbal arena can restore the encounter.

T.: I would like to know how you feel right now.

M.: [*without looking up*] Sad and hopeless.

T.: [*attending the obstacle rather than the sadness, since this is her observable behavior*] Sharing your sadness and hopelessness with us seems difficult for you. [*The invitation is accepted and she begins crying softly.*] Now let's hear the words that go with the tears.

The mother shakes her head evidencing a clear "No." The therapist decides not to push further at this time. Even though reluctant to continue, she is, in this moment, more negotiable than father. The therapist's attention turns to him.

T.: You sit silently. I'd like to know where you are now.

F.: [*ignoring mother's sadness and criticism of him, he responds on his safest ground*] I tell the kids to listen to her.

M.: [*angrily to father through her tearfulness*] But you're not effective. They don't listen to you either and then you blow up at them. That's not the way to treat kids. You can't be hitting them all the time.

F.: [*whining*] You always stop me. They'd listen to me, but they know you'll come in and stop me.

T.:   You're whining at your wife.

F.:   What else can I do? She stops me at every turn.

Until now the therapist has been a catalyst. However, he may be getting annoyed with the husband who transiently engages with his wife and then retreats to the posture of a whimpering child. He may also be annoyed with the wife who double-binds her husband by asking him to be the father, while treating him as a child. The therapist's attention, however, goes to the encounter. The wife is ready to engage but her husband is not. The therapist's attention then must go to him in order to bring him to a negotiating posture. To do this, he now must engage more vigorously and become a principal. There are several ways he can do this.

Should he sense that the father is fragile and truly needs a good mother, the therapist is likely to become one by remaining at a content level and suggesting, for instance, that the father stop whimpering, take his rightful place as leader in his family, and demand from his wife the behavior he requires to enjoy his home. This backing may be given by specific suggestions, such as advising him to demand from his wife that she settle her problems with the children instead of saving them up for him, or by the therapist's vigorously confronting the wife himself by way of example.

Whenever possible, however, the patient should do his own work. Should the therapist conclude that the person (in this instance, the husband) is capable of an oppositional engagement—as indeed he assumes from the report of this father's angrily spanking his children on occasion—then this opportunity for the father to experience his power with adults should not be denied him. The therapeutic task is to bring this available power into the husband's relationship with his wife. The therapist can best do this by directing his own angry frustration into a vigorous attack on this man's whimpering posture.

Before going further, a word is needed about the transition from catalyst or interloper to a more active participant. This transition is largely related to the therapist's needs—his frustration and how he directs his frustration.

In an existential model, the therapist does not suffer from a need for "objectivity." He knows that this concept of the immaculate perception is a myth and that at every moment he is subjective. He believes that therapeutic interventions are most appropriate when they are the richest possible distillation of the therapist's presence. It is not necessary to justify or explain one's behavior in terms of an existing theory so that it may be labeled scientific. In a therapeutic encounter the existence of the therapist-person is more pertinent than the existence of a supportive theory.

The word *spontaneous* may be applied to such behavior. However, it is incumbent on any therapist, existential or not, to distinguish clearly within himself the difference between spontaneous and impulsive behavior. Impulsive behavior is not a thorough representation of a person but rather a fractional escape of behavior in a constricted individual.

For this therapist, frustration leads to action and to further engagement with people. For each therapist the intensity and direction will vary. Those who become passive in the face of their frustration are not likely to become experiential family psychotherapists. They are not likely to become family therapists at all. *Family therapy requires active participation if the therapist is to survive.*

The husband in the case above has now whimpered at his wife and, when confronted by the therapist, whimpers at him also, helplessly asking, "What can I do? She stops me at every turn."

T.: [*sarcastically, to provoke him*] You poor thing, overpowered by that terrible lady over there.

F.: [*ducking*] She means well.

T.: You're whimpering at me, and I can't stand to see a grown man whimpering.

F.: [*firmer*] I tell you I don't know what to do.

T.: Like hell you don't [*offering and at the same time pushing*]. You know as well as I that if you want her off your back, you just have to tell her to get the hell off your back and mean it. That's one thing you could do instead of that mealy-mouthed apology: "She means well."

F.: [*looks quizzical; obviously he is not sure if he wants to chance it with either wife or therapist, but is reluctant to retreat to the whimpering-child posture again*] I'm not used to talking that way to people.

T.: Then you'd better get used to it. You're going to have to shape up this family into a group that's worth living with, instead of a menagerie where your job is to come in periodically and crack the whip on the little wild animals.

F.: You sure paint a bad picture.

T.: If I'm wrong, be man enough to disagree with me, and don't wait to get outside of here to whimper to your wife about how you didn't know what to say here.

F.: [*visibly bristling and speaking more forcefully*] I don't know that you're wrong about what you're saying.

T.: But now do you like what I'm saying?"

F.: I don't. Nor do I like the way you're going about things either.

T.: I don't like the way you're going about things either.

F.: There must be a more friendly way than this.

T.: Sure, you know, whimper.

F.: [*with deliberate softness*] You're really a pusher, aren't you?

T.: How do you like me?"

F.: I don't.

T.: You keep forgetting to say that part of your message. I can see it all over you, but you never say it.

F.: [*finally in anger*] I'll say what I damn please. You're not going to tell me how to talk . . . and how do you like that? [*He socks his hand.*]

T.: I like it a helluva lot better than your whimpering. What is your hand saying?

F.: I'd like to punch you right in the nose, I suppose.

T.: You suppose?

F.: [*firmly*] Enough. Get off my back and stay off.

T.: [*delighted to see his assertion*] Great. Now, about the rest of them (*waving to his family*). I'd like you to see if there's anything you'd like to say to them.

F.: [*looks at each of them then settles on his wife*] He's right. I take an awful lot of nonsense from you and I hate it [*still socking his hand*]. I don't intend to take any more. I'll settle with the kids my way. If you don't like it, that's too bad.

His wife says nothing. The children look pleased. The therapist wonders if he will be too harsh on the children but thinks that if he has his power with her, less will spill over onto the children. The father is no longer socking his hand. He sits up straight for the first time and sits back in the chair looking over his family.

T.: What do you kids think about all this?

S.: Okay. [*He looks comfortable.*]

T.: Do you want to come back?

S.: It's okay with me.

T.: Daryl?

D.: I think it's helpful. [*He looks proudly at his father without saying anything but is obviously pleased.*]

The therapist, also pleased with what he sees, tells the father, "I like you better when you are being the man I know you are. I had the fleeting thought that maybe you will become a tyrant, but I know you won't. I'm not afraid of your power. I saw you taste it here and use it very justly with us."

The father doesn't answer. When the therapist inquires about further visits, the father answers without consulting his wife. "We'd better have a couple more."

On the few subsequent visits, the father ushered his family in.

In this approach, the therapist becomes a family member during the interviews, participating as fully as he is able, hopefully available for appreciation and criticism as well as dispensing it. He laughs, cries, and rages. He feels and shares his embarrassments, confusions, and helplessness. He shares his fears of revealing himself when these feelings are a part of his current total person. He sometimes cannot share himself, and hopefully he is able to say at least that much.

One practical consequence of such negotiating with families, then, is the therapist's lack of concern with "taking sides." On the contrary, it is more suspicious when he is never on a side. A feeling therapist often has a side and is comfortable with it. Hopefully, he is sensitive to his own needs. If he is, he will find himself changing sides often enough to be inspiring to everyone. If not, the family will let him know, provided he has clearly established an atmosphere conducive to free exchange.

Another family of mother, father, and twenty-one-year-old daughter are seen for the first time. The daughter has just been released from a psychiatric hospital, where she was briefly hospitalized with the label of an acute psychotic reaction. At present she is at home, heavily tranquilized, spending most of her time in bed.

The mother begins (as seems remarkably usual) with the aforementioned story. She not only begins but she never ends. Her excited, charm-laden loquaciousness is occasionally interspersed with remarks to her husband, such as "Isn't that so dear?" or "What do you think?" She never waits for an answer but babbles on. The therapist is the only one apparently annoyed enough to object. "Oh, I do talk a lot I know. Why don't one of you (turning to husband and daughter) say something?" Before they can, she is off and running again.

This time the therapist tells her to be quiet and invites the father to comment on the babbling. "Oh, she's like that all the time. I'm used to it." Then he offers the observation, "All our daughter needs is a good job. I tell her that all the time but she won't listen." The mother picks up on this and verbally runs nowhere with it. The father permits it.

After several more futile attempts to invite each of them, including the daughter (who remains silent), to look at their behavior and consider altering their encounter-diminishing behaviors, the therapist with great exasperation turns on both parents, telling them in no uncertain terms of their destructive behavior: the mother's incessant babbling, the father's absurd tolerance of it, and further, the absence of any constructive working with each other.

At the end of the therapist's harangue, the daughter smilingly speaks for the first time. "We should have had you when I was ten years old." With some residual grouchiness, the therapist retorts, "But you're not ten now, so get started changing things for yourself."

The mother and father both cheered. Therapy had begun with the therapist siding twice in this first encounter. Within two months, the daughter was working. At three months, therapy had terminated by concensus, and a year later, the therapist was invited to attend the daughter's wedding.

There is no obscuring of the therapist behind a title. He brings his personality and life experiences to the family encounter. It is his uniqueness in this family (he is not likely to be caught up in its painful, interlocking behavior patterns—at least not initially) and his willingness to engage fully with others that are his most valuable therapeutic "techniques." In other words, in experiential psychotherapy within families, there are no "techniques," only people. At every turn, the therapist is obliged to struggle for his right to be seen as he perceives himself, and not to permit distortions such as, for instance, an implication that he is all-knowing or all-powerful. By such example, the family members are likewise encouraged to struggle for what they perceive as their identities. It is during the vigorous clarification of who we are to each other that therapy occurs.

The illustrative samples are admittedly one-dimensional. This seems necessary for clarity of exposition. However, this should not prevent translating the basic principles to more complex moments in therapy when many needs seem to arise at once or when chaos seems temporarily to prevail. At such moments, it behooves the experientially oriented family therapist to turn to his own needs first. Perhaps he will demand a moment's moratorium from bedlam in order to see in which direction he arbitrarily wishes to proceed. Possibly he will request some assistance from the working family in this matter. His own transient uncertainty is a welcome expression in a good experientially-oriented family encounter.

During the course of such encounters, personal growth and family integration for each family member becomes excitingly possible. Even therapists grow in such an atmosphere.

The degree to which the therapist is capable of encountering in the here and now is the degree to which experiential family therapy is propelled on its way.

CHAPTER 13

MARY: A Session with a Passive Patient*

James Simkin

M.: I was aware, when I sat down in the chair and put my hands on the arms right here, of the warmth that was still here from Leo and experiencing the warmth in my cold hands. [*Flat voice.*] And . . . I'm perspiring, and . . . my heart's beating fast, and I'm feeling . . . I'm swallowing, I'm holding my breath. [*Pause.*] A feeling, a stiffness in my shoulders and . . .

T.: Sounds like you're doing a lot of squeezing.

M.: Yes, I'm squeezing, squeezing in.

T.: Can you either go with your squeezing in, or the reverse?

M.: Squeezing in and pulling. Being very cl-close, closed . . . just kinda all in a knot. [*Sigh, tremulous voice.*] And when I can open [*arms unfolded, legs uncrossed*], when I'm not like this, I feel like I let people—the room—come in, and can be aware of what is going on in the room or aware of Jim, Leo, Bill, and all the rest, and then when I'm like this [*arms folded, legs crossed*], then the rest of it—you—begin to disappear. I'm aware of only me.

T.: Yeah. What did you just do?

M.: I swallowed. And I experienced a cutting off of my breath, the jerkiness of it in here and here [*points to chest*].

T.: [*talking ostensibly to the group*] I'm always impressed with the phenomenon that I see over and over again—somebody will learn something about himself: if he does this, something nappens; if he does that, something happens—and then he discards what he's learned immediately. I don't understand.

---

*Transcription of a therapy demonstration presented at a professional workshop in Gestalt therapy, Esalen Institute, 1966.

M.: It's a beautiful avoidance.

T.: Yes. "I'll work on this tomorrow." "I'll tuck it into my computer and explore it next week."

M.: Um-hum. [*Pause.*] And it always leaves me with unfinished business.

T.: *It?*

M.: *I* leave myself with unfinished business.

T.: How?

M.: By not staying with my feelings.

T.: I'd like to reinforce your *this* and *this* [*referring to Mary's hand gestures of squeezing in*]. And I object to your avoiding the experiment. [*Pause*] Now I'm stuck. If I don't do anything, Mary will sit there. [*Sighs.*] A perfect trap.

M.: You—you are saying to go ahead with the experiment of the squeezing, with the feeling I get with it, or from it?

T.: I wish I had Fritz's cigarette [*to wait out Mary's helplessness*].

M.: I don't know where to go from here.

T.: [*beginning dialogue with himself*] Jim, shall Mary squeeze herself? Yes, but if you ask Mary to squeeze herself, then *she* isn't doing anything. She's just doing what *you* want. So how can Mary get out of her bind, Jim? The hell with Mary, how can I get out of my bind? [*General gentle laughter.*] You've got *yourself* stuck. [*Long pause.*] What do you experience now?

M.: I experience wanting to . . . giving you the power . . . to get me out of the bind . . . and I'm feeling helpless and . . . "What do *I* do?"

T.: What *are* you doing?

M.: I'm sitting here, in the chair, and my left leg is over my right, and I'm looking at you. [*T.: Um-hum.*] And I swallowed. And my hand is going in and out over the arm of the chair. [*Pause.*] I want to—to push away, to move about. [*Pause.*] I want you to reach out and pull me back in.

T.: I know. This is what I've been experiencing with you from the very beginning. And I think this is the *key* to how I get stuck with you and how you get stuck. What you want from me is for me to pull you. What I want from you is for you to support yourself. So I set up an experiment where you can learn to support yourself and do something for yourself, and I sit back and expect, "Ah! Now Mary's going to work on this." But [*laughing*] Mary wants *Jim* to pull her. [*Pause.*] And so your expectation and my expectation just don't get along.

M.: They can't. [*Laughs.*] At least I'm aware of this, which I haven't been aware of before. [*Voice stronger.*] And this clearly. I would like to try again and see if I can find out if I *can* support myself.

T.: I'm perfectly willing.

M.: [*Pause.*] I'm supporting myself here in the chair. [*T.: Um-hum.*] And I'm breathing for myself, and all the body parts of it I'm doing for myself.

T.: All the body parts of *it* you're doing for yourself?

M.: For me. Breathing, my heart's beating—it's not like what I'm doing now.

T.: What are you doing now?

M.: [*Pause.*] Queer, when I am responding to *please* you—to get recognition in this way [*thoughtful voice*]—

T.: OK, do you want my recognition?

M.: Er . . . yes.

T.: I'm willing to acknowledge you and recognize you when you do the experiment.

M.: OK. [*Pause.*] Would you tell me again what the experiment is that you want me to do?

T.: *Oh, no!* Absolutely not. I've told you once.

M.: [*Long pause, then very fast*] Well, I'm not sure at this point, but I *think* the experiment is to go back and experience what I am feeling when I'm all, well, when I'm tense and all tied up like *this*. [*Wraps arms around her body and pauses.*] And when I'm here pulling in . . . and with my eyes closed . . . it's the feeling that it's dark—

T.: *It's* dark?

M.: I'm dark. I'm alone, [*Pause.*] And I'm frightened.

T.: Right.

M.: [*Pause.*] I want to scream and somehow I can't. [*Voice becomes tight.*]

T.: Do you have any idea what you want to scream?

M.: [*Pause.*] HELP! HELP!!!

T.: Did you see what you did with your feet when you screamed, "Help"?

M.: I brought them up.

T.: Go through the movement again.

M.: [*Brings feet up. Long pause. Very scared voice.*] My hands are tied.

T.: Yes.

M.: [*crying*] I can't get away. Somebody's beating me. I scream [*catches breath*], but even if I scream nobody hears. [*Sob and sharp intake of breath. Cries.*] And I have the feeling—I remember being tied to a post [*sobbing*] . . . when I was a little girl. [*Pause. Continues crying.*] And they're leaving me here. And I can't get loose.

T.: This is when you were a little girl. Yes? [*Voice very gentle.*]

M.: Um-hum.

T.: Are you still a little girl?

M.: [*voice stronger*] No, but—

T.: Can you untie yourself?

M.: [*Blows nose.*] Yes, I can untie myself.

T.: I'd like to see you.

M.: [*Long pause, voice controlled.*] Now, I'm back here in this room, but I'm still a little girl all tied.

T.: Right.

M.: I'm closed in—alone.

T.: [*softly*] Now I want you to talk to your little girl—to tell your little girl that she knows exactly how to untie herself and how to open up, and I care too much for that little girl to do anything that would interfere with her doing it for herself.

M.: Um-hum. [*Long pause.*] "Little girl, you don't . . . you've been . . . you no longer need to stay tied. OK now, open your eyes."

Seeing where I am—here in this room with Sandy, Abe, Bill, Bob, Jim, Leo, Joen, Elizabeth, Art, Miriam, and Cooper. [*Slowly.*] And the ropes are getting looser, and I can take the hands and . . . [*sigh*]. I'm beginning to breathe. [*Voice gets firmer.*] I have some space there to take in. [*Pause.*] My feet are untied. I can move. [*Gets up slowly, stretches.*] Support myself way up to the ceiling and back. I can move around.

T.: Now I recognize you.

M.: I can see! I can feel!

T.: Yeah. I'm very interested in what you do next.

M.: [*Laughs.*] You, son of a bitch! [*General laughter.*] No, I'm not going to do anything.

T.: Yes, you are. [*Mary continues to laugh.*] You're laughing.

M.: I'm enjoying it.

T.: Who's the *it* you're enjoying?

M.: I'm enjoying *me.* I'm enjoying *you.* I feel wonderful. [*More softly.*] I feel almost as if—my head feels lighter.

T.: I'm still interested in what you're going to do next. [*Pause.*] What are you doing?

M.: I'm pushing back. [*Um hum.*] I can get up, and I can sit over here, and say "thank you," and pick up my chair, and move over here, and sit down. [*Picks chair up and moves it back as she is talking.*]

Woman: That's clearly what I was doing all day yesterday with Fritz, just what you were experiencing with Jim just this morning, playing helpless and waiting. It was very painful for me to watch you go through it, because of how much I didn't see in me. And my fantasy is that there is a bit of the bad girl in you, like me, that I'd love to see you play. [*General laughter.*]

M.: We'll do that in real life.

Woman: *We* will?

M.: *I* will. [*Laughs.*]

Man: I have a feeling of a person awakening from a deep long sleep.

T.: I'm very fascinated with your voice now as compared to your first session this week.

M.: There's room to breathe down here now.

T.: Oh, boy! [*Laughter.*]

M.: Such a relief!

Man: [*to Jim*] You took the ropes off of me too a while ago there. [*To Mary*] I remember your voice the first week, too, and how deep and resonant it is now!

T.: Now, as therapists, you see here a beautiful demonstration of a dilemma, a therapeutic dilemma. Somebody plays helpless, and you want to help, and *part* of you is aware that if I were going to help, I would reinforce Mary's helplessness. *But* if I don't help, am I being a therapist?

M.: I'm real good at this game. [*Laughter.*] I've been playing it for a long time, and it's so familiar.

Woman: My identification in this was more with you, Jim, in feeling how often, as I went along with you in this session, I might have been the Jewish mother and run in and sort of tried to help or gotten pushed away and gotten furious. I felt that this was just a *beautiful* thing, watching you help her without overcommitting yourself.

T.: And here's another thought for the rest of you, and for you, Mary: At the moment of the therapeutic impasse, when I said to you that now you know what to do, I was thinking that I've seen this over and over and over again. As soon as a person learns what to do, he promptly forgets it. He does the experiment, and has the "aha" reaction, and then asks, "What shall I do next, Doc?" Even pointing this out has no real effect.

Woman: Somehow Mary has to feel it up and down her backbone and in her gut and blood vessels.

Man: One thing that Mary did with that was to really experience her suffering, but in the fantasy of being tied up, she experienced the discomfort of being the way she usually is, only much more vividly.

M.: This came as, well, as I suddenly found myself there and began to realize . . . I mean, this came as a complete surprise to me, and I think it's silly, I've been . . . there's awareness *way* back there, but I wasn't making the connection. I *felt* it.

T.: What I experienced as the transition point was when Mary was able to differentiate between herself *now*, that she is no longer a child, that she can untie herself, and was willing to do it.

Man.: Mary, I've seen, and I know you've seen too, many people who finally work through an impasse and don't know when to quit. They sit there and get right back into another one. I was delighted to see you quit, stop when you found what you wanted.

M.: Me too!

CHAPTER 14

ANNE: Gestalt Techniques with a Woman with Expressive Difficulties

Joen Fagan

Anne was a twenty-eight-year-old student, married, with two children, who enrolled in my class in Abnormal Psychology. She did nothing that would call attention to her until the first test. She showed a high degree of mastery of material and clear indications of intuitive sensitivity, but expressed her ideas in extremely poor English with many errors in grammar, spelling, and punctuation. Her second test presented even more impressive evidence of her ability—and of her expressive handicap.

Fig. 1.   Examples of Anne's Test Answers

(Marasmus) a reactions of infants who are deprived of maternial
affection, a severe physical conditions resulting in body and mental
deteriation
(Undoing) an ego-defense mechanism characterized by a effort to
atone for undesirable thoughts or impules. Like a child we are taught
to apoligizes type of constance apoligizing to make things right.
(Parkinson's symptoms) A brain disease of unknown orgin, the
patient has rythumic tremurs, difficulties with gait. No loss of mental
ability but lose of ability to make muscles do what the patient desires.
(Korsakoff's syndrome) In chronic acoholics and senile pyschoes, the
patient has poor memory and uses conflagulation.
(Huntington's chorea) A brain disease of unknown order which a pre-
senile deteriotion of the brain. Only brain disease which follows
Mendle's gentics. Patient has jerky involintory tremers. Mental
deteriotation.

After the second test, I suggested a conference. Both pleased and frightened by my interest, Anne wrote me a letter to say that she also had difficulty in talking about her problem. She did come, however, and indicated in a hesitant, apologetic way that her inability to spell and express herself clearly and correctly had existed since the first grade. Neither her own efforts, spurred by her continued embarrassment and considerable tutoring, nor a year of psychotherapy had resulted in any noticeable improvements.

Since I perceived that her high potential in many areas was clearly handicapped by her problems in expressing her abilities, I asked if she wished to participate in an experiment that would consist of a series of tasks that she would perform by herself with minimal direction from me. While I could not guarantee that this would help her, her past lack of success at getting help through the usual channels suggested that there was little to lose. Anne agreed eagerly, and arrangements were made to begin the following quarter.

In Anne's diary of her experiences, she describes in detail the instructions and techniques that were used. Briefly, the tasks were:

1. Write in free-association style your thoughts about *play*.

2. Look up in an unabridged dictionary the derivation of the following words: *tantalize*, *prejudice*, *agony*, *gentle*, *responsible*, *devil*, *fool*.

3. Write your associations to *anxiety*.

4. Draw or copy a picture, first with your right, then with your left hand.

5. Write ten reasons why people should not obey rules, misspelling every word.

6. Write your associations to *anger*.

7. Read poetry selections aloud.

8. Finger-paint left-handed.

9. Listen to a tape (selections sung by Leontyne Price) and write what you hear.

10. Listen to a tape (orchestral selections) and finger-paint with your left hand.

11. Listen to a tape (orchestral) and write your emotional responses in adjectives.

12. Study a flower intensely and then finger-paint it.

13. Write three criticisms of other people and five of yourself.

Each task was designed to be completed in a thirty-minute session; sessions were twice a week. While several other tasks had been intended, Anne had to stop the experiment prematurely so they could not be included. (It is also clear from the diary that the tasks had fulfilled much of their purpose and might have been discontinued, even had the interruption not occurred.)

The general procedure of self-experimentation was based on Perls's *Gestalt Therapy*, which describes a series of instructions the student reads and follows, the purpose being to increase his awareness of his sensory, visceral, perceptual, emotional, and motoric functioning. The specific tasks I chose came from several sources. Those involving drawing, painting, and emphasis on the right-left dichotomy were based on techniques and procedures used by Perls in his workshops at Esalen Institute. The use of free-association writing was modified from Hayakawa[1] to assist in freeing written expression.

The use of the self-experiment procedure was chosen for a number of reasons: (1) my knowledge of the power of such methods; (2) evidence of the failure of more direct or specific approaches with Anne; (3) my perception of Anne as being so blocked by other people's actual or potential evaluations that she could get most from a situation where she was in charge with no external evaluations, only clearly implied support and interest; (4) limitations on my time; (5) the opportunity to test the power of Gestalt techniques in a challenging situation; and (6) my wish to assist this potentially able person. While I was aware of the possibility that some organic damage might have been partially responsible for Anne's expressive problem, there seemed more to be gained by viewing her problem as modifiable.

The specific tasks were chosen partly for theoretical or dynamic reasons, partly from hunch. It seemed that Anne's failure to "follow the rules" was related to an inability to rebel more openly, to express anger or say "no" more directly. It was apparent that she perceived and projected much criticism from others and criticized herself severely. Almost any form of expression was a painful and anxiety-producing event for her, with words being perceived as difficult, demanding, immovable objects rather than actual or potential objects of play or beauty. These thoughts helped determine the selection of the tasks involving writing. I also wanted the first few tasks to have "face validity" for her and to be neutral emotionally. The tasks involving noncognitive expressiveness were chosen because of my perception of Anne as a blocked and tightly bound woman whose prime difficulty was in expression in a global sense. Listening, looking, touching, moving, and the combination of these were utilized in a number of tasks with the hope that some sense modality would be relatively more open and could be used to tap into the area where her feelings and responsiveness were buried. The use of the left hand in a number of tasks was based on Perls's ideas about the right-left split. I hoped also to encourage her to stop thinking of her responses as having to be "right." The goal of all the techniques was to increase Anne's sensory awareness, emotional responsiveness, motoric expressiveness, and personal integration. If this could be accomplished, then it was hypothesized that the more specific spelling and grammatical problems would tend to solve themselves.

The diary that follows was begun spontaneously by Anne at the start of the experiment. She did not tell me she was keeping it until a number of

---

[1] Hayakawa, S. I. Learning to think and to write: Semantics in freshman English. *ETC.*, 1962, 18, 419-426.

weeks later, and showed me the first part only toward the end of the experiment. The diary has received minimal editing, with spelling corrections made for ease of reading; some sections were deleted because of being unrelated to the experiment, embarrassing to Anne, or identifying of her or others.

As Anne's account of her experiences begins, it is obvious how hard she tried to get the instructions right, to follow them exactly, and to do what was expected of her. Another major theme is her frequent effort to to find reasons and explanations for the tasks—usually totally incorrect. Only as more sensory involvement and "body" entered did she become aware of her own responses and find meaning "inside." It is likely that the first few tasks did build a base of support that facilitated the later release. The unblocking of Anne's sensory and emotional responsiveness was closely followed by her wish for more direct contact with me, and the ability to express herself more directly to me, her husband, and others.

As far as specific accomplishments, there was some improvement in Anne's written expression before the end of the quarter in which the experiment was conducted. Her spelling and ability to express herself in writing have continued to improve and now fall within the normal range for college graduates. Three months after the experiment, Anne went back into therapy and was able to make much fuller use of it. (She had terminated therapy earlier because of her inability to tell her therapist her feelings about him.) She has since graduated from college and has made a much more adequate adjustment in all aspects of her life. She has pursued in a determined way her area of special interest and has made some considerable contributions, her recent work demonstrating ingenuity and clear indications of creativity.

I am more than satisfied with the results of the experiment with Anne. In considering the factors that produced the change, I see several of major importance. It is obvious that Anne had strong motivation to change, but this had existed for many years. It is also obvious that I became a very important person to her, toward whom she had strong positive feelings. However, she had had similar feelings toward her therapist, and her earlier response had been to leave therapy because of her inability to express and explore these. I am certain that my clear interest in her and my appreciation of her potentialities were communicated to her, but the actual amount of time I spent in talking with her during the previous quarter and the first four weeks of the experiment did not exceed a total of thirty minutes. Finally, the techniques used facilitated emotional unblocking and acted as catalysts for change. In the final analysis, all of the above factors probably contributed to the growth that is so apparent in the diary.

As I reread Anne's diary; I find that the experiment itself, Anne's response to specific tasks, and my own role fade into the background. I become most aware of a person, initially frozen into immobility, who slowly, then rapidly, begins to grow with a vividness and excitement that I find breathtaking and awesome—and which leaves me with renewed faith in human courage and human possibilities. Anne's diary, in my final judgment, is less an example of Gestalt techniques than a testimonial to human capacity for growth.

ANNE'S DIARY[2]

This is the story of a girl (she was really a woman, but she didn't know how to behave like one) who had a problem (well, actually she had quite a few problems, but one particular one which was extremely apparent) and what helped this girl become a woman and to overcome some of her problems.

It all began when this girl was in an Abnormal Psychology class. Now the problem that this girl had which was so apparent was a spelling problem. This spelling problem greatly hindered her in her school work. However this particular teacher tried to see what the student was trying to say rather than just how she was able to say (or spell) it. On the second test in this course, this girl made a 98, now that's a pretty high grade for anyone, but for a girl who can't spell it's not only high it's downright remarkable. The teacher had written on this paper. "How about that?" and "Please see me." After class the girl went up to see the teacher.

G.: "You wanted to see me?"

T.: "Yes, what are we going to do about your spelling problem?"

G.: "Well, I guess teachers have been wondering that since I was in the first grade."

The girl thanked the teacher for not counting off for the spelling errors. The teacher said come and talk to me some time. But the teacher didn't know that one of this girl's other problems was that she couldn't talk, particularly about her problems.

The girl decided to write the teacher a letter explaining the problem and why she couldn't talk about it. This is the letter:

Dear Dr. Fagan,

Although my problem to a great extent centers around writing, I find it much easier to write about than to talk about. In fact any close emotional problem is very difficult for me to communicate, written or verbally, my feelings on the subject. I usually become silent. I withdraw because the stress that I experience when placed again in the frustrating position of explaining my problem is too great for me to cope with.

[2]The diary was originally titled, "Diary of a Girl with Blue Paint on Her Nose." The introduction was written at the end of the quarter, after the rest of the diary was finished. Some spelling corrections have been made for easier reading.

The problem when it is in its full glory includes not just spelling, but grammar, coherence of thoughts, reading comprehension, and verbal expression. There have been times when I could not write a coherent sentence. There have been times when speaking was so difficult that I could only mutter a halting, faltering statement. Under stress I use the wrong words, mix words up, or combine them in an unheard of fashion.

I want very much to be able to completely overcome these difficulties, but I do not know what else to do. I have really come a long way. Spelling is the last stronghold which I cannot break through. I have almost decided to let this ride and hope that as each part of me experiences growth, spelling like the caboose on a train will come tagging along, making progress but at a slower pace.

I could give you reasons and explanations about this problem, but they are long and drawn out. After I finished telling them, I would still have my problem. I do not know why I have this problem or why I cannot get rid of it.

I appreciate your interest in me. My first reaction was that you probably do not have time to talk with me. When you can, I would like to talk with you, but you have to realize the extreme fear I have for this subject. I have experienced shame and guilt, I have tried to cover up, hide, change, but it's still there.

You have probably known that there is more involved here than just the overt symptoms. I have only a few suggestions that might over the years help me. If I could feel that people would accept me with my problem (just like one who stutters or who has a tic), if I could feel that I am enough of a person not to be destroyed by criticism or ridicule, if I can become an achiever rather than a nonachiever, if I could feel that I am not going to be discriminated against because of the particular type (academic) of problem that I have, then I feel that maybe I would not manifest my confusion and anxiety by difficulties in written and verbal communication. I sometimes feel that my brain is a switchboard and I just cannot plug in the right switches for communication.

I have only found a handful of people during my life who had the patience, kindness, and understanding to extend a helping hand to me. Thank you for being one of these people. In my classroom work there has usually been a high correlation between the teacher's ability to understand me and my performance in class.

This is a pretty sick sounding letter, but if I wrote it any other way it wouldn't be real.

                                                                    Anne

The girl really did not ever expect to talk with the teacher, but after the exam the teacher offered to help the girl next quarter during the break (a "free" forty-minute period in the morning schedule) with her problem. The girl was delighted because there was someone who thought that something could be done about her problem. All during Christmas holidays the girl thought about what was going to be done about her problem. In 1967 at Georgia State College, in the girl's junior year of college, the adventure began. The cure for the spelling problem was to be two thirty-minute sessions a week. These sessions turned into the most traumatic, exciting, miserable, and marvelous adventure this girl had ever entered into. I know so much about this girl, because I am the girl and this is my story.

January 7

I had my first session with Dr. Fagan. I was surprised when she handed me a stack of paper. I had to borrow a pen. She gave me the instructions to write free-association, no regard to grammar, spelling, punctuation. The topic—play. There is no need to restate what I wrote—she has it in a file, although she told me I was writing for myself, and that she would not read what I wrote unless I wanted her to.

I was concerned about not finishing a thought so the next day requested to finish. She said I could and asked why I had not come that day. I had not understood I was to come—thinking she had said Thursday *or* Friday. She laughed and said I was in for the duration.

January 12

I gave Dr. Fagan the completed thought written on a piece of notebook paper. This feeling of incompletion had disturbed me—like a conversation with rapport established and interrupted before completion of thoughts. Phone calls, children, time are interruptions.

My second assignment was a list of words to look up in the dictionary. I was disappointed for I had wanted to write some more, and wondered what subject I would be told to write about.

While looking up the words, I had a funny feeling that I had misunderstood my instructions. She used a word which I assumed was definition.[2] I need to find out that word.

I looked up the words, reading and writing the meanings. While only on the fourth word, the bell rang. I read the last two and was unable to look up two of them. I will go back later and look them up.

---

[2]What I had told her was *derivation*, choosing words (sincere, tantalize, agony, etc.) whose origins illuminate their meaning. I had hoped that she would be able to get some feeling of play in relation to words, but she instead clearly turned the assignment into work. This paralleled her writing about "play" which ended with a disphoric association to sex play. — J.F.

Fig. 2.   Anne's Associations to "Anxiety"

ani
this thought distressing I can't even spell it ~~ange~~ anger, tention
frustration I can't make people understand me aniety anxity
~~an anxiety~~
I talk with my husband he cannot understand what I am trying to
communicate. I feel tight in side. We have had an arguement every
night this week
I have to deside what I am going to be and be it no one can interfer
with my being
pulled in too many different directions like ropes tied to my hands,
feets being pulled apart
what I have to be and what others need for me to be I know when I hand
someone a paper I have written the errors bother them they laugh at
mistakes or cannot believe I am that incapable of being able to ~~sple~~
spell or write correctly,
I am ashamed about my writing to test a friend I see if they can stand
the extend of my problem by asking or letting them read something I
have written pass test my husband has not passed, every time I ask
for his help I get a lecture on spelling or basic English he gets angry
I become anxious
School not anxious any more except on test being tested or examined
being judged by my writing I can not get my knowledge on paper
last night arguement with my husband has never like how or way we
live He is thinking of buying new dinning room table this makes me
sick all he wants is a neat well furnitured house who is there or what
happened doesn't matter
I am freer from aniexty than used to be When I feel it I try to do
something look at me look at problem - look look look I should not have
left treatment when I did
I feel like I failed Gail I feel never well be a family have unity or
growth or love or freedom or life husband asked if I had been happy
way we life I had to think of happiness as basied on material item
used to need material china, silver, furniture, pianio I was
miserable
Happeness being free from ~~anie anxeit~~ anxiety happeness people growth
maturity productive work husband fussed at Gail about her spelling
fussed at Robbie for not writing neatly on homework this disturbs me
am I too permissive does growth come from producing anxiety about
problem fussing or growth comes from support you are alright in
enough was that I can over look or help you with you problems
not as anxious now as when first started ~~writt~~ writing yes I am I am
scared about something don't know what
can't write just think life end nothing sadness work happiness
is someone believing in me struggle fight nag fuss acceptance
success college work which way to go what can I do to free myself
from anxiety
what can I do to solve my problem I am anxious now why subject
writing was I already anxious I hate to read what I write

I went back to pick up my coat and books and reported to Dr. Fagan that I had not completed my task.

January 15

Again, I went to Dr. Fagan. I felt in a happy mood. I followed her into another office stating that I had completed the list of words. She said I was not to feel that I should complete what I started on these days. She also said not to write using correct style—that I was to free-associate. She assigned me a subject—anxiety.

From the moment she uttered the word, I became anxious and remained so in varying degrees during the entire session. At one point I did not see how I could turn in the paper or go to class. When the bell rang, I was less anxious and very willing to stop.

My sessions with her seem unstructured. I am to come two days a week, but can choose the days. There is something very comfortable about this non-structured element.

I can't understand why it displeased her that I had continued and finished the words. Since I am doing this to learn and improve my language, I thought this was what I was supposed to do.

January 17

I am angry—I hate to draw. Today Dr. Fagan gave me some colored pencils and told me to draw. She gave me a calendar picture of mountains and valley in either Switzerland or Germany. Fog, mist, color, sunlight, trees, I can't stand to look at my drawings. It was painful to try to get such a beautiful picture on a piece of white paper. I couldn't draw the house. I didn't know how to give the impression of mist, fog. In any other position, I would have chucked the whole thing and said I can't draw, but I tried as much as my extreme dislike and lack of ability would allow.

And when I finished all this effort, she gave me another piece of paper to draw with my left hand. I looked at her more astonished than before. And then began the painful task, eagerly awaiting the bell. When I gave her my pictures, she asked if I had compared them. I said no. She said it might be wise if I did sometimes. I do not want to look at the pictures. But I think I know what she is getting at. I have thought I should be left handed. Maybe she thinks so too and feels that some of my language problems come from this.

January 22

Dr. Fagan handed me a dictionary and paper. Her instructions were to write an essay on ten reasons why people should not obey rules and that I should not spell any words right even if I had to look them up to spell them wrong. I laughed and said I doubted if I would need the dictionary.

After my initial surprise over the instructions, I enjoyed misspelling the words and writing about breaking rules. I see two methods behind this, first

Fig. 3. Anne's Associations to "Anger"

Anger
I ca'nt write about anger. I am not angry happy joy blue mist over
distanct mountains
Maybe I misspell because I an angry with people, particularly people
who try to teach me something I learn best by inspiration and wanted
to achieve
Anger, anger if I can't feel it I can't write about in this is
interesting because I became anxiety the moment Dr. Fagan spoke
the word but I cannot feel anger
What makes me angry it makes me angry when I can't communicate
with people or they with me I want to take their heads and hold them
in my hands shake them and demand rapport Now I am angry
frustrated because of all the people who would not take the time to
listen to me.
I hate my mother when she says thing like when she views Mark's
old work and new ones she is discussed (disgusted) with the new one
and prononces them as bad, narror mind, ignorant she can not
tell good and does'nt want anyone else to either
hard throbbing in head sick feeling in stomach I feel like nothing is
ever going to change weary, tired of struggling anger gets no wear
were people angry with me and I can't trust them how can I be one and
reveal my inner self when all that happens when confronted with this is
lectures and anger What do you do with anger what what what
if you show anger and it is not appropreate you are wrong in dog
house when you keep the anger inside you find other people don't
know how you feel and that even though you put up with them, they
won't put up with you. Anger inside keeps building up up up up and
you want to explode or stop exsisting
half time I feel like a little girl rest of time I feel like a weary old
woman How do I feel when I am angry I don't know. What do I do with
anger. I try to show it when I can, but constantly feel people telling
me this is not allow They say you have to take it from me, but you
can't give it back to us
when you love some one it hurts so much to have them angry with you
but even more for you to be angry with them
What is anger like like a boiling pot on the stove if it spills
someone gets burnt like the wind blowing so hard the branches creake
and breaks off like a child spell stepping on a bug and squashing it
like a bruise on your kee knee black, blue, yellowish in contrast
with white skin
Anger is like having a kin knife in your guts and having it pulled and
pushed until nothing is lift left. Worse than anger is what follows
   hollow, pain, nothingness and what to do how to a aee aeh act
how to learn and not let it happen again, but it happens again & again
& again with the same miserable feeling

that I could concentrate on misspelling and possibly begin to be conscious of the way letters are placed and second, that possibly I show my rebellious nature in spelling or rather not spelling. I liked what I said about rules. I reminds me of how pleased I was in my phonetics course to learn how common the errors I make are and some of the reasons behind these errors.

January 25

Today she asked me to get a copy of Milton's *Paradise Lost* and Keats from the library. Then she told me to write on anger, but I couldn't because I was not angry. I felt no anger.

January 26

I went back again today. I wonder if she was surprised to see me two days in a row. She looked around her files for something, but couldn't find it. I was afraid she was going to ask me to look at the pictures I had drawn. She asked if I had the books, I did—I had brought the Milton from home and had just checked Keats out of the library. She sat down and first marked Milton and then Keats. She handed them back to me and told me to read them aloud until I could do it well. As she unlocked the door to another office I said but it isn't sound proof— she said well you don't have to shout.

So I sat, reading softly aloud. In Milton book 1, *Paradise Lost*, I found two particular passages I liked. I am sure I am reading in my own meanings.

> . . . What in me is dark illumine,
> What is low raise and support:
> . . . One who brings
> A Mind not to be changed by place or time
> The mind is its own place, and in itself
> Can make a heaven of hell, a hell of heaven.
> What matter where, if I be still the same
> And what I should be, all but less than he
> Whom thunder hath made greater? Here at least
> We shall be *free*.

From Keats "Ode to a Nightingale".

> This not through envy of thy happy lot
> But being too happy in thine happiness.

There were some words I could not pronounce and places where because I did not know the meaning, I could not phrase it right. I read a little past the bell (I plan to do some more later) and I asked Dr. Fagan if I could come tomorrow. She said I could.

January 27

Dr. Fagan suggested that this might be a good time to think about what we had done. I thought she meant for me to write that day my feelings, so I told her I was keeping a diary. I think she was pleased. She said thus far she had avoided any communications about what I felt about what was happening—I said did she want to read my diary? She let me know she wanted me to talk about anything I had been thinking.

First, I asked about the left-handed drawing and told my story about perhaps experiencing a change in dominance. She said this was not what she was indicating or had interest in. She did it because in class this summer in California some drawings had been done left handed and some interesting different approaches had been discovered.

I then brought up something that had bothered me. Since she was working with me and might also teach me, I was afraid if I took a test under her and didn't show some improvement, she might feel her time wasted on me, or feel that her method had failed or something. In my effort to please her I would be under such stress that I wouldn't be able to do anything—she said she had nothing invested in me—I can't remember exactly what she said, but it was trying to help me know that what I did she was not ego-involved in. I said that she was a special person to me right now and I appreciated what she was doing for me and thinking I was worth helping—the only way I knew to show how I felt was by achieving and yet this would place me under stress. I am not sure the exact way the rest of the conversation went, but this is as I remember it—she said on a test to start off and misspell the first couple of sentences deliberately. This surprised me (my, how I use that word, *surprise*, but that's exactly the feeling I get when she says something). I reacted by telling her that I had the feeling while writing the rules that perhaps I had used spelling as a way of rebelling—she smiled at this. I felt I had hit the nail on the head. Only, I continued, when I stopped rebelling I was left with the habit which I couldn't break—she said something about my achieving and my family's achieving—I couldn't get this—and what I said was rather incoherent. She could see I was struggling with it and said that this was something I could not expect to grasp right off.

I said what first came into my mind that mother had not reacted to my making the dean's list. Dr. Fagan told me about a man from the slums who had gotten a Ph.D. and his mother would not believe it. I know this feeling.

She also said that she could read through my spelling errors and see what I was trying to say. This didn't bother her. She wanted me to know, I think, that I should relax, not be under stress and just be me and experience what growth I could.

She said she wanted to help with the problem because she felt it interfered with my doing, expressing what I wanted to. And that's the understatement of the year—I might as well be deaf and blind, or armless and legless.

I told her that I am ashamed for people to see my work. When she let me know our talk was over—I left feeling pretty good.

February 1

She had a box under her arm and paper. Earlier when asked if she were cut she said no, red finger paint. Without being told I followed her. We stopped for water in a coke bottle, after which I carried the papers and we entered the Experimental Psychology Laboratory. In one of the compartments, she put the paper, paints, coke bottle and paper towels down. She asked if I knew how to fingerpaint and I said I had two kids. She said paint left-handed using, if the paints held out, black, blue and red.

I began to paint attempting a dark black and blue cloudy sky with an ocean underneath, but then I realized I was using my right hand. I left that painting and began another—with my left hand. I think I am freer with my left hand, more rigid with my right. So I let go and just smeared paint. Mostly blue, but then I added red and ended with a painting with blue on each side and lavender in the middle. I just swirled, rolled and blended—I wanted a rhythm and grace, but am never able to achieve in art work. I went back and wet the other painting and did one with my left hand. I think a lot more went on in my mind while painting than I am able to remember.

When I finished, I washed up and headed back to take the paints to Dr. Fagan. On the way I met her—she said that I had blue paint on my nose.

February 5

Dr. Fagan brought a tape recorder into another office but couldn't find a plug. I said shall I find an empty room? She said yes and gave me a tape with Nos. 1, 41, 80, etc., written on the box and a handful of paper, and told me to listen to it two times and then write what I had heard. I think she said the first two and that they might not start at exactly on 1 and 40, but I was not sure of the instructions. I thought I would be transcribing and unpleasant memories arose from failing all my German transcriptions.

So off I went to a classroom, plugged in the recorder—and it was music—how surprised I was and delighted, but I thought I must have not listened to the instructions, so I listened to spots on the tape—all music. I started at the beginning and listened to a girl sing. Was I supposed to write the words or the sounds that I thought I heard? Then I knew that was not it—music is not words, songs are not words, they are only the feeling responses which people experience while listening to them. So I listened, it was breathtaking. I decided for the first time, I would have to go back and tell Dr. Fagan that I found it impossible to do what she said. I wished I could have written my feelings while listening, but I have not developed the ability to express that type of response.

The bell rang and I picked up the recorder thrilled with the music I had heard and excited about it.

February 8

It had been raining and stopped. The day was warm and the skies clear. For some reason it was a particularly lovely. I stood in the hall talking to some students before Dr. Fagan came. She presented me with a set of keys and the same tape I had used Friday. She instructed me to get the recorder from the supply room, pointed to a selection and told me to finger paint with my left hand while listening to the tape. I could hardly help from chuckling and asking should I whistle "Dixie" and write free association with my right hand while stringing beads with my toes? Then I said where is the supply room? She said the door next to the men's rest room. I said shall I put a sign on me? She said no, just don't go in the door marked Men. So off I went, picked up my pocketbook, the bag of materials, the tape and recorder and I couldn't find an empty room. I decided if I went to Experimental Psychology Laboratory I would waste time. Then I remembered the little room off the women's rest room. If it had a plug in it I was set. It did and after getting the tape on the recorder, the paper wet, and the paints ready, I began. My first thought—how the hell do you paint to music, second thought—how the hell do you paint? I chose red, smeared it over the entire paper. The musical selection was over and another one began which indicated to me I had the tape on the wrong speed—perhaps that's why I chose red.

In the midst of this rather disorganized, ridiculous situation (a 28-year-old woman finger-painting to music in a college rest room; there are probably people who have been locked up for less) I was able to achieve some rather unique and beautiful feelings. The music aroused in me some sensitive, sensuous, exotic feelings which lead me to believe that if I were totally without language, every feeling and emotion could be communicated to me through music. So the music spoke to me and I tried with all my heart to get the rhythm into my left hand and thus onto the paper. I listened again and again each time erasing (by smoothing out) the patterns I had previously stroked through the red paint. How many different times I did this I couldn't say, but I was surged with an intense desire to manipulate that paint in a rhythmic pattern similar to the music. As usual, I was unsuccessful, but the depth of my pleasure was reward enough. I cleaned up, left the painting on the floor and ran to class late.

February 11

Now I have time to sit down and write my feelings about this fascinating therapy Dr. Fagan has involved me in. Since I had a test today, I studied yesterday rather than take time to write. I can only say I am happy, pleased, and rather delighted to be writing again.

Before describing the last session I must go back and write some of the remarkable discoveries, or revelations which occurred to me since Monday's session. Either this first discovery is so basic that everyone already knows it, or it is so foolish that no one is impressed by it. I am inspired by the discovery. It began when I wanted to bring back the music I had listened to. The tune couldn't come nor the rhythm—but when I moved my left hand in the patterns (or to the music) which I had attempted to blend into the paint, the total sounds of the music came to me. I discovered the way I remember music (perhaps other things too) is not by intonation or the rhythm but by the patterns—the patterns of music. A combination of patterns of feelings, volume, tone, tune, rhythm. I can't really say why this is so fascinating to me except that now that I have identified it, it facilitates my use of it. Not too long ago after seeing the movie *Lilith*, I was impressed with the music, particularly the theme, but couldn't at a given moment recall (bring back the music). It would just occur to me (sometimes at rather unpredicatable times) and then it would be gone. Once when I remembered it, I said I must do something to facilitate my being able to bring back the music when I want to. So I chose five descending notes, by remembering this scale, I thought I was using intonation as a memory device, but what I was doing was remembering a pattern and through this pattern the rest of the music came. So I had used a device which I myself had identified. It worked and does work because with both sets of music I am able to completely recall every aspect.

The second discovery has probably a more personal intent. Quite a few years ago, I placed my violin softly on its case and snapped the locks shut—I don't want this to sound soapy—I am not implying by this that the world or community lost something when I reached the decision to play no more, or that anything would be gained by my going back to it. I did not play well, but I loved my violin, I struggled with it, the rewards involved were totally personal. I still am not at the point in written expression that I could adequately explain what playing the violin alone or in an orchestra did for me. Somehow it filled a tremendous gap (void). When I made the decision to put it up, to play no more, it was painful, like part of me dying and no one, not a living soul, knew the depths of my loss. So the conclusion I arrived at is that I cannot take a part of me which has meaning to me, which fills a need, and decide that it no longer exists or that it can be packed in a case and the locks snapped. I think I have quite a few cases to go back and unsnap, unlock and reexplore.

When Dr. Fagan first mentioned my problem to me—she handed back a test with a "please see me" written on it. Then she said something that really hit me—I may have mentioned it before, but if so it has reoccurred to me— "What are we going to do about your spelling?"—not how did I get this way or why hadn't I done something about it.

There are other ideas running through my head, but not clearly. Somehow the freedom with which I moved the paints to the music made me feel that I had never been that free with emotions, so as my emotions were confused, distorted (lacked perceptions) and flowed in uneven jerks—so my communications developed along the same lines.

The thing I hate most is to be wrong and yet I have spent my whole life being wrong. Did I or do I have the need to be wrong? If so, when I do not need that any longer, will not my communications clear?

February 11

The questions is why was this particular session so intense for me? It could be that I started my answer in the previous paragraphs. Maybe I had more invested in this (one almost missed, or particularly granted) session. Verbally she said (while handing me the keys) listen to this and write only adjectives or feelings. But somehow I think I received more communication than that. It was as if she were asking me to allow myself full emotional exposure to every feeling that the music conveyed to me. I got the recorder and tried two rooms, but the recorder wouldn't work. I had on a sweater, I was getting hot, the recorder was heavy, and I had my pocketbook and notebook. I decided maybe the wall outlets weren't working, so returned to the little room off the restroom. Still would not work, I was almost on the verge of getting Dr. Fagan to help me when I discovered that there were two off-on switches. So, I sat on the floor and listened. Why was that experience so intense—why did that music speak to me so—

why, why, why? There are no words in the English language to really describe it. I experienced a wide range of emotions in an intense degree. It was like experiencing all at once every type of emotion I had ever felt. The height of ecstasy and the depth of miserable confusion and pain. I made an inadequate list of adjectives and feelings. When the bell rang, there were tears in my eyes, I experienced a complete inability to control myself and a feeling of being extremely vulnerable.

I just couldn't come back. I put up the recorder. When I walked down the hall, Dr. Fagan was at her door. I couldn't look up, when I feel this vulnerable I can't let anyone see me. I handed her the keys, tape, and paper and walked to pick up my books. And then something tremendous happened. Dr. Fagan began whistling the music I had just listened to—I did an about-face and entered her office. This was just the link I needed to be able to go in and risk exposing my emotions. I asked would you like to hear a few discoveries I made Monday? She said sure. She really looked so pleased, I was almost sorry I had not made more of an effort at communicating with her before. So I told her about the patterns of music and about her saying what can *we* do about your spelling. The experience that I had just been through had so shaken me that I spoke in a faltering voice. I was unable to determine what effect I had on her. I lowered my head and said those are just a few of the discoveries.

All during the class which followed, I was withdrawn. I had experienced something I couldn't handle, cope with. I could not come back, I could not look at people.

February 13 (Saturday)

Friday my husband and I had a particularly meaningful, inspirational talk. I can't remember all of it, but I did tell him about my experience Thursday. After a while he commented that he thought he saw what Dr. Fagan was trying to do for me. Then later he commented maybe many of my problems stem from a frustrated creativity. I don't think ever in our married life has he in one evening been so close to grasping some concept of me.

February 15

I was extremely excited this morning. While waiting for Dr. Fagan, the secretaries asked me what I did. They didn't believe me and tried to say I was taking a reading course. I tried to explain some of the things happening to me, but I don't think they really understood. Dr. Fagan walked up—the place was cold and she began putting on her coat. She looked in the other office saying someone had taken her chair. She asked me to come into her office and I did. She handed me a daffodil. I can't remember ever before being handed a single flower. She told me to Zen it. (I knew this had something to do with Zen Buddhism, but I have not read a book on the subject—I must do so soon.) I said "What?" I looked at her and I think we were both a little amused. Then she said look at the flower for 20 minutes, that should give you 10 minutes to paint it. She handed me the bag of paints and started opening the door. But I began talking and I told her about Thursday. She said she wanted to talk with me about it, to come back at 10:30.

So, with my bag of paints and my yellow daffodil, I headed toward the Experimental Psychology Laboratory. There

> I sat and I looked
> So this might be called thoughts
> While looking at a daffodil.
> I thought how little the names
> I had learned in biology had to do
> What what a flower is, stamen,
> Pistil, and all the parts, what is
> Important is the whole, the flower
> And its beauty—the feeling emitted to
> People. I wanted to be small enough to
> Step inside the horn of the daffodil and
> Follow the tunnel, to be engulfed by its
> Power, its beauty, its existance. How like
> Crepe paper the rim of the horn is, how can
> Nature crinkle its products in such a delightful way.
>
> Then I thought I must look at its form,
> Its structure, if I am to know how to draw it.
> I looked, I saw the texture, the strength and
> Yet the fragility, the softness and yet the
> Roughness. I saw the delicate petals, their points
> Reaching out. I saw that they were not formed in
> Perfect evenness, but nature formed them in a
> Pleasing informal unevenness. Because the flower was
> Not quite open, I tenderly opened the petals to
> Their extention. So before me a full mature flower.
> But somehow I thought of it as a baby,
> Proud on its green stem, but it did not know
> That it was going to die, in fact,
> It was already dead.

And now to paint, I wet the paper and applied yellow paint. I can never get over the surge of pleasure I feel when I place my left hand into the paint and begin to move and manipulate the wet paint into some rhythm, grace, pattern. I could not get a front view of the daffodil, so I attempted a profile. Somewhere along the line, I decided that flowers have rhythm and if I could paint I would not portray them with realistic, structure forms, but as a rhythm and feeling presented by that particular flower. So I placed a full horn (trumpet) and swirled around it the petals. Again I was not pleased with the results. I attempted several. The pleasure I felt was one of having experienced something that had meaning for me.

The bell rang and I hurriedly cleaned up in order to get back and talk to Dr. Fagan. I said I brought your flower back. She said it's opening right up.

I said I think I helped it some. Then a brief moment of uncomfortableness on my part, not knowing what to do. She said sit down (her chair was back). So I picked up the bag of paints I had placed there and plopped my pocketbook on the floor and sat down. I for some reason can't remember what I said—oh, yes, I began by saying I felt I had a greater capacity for feelings than most people, a greater range and intensity. I continued that for some reason the music had disturbed me, I felt shaken, couldn't cope with it. She said anything that bothered me I didn't have to do, I could stop. I said no that's not what I want to do. I want to know why? Why on that day with that music, what happened? Why should being in a room with a tape recorder bring such an intense emotional response from me? Other sessions had been intense, but I could handle them and had often been elated—(she said earlier in the conversation that I should have talked with her on Thursday). But I couldn't handle Thursday. She said she felt the need for feedback and suggested I come back and talk a few minutes each time, even though there was so little time. I said well I'm not sure that will do much good because that's me. I can talk about Thursday on Monday and Monday on Thursday but not Monday on Monday. Sometime in the conversation she said she needed to know if I were still in treatment, wouldn't want to interfere with that. I said no, I had quit last May.

I can't remember the exact words, I talked about the fact that almost missing the session might have made me more sensitive than usual. The bell rang and I left because we were both late for class.

February 16

Yesterday after or while writing I began to see some answers to why Thursday had been so intense. First I began to analyze the music that I had listened to. The first music was the two selections each with its own circle of emotions, although each was at a different end of the continuum, not intermixed. So I could listen with one set of feelings and then switch after the pause to another set of feelings opposite from the first. The second music had only one change, this from a powerful to a soft interlude. But the music I heard Thursday was varied— the patterns, the type, the extremes—produced in me a variability of emotions, like therapy in a capsule (or nutshell), like every emotion I had ever felt all together, like I was an instrument and every note had been played upon me in every possible combination.

Now this explains why that particular music hit me so. But there is more, I was predisposed to question how meaningful the situation should be, how foolish I can feel about some situations, how vulnerable I feel. I may have written this before but I will write it again to work through it. I knew Monday that Dr. Fagan might be out of town on Friday. On Monday I had wanted to ask if she would be out of town Friday and if so could I come on another day, but I didn't get to ask. On Wednesday, when she told me, I felt unhappy although I should have been glad because I had an Experimental Psychology test and could use that extra study time. Somehow I still felt foolish not being able to miss a session. During the next class I was painfully aware that missing was going to bother me. That's when I went by and asked Dr. Fagan if I could come Thursday. So the music reinforced my feelings of why things mean so much to me, why I feel foolish that they do, and why I feel so vulnerable.

February 16

I decided last night that I wanted to tell Dr. Fagan the answers I had come up with and that I felt better about it now. I told her I had come up with some answers about Thursday, would she like to hear them? She said yes and to sit down. She moved some books from the chair and I sat down. I did not experience the usual uncomfortable feeling that I have when I attempt to communicate with someone, particularly someone who means something to me. I began with my analysis about the music and then continued through the feelings of desertion and vulnerability. Then I said I felt better and hopped up and started to leave.

She said hold on, she wanted to have her say. So I sat back down. I can't remember how she started but she did say something like—there is more going on here than she knew about or was getting told about. I said I was worried about taking up too much of her time. She was angry, she said for me not to be hostile, let *her* handle her time. She said something about wanting the communications to come from me. She said if I couldn't talk, then she would suggest I write, but I had already said I was doing that. Yes, I said, I asked if she wanted to read it? She said whatever I wanted. I said I had planned to type it and give it to her at the end of the quarter. She said it was up to me. I said I wanted her to read it now, if she didn't mind the writing, etc. I was pleased to be able to give it to her. I opened my notebook and took it out (all on notebook paper) and said you will notice one effect of what you have done for me is more quantity of words. She took the papers and placed them on her desk. I said one other thing I wanted to say was that on an Experimental Psychology test I had gotten all the points on the essay questions, although I had not done well on the test as a whole. My husband and I noticed a significant improvement in endings, spelling, and ability to express myself.

February 17

I began by saying I was sorry that I had not talked with her about what I was experiencing, because she could have no way of knowing how I felt without my telling her. She sure couldn't judge from my behavior. And I felt sorry for all the people I hadn't talked to, particularly my husband.

I can't recall all she said or how she said it. She began by saying that reading the diary had been a moving experience for her. She listed some underlying trends running through it and at the time they all seemed so clear and now I can't remember them. (My not believing I had a right to feelings. Rejection, do I have to go ahead with my response and accept what follows.) I said that I can't believe anyone would see me as worth helping. That my enthusiasm has to be controlled. I drive people away with my enthusiasm. She said so you know what you are calling me? I said no. She said think about it. I did (with bowed head) but couldn't think. So she said I'll give you a few adjectives bored, deceived, etc. You are saying that I am the kind of person who can be bored by you, etc. She counted the adjectives and then the phrases on her fingers. I can't remember the exact words, but she was saying that my low self-concept was calling her names. She asked if I thought that was nice. No I said. She said I think it's pretty nasty (mean).

Silence (when I was so thankful she didn't say can't you tell me about what you are thinking, or something similar).

I began again, I am afraid to talk and expose myself for fear of getting hurt. I used to say if I ever became psychotic, I would be catatonic. Then I would not be hurt any more.

She said more to me, prison, power, little details messed up, picking people in my life, behavior, response. She said that I felt everyone else was born knowing how to behave. No one perfect, everyone has a bellybutton. Power, I always felt that if I really released myself on the world, it just could not take it.

So she told me about the misconcepts I had of myself and the world. Somehow all of it was rather nice, painful but nice, because they were all things about me that I would rather not have affirmed. When she finished talking, she said she would like to read me some poems. I was amazed. She read several from one book and then from another. I asked if I could borrow the book, she said yes. She picked up another book, but I have some more to read. Then she said no you can't borrow them, but I will reread any that you want.

February 18

I had so much to say today. I felt that I had 100,000,000 things to say and there will never be enough time to do so. I went by her office but the bell had already rung and I met her coming out of the door. She said did you want to see me? I said well I think I'm late. We started walking down the stairs. I said I just wanted her to know that I had a pretty exciting afternoon. I showed the book I had gotten and I was pleased with it. She said that's not the best one, Alan Watts is better. We parted, but I wanted to talk. I felt frustrated by not knowing what to do. I felt that I had learned a thousand new concepts about myself and life in the past three days. I wanted to tell her about yesterday, that after leaving her I had gone by the library and selected three books, one on Zen, one on loneliness, and one on the need to love. Then I walked out with Margaret—into the rain. I told Margaret let's walk through the park and I stepped in puddles and held my mouth up to taste the rain. It was like I had been in the hospital for months, years, and suddenly I could step back into the world and once again perceive all the wonders that I had almost forgotten existed.

All afternoon I either read Zen or thought about our talk. I was in a state of complete wonderment. Like I wanted to go saying wow, wow, wow! Like the poem. I felt like a hen who had suddenly been transformed into a sea gull and someone had said fly and I flew. Or rather like (after reading Zen and feeling that some of my own ideas were unfolding before my eyes in a more sensible form) I had been a sea gull all the time but thought I was a chicken. Now Dr. Fagan says YOU ARE A SEA GULL and I know that I am. But best of all is that way up there are a thousand other sea gulls for me to soar with. I am not alone.

February 19

So the sea gull swooped into Georgia State via her old Chevrolet, unloaded some frames and raced to see if there really are other sea gulls and if she were really a sea gull. But, alas, she was still a chicken.

I stood in the hall. She opened her office door and went in. She opened the other door and then went back to hers. I walked over to her door and stood on the outside looking in. She thought a moment and reached for three sheets of paper. I followed her into the other office. She said write three criticisms I have of other people and then five of myself, and write big.

And I was furious, I was so mad. I wanted to talk and she put me in there to write. I wrote large and I was so mad that I looked up the words I couldn't spell. Twice the phone rang and I answered it. I kept writing and getting madder and madder. I wanted to stop and go turn in the paper, but I couldn't. I thought maybe if I fill up all the paper I can go turn it in. But I sat there. NO BELL. Dr. Fagan knocked on the door and said that it was almost time for class—they're not ringing bells today. I said, oh, they aren't.

So I folded up my mad paper, picked up my books, and walked over to give the paper to her and turned to go. She said something—wait a minute or something and I turned back. She put my paper into the file and brought out the papers which I had written my diary on. I took them and then she handed me a book and said, "This may clear up some things for you." I took it and left. I don't think I said thank you, but may have. I went over to use the calculator and I sat in that little room and closed the door. And I said I am so damn mad I can't go to class. I will go and see her after class and I hope she has read my paper. I sat and read the book she had given me (*Psychotherapy East and West*) which I had ordered in the bookstore yesterday out of a list of ten of Watt's books.

I stomped up to her office and waited. She arrived and we went in. I said "Did you read what I wrote?" She said No, I never read it unless you tell (or want) me to. I said "Well read it." She reached up and took it out of her file and read it. My anger blared out in every word. I had written the criticisms as I was told. She finished reading. She asked "What do you do with your anger?"

"I don't know." I said I appreciated her not saying during my silences—can't you tell me about or something soapy like that. I struggled to think and to answer her.

A.: I am angry at you and at me.

F.: Why are you angry at me?

A.: I think because you told me to write and should have known that I needed to talk.

F.: What else, are you disappointed with me?

A.: Yes, I thought you should have known better.

F.: Why are you angry at yourself?

Fig. 4.　Anne's Criticisms of Other People and Herself

Criticism

I dont want to write any damn criticism I want to talk to you, I have
100,000,000 things to say and there will never be enough time to say
it in.

Criticism of other people

They are narrow minded, stupid, and unflexiable. They won't listen to
me or attempt to understand what I am saying. If they appear to
understand they start off with "I understand, <u>but</u>" and then they let
you know they didn't understand at all.

They will not take the time to look around at all the lovely things in
life. If you do and if you appreciate these, they can't understand --
they look at you like you're crazy. And they misinterpretate like to
such an extent that they don't even know where the beauty lies.

What I hate most about me

I hate not being able to let someone know when I need them -- the
hardest thing in the world is to admit you need someone and the second
hardest is to tell them about it and when I need someone I want to
say please don't leave me and I can't,

When I experience something it hits me so completely that it engulfs
my whole life. I can't make it go away or handle in a nonchalant
manner. I think and think and think and can't turn it off.

I can't respond angrily when I want to. I can be mad as hell and I
won't do anything about it, I just smolder. It takes me awhile to
incorporate new ideas and concepts into myself. I can't just hear it
once, I have to hear it over and over and over. I have to feel complete
wonderment and awe, I have to rehash each new idea a million times. I
wish I could hear something once and have it and not be so stupid.

I feel foolish so much of the time and I hate it. I don't know what
to do about it. In fact I don't really know what to do about a lot of
things.

I want to be brilliant and I just can't quite manage it. I run and I
run and I run and I keep saying I am not going to run any more and I
do.

I get so completely absorbed in what I am doing that I can't analysis
it until much later, all of me is experiencing there is nothing left
w̶h̶ with which to analysis or make judgements.

I feel humble and I don't want to go around feeling humble. I want to
demand and have a right to demand and have my demands responded to.
(I keep ending sentences in prep.)

Right now I could knock a whole in the wall or e̶x̶p̶l̶e̶y̶e̶d̶ e̶x̶p̶l̶e̶r̶e̶d̶
explode -- (when I am mad with a word I can't s̶l̶e̶ spell it) and I
won't do anything about it. I'll just sit here and write.

If I have power over people I have not been aware of it. I want the
power but I want to recognize it and use it appropriately.

Words that I hate right now -- power, control, conform, good, sweet,
behave, details, anxiety, explode, anger, fear, need, humble, foolish,
embarrass, complement, vulnerable, intense, baby, crying.

A.:   Because I did not say anything about it, because I did what I was told, because I sat in there and wrote when I wanted to come out.

F.:   How are you going to punish yourself?

A.:   Well, I didn't go to class, I guess that's a punishment, otherwise I don't know.

F.:   So, you're calling yourself names. [How nervous I was, I kept flipping the pages of my book.]

She held out her hand, palm up and told me to put my hand against it. I said "Why?" She said go ahead and do it. So I put my hand up to hers. She pushed and I pushed—rather like Indian wrestling, but she would ease up at times and never really pushed hard. She took her hand away and I put mine down.

F.:   What did you feel?

A.:   Pressure.

F.:   Go on, what else? [Pause.] What else? [She was smiling but I could not continue.]

OK. I'll tell you what hopefully you felt. That when I meet you half-way, no one wins, no one loses. I hoped you were aware of your arm, your shoulder because awareness of self comes from pushing against someone else. [And she said something I can't remember which I asked her to repeat.] OK, let's put it another way. You are more afraid of your fears than I am. [Pause.]

A.:   OK, what am I afraid of? [Pause.] Am I afraid of me, or anger, or you?

F.:   That's not a question that gets answered right away. [I knew it was time to go and began picking up my things. She looked at my paper again.] I am glad to see this firm writing.

A.:   And big.

F.:   Yes, you are big and John Hancock said he wrote his name big so the king wouldn't need his spectacles.

I said thank you and left.

Friday while sitting in the car at the Y, a poem came to me, I took a piece of cardboard and jotted it down. When I came home I wrote it out, and corrected a few prepositions to keep the rhythm smooth. I was pleased with the poem. All through my personal belongings are snatches of paper with poems on them. Only none of the poems are any good—they are good ideas poorly executed. They are jerky and lack rhythm. But this poem flowed smoothly (or so I thought) and it expressed exactly what I wanted it to say. I was delighted. I really felt like a sea gull, or like a sea gull who had thought she was a chicken and never knew the difference until another sea gull told her how to fly. And I flew. All weekend I soared and swooped and glided so filled with feelings and ideas and thoughts and freedom. I felt like a jet plane mind in a Model T body. I felt like I had been around the world several times in the past few days.

Anyway. I was in seventh heaven, I had communicated, I was growing, I was reading Alan Watts. I was happy, busy, and up on my schoolwork, looking forward to having more time to read on my own.

NOW IN THE MIDDLE OF THIS ROSY PICTURE ALL HELL BROKE LOOSE.

(On February 23rd a crisis arose for Anne that occupied all her time outside the basic requirements of family and courses. The experiment as such had to be discontinued, and in essence ends here. Anne's diary describes this problem, the difficulties involved, and her surprise and pleasure when in spite of her fears and self-doubts she was able to cope with it successfully.)

March 17

I have not written anything in this diary since February 19. The events which have occurred will explain why. But before I try to catch up, I have to write about today. I went up to say goodby to Dr. Fagan.

F.:   Would you like the tape you listened to?

A.:   Yes.

F.:   What do you want to do with your materials?

A.:   I don't know.

There was a woman at the door with a little boy, who needed her card signed. While Dr. Fagan signed it I tried to think what she meant by the question and what I should answer.

A.:   I think I would like to take them with me.

F.:   OK.

She went back to her office and handed me the manila folder and the tape. I was rather puzzled, a little confused. I didn't know if she only meant for me to listen to it (which I had wanted to do again since the first hearing) or whether she was giving it to me. I asked. She said, "You may have it if you want." When she offered me the tape, I knew she understood how much the whole thing had meant to me and she knew I would want to keep it. I still did not know what to think about her asking about the materials. After thinking about it I decided she asked me to see what I would do. And that I had taken them because I felt that I could not go back to the stages of finger-painting, free-association writing, and writing what I heard to music. I wanted to continue, I hated to think it had passed, and yet I had the feeling more exciting adventures lay waiting for me to discover in light of my past experiences.

I wondered if somehow Dr. Fagan feels this also, that I have gained a great deal from what has happened, but am ready to go on to something else.

Can this be the end? Is it all here in this manila folder? I can't believe it. I walked away aware of every pressure of my feet on the stairs, aware of the bent folder and its contents, aware of every sensation I was feeling. I opened the door and walked out. The wind blew my hair. I felt the wind on my face and the hair blowing around it. I smelled rain in the air.

CHAPTER 15

GROSS EXAGGERATION WITH A SCHIZOPHRENIC PATIENT

Henry T. Close

Gross exaggeration has been used by therapists of many persuasions in communicating with their severely disturbed patients.[1] However, this exaggeration has been used in the service of communication and has not been commented on as a specific technique in and of itself, with its own theoretical rationale. Here I would like to present an example of gross exaggeration, and suggest some theoretical points of view that would support this kind of intervention.

The patient discussed here is a twenty-four-year-old male who had dropped out of several colleges, finally suffering a severe breakdown shortly after being drafted into the army. He had recently been driving his parents to distraction by his incessant rambling and incoherent communications, which were full of bizarre sexual symbolism. Two incidents will serve to introduce him: His first appointment with me was with his parents for the evaluation interview. I asked them, "What brings you here?" The patient volunteered, "We got this letter that said to be here at 8:30." On another occasion, he and his parents walked into the office for a family interview, and he opened the conversation by saying, "Mamma told me not to say anything to open the conversation today."

After two months of outpatient therapy, the patient was hospitalized. I had seen him daily for two months preceding the following interchange, which occurred during a session in his room:

The patient reported feeling that he was a nothing and had to bend over backward to avoid offending people. He said that he was keeping his shirts in his drawer instead of hanging them up in the closet because the rattling of the coat hangers might disturb the patients in the other rooms.

T.: [*With exaggerated affect and gestures*] I certainly agree with you. I can't imagine anything worse than your disturbing the tranquility of the ward by rattling your coat hangers. After all, what right do *you* have to make all the racket?

---

[1] Perhaps the best known is John Rosen, who yells at, caresses, bullies his patients in a highly dramatic and effective manner.

P.: I can hear M——when he rattles his coat hangers in his room.

T.: That is different! M——is *somebody*. He has a right to make noise. You do not! You certainly don't think that you are as good as *he* is, do you? It would be terrible for *you* to make that kind of noise. You will just have to keep your shirts in the drawer.

P.: But even the drawer makes some noise when you open it and close it.

T.: By golly, you're right. I'd forgotten about that. I guess the only thing for you to do is pile your shirts over there on the floor—but don't unwrap them—the crumpling of the paper would make *way* too much noise!

P.: That's right! I remember once I unwrapped a big package, and instead of crumpling up that big piece of paper, I laid it under the bed. I did right, didn't I?

T.: You sure did. That was absolutely right. The only thing you should have done differently· is to have covered it with a blanket, lest a mosquito land on it.

P.: [*Warm, spontaneous laughter.*]

T.: Look, I'll tell you one way you might be able to get your shirts hung up. If you will go out to the TV room and turn the TV up full blast, then you could dash madly back to your room before anybody turned it down, and the TV would drown out the rattling of the hangers. Or, even better than that, turn up the stereo and the TV, and make this coincide with R——'s singing [a constant nuisance on the ward], *then* dash madly back to your room. I'll bet you could get your shirts hung up before all the chaos outside subsided. No one at all would hear the coat hangers.

P.: [*Smiling warmly, starts to make some comment.*]

T.: Wait a minute. I've got another idea. If you really wanted to do this right, you could set off the *fire alarm*—that would get the staff all upset, as well as the patients, and you would have plenty of time to hang up your shirts.

P.: [*Laughs warmly.*]

T.: An even better way than that would be to turn up the stereo and the TV, get R——to start singing, and then *start* a fire in the sitting room. That would *really* cause a racket, and while everybody was running around wildly, screaming and hollering, you could be in here hanging up your shirts in complete serenity.

The patient appeared to enjoy this interaction very much. Following the interview, staff members commented that he seemed to be a bit more assertive with other people, and a few days later it was noticed that his shirts were hanging in the closet.

The rationale for this kind of gross exaggeration can be made from several theoretical frameworks.

Gestalt therapy would view the patient as playing the fearful "good boy" dominated by the catastrophic expectations and *should*s propounded by the tyrannical top-dog. Instead of asserting himself appropriately and directing his aggression toward the outside, he directs it against himself, punishing himself to a ridiculous extent. The therapist then assumes the role of the patient's top-dog and makes explicit the internalized conversation. The patient can then come to a centering, with the extremes of self-effacement and external manipulation having been explored.

The "double-bind" theory of Bateson, Haley, and Jackson would suggest that in the past, when the patient has tried to assert himself, he has been placed in a position where he cannot win. The therapist places the patient in another double-bind, whose significant instructions go: (1) Display no aggression; make no noise (with coat hangers). (2) Display much aggression; make much noise (setting fire to the lobby). (3) Do not take any of this literally; do not obey me. (4) Recognize that all of this is sarcasm. The exaggeration of the therapist makes it impossible for the patient to avoid recognizing this as an impossible message, which can be responded to with pleasure and humor rather than anxiety.

Finally, regardless of other reasons, the use of gross exaggeration is fun and can be an opportunity for warm interaction and enjoyment between patient and therapist.

CHAPTER 16

A CHILD WITH A STOMACHACHE:
Fusion of Psychoanalytic Concepts and Gestalt Techniques
Ruth C. Cohn

Nine-year-old Laura is the daughter of friends of mine. Both parents are psychotherapists who enjoy a close relationship with their three daughters. Over the past few years I have spent several weekends at their home in the country.

Several months ago, Elaine (Laura's mother), while driving me to their house, told me that she was upset about Laura, who had complained about constant severe stomachaches for several weeks. Laura described them as being very distressing, and she had frequent crying spells. Elaine's father had recently died after a prolonged illness and several operations. The parents had spent a great deal of time away from their children, caring for the failing father and supporting anxious family members.

Laura had previously suffered from severe stomachaches when she was upset. Elaine remembered the first incident as occurring after the dismissal of her baby nurse, when Laura was one year old. But at all previous times the stomach pains had subsided quickly. This time the symptoms were so persistent that the physician suggested a G.I. series, even though there had been some lessening of the pain when the grandmother had spent a few days in their house.

Elaine, in telling me about Laura's trouble, appeared low in energy and spirit. She felt physically and emotionally drained by the demands of her family and the loss of her father. She had failed to get as close to him as she would have wished before the finality of his death. When I suggested that she take a short vacation away from the family and her other obligations, she responded that Laura's physical pain and emotional distress would make this impossible.

I offered to speak with Laura who, two years earlier, had participated in an experimental Two-Family Weekend Workshop under my guidance.[1] Upon our arrival at the house, Laura behaved as if she had been present during my conversation with her mother. Several times she approached me with a warm, entreating smile and words such as, "I'm so glad you are here"; . . . "I'm so glad you could come." We had planned that Laura's mother would talk to her about a session with me in her father's office. However, since Laura approached me directly, I responded by stating that I knew something about bad stomachaches and sometimes could be of help. Laura excitedly told her family about my suggestion and rushed me into the guest room for her "private session."

I had Laura lie on the bed and placed my hand on her stomach, asking her to tell me where it hurt. She pointed to the right side to a spot just under her rib cage. This spot remained the site of the pain throughout the session.

I asked her what kind of pain it was, and she said that the doctor had asked her the same question. "But it's not like a knife or fire or burning."

After more questioning, she said, "It's like a weight."

I asked what kind of weight it was: "Like a thing, or an animal, or something else?"

She said without hesitation; "It's like a person."

"Give the person a name, Laura."

"His name is Chuck. All Chucks I know are overweight."

I asked her about the Chucks she knew.

"Chuck is a lawyer, and I know one other Chuck."

"Who is the other Chuck?"

"Another very nice man."

Repeatedly throughout the session I suggested she stay with the physical symptom and describe it fully, or "let it talk." Meanwhile I moved my hand slightly over the place where it hurt, sometimes putting varying degrees of pressure on the painful spot.

"How does my hand feel now?"

"Like a weight."

"And now, when I take it off?"

"The weight is still there."

Gradually, as the session continued, Laura observed that there was less pain, but that it was still there.

"Is the pain usually the same, or does it get worse at times?"

"It's always worse at night or when I have a fight with Kathy. But, it's always there, even when I am happy and don't feel it much. It's always there, even when I don't know it's there."

---

[1]This workshop was held under the auspices of the Membership Workshop of the American Academy of Psychotherapists.

"What does the pain say at night . . . to Kathy?"

"It says, 'Kathy, drop dead.' Mommy is always on Kathy's side. She is always getting her way, and Mommy believes what she says."

"And then you would like to say, 'Mommy, drop dead.' "

"No, but at night I am so scared."

"What does the night say?"

"There is an evil spirit in the house, and it says, 'You have committed a mortal sin.' "

"What else does the evil spirit say?"

"He has come from Grandpa's graveyard. He has come to us because he cannot go to Grandma because she would be too old and frightened. And we are the next after Grandma. Grandpa has done something that he didn't like, and so he is haunting him. I touched Grandpa, and so the scent (Laura pronounced it 'skent') of death is on me and all of us."

"And so the evil spirit says someone else has to die?"

"Yes, and I always think next will be Grandma, but after that it will be me."

"Grandma is the oldest, but you are the youngest. How come it will be you?"

"Because I am so bad."

"You really are? Isn't it Kathy who you think is really bad? And Mommy?"

(Laura smiled.)

"Pretend you are the evil spirit. Now be very evil and go through the house scaring people."

"There is a big meeting downstairs with the president and all the big ministers, and they are talking about rockets which will blow up the world if they don't do something. And the evil spirit blows up all the papers and things, and so the world will come to an end."

"Do it all over again now, Laura, in your own house. There is a meeting and *you* are the evil spirit. Not 'it' or 'he.' You play the evil spirit and say, 'I, the evil spirit . . .' "

"Okay, Daddy has a meeting and he talks, and I am the evil spirit and the evil spirit unties Daddy's shoelaces and pushes his fingers through his hair so all the dandruff gets into his eyes and he has trouble looking around."

"Laura, do you think your father has trouble looking around with all the dandruff in his eyes?"

"No."

"But you thought, as the evil spirit, that you could do that, make him not see what you don't want him to see. You can think Kathy should drop dead, and your mother should drop dead, and you can wish this, and you can feel this—but that doesn't make it happen. This is very important to learn, Laura, that we can wish and feel an awful lot of things, and this is fun and good to do, but it doesn't make them happen.

"Did you wish your grandfather would die when your parents visited him so often and everybody was concerned about him rather than about anybody else, and you were alone so often?"

"No, I didn't wish him dead, but when I didn't go to my lesson, I told a friend to tell the teacher I had to go to my grandfather's funeral, and then he really died. And a friend of mine told me the same thing happened to her when she told a lie."

Laura then went into details about the noises the evil spirit made at night and her symptoms of anxiety.

I advised her to use her loudest voice in the dark when the evil spirit came around, and to talk back, playing the evil spirit as she had just done. I also made some practical suggestions such as remaining on a bland diet and using a hot-water bottle on her stomach.

The next morning Laura saw me and her father together and asked whether I had "told him the whole thing." I said truthfully that I had given him a summarizing report, but not any facts. Laura immediately, almost verbatim, told him what had happened in the session, forgetting only my saying that wishes didn't have the power of deed. She also demonstrated the same difficulty in pretending that she was the evil spirit that she had experienced in her session, and repeatedly verbalized, ". . . and *he* untied Daddy's shoelaces." I consistently corrected this into, *"I, the evil spirit, untied Daddy's shoelaces."*

Shortly thereafter, Laura repeated the story to her mother, this time stressing "the most important thing" she had learned, that "wishes are feelings and don't make things happen, like dying."

Later in the day she asked for another session. But both of us were tired, and little additional transpired. She did, however, report that while she was telling her father the story of the session in my presence, she had the fantasy, "What would Mamma think if she came in when the evil spirit spoke about dandruff in Daddy's eyes?"

In this second session Laura inquired about the likelihood of her grandfather's ghost being in the house. I told her that I would rather believe that it was not ghosts walking about, but old wooden floors cracking because of temperature changes, or her father's steps walking to the bathroom.[2]

---

[2]Prior to Laura's telling the evil-spirit story to her father, I had spent some time alone with him. He told me about his personal experience during his father-in-law's illness and his own feelings of helplessness about the medical problems involved. He also felt upset and anxious alone with the children while his wife stayed with her parents. Several nights he awoke at 2 a.m., vaguely feeling a "presence" in the house. He turned on the light, went to the bathroom, and then went back to sleep.

Seven weeks later I revisited the family. In the interim Laura had not suffered from stomachaches or crying spells, nor had she mentioned me in either a positive or negative way. When I entered the house, she greeted me in her usual friendly manner and immediately said, "I have no more stomachaches." She remained friendly, but showed no special interest in me throughout my weekend visit. Four months later, when I visited again, she did not mention her stomachache or our "special relationship" at all. Her parents confirmed the disappearance of all symptoms.

COMMENTS AND DISCUSSION

The existing training and experience barriers among psychotherapeutic schools have been my concern for a long time. It seems timely to declare these barriers obsolete, so that the choice of treatment can be based on the patient's needs in terms of diagnosis, history, and present life situation, as well as on the therapist's personality. Therapists-in-training should be exposed to the various concepts, methods, and techniques of all relevant schools of therapy.

In former years I would never have offered assistance involving any psychotherapeutic intent or techniques to a friend. As a psychoanalyst I found myself in agreement with my colleagues, that the transference and reality confusion would interfere with both the personal relationship and the therapeutic intent. In fact, it was an analyst friend (John Brinley) and I who coined the aphorism: "Never practice on a friend—you will have neither."

However, in recent years, employing a variety of therapeutic skills, I have occasionally and under very special circumstances used Gestalt therapeutic techniques with colleagues and other friends in situations of acute psychosomatic pain, panic, or depressions (often as a bridge to psychotherapy with someone else). Under these carefully selected circumstances, no detrimental results to either the person in distress or the friendship have occurred. The use of the Gestalt therapeutic maxim of staying close to the patient's immediate experience and recognition of his feeling in the present appears to diminish the danger of inducing surplus transferential elements into the personal relationship.

I chose to have a therapeutic session with Laura because of the possibility that one interview with me might be helpful in determining the weight of psychosomatic components in her stomachaches and distress, prior to, or instead of, a G.I. series. Since the child as well as the family had had a previous psychotherapeutic experience with me through the experimental Family Workshop two years earlier, and a generally trusting relationship already existed, a session with Laura seemed more appropriate in this specific situation than placing on mother and child the additional stress of visiting with another therapist.

The described session contains both Gestalt and psychoanalytic techniques, filtered through my personal style of therapy, which is an outgrowth of my interest in psychosomatic approaches in psychoanalysis and training of emotional skill.[3] The placing of my hand on the little girl's stomach and asking, "Where and how does it hurt?" and "How does my hand feel?" reflects the immediacy of Gestalt techniques, which promote awareness of body and feeling. Laura's response led to a description of "a weight which feels like a person"—a man, a lovable (but heavy) man. My thoughts connected her words to a psychoanalytic frame of reference. I perceived the statement as an expression of a positive but "weightful" relationship to, and desire for, intimate contact with her father. My question, however, remained within the noninterpretative here-and-now technique: "How does my hand feel now?". . ."What does the night say?" . . ."What does the evil spirit say?" Psychoanalytic questions would have been: "Why are you scared at night?". . ."What do you think about in the night?". . ."What do you hear at night?". . ."What bad things have happened to you at night?" Cruder, premature psychoanalytic interpretations would have been: "Perhaps you have bad thoughts, or do things you feel are bad like playing with yourself." The simple question, "What does the night say?" led directly into the immediate, painful area of conflict expressed as the "evil spirit." Again I avoided questions about the meaning of the "evil spirit" or "mortal sin." I did not investigate how the Catholic concept of mortal sin had entered this Jewish girl's mind, but simply asked what the evil spirit said. This led to an emotionally alive description of Laura's fears.

Preceding the evil-spirit theme, I used one analytic "there-and-then" question: "Is the pain usually the same, or does it get worse at times?" This question, as well as the interpretative hunch that she would like to see her mother or sister, or both, drop dead, represent psychoanalytic hypotheses. They were meant to lead, and did, into the awareness of connections between the acute symptoms of increasing pain at night and rivalry conflicts. Yet, again, rather than analytically pursuing interpretations of night and rivalry episodes, I simply asked the here-and-now question, "What does the pain say?" Although Laura overtly rejected the interpretation of wishing Mommy to drop dead, she responded immediately by talking about the "evil spirit," which to me seemed to confirm the

---

[3] I have introduced the concept of "Emotional Skill" in teaching how a person can be trained to employ his emotions consistently for useful purposes. In psychotherapy as well as in other living and creative endeavors, we can feel, acknowledge, and use our feelings such as tenderness, hostility, fear, and rage, consciously and constructively. We can train such awareness of emotions with special techniques, that is, in theme-centered interactional workshops. A description of my work in this area is presently being prepared for publication.

analytic interpretation: the evil spirit wants to explode the world or to invade the man-father world in which a little girl cannot succeed.

I used Laura's evil-spirit concept for therapeutic and educational purposes:

1. Feelings, even bad ones, are good to experience; they are essential for living.

2. In themselves, feelings and wishes have no outside power. They are expressions, not deeds—they do not kill.

3. The "evil spirit" is a projection from inner feelings into the outer world. The evil spirit needs to be experienced as something within, as a legitimate feeling, and not as an outside powerful agent.

These thoughts belong in the psychoanalytic conceptual framework but were used here in combination with Frederick Perls's techniques, such as "speak of *I,* not of *it* or *he*" and his encouraging, sometimes even insisting on, direct speech, such as "*I,* the evil spirit, want to . . ."

Another analytic there-and-then interpretation was, "Did you wish your grandfather would die?" Again Laura overtly rejected the interpretation but responded with the communication of her fear that she had omnipotent power to kill her grandfather—by her lie to the teacher.

The practical suggestions about diet, hot-water bottle, and importance of medical care had been discussed with her parents prior to the session and served as a bridge to their authority.

CHAPTER 17

DREAM SEMINARS*

Frederick S. Perls

I

Freud once called the dream "the royal road to the unconscious." I believe that it is really the royal road to *integration*. I never know what the unconscious is, but we know that the dream is definitely the most spontaneous production we have. It comes about with our intention, work, or deliberation. If you want to understand what you do with the dream, there is no better way than the way I will show you.

If you want to work on your own dreams, do it together with somebody else, because, as I will try to point out, around the sick point you will get phobic. You will try to avoid—run away—suddenly get sleepy, or have something very important to do. If you have a partner to work with, he can see this phobic attitude. Generally, the neurotic only fools himself—he only thinks he fools other people.

Now I'd like to do a little bit of systematic work. Dreamwork can be fun. Actually it's very sincere work. You will notice those who work on dreams the way I suggest—namely, *without interpretations, without interference* by your computer, the thinker—derive a great benefit from it.

Before I go further in theory, I would like somebody to come up here with me. I had two offers—one from Mary Anne, who has worked with me before and is willing to come up and work on a dream.

Now, we do the dream. To be systematic, we do it in several stages. We want to bring the dream back to life. First the patient tells her dream like a story—something that happened to her.

---

*Transcribed from workshops held at Esalen Institute, 1966.

MARY ANNE'S DREAM

M. A.: My dream—the first part of the dream—I was sitting, looking, watching, off to the side of the shore. There were some rather fat naked women, and I could only see their backs.

Then the next part of the dream that I remember, I was on a promontory overlooking the ocean. It was a very steep cliff—down. And a cow came out of the water with horns, with a little calf beside her. And there was a man dressed in white. He reminded me of my father. And he yelled—I don't remember what he said. But, whatever he yelled—there was a man over here—and a man over here, also dressed in white—with megaphones. And, they did something. And so all these cows that were starting to come out of the water with their calves went back. And there were a lot of . . . then some other people came along. They were sort of . . . and they—why doesn't he let them come? It's time for them to come, and I felt it was time for them to come. Why doesn't he make them come? And he said something about the shore. He didn't want to let them come. It wasn't time. So I decided to go in swimming. And so I asked him if it would disturb the cows if I went in swimming. And he said no.

So, I took off my shift and went in swimming. And as I was swimming, something grabbed my hand—a jaw. And then something grabbed my other hand. It didn't bite it though, but it just held it firmly. And I don't know how I got back out of the water. I think I got my left hand free—got back out of the water. And on my right hand was a little Pekinese dog, sort of a bedraggled one. He was a cow-herding dog. And he let loose. He didn't hurt my hand. That was the end of the dream.

Perls: There's so much material in this dream—can you pick up a little part of the dream, and say it again in the *present tense*: as if you were dreaming it *now*?

M. A.: I like the part about the cows coming out of the water. I see the cows. First, I see the cow coming out of the water with her calf. And then I see the man, making the other men sending the cows back. I see all these cows in the water with their noses up, like water buffaloes sniffing when they come up for air. Then they sink down.

Perls: Do you actually see them now? Or do you just say so?

M.A.:   I remember.

Perls: But you don't see them.

M.A.:   No.

Perls: Could you tell the same thing again and try to *see*.

M.A.:   I see the cow coming out of the water with her calf. And I see
the man yelling to the other man. And the cow goes *back* in
the water, and all the cows *stay*. I see them snuffing around.

Perls: Did you see it this time? Now can you set the scene? You're
now the stage director. Where is the ocean? Where are the
cows? You begin to psychodramatize—

M.A.:   The ocean's out there. All these people are the cows. And
they're all under water, sniffing. And there's a little bit of shore
between the ocean and the cliff. I'm on top of the cliff. And
I'm very resentful that this man doesn't let the cows come out.

Perls: Now, let's start acting it out. Tell this to the man. Talk to the
man—express your resentment.

M.A.:   I want those cows to come out! You have no business telling
those other men to yell with their megaphones for the cows
to stay back in. And I don't see how you can get cows to stay
in the water by yelling at them, anyway.

Perls: What does he answer?

M.A.:   He answers, "But *I* am the person who knows about cows. I
know when they come out, and when they shouldn't come out.
And I can control those men with the megaphones. And I have
some magic noises that the cows respond to—that keep them
in the water. And I know best."

Perls: Now, play this role again, and tell this to the audience.

M.A.:   I know best about those cows. I have some kind of inner vision,
and I know that they shouldn't come out of the water at this
time. They don't belong here right now. I don't want them
here. I tell these other . . . I don't have to even bother doing it
myself. I tell these other men to keep them back—and they
stay back.

Perls: Now, say this to the cows.

M.A.:   Stay back cows . . . Oh-h—I don't want them to stay back. I
want them to come.

Perls: You have to fight for control.

M.A.:   Yes.

Perls: Now, go on. Have it out with them. Let's see who wins.

M. A.:   You have that secret message, and the know-how. And I partly feel that you know what you're doing, but partly feel that
I want those cows to come out—now. And all these other
people over here want them to come out now. So, you tell
them to come out. I don't sound very convincing.

Perls: Who says that?

M.A.:   Me. You see, I really think he probably knows what he's
doing.

Perls: Can you say this to me?

M.A.:   Do you know what your doing? Part of the time, you do.

Perls: Well, I don't see any integration yet between you and this
man. You're still at loggerheads.

M.A.:   I am the man [*pounding*]. And those cows do what I say! And
I don't give a—

Perls: Who are you hitting?

M.A.:   [*Pounding*] You!

Perls: You are hitting me?

M.A.:   I don't know.

Perls: Is he hitting Mary Anne?

M.A.:   Yes, he's hitting me.

Perls: How do you feel when he is hitting you?

M. A.:   . . . Oh, God!

Perls: You feel, oh, God?

M. A.:   Um-hum.

Perls: When he is hitting you, you suddenly become religious. Does
this mean anything to you?

M. A.:   God?

Perls: Yes. When you are being hit, you discover God?

M. A.:   No.

Perls: But is he God, by any chance?

M. A.: I don't know. Yeah, I feel . . . I suppose so, he's God. He's an all-powerful hitter!

Perls: So, God is a hitter?

M. A.: Yeah [*pounding*]! And he has a hell of a good time!

Perls: All right now. You be God and hit with vengeance.

M. A.: [*pounding*] I hate people that don't want cows to come out! Sit down, cows! Sit down, nice cows. I encompass everything.

Perls: OK. I think you have gained a bit of strength. Now I want you to play the cows. I think you have to go over there.

M. A.: With all these other cows? I'm the cow that comes out of the water first, sneaks up the shore . . . I am the cow—with horns. And I've got a little calf. I think the little calf has horns, too. We come up around the edge of the promontory. We're very happy about coming out. It's great to be out of the water. And here's this horn yelling at us. And, my God, why should we pay any attention to a horn! So we—

Perls: You are the cow. Talk to him. You are a happy cow.

M. A.: Yeah, coming out of the water. "And, listen. You're so damn high up there [*raising her voice*]. You're telling *me* to go back in the water? I'll stay right up here!" And then I go up and kick him.

Perls: Now, change roles. Become God again.

M. A.: Listen, you cow. I don't give a shit, if you kick me. I've been kicked before. And I've got this big horn. And I know, God damn well, that you're going to go back when I blow it.

Perls: How does the cow respond?

M. A.: That cow's kind of beaten down. The cow says, "I don't dare— I don't dare gore you like I want to do!"

Perls: Oh-h. Say this again.

M. A.: I don't dare gore you like I want to.

Perls: Say it again.

M. A.: I don't dare *gore* you like I *want* to! [*Pause*] But I *want* to!

Perls: Now, the power part is wanting to open again.

M. A.: Yeah. The cow is standing there. The cow doesn't see what this horn has to do with it—you know—if that man is up there pushing with pitchforks, that would be all right. But this horn—

Perls: What role are you playing? *Be* the cow.

M. A.: I don't understnad why this horn just paralyzes me. *Your* horn paralyzes me—I am *paralyzed* by that horn!

Perls: He has a horn?

M. A.: He's got . . . well, that man over there is talking to this man who has the horn.

Perls: But the cows also have horns.

M. A.: Yeah. *I* have horns, *too*! I could go right in your horn and gore your mouth out. But I am going to stand here in the sand and not move back, anyway. And you can sit up there with your horn, and toot—and I'm *still* paralyzed, but I *won't* go back!

Perls: Say this again.

M. A.: I *won't go* back!

Perls: Louder.

M. A.: I *won't go* back!

Perls: What does he say now?

M. A.: He says . . . "My God" . . . he says, "if . . . This horn isn't that effective." He says, "To Hell with it." He throws it away.

Perls: So the under-dog wins again. What do you feel now?

M. A.: Oh, I don't know. I feel kind of . . . just depleted. I'm wondering if this cow is really—has the strength to stay there, or if she's just pretending to herself, or if—if she's just defiant for nothing at all. This horn is just *nothing*. All this defiance and this turning back is just for nothing, you know, just for nothing. And yet, all this time . . . with the energy wasted. She could go out there with her calf and have her grass and her water. And she just sits there in the sand. That's better to be there than in the water.

Perls: Let's find out. Go back to the water and play the water. What kind of water is this? The ocean?

M. A.:   Yes, it's the ocean. It's calm—

Perls: Play the ocean, *I* am . . .

M. A.:   I am the ocean. And I, sort of, surround all these cows. And I've nurtured them, and I love them and here, they want to go away.

Perls: Talk to them.

M. A.:   Here, you all cows, I try to let you become alive and live in this ocean, that I am, and I surround you, and you have your calves, and I don't see why you're not happy. So, why don't you just stay here. It's pleasant. You can come up for air— You've got somebody up there on the shore telling you what to do—it's safe. Just stay here, cows, and be with me. Let me, sort of, lap around you. We'll have a pleasant time.

Perls: What do the cows ask?

M. A.:   Oh, the cows say, "*God, no!* We're restless and unhappy in this ocean. We want *more* air than just a sniff, and—than just a sniff now and then. We want to have grass and clear water. We want to live. So we're going to leave you."

Perls: Now, which parts of the dream can you really identify as being *yourself*?

M. A.:   I'm the cow, and I'm the man that's keeping them back, and I'm the onlooker, and I'm the little dog that bites my hand— I don't know about the ocean. The more I think about this ocean, the more insidious it gets—and the more it's like saying, "stay with me and I'll give you honey forever—a little LSD, and peace and quiet, and you'll be happy."

Perls: You're not mistaken, the ocean represents safety?

M. A.:   I guess so, yeah.

Perls: Protection?

M. A.:   Yeah. And it's knowing where you are. I can't identify—

Perls: You can't identify? Say this to the ocean.

M. A.:   I'm sorry, ocean. I just don't dig you. I don't feel that I'm you. I feel that you *engulf* me—I want to get rid of you, this waving ocean, all that you do to me—the salt water that gets in my nose. And yet, this ocean is—kind of loving, and nice, and slippery, and—I don't know if *I* am loving, slippery— Maybe I could be the ocean.

Perls: Yeah?

M. A.: I am the ocean. I am loving and slipping over you cows, and there's some seaweed that's around, that you can eat. And some sea otters to give you a little entertainment. And, I *am* the ocean, because the ocean—I am everything being the ocean. I cover—but I know I don't really, because I know there's that land up there, and there's that man with the horn— I guess that the real problem is the man and the ocean.

Perls: The ocean representing what, and the man representing what?

M. A.: I don't know. The man, I—sort of, think of as my father—a controlling, repellent force that I *want* to go to, and yet I don't want to go to. And the ocean, I think. I . . . it's awfully hard for me to feel for this ocean. I don't know what this ocean is—what *you* are, ocean. I don't know what you are. But, partly, you're going to suffocate me, and I think that this ocean is *much* harder for me to deal with than this man. Then I think, well—the ocean is my mother, but then—maybe, this is true, though. Maybe this ocean is—very slippery and—

Perls: You know, I don't like to interpret, but to me, this is so obvious that I think I will interfere here. To me, it seems the ocean represents your female part, and the other is the male part. It's the female—the *caring, loving* part—and the other is the fighting, domineering, controlling part of you. So, I think you are right when you say those are the two antagonists. So could you have an encounter with these two parts of you?

M. A.: Well, it's a million times easier. The man part: As the man, I boss people around—keep things back, and I've got my feet on the ground, and . . . It's the woman—this is very hard.

Perls: I want you to just let the man go into the ocean and see what happens.

M. A.: I, the man, go into the ocean?

Perls: Yes, you as the man.

M. A.: Well, I—as the man, I won't have anything to do with that ocean. But, if you tell me to go in—

Perls: Yeah. I'm interested in how this man would control the ocean. He can control cows, apparently.

M. A.: I take off my clothes, and I go into the ocean. And I'd just be a little tiny, itty-bitty speck swimming around in that ocean, with all those cows and all that seaweed. I wouldn't amount to a hill of beans, so I'd have to come right out!

Perls: What would happen if the ocean came to the man?

M. A.:   Then the ocean would lose her identity, because she'd have to come up onto the land, and she wouldn't be an ocean any- more—she'd be a little stream. And, I, as the ocean—I don't want to be a little stream. I want to be an ocean. And I, as the ocean, *resent* that man. He's *different* from me. *He stands up*, and *I* spread out. And I don't like anything different.

Perls: Say this again.

M. A.:   I don't like anything different from me. I want to be it all.

Perls: So, be it all! Be the ocean, and be the man. This is the es- sence. Instead of having a conflict—either/or—the male or the female—be both. This has been known for ages, that the conflict between the male and female cycle in a person pro- duces neurosis. Integration produces the genius. All geniuses have *both* male *and* female aspects. The really mature person is ambidextrous. He not only uses both hands, he reacts both emotionally and aggressively toward the world.

  Well, I think you can now do some more work on your own. Thank you.

You see, we've demonstrated that all the different parts, *any* part in the dream—is yourself, is a projection of yourself. If there are incon- sistent sides, contradictory sides, and you use them up to fight each other, you come again to the eternal *inner conflict game.* You find in all these encounters that the two parties are usually hostile at first. But if we work long enough, then you come through to an understanding and . . . an appreciation of differences.

We couldn't get to the point, yet, where Mary Anne could *appreciate* the difference. An ocean is *not* a he-man, and a he-man is not an ocean. But, both have potentials which might be useful and valuable by them- selves.

So, since all impoverishment of the personality comes about by self-alienation—by disowning parts of ourselves, either by repression or by projection—the remedy is, of course, *re-identification.* We achieve the identification by *playing* the parts of the dream. We *become* the part until we begin to recognize it as a bit of ourselves—and then it becomes our own again. Then, we begin to grow and gain in potential and matur- ation.

The psychoanalytical approach to a dream is to make it an intellectual game by interpretations and fixed pseudosymbolic statements: this is sexual, the horn is a phallus symbol, the cow is the mother symbol. But we don't get very far by interpretation.

All right, who would like to work on a dream now?

CAROL'S DREAM

C.: I dreamed that I saw a lake drying up. There's a small island in the middle of the lake and a circle of, well, porpoises. They're like porpoises except they can stand up, so, they're like porpoises that are like people. They're in a circle—sort of like a religious ceremony—and it's very sad. I feel very sad, because . . . they can breathe—they are sort of dancing around in a circle—but the water, their element, is drying up. So, it's like a dying—like watching a race of people or a race of creatures dying. And they're mostly females, but a few of them have a small male organ so there are a few males there. But they won't live long enough to reproduce—and their element is drying up. One is sitting over here near me. I'm talking to him, and he has prickles on his tummy—sort of—like a porcupine. They don't seem to be a part of him. And, I think there's one good point about the water drying up. I think—well, at least at the bottom, when all the water dries up, there will probably be some sort of treasure there, because at the bottom of the lake there should be things that have fallen, like coins or something like that. I look carefully, and all I can find is an old license plate. That's the dream.

Perls: Will you please play this license plate.

C.: I am an old license plate, thrown in the bottom of a lake. I have no use because I'm of no value. I'm not rusted, I'm outdated. So, I can't be used. I'm just thrown on the rubbish heap. That's what I did with the license plate—I threw it in the rubbish heap.

Perls: Well, what do you feel about the dream?

C.: I don't like it. I don't like being an old license plate—useless.

Perls: Could you talk about it until you come to be the license plate.

C.: Useless—outdated. The use of the license plate is to allow—to give a car permission to go—and I can't give anyone permission to do anything because I'm outdated. In California they

just paste a little—you buy a sticker and stick it on the car—
on the old license plates. So, maybe someone would put me
on their car and stick a new sticker on me. I don't . . .

Perls: OK. Play now the lake.

C.: I am a lake. I am drying up and disappearing—soaking into
the earth—*dying*. But, when I soak into the earth and become
part of the earth maybe, I water the surrounding area, so—
even the lake—even in my bed—flowers can grow. New, like
can grow [*starting to cry*] from me—

Perls: Do you get the existential message?

C.: Yes, I can—I can create. I can create beauty—I can no longer
reproduce. I'm like the porpoise—I'm . . . But, I—I keep
wanting to say, "food." I—as water, become—I *water* the
earth and give life—growing things. The water—they need
both the earth and the water—and the air and sun. But, as
the water and the lake, I can play a part.

Perls: You see the contrast—on the surface you find some *thing*,
some artifact—the license plate—the artificial you. But, when
you go deeper, you find the apparent *death* of the lake is
actually fertility.

C.: I don't really like this plate—or permission—or a license
plate in order to—

Perls: Nature doesn't need a license plate to grow. You don't have
to be useless if you are organically creative—and you just
found that you are. Thank you.

JEAN'S DREAM

J.: This was a long time ago. I'm not sure how it started. I think
it, sort of, started in the—the New York subway—and kind of,
paying—putting a token in and going through the turnstile,
and walking a little ways down the corridors and then, kind of,
turning a corner. And I realized that somewhere or another in
here—instead of being a subway, it seemed like—there was,
sort of like—inclines that started going down into the earth.

Somewhere or another at just about this point, as I discovered this incline, my mother was with me. Or, well, maybe
she was when I started—I can't remember. At any rate, there
was this incline. It was sort—of muddy; sort—of slippery.

And I thought, "Oh, we can go down this!" On the side or somewhere, I picked up a leftover carton. It was flattened out, or maybe I flattened it out. At any rate, I said, "Let's sit down on this." And I sat down on the edge and kind of made a toboggan out of it. And I said, "Mom, you sit down behind me," and we started going down. And it sort of went around—and there were other people—it seemed like, waiting in line. But then they kind of disappeared.

Anyway, we were just going down and around. And it was—it just kept going down and down and down—and I was sort of realizing—I was going down into the bowels of the earth. And every once in awhile, I'd turn around and say, "Fun?" Maybe I was a little scared, but it seemed like it was fun. Yet I wondered what would be found at the bottom of this.

Then, finally, it leveled out. And we got up, and I was just astounded! Because here I thought, "Oh, my God—this is the bowels of the earth." And yet, instead of being dark—it was like there was sunlight coming from somewhere—and this beautiful—oh—I've never been to Florida, but it seemed like Florida—everglades, with lagoons and things like that. And I don't remember *saying* anything particular except—maybe something like, "Who would have ever expected this?"

Now, when the dreamer tells a story like this, you take it just as a single incident, or an unfinished situation, or wish fulfillment. But, if he tells it in the present—as *mirroring* his existence—it immediately has a different aspect. It's not just an occasional happening.

We think of dreams as *night* dreams. But, what we don't realize enough, is that we devote our lives to dreams—of glory, usefulness, being a do-gooder, or whatever we dream of. For many people, through self-frustration, the dream turns into a nightmare. The task of *all* deep religions, especially Zen Buddhism, or of good therapy, is the Great Awakening—the coming *to one's senses*—waking up from one's dream, especially from one's nightmare.

We start to see, to feel, to experience our needs, to find satisfaction instead of playing the roles and needing such a lot of props—houses, motor cars, dozens and dozens of costumes. We burden ourselves with millions of unnecessary ballasts, not realizing that all property is given to us only for the duration, anyhow. We can't take it with us.

This idea of *waking up* and becoming real—of existing with what we have—the real full potential—the rich life, deep experiences, joy, anger, being *real*—not zombies . . . . that's the meaning of *real* therapy—

of real maturation—of *real* waking up—instead of this permanent self-deception and fantasizing, seeking impossible goals, feeling sorry for ourselves that we can't play the part we want to play, and so, on and on.

Well, let's return to our lady.

Perls: So, Jean, could you tell again, the dream? Live it through, as if it were your existence, and see whether you can understand more about your life.

J.: Well, I know it doesn't really seem clear until I find myself—the place has become, kind of—top of the shoot. I don't remember whether at first I was afraid or not, possibly. Oh, I shouldn't say this now—I mean. I guess I'm—

Perls: Are you afraid to go down?

J.: I guess I'm a little afraid to go down. But then it seems like—

Perls: But you have to go down.

J.: I guess I'm afraid to find out what's there.

Perls: Does it point to a false ambition—that you are too high up?

J.: That's true.

Perls: So the existentialists say, "Go down—it's fun." Of course, again our mentality says, "High up, is better than down." We always want to go somewhere *higher than*.

J.: Anyway, I seem a little afraid to go down.

Perls: Talk to the chute.

J.: Why are you muddy? You're slippery and slidey, and I might fall on you and slip.

Perls: Now, play the chute. "I'm slippery and muddy . . . "

J.: I'm slippery and muddy—the better to slide, and the faster to get down. (*Laughter*)

Perls: Well, now, what's the joke?

J.: I'm slippery! (*With laughter*)

Perls: Can you accept yourself as slippery?

J.: I guess so. Yes, I can never seem to—you know—always just when I think I'm about to—you know, say, "Aha. I caught you now," it slips away—rationalization. I'm slippery and slidey. Hm-m-m.

Anyway, I'm going to go down, because it looks like it would be fun. And I want to find out where it goes and what's going to be at the end. And it seems perhaps—only now . . . I . . . in turning around and looking to see what I could use—to protect my britches, or maybe make a better slide—I discover this cardboard.

Perls: Can you play this cardboard? What's your function?

J.: I'm just to make things easier. I'm just kind of lying around there—almost left over—but, aha, I have a use for—I can be useful. And I'm not just left over and lying around—and we can make it easier to get down.

Perls: Is it important for you to be useful?

J.: Yes. I want to benefit somebody. Is that enough for being the cardboard? Maybe, I just want to be sat on. (*Laughter*) Isn't that part in the book about, "Who wants to pity whom?" I want to be pitied—or I want to be sat on—and scrunched down.

Perls: Say this again.

J.: I want to be sat on and scrunched down.

Perls: Tell this to the group.

J.: Wow—this is hard to do! (*Slowly turning to group*) I want to be sat on and scrunched down! Hm-m-m-m. (*Yells*) I WANT TO BE SAT ON AND SCRUNCHED DOWN! (*Pounds*)

Perls: Who are you hitting?

J.: Me.

Perls: Besides you.

J.: I'm hitting my mother who is turning—who is behind me—and I look around and see her.

Perls: All right. Now hit her.

J.: Mother, I'm scrunching down on (ouch) you! And *I* am going to take *you* for a ride, instead of you telling me to go, and taking me wherever you want to. (*Yells*) *I'm taking you along for a ride with me!*

Perls: Did you notice anything in your behavior with your mother?

J.: Just now?

Perls: I had the impression is was *too much* to be convincing. It was spoken with anger—not with firmness.

J.: I think I'm still a little afraid of her.

Perls: That's it. You tell her that.

J.: Mom, I'm *still* afraid of you, but I'm going to take you for a ride anyway.

Perls: OK. Let's put Mama on the sled.

J.: There. You have to sit behind this time. Are you ready? OK?

Perls: You're taking the lead?

J.: Yeah. I'm—I'm in control.

Perls: You are in the driver's seat.

J.: I'm not only driving—I'm doing this with, you know, balance.

Perls: Do you ride a bobsled?

J.: I've never ridden a bobsled, but, I've skied. OK. Here we go. I don't know where we're going at this point. We're just going off.

Perls: Well, you said that it's a journey into the bowels of the earth.

J.: Yes, but I'm not really sure of that now. I think—I don't really—It doesn't really dawn on me until I realize just how far we keep going.

Perls: So, start out.

J.: We're going down now. And we're sliding down, and then we come to a turn, and we go around—around—around. I'll see if she's still there. She's still there.

Perls: Always make it an encounter. This is the most important thing. Change everything into an encounter, instead of gossiping *about.*

J.: Are you still there?

Perls: What does she answer?

J.: "Yes. I'm still here, but it's kind of scary," she says. Don't worry! I've got it all taken care of! We're having fun. I don't know where this is going, but we're going to find out. "I'm scared," she says. I think I . . . *Don't be scared!*

It's just going down and down and down. I wonder what's going to be down here—if it'll just be black. I don't know what she says.

Perls: What's your left hand doing?

J.: Right this instant?

Perls: Yes.

J.: Holding my head. I'm—

Perls: As if?

J.: Not to see?

Perls: You don't want to see where you are going—not to see the danger.

J.: I'm a little afraid of what will be down there. It could be terrible, or just blackness, or just maybe even oblivion.

Perls: I would like you to go now into this *blackness*. We haven't come, in this seminar, to talk about *nothingness*—the blankness, the sterile void. But I would like to make a little excursion with you right now. What does it feel like to be in this nothingness?

J.: The only nothingness is that I'm going down, now. I still have a feeling that I'm going down, and so it's kind of exciting and exhilarating because I'm—just because I'm moving, and very much alive. I'm not really afraid. It's more, a kind of terribly exciting and—the anticipation of what I will discover at this end—at the end of this. It's not really black. You see, at the time, it's sort of like I'm going down—somehow there's *some* light. I don't know where from, but just a little.

Perls: Yeah. I want to make a little bit of a shortcut. Are you aware of what you are avoiding in this dream?

J.: Am I aware of what I am avoiding?

Perls: Having legs.

J.: Having legs?

Perls: Yes.

J.: Legs that carry me—

Perls: Yes. You rely on the support of the cardboard—and you're relying on gravitation to carry you.

J.:   Possibly—passively through the time—through life.

Perls: What's your objection to having legs?

J.:   I just—First thing that come to my head is that—somebody might knock me down. Then I realized that, I guess I was afraid that my mother would—knock me down. She doesn't want me to have legs.

Perls: Now have another encounter with her about this—that she doesn't want you stand on your own legs, on your own feet.

J.:   Why don't you want me to stand on my own legs? She says, "Cause you're helpless, you need me." I don't need you. I can go through life, all by myself. (*Pause*) I can! She must have said, "You can't."

Perls: Notice the same anger, and lack of firmness—lack of support. You see, the lower carriage is for support, and the upper is for contact. But, without firm support, the contact is wobbly, too.

J.:   I shouldn't be angry.

Perls: I didn't say you shouldn't be angry, but the anger is still—

J.:   It's too wobbly.

Perls: Too wobbly, yes.

J.:   I'm afraid to stand on my own two legs and to be angry at her.

Perls: And to face her really. Stand on your legs, and now encounter your mother and see whether you can talk to her.

J.:   I'm still afraid to look at her.

Perls: Say this to her.

J.:   I'm afraid to look at you, Mother.

Perls: What would you see?

J.:   What do I see? I see I *hate* her. I *hate you* for holding me back every time I wanted to even go across the aisle in the damn department store. [*High, mimicking voice*] "Come back here. Don't go on the other side of the aisle!" I can't even walk across the damned aisle. Can't go to Flushing when I want to go on the bus! Can't go to New York, not until I go to college! Damn you! [*Screams*]

Perls: How old are you when you play this part?

J.: Well. I'm—in the department store, I'm only—anywhere from six to ten or twelve, or, who knows?

Perls: How old are you, really?

J.: Really? Thirty-one.

Perls: Thirty-one.

J.: And she's even dead.

Perls: Can you talk as a thirty-one-year-old, to your mother? Can you be your age?

J.: Mother, I am thirty-one years old. I am *quite* capable of walking on my own two legs.

Perls: You notice the difference? Much less noise, and much more substance.

J.: I can stand on my own legs. I can do anything I want to do. And I can *know* what I want to do. I *don't need* you. In fact, you're not even here when I *did need* you. So, why do you hang around?

Perls: Can you say goodbye to her? Can you bury her?

J.: Well, I can now, because I'm at the bottom of the slope, and when I come to the bottom, I stand up. I stand up, and I walk around in this beautiful place.

Perls: Can you say to your mother, "Goodbye, Mother, rest in peace."

J.: I think I did that in the dream. Bye, Mother . . . Bye. [*Weeps*]

Perls: Talk, Jean. You're doing great when you talk to your mother.

J.: Bye, Mom. You couldn't help what you did. You didn't know any better. It wasn't your fault that you had three boys first, and then you got me. You wanted another boy, and you didn't want me—and you felt so bad after you found out I was a girl. You just tried to make it up to me—that's all. You didn't have to smother me. I forgive you, Mom. Just rest, mama . . . . I can go now. Sure, I can go—

Perls: You're still holding your breath, Jean.

J.: (*Pause*) "Are you really sure, Jean?" Mama, let me go—

Perls: What would she say?

  J.: "I *can't* let you go."

Perls: Now, *you* say this to your mother.

  J.: I can't let you go?

Perls: Keep her—you're holding control.

  J.: Mama, I can't let you go. I need you. No. I *don't* need you.

Perls: But, you still miss her, don't you?

  J.: A little. There's somebody there. Well, what if nobody was there? What if it was all empty? and dark? It's all empty and dark—it's beautiful. I'll let you go. I'll let you go Mama. [*Softly*] Please go—

I am very glad that we had this last experience, because we can learn such a lot from it. You notice, this was not play-acting, not crying for sympathy, not crying to get control. This showed the ability to explode into *grief*. And this "mourning-labor," as Freud called it, is necessary *to grow up*—to say, good-bye to the image of the child.

This is very essential. Very few people can really see themselves as adults. They always have to have a mother or father image around.

This is one of the few places where Freud went completely astray. Freud thought a person does not mature because he has childhood problems—this is utterly wrong. It is because he doesn't want to take on the responsibility of the adult person. To grow up means to be alone, and to be alone is the prerequisite for maturity and contact. Loneliness is still *longing for* support.

Jean has just made a big step toward growing.

BARRY'S DREAM

  B.: I'd like to work on a dream I had, Fritz. In this dream, I'm on some kind of a toboggan run, in a sleigh, and the dream starts where I pick a sleigh to go down this run. It's in the woods, and I deliberately pick a sleigh that's too wide, and the trail is narrow. There are a lot of people around. They see me do this, and I'm aware that I'm doing it. They're watching me. I want them to see I'm picking a more difficult sleigh. So I get in this, and I go up to the top of the run, and I start down. On one side is a precipice and on the other side is a hill.

Perls: On what side is the precipice?

B.:   On the right side.

Perls: On the right. On the left is the . . . ?

B.:   The hill. And I'm doing fine. As I get to the part around the corner—around the turn—sort of at the peak really of the whole run—an animal comes out from the right side, from where the precipice is. It's like a two-headed mountain goat with one head above the other—one head on top. And it comes at me menacingly as I'm going by. I take out my pocket knife, and I jab at it in the mouth, and it stops menacing me. Then I finish the run. And that's the end of the dream.

Perls: Well, I would like you to continue this. Please continue, what did you do?

B.:   I am down at the bottom of the hill. I'm in the sleigh. It's in an open clearing, like it's wooded area. And there are people lined up one or two deep—all just standing there. The sleigh stops. I'm about thirty feet away, and I get out and look toward them. Nobody is moving. Nobody is saying anything. Now, I see myself walking first to the right and then to the left, toward them but in a little zigzagged way.

Perls: All right. I would like you to repeat the dream. Again use the present tense. And this time be aware of your voice.

B.:   I'm going to run a toboggan run in a sleigh made out of bamboo. This is in a wooded area, and I pick a sleigh that's extra wide for the narrow trail, which makes it more dangerous. There are a lot of—

Perls: Can you hear your voice?

B.:   Yes.

Perls: What does your voice say about the content of the dream?

B.:   My voice sounds firmer than my fear. I think I'm more afraid than my voice shows. I also feel my voice is firmer now than it was the first time I told the dream.

Perls: And can you take your fear along to the dream—to the telling of the dream?

B.:   OK. I have to run this race, and it's a toboggan run. It's a dangerous run, and I know it's dangerous because it's a narrow trail and there's a deep precipice on one side. Just one slip and I've had it, and so—

Perls: Go back once more. To whom are you telling the dream?

B.: I think I'm telling it to everybody here and you.

Perls: No. I'm thinking you are telling it to your head.

B.: I have to run this toboggan race, and it's a dangerous race because this run is very narrow and there's a deep—

Perls: Listen to your voice. Just feel again the difference, the discrepancy between the tone of your voice and what you're saying.

B.: I have to run this race, and it's a dangerous race that I have to run, and it scares the hell out of me.

Perls: Is it really very dangerous?

B.: Yes it is. I'm very frightened about it.

Perls: And still you're going to do it?

B.: Yes, I'm still going to do it. I don't feel I have any choice.

Perls: You don't have any choice?

B.: No. All the people are watching. You all are watching me.

Perls: Oh! So if you don't do it for yourself, you do it for us.

B.: I have to show you—uh—I have to show you something.

Perls: Who am I that you have to show me something?

B.: [Long pause] I don't know who you are. All I know is that I have to show you, and I am afraid. I'm afraid of you and I'm afraid of what I have to do.

Perls: You get already part of the message of the dream?

B.: I'm not sure I know what you mean.

Perls: Well, I mean that you have to show that you're not afraid—that you're not a coward. It's from your own very important existential message.

B.: So far that was the most—the most difficult thing I've ever experienced—when you told me to sound like I'm afraid in my voice. That was the hardest thing.

Perls: Will you follow this up a little more and tell members of the group something you are afraid of and don't want to show.

B.:   Yeah. I'm afraid of—uh—Bob. So I sat down next to him yesterday. I'm afraid of Bob, so when we're going to think quiet thoughts I look at him first and say to myself, "I'm afraid you're going to strangle me, but I'd like to be your friend."

Perls: All right. Could you show me? Come up here. Could you rehearse this with me? How is Bob going to strangle you?

B.:   You mean—uh—should I be Bob or—

Perls: I don't know whether you should be Bob. I would just like to know what your fantasy is—how he strangled you.

B.:   You're me and I'm Bob and you say —

Perls: What do I say?

B.:   Uh—I'm afraid that you're going to strangle me and so I start to go like this. [*Moves hands toward Perls's throat.*]

Perls: Wait a moment. What do you experience?

B.:   You're right! That's right! That's what I'm going to do.

Perls: But one does not strangle people just out of the blue? You must feel something.

B.:   Well, that doesn't seem important.

Perls: It's very important to me, because I'm going to be the victim. I like to know with whom do I have the pleasure.

B.:   I don't think I could justify why you should die. This is—uh—this is what comes. This is what I feel. And, of course, now I don't feel it. I'm sort of out of it. I'm just standing here.

Perls: I don't think you are.

B.:   I don't know. My left hand is up.

Perls: Are you just standing there like the Bob of your fantasies?

B.:   No. Not now. I started to.

Perls: Let's go back. How was Bob in your fantasies?

B.:   He stands like this.

Perls: Go on.

B.: That's all. He just develops more and more power, and then he comes in and he puts his hands on your throat. But I'm not Bob.

Perls: If you start—

B.: I didn't want you to be afraid of me.

Perls: If you put your smile on your face, I'm not afraid of you?

B.: It sounds very stupid.

Perls: Yes. I think it is stupid. Somebody is stupid.

B.: How would I make you not afraid of me?

Perls: This is rubbish. The Bob of your dream or how you fantasied him is somebody to be afraid of. You try to avoid now the frightening part.

B.: The frightening part would be if I had to strangle you.

Perls: Yeah, yeah. And you want to avoid this. Now try once more.

B.: I feel both fear and trying to reject Bob. I feel frightened at the same time that I'm trying to become Bob. [*Sighs*] I'm shaking.

Perls: Can you allow yourself to shake?

B.: It's a pleasure.

Perls: Could you include your muscles and your shoulders in your shaking? [*Exaggerates trembling*] All right, let's start the job again.

B.: I have to strangle you. Barry, because you said that's what you are afraid of so now I have to do this to you.

Perls: That's nice strangling. How did you prevent yourself from actually strangling me? What did you feel?

B.: I just felt I had a good grip on you and that's all I needed.

Perls: Ho! Thank you. Getting a good grip on something, doesn't this frighten you?

B.: That's what I wanted from you anyway—to get a good grip on you.

[*Perls holds Barry. Barry shows much feeling.*]

B.: Thought I needed to cry, but I don't.

Perls: Oh, yes. You still have a grip on yourself. Let's take somebody else. Tell somebody else what you're frightened of.

B.: [*Long pause*] I'm trying to do two things at once. I'm trying to pick somebody and trying to find out what I'm frightened about.

Perls: Can you stay with this process? Tell us what you're rehearsing.

B.: I decided to first try to search for something that I'm frightened of.

Perls: How do you do this?

B.: Well, I start to picture something and just before you said that I—

Perls: Oh no, you do not just picture something. Picture some *thing*?

B.: I pictured myself out on this point out here by the—

Perls: Oh, it's yourself you picture.

B.: By the precipice—

Perls: Yeah.

B.: Where I was yesterday with somebody. She walked out there. I was frightened to go out because there is a narrow place, so I—but I wouldn't stop. I went out there anyway, but I got down on my hands and knees. But I went out there. I was willing to show her I was afraid, but I wasn't willing not to go out there.

Perls: Do you see the connection to the dream?

B.: Well, I thought of the precipice again, but that's the only connection with the—well, it's just that I have to deny that I'm afraid. I have to show that I'm not. And I wanted to tell about my experience yesterday. I—uh—just met this girl, and she was pretty, and I wanted her to like me. So she says, "Come on, I want to show you this point out here on the precipice." And I said, "I want you to." And right away, I began to get apprehensive because I couldn't see where we were going yet. So we get there, and she—she just walks right out. There's about five or six feet of narrow part and then there's a wide place.

Perls: Stop this now, and tell us about the girl. Let's start the girl. Write a script between you and the girl. "Come on, let's go out on this ledge."

B.: She says, "Let's go out on this. Come on, I want to show you what this ledge looks like. I want you to see the view from this ledge out here." Me: "Can't we just stay here? I'd like to be friends with you, but I don't want to go out there. I'm scared I might fall off. She: "Oh Jesus! Get lost." Me: "Wait a minute. Wait a minute. I'll go with you. I changed my mind." And she's shaking her head, "Too late, Buster."— One slip. Now, I'm kicking myself. "Chicken. Why don't you just go out there and take a chance." But she's gone.

Perls: So we get the second message. You have to avoid rejection by a girl. Her esteem is so important to you that you're willing to risk your life.

B.: Well, of course, when I hear that, I—uh—it makes me cringe. It is all so absurd.

Perls: Cringe so. Cringe and get sick.

B.: "Ah! Well!"

Perls: Now say that to the girl.

B.: [Angrily] God damn you!

Perls: Get all this into the girl.

B.: You mean that if I don't go out there with you, then you're going to just walk away? You go straight to hell! Get lost! Who needs you! Ahh! [Disgust] Sickening! [Voice very strong] I'm about half way with this one.

Perls: It's difficult to undo the projection of rejection. We love our ability to reject people who reject us. We love to project that. We'd rather feel rejected than have the courage to reject. The question is how much poorer would the world be without this girl?

B.: Well, now that's—you know, that's not me talking. That's you talking.

Perls: I would like to have your opinion. I know I'm giving you a leading suggestion. I know that I feel if she doesn't take you as you are, but puts you through such a test, she's hardly worthwhile to be in your world. This is my opinion, but I'm not you.

B.: No. I—uh—I can't take any chances. I can't afford any slips. I can't miss once. It just seems like—uh—a person—a person is—the feeling is—you know, how horrible that would be. But when I say it, I know it doesn't make sense, but that's what I feel in here.

Perls: Exactly. That's what I wanted to point out. This is one of those catastrophic expectations, and you rehearse, and you live on the basis of this expectation without testing whether the catastrophe will really come about if you tell the girl to go to hell. All right, let's find out what kind of death you would risk. Could you now take it up again and go to your death over this precipice? Go and die. Get over with it.

B.: All right. She's out there. And I'm on the wide part. I'm starting to crawl across the narrow part, and it's real steep on both sides. I'm going slowly, and my one hand misses on this side and—[*Scream*]

Perls: Now, speak of your present experience. What do you feel?

B.: Relief when I hit the bottom. It wasn't so bad. It wasn't bad at all—only bad falling down.

Perls: Oh, so the death of a fake hero isn't so bad?

B.: I'm still shaky.

Perls: Let go. I think the shaking is very important, because when you stood here, you stood like this. [*Imitates*] You had an armor plate on your back.

B.: Well, I don't. I want to hide the shaking. I still want to hide it. I feel that I don't want everybody to see my hands shaking. I don't like the way my voice is shaking—I know it is.

Perls: Tell this to these people. Pick someone it would be most difficult to confess to.

B.: I don't want you to see that I'm afraid. I don't want you to see that I'm shaking, because then you wouldn't want anything to do with me. You wouldn't think it was worth-while to bother with me. Or you would just turn away. I didn't want you to see it. I would feel I had lost you. And I've stayed away from you all the time anyway, so how could I lose you?

Perls: Who's *it*?

B.: My hands feel warm.

Perls: Who's *it*? Who's *it*?

B.: You. I said you.

Perls: But say this to *me*. What you said.

B.: What I said to you?

Perls: Something about your fear of shaking.

B.: I don't want you to see that I'm shaking.

Perls: Go on.

B.: You're getting me out of the mood. [*Perls stands up and demonstrates shaking.*] You don't shake like I shake.

Perls: Show me how you shake.

B.: I shake like this, but I mean it. You don't do it as good as I do. Try to shake the back. It doesn't shake fast enough.

Perls: Tell this to your back.

B.: You don't shake fast enough.

Perls: What does your back say?

B.: I'm too big to shake that fast.

Perls: What do you feel?

B.: Well, now all of a sudden I feel some strength in my back. That's the part of me that says you don't need to shake. Just stand up straight and don't shake. Don't act like an ass.

Perls: What does an ass act like?

B.: He shakes.

Perls: Huh?

B.: The ass shakes.

Perls: Could you shake your ass? The fact that you can tell us that you're frightened to shake your ass, is that frightening?

B.: I'm embarrassed to shake my ass in your presence.

Perls: Could you show us that you're not embarrassed to shake your ass in front of us? [*Laughter*]

B.: For what I'm about to do, I apologize. [*Laughter*]

Perls: All right. Let's go a step further. When you use the toboggan or slide, you can immobilize your ass, can't you? So there's no need of shaking your ass there.

B.: The danger is falling *off* the precipice. The whole of me, the sled, and everything.

Perls: But there's no need of shaking your ass. I'm sure that you do not have to shake your ass. You put yourself in that carriage and it immobilizes your backside. I want to go down the same slide, without using the toboggan but to go down yourself and shake your ass.

B.: I picture myself up on top of this hill. The pass sweeps around like that, back down to the bottom—

Perls: Shoot to the bottom. Go to the bottom.

B.: Shoot to the bottom?

Perls: Shoot to the bottom. So I would even use this part of the dream. Start shaking from here until you come down to the bottom. Start shaking at your head or shoulders.

B.: My ass shakes first.

Perls: OK.

B.: I just picture myself sliding down on my ass with my feet up in the air. And my hands are flying out, and my feet are flying out, and I'm shaking all over. I'm going around this curve and all the way down to the bottom. [*Voice tremulous*]

Perls: I want you to continue it again and again until you get a spine—thirty-two joints.

B.: Well, now I feel like my whole back is stiffening up. And I— now I sort of see myself again on the top of the hill. I'm in the same position. I'm on my rear end, but I'm sort of arched—in the same position except I'm in control. And I'm sliding down the hill on my butt, and I just go right on down. I'm perfectly fine. I have complete control, and I head right on down to the bottom.

Perls: Do it again—quicker and quicker and quicker. Go round and round and round.

B.: Can't get a lot of momentum here.

Perls: Can you feel how you're still holding on to this?

B.: I'm trying to. I'm trying to maintain control as I go down.

Perls: And you put on control by cramping your muscles?

B.: I am in better control if I'm sliding and I hold.

Perls: Uh-uh. Absolutely not. You're only in control if you have adequate coordination.

B.: That's so simple that it doesn't fit my—what I think I have to do.

Perls: How many muscles would it take, really, to give you the coordination to make that turn?

B.: Very little. I could just relax and just slide on down. I've done that a lot—

Perls: Oh yeah. Good. Come on and talk about it.

B.: I could just relax and slide right on down the hill. I've done this.

Perls: Come on. Do it.

B.: I'm just sliding.

Perls: Are you dead?

B.: 'Course not.

Perls: 'Course not.

B.: Can't get killed that easily.

Perls: Thank you.

Obs.: When did you have that dream?

B.: Just about a week ago. Before I got here.

Obs.: My fantasy when you spoke of the mountain goat was that it was sex.

B.: Ha! My feeling about the mountain goat was that it was important. The only thing that I felt about it was that it—it disappeared so easily. I gave it a few jabs with my pocket knife as I went by and it was gone.

Perls: I don't want, at this time, to go into the detail of the fantasy content. I think I got the main message that you have to protect your back, your backside, thereby creating bad co-ordination. You limit your coordination by stifling your trembling because you think shaking is bad. But if you are not free to shake, you are not free to use your physical organism.

CHAPTER 18

LIMITATIONS AND CAUTIONS IN THE GESTALT APPROACH

Irma Lee Shepherd

New approaches and innovations, often welcomed by jaded professionals, may stir up both enthusiasm and skepticism. The skeptic may avoid discovering and utilizing valuable insights and skills; the enthusiast may overextend the usefulness into indiscriminate application, with glowing promises that cannot be fulfilled. It is to the latter that this article is directed. Gestalt therapy offers powerful techniques for intervention into neurotic and self-defeating behaviors, and for mobilizing and redirecting human energy into self-supporting and creative development. The work of Perls, Simkin, and others, as reported in articles and shown in films, tapes, and demonstrations, attests to this. Rarely in the literature of Gestalt therapy, however, is there reference to the limitations and contraindications essential to effective practice.

The most immediate limitation of Gestalt or any other therapy is the skill, training, experience, and judgment of the therapist. Since Gestalt techniques facilitate access to and release of intense affect, a therapist using this approach must neither be afraid nor inept in allowing the patient to follow through and finish the experience of grief, rage, fear, or joy. The capacity to live in the present and to offer solid presence standing by are essential. Without such presence and skill the therapist may leave the patient aborted, unfinished, opened, and vulnerable—out of touch with any base of support, either in himself or available from the therapist. The therapist's capacity for I-thou, here-and-now relationships is a basic requisite and is developed through extensive integration of learning and experience. Probably the most effective application of Gestalt techniques (or any other therapeutic techniques) comes with personal therapeutic experiences gained in professional training workshops and work with competent therapists and supervisors.

Beyond the basic issue of therapist competence, the use of appropriate application of Gestalt techniques hinges on questions of *when,* *with whom,* and *in what situation.* In general, Gestalt therapy is most effective with overly socialized, restrained, constricted individuals—often described as neurotic, phobic, perfectionistic, ineffective, depressed, etc.—whose functioning is limited or inconsistent, primarily due to their internal restrictions, and whose enjoyment of living is minimal. Most efforts of Gestalt therapy have therefore been directed toward persons with these characteristics.

Work with less organized, more severely disturbed or psychotic individuals is more problematic and requires caution, sensitivity, and patience. Such work should not be undertaken where long-term commitment to the patient is not feasible. The patient needs considerable support from the therapist and beginning faith in his own self-healing process before he can undertake to experience in depth and intensity the overwhelming pain, hurt, rage, and despair underlying most psychotic processes. It is preferable, then, in the initial stages of therapy with a severely disturbed patient to limit therapeutic activity to procedures that strengthen the patient's contact with reality, his confidence in his own organism and the good will and competence of the therapist, rather than involving him in role-playing or reenactment of past experiences of pain or conflict. In short, with the deeper struggles the therapist postpones those techniques that release the most intense affect, although these must be dealt with later in time to reduce major aspects of unfinished business and develop freedom to move on. It is helpful to use techniques to facilitate the patient's reclaiming freedom to use eyes, hands, ears, body; in general, to increase sensory, perceptual, and motor capacities toward self-support and mastery of his environment.

The therapist's willingness to encounter the patient with his honest and immediate responses and his ability to challenge the patient's manipulative use of his symptoms without rejecting him are crucial. It is important for the therapist to listen to the patient's refusal to undertake experiments, at times exploring his catastrophic expectations, at times simply accepting his judgment that he does not have access to sufficient support in himself or from the therapist to risk open confrontation with the terrors within. The challenge to the therapist lies in discerning the fine line between overprotection and genuine acceptance of the patient's final wisdom in the moment. In some instances, the acceptance of the patient's appraisal of the situation is sufficient support for the patient to undertake spontaneously that which he avoided only moments before.

Individuals whose problems center in lack of impulse control—acting out, delinquency, sociopathy, etc.—require a different approach. Obviously, techniques that are useful in freeing expression imply this as a desired goal and may be used by the patient for rationalization of his actions with disregard for consequences and responsibility. Carelessly used, such techniques further arm the patient to continue avoiding the deeper levels of pain that he early learned to avoid through acting rather than experiencing. Here the therapist needs to be able to determine genuine from manipulative expressions of affect, to confront without rejecting, and to support without being exploited. Gestalt exercises in "taking responsibility for" (described in '"The Rules and Games of Gestalt Therapy," page 140) are often useful. So is the therapist's willingness to confront patient response or behavior not experienced as genuine with "I don't believe you," or "I don't believe you are finished now," or similar reports of the therapist's own response and perception. At the same time, the therapist needs to be aware of the patient's severely damaged sense of trust and the despair and hopelessness that he wards off by his aggressiveness, manipulativeness, and acting out.

A skillful Gestalt therapist will design experiments to facilitate the patient's working within the therapy session, thus reducing his need to act outside. However, work with acting-out individuals, as with psychotics, cannot be considered without commitment to a longer and often slower process than many Gestalt therapists are willing to undertake.

Because Gestalt techniques, in general, facilitate the discovering, facing, and resolution of the patient's major conflicts in often dramatically short time, the inexperienced therapist-observer or patient may assume that Gestalt therapy offers "instant cure." Even in experienced Gestalt therapists, the temptation to direct or push the patient to a stance of full self-support too fast, too soon, may result in pseudointegration and subsequent disappointment. In many patients, the task of relinquishing their immaturities is a tedious and long-term process filled with tentative risking and retreating, requiring the steadfast presence and support of the therapist. He constantly asks the patient to face his responsibility and at the same time encourages him to take risks in order to find his own support, thus reducing the likelihood of the pathological dependencies potential in any therapeutic endeavor. In an effort to reduce or eliminate transferences, it is easy for the Gestalt therapist to reject the patient along with rejecting his manipulative efforts at avoiding self-support. While the patient is to be encouraged to discover his own values and identity, it is absurd to disclaim the influence of the therapist as model; in many instances, he is a good model of a parenting adult who values the growth and freedom of his "children" (patients or students). Sometimes, however, the therapist's goal of patient self-support may be short-circuited by his own impatience in much the same way that parents restrict their child's development by demanding adult behaviors prematurely.

The use of Gestalt therapy with groups is common, but frequently this amounts to individual therapy in a group setting rather than the usual group approach of extensive interaction and "group process." While there is often a high degree of involvement on the part of the group participants, at times with considerable affect and self-insight as they watch one patient working with the therapist, this approach inevitably reduces time for potentially useful spontaneous group interaction. A skillful therapist may reduce this limitation by directing the individual to confront the group as individuals, to use them for trying out new perceptions or communication skills, or to deal with his projections with them and to get their feedback in return. The degree of individual growth and development in such groups may well compensate for the loss of more traditional group experiences.

A major hazard, however, is the therapist's assuming excessive responsibility for the direction of the group by too much activity, thus fostering patient passivity and defeating his own goal of patient self-support. In this case, the group too responds passively, regarding the therapist as an expert or magician, and themselves as having little to contribute without his special techniques and skill. Certainly this is not inevitable, but can be decreased and modified by therapist judgment and action.

One of Perls's most valuable contributions is his approach to projections as the patient's disowned attributes that he has failed to assimilate in the process of growing up. The technique of "playing" the projections (the disowned roles or characteristics) has proven valuable in helping the patient regain and integrate much lost power, energy, and self-support. However, since any statement that a patient makes about another person can, within this system, be described as a projection, caution should be exerted before denying the reality factors in the perception. When one patient confronts another with his dislike or other strong response, the therapist will have to make a decision as to whether to deal with this in terms of the interaction and relationship between the people—whether to encourage the object of attack to explore his stimulus value—or whether to deal with it as a projection of the attacker. This distinction is especially important in patient evaluations of or confrontations with the therapist. A defensive therapist holds a powerful weapon if he labels all statements about himself as projections and fails to differentiate accurately. If honest encountering is valued, it must be a two-way process. The therapist needs to listen carefully and admit, "What you say is true of me" if it fits, rather than dealing with this as the patient's fantasy, and implying inaccuracy or distortion of perception. The exercise of taking both sides—that is, "This is true of me" or "This is not true"—may provide the most comfortable solution for both therapist and patient. In any case, personal openness and reappraisal is essential.

The theoretical emphasis in Gestalt therapy on awareness, self-support, etc., tends to magnify the role of the individual as individual, master of his own fate, separate and distinct from other people, often with little emphasis on his important ongoing relationships and the effects of the vocational, institutional, and cultural systems of which he is a part. This may mean that relationships may too often by viewed as projections and as clearly secondary in importance to the internal happenings, and the marked influence of family and other external pressures and difficulties may be ignored. The emphasis on the patient himself as being solely in possession of the key to his own destiny and happiness can distort the realities of everyday existence. There is a risk in the temptation to make a valid growing and emerging process into a dictum, a *should*, and thus substitute a new tyranny for the old. Full functioning, integration, and actualization, unless experienced in the moment rather than viewed as end states, can become as cruel an expectation and requirement as salvation. Gestalt therapy's focus on a Zen-like way of knowing and growing presents Western man with a dilemma, both experiencing the value of this process, yet finding little in the environment that supports this way of life. Gestalt therapy may often offer a promise of integration, freedom, and satori that is very difficult to achieve in this culture.

The consequences of successful Gestalt therapy may be that by teaching the patient to be more genuinely in touch with himself, he will experience more dissatisfaction with conventional goals and relationships, with the hypocrisy and pretense of much social interaction, and may experience the pain of seeing the deficiencies and destructiveness of many social and cultural forces and institutions. Simply stated, extensive experience with Gestalt therapy will likely make patients more unfit for or unadjusted to contemporary society. However, at the same time, they may hopefully be more motivated to work toward changing the world into a more compassionate and productive milieu in which human beings can develop, work, and enjoy their full humanness.

PART III

APPLICATIONS OF GESTALT THERAPY

Just as new techniques are constantly being devised by therapists as they respond to the needs of a patient in the therapeutic situation, so applications of Gestalt theory and techniques are being increasingly extended to many problems and situations that differ from the more narrowly defined therapeutic endeavor. Gestalt therapists may use their skills in such areas as the crises of normal college students, visual problems, and awareness training of professional groups. Persons with special skills in other fields may combine these with Gestalt techniques, resulting in productive combinations such as art therapy. Gestalt approaches may be used in a classroom for disturbed children or in a day-care center. These applications are described in the papers that follow in this section. They, of course, represent only a limited sample of the applications being made at present, which extend to such areas as creativity training, city planning, experimental college utilization, and group confrontation. What uses may develop tomorrow is impossible to predict.

It must be noted again that a "reading knowledge" of Gestalt theory and techniques is not adequate for extensive use of them. The techniques should not be considered as magic formulas that are sufficient in themselves to compensate for the user's lack of adequate training, experience, and supervision. The story of the sorcerer's apprentice provides an illustrative warning.

In the first three papers, experienced Gestalt therapists extend the range of therapeutic approaches into other than routine therapy situations. In "Person, Dialogue, and the Organismic Event: A Point of View Regarding Crisis Psychotherapy" O'Connell writes a poetic account of crisis experiences in "normal" college students. He views crises as points at which a person is called on to make a step forward in his development. However, as growth often involves conflict and suffering, many will hang back and try to maintain the status quo or attempt to solve the problem "in their heads." O'Connell emphasizes the importance of the personal involvement of the therapist and the need to avoid making the student into a patient by overconcern with his symptoms rather than with his struggles. He sees crisis resolution as first dealing with the actual environmental pressures and then utilizing other environmental supports. When the environmental pressures have been reduced, the student can focus on the internal changes necessary. Final resolution occurs in four steps: allowing oneself to be processed, saying good-by, forgiveness, and allowing oneself to love.

Despite the many physical conditions that are now regarded as psychosomatic, there has been an almost total disregard of the emotional or personal problems that produce or intensify visual difficulties. In "Gestalt Therapy as an Adjunct Treatment for Some Visual Problems," Rosanes-Berrett, from a background of both research and therapeutic experience, approaches vision from the standpoint of the meaning of seeing to the individual. She experiments with visual awareness, finding that when blocks are removed, visual distortions may be available to voluntary or conscious modification. She presents three cases in which blocks or distortions in vision were related to personal and emotional factors.

For the most part, there has been no formalized effort at fostering internal and personal awareness in therapists, even though the therapist's inner awareness provides very important cues as to what is occurring in the patient and the relationship, well before overt signals occur. If the therapist, because of training emphasis or his own lack of sensitivity to his inner responses, spends much of his time "in his head" planning, computing, and rehearsing, he cannot attend fully to more direct experiencing; thus he will miss nuances and dim his perceptions and memory. In "Awareness Training in the Mental Health Professions," Enright describes some of the usual processes, including attribution and denial, and gives examples of his responses in training groups. He discusses handling of such problems as the reluctant participant and indicates the distinction between awareness training and therapy.

"The Gestalt Art Experience" (Rhyne) describes how the author has combined an extensive background in art with experience in Gestalt therapy. The result is an approach in which the emphasis is neither on artistic skills and products nor on therapeutic change, but rather on fostering increased awareness of oneself through a variety of expressive, nonverbal media. Rhyne describes her procedures and then details a sequence of eleven art experiences that can be used with individuals and/or groups, including involvement with and expressions of various aspects of oneself and one's experiencing of time, space, the environment, etc.

The next two papers tell how teachers working with young children have each used their experiences in Gestalt and awareness groups to create new approaches to the demands of their work situations. In "Anger and the Rocking Chair," Lederman gives a vivid account of a sensitive teacher's approach to emotionally disturbed ghetto children. Ennis and Mitchell, in "A Program for Staff Development in a Day-Care Center," describe their perception of a need for increased awareness and interpersonal competence among staff members caring for young children, and the initiation of a program for accomplishing this. They indicate the early difficulties and uncertainties, and report some of the changes that occurred in the relationships among staff members and with the children as a result of the program.

The final paper raises the issue of research in Gestalt therapy. Until recently, the energies connected with Gestalt therapy have been devoted to exploring its possibilities and extending its usefulness. While the Gestalt therapist attempts personally and in his work with his patients to be open to experimentation in the true sense of the word, in the more scientific sense this is still to be accomplished. This is an ongoing criticism and a challenge to psychotherapists of all orientations. Most often, hard data are difficult to obtain; the important variables resist quantification; the complexity and multiplicity of variables in therapist, patient, and the interactional processes are almost impossible to unravel; and the crudeness and restrictiveness of the measuring devices available cannot adequately reflect the subtlety of the process. However, the fact that the task is difficult does not reduce its importance, and the need for many questions to be asked and answered by the more formal procedures available to researchers.

"Deception, Decision-Making, and Gestalt Therapy" (Denner) represents one approach to an intersection of Gestalt therapy and research procedures. Denner is concerned with the problem of the reluctant witness, the person who has observed a crime but does not report it. Previous research suggests that reluctant witnessing and preoccupation with "reality" are related to a dislike of acting with little information, as measured by perception of autokinetic movement and reporting ambiguous visual material. Denner relates this cognitive perceptual style to Perls's discussions of persons who are out of touch with concrete objects and who fail to respond adequately to happenings or events in the environment. He hypothesizes that reluctant witnesses, defined as persons with high needs for information and high concern with real-unreal distinctions, would perform differently in response to Gestalt therapy exercises than would subjects with opposite characteristics. The results were all significant in the predicted directions. He discusses at length the possible relationship between reluctance to describe experiences and deception—possibly pathology. It is hoped that Denner's study will encourage other researchers to attempt systematic investigations into many aspects of Gestalt theory and therapy.

CHAPTER 19

CRISIS PSYCHOTHERAPY:
Person, Dialogue, and the Organismic Event

Vincent F. O'Connell

The journey which is the lived life is not an evenly spaced event in space and time as is the highway that is laid down by the engineer. It is more like music, a process of rhythm and change that unfolds in time and space, according to its own nature. This rhythm and change of life is not metaphysical, it is a concrete matter. It is an affair of the heart and the guts, of works done, of joys felt, of sufferings endured. It is also a matter of feeling. Feelings are always concrete and not metaphysical. They have to do with the heart, the blood, the muscles—with the blocks and expressions, the joys and agonies of living. Nowhere is this more evident than in the situation of crisis—that period of time wherein the person is being called on to make a step forward in his development.

In a crisis, the person comes on a crossroads. He encounters there both what he is and what he can be if he changes himself. A crisis occurs when a person is confronted by the community demands on him—when he must come to know himself as limited. Without this community processing, a person does not grow—he knows himself only as an isolated individual. The path to becoming a person and the crises of that journey are at once the hope of an individual's salvation and his purgatory also. He longs for growth, strains toward growth, yet he hangs back as well from the suffering that all growing entails. And this is how the crossroads come into being.

A person enters the crisis situation when his accustomed mode of living in the community has become less viable. This is when awareness dawns that all is not well with him. Should he heed that signal, and make the necessary changes in himself by adapting himself to the present demands, he will move forward in his development almost without hesitation or pause. Since there are inherent rigidities in personality, however, the organismic signal is sometimes ignored and the path of comfort and avoidance is chosen instead. But the processing demands continue steadily (or intermittently) until the conflict once again becomes acute—until the person's awareness of himself as a conflicted organism becomes the orienting factor in his living. Depending on who he is and how acute his suffering has become, he may at this moment come to psychotherapy for help.

What is a crisis? Paul Tillich calls it "the walk through Hell," which is apt, descriptive, and phenomenologically precise. It has been called also "the passage through fire," (Montaurier, 1966) and described as the struggle with the Biblical angel—and it is all of these when it is the real crisis.

For it to be the real crisis and not merely a fantasy crisis (a matter of life and death and not merely a wish fulfillment), the person needs to be in the mode of conflict and suffering. That is what makes crisis, that the person already senses the "fire," but that he holds back from the journey in which he will be processed and changed.

Occasionally a person will attempt to go through the crisis "in his head" (as many think they can)—to be analyzing, that is, what happens at the same time it is happening. That is the fantasy crisis. And it does not foster growth in an essential way since the rational aspect of the personality inevitably takes over. To put it in another way: We may be able to cheat our way in the world of men, but we can never "cheat our way into heaven." (What I call "heaven" and others might prefer to call "reality," has nothing to do with pre-conceptions, projections, or rationalizations. That is what makes it heaven, that things are just the way they are, and none other!)

THE PATIENT AND THE PERSON

The person in crisis sweats and squirms and has his psychic balance shaken up in giving himself to the struggle, and the therapist must also expect to be processed in some measure as he takes "the walk through hell" with the person. He cannot expect to come close to the "fire" and not himself to be processed a little. He can be of no essential help if he plans to be a fence-sitter, since any kind of gamesmanship, any kind of therapeutic manipulation that is aimed at diminishing the therapist's participation, will result in closing off the growing edge of the person. This growing edge, and the work of moving toward it, depend on encounter—on the giving of oneself to what is there, while placing one's trust in the organism to guide and support the partners until they reach the core of the crisis. It is therefore necessary for the therapist to participate in what is taking place, to enable the person to stay with the growing edge of himself until the work is done.

The "walk through hell" is the encounter with one's conditioned state of behavior, with what I call "one's state of hypnosis." It involves, in brief, the processing, or changing, of those behavior patterns that are now blocking the person's coming forward in his development. It is a destructive process, in the sense that the attitudes and behaviors that no longer have survival value for the organism will be destructured so that the person may evolve new patterns of behavior more supportive of his present stage of development (Perls, 1951).

In the destructuring process, the crisis moves from the peripheral level to become a matter of acute and central concern for the person. Since he is at that moment, so to speak, in sight of the "fire," it is at that moment that symptoms also become acute. What are the symptoms? They can be legion: depressions, anxiety, fears, conversions, manipulations, helplessness, etc.—the gamut of human creativeness.

Although the person will select a limited palette to illustrate and express his suffering (and for this we can only be grateful!), an important consideration for the future progress of this therapy is the therapist's perception of symptoms. Does he, for example, interpret symptoms as forms of *resistance*—as something that interferes with the therapy process and thus something to be rid of as quickly as possible? In this case, symptoms can be a nuisance both to the person and to the therapist. Attention will be directed toward eliminating them—attention that should be directed elsewhere. Or, the therapist can view the symptoms as expressions of some pathological process going on within the person. In that event, the person is seen as "ill," and in need of some form of psychic treatment.

I prefer to approach symptoms as valuable pieces of behavior that can be turned to the person's support once he learns to decipher what he is saying on these levels of his being. Rather than being simply a reactive system of "neurotic" processes, he is seen as an open-ended center of consciousness who is moving forward in his development, as evidenced by these very symptoms. Because of this, there is no "treatment" necessary to work the crisis through. What happens is education, teaching, exploring, conversation—an experimental investigation into the person's present methods of journeying in the world with others. The person remains a *person* from the beginning to the end of the relationship. He does not need to become a *patient* for therapy to work. Indeed, the approach is oriented toward preventing the "patient syndrome" from occurring, whenever possible. The work is not something a therapist does to a patient so much as it is the study of ways of being together with this person so that ultimately he can be together with other persons.

In work with college students, this is relatively easily accomplished. Students, for the most part, are essentially "healthy" persons who can work out their living difficulties on their own. The therapist seldom needs to provide more than momentary support for the crisis situation to be resolved. His approach to them involves the same skills as are in the repertoire of any experienced therapist. But his perception of himself and his function *vis à vis* the person will need to change if he sees the patient-therapist dyad as the *sine qua non* of therapeutic movement and behavior change.

Crisis therapy in the college setting differs in important ways from crisis therapy in out-patient and in-patient settings. Whereas in the college situation we deal with, as I have said, persons who can for the most part work out their living difficulties on their own, in the latter settings we all too often meet alienated persons who have failed to resolve the crises of growth (largely because at certain crisis points there was no one to intervene to help them). In so many of the latter instances, we must deal with *scotomata* rather than *living difficulties*; and with varying degrees of hypnotic trance states (character disorders, neuroses, psychoses), which are substitute behaviors and attempts to make up for the desensitizations of the organism.

While all of these "substitute" methods of integration are to be found in the work with college students (and crisis therapy with a "borderline" person can be just as much an around-the-clock situation of hard work in the college situation as it is elsewhere), in most instances of crisis intervention with students, we begin with a person who has youth on his side and who brings the *living difficulty* with him into the therapy. The therapy can thus begin at the beginning, in the period when the conflict first arises and when it is more accessible to brief, intensive work. The student is more likely to resolve his conflict successfully. Because someone meets him at the crossroads and provides the support he needs at that time, he is strengthened enough in himself to go through the agony of being processed and changed.

TECHNIQUE, RELATIONSHIP, AND ENCOUNTER

The approach to crisis intervention may become clearer if we pose two questions I shall now attempt to answer:

1.   How does the therapist involve himself in the crisis so it remains a living difficulty and does not become a "neurotic" problem in need of analysis?

2.   How does the therapist enable the person to meet the crisis so that he takes "the walk through hell" and resolves the crisis for himself?

When we speak of the therapist's involvement with another person in therapy, we come to subtle and fugitive factors in the therapist's personality arising from his theory of man and of health and illness. His approach to involvement will express (and I realize this oversimplifies the matter) how much he needs to be needed by a patient, as compared with his willingness simply to be useful to this person for a time. True, the relationship begins with the essential inequality of the persons. It is the student, for example, who comes for therapy since it is he, and not the therapist, who has become problematical for himself. But being in need, or confused, or conflicted does not abridge his ability to do something for himself once there is someone who can help him for a time, unless his therapist enters the relationship with the attitude that being in a state of symptomatic crisis makes the student somehow less a person than himself. That approach seems short-sighted, for it fails to perceive that in this very inequality may reside the needed solvent of *this* person's situation. On occasion the turning point in a therapy is not reached until the therapist allows the other person to become problematical for the therapist himself!

The extent to which a therapist will permit that level of encounter to happen to him is a matter of individual choice. As I see it, the problematical aspect does not always have to fall full force on the therapist. For example, some persons in crisis need only to be taught some techniques of unblocking themselves to enable them to resolve the situation almost immediately on their own. These are the ones who, so to speak, bring "adequate relationships" with them into the crisis. They need little in the way of nourishment from the therapist's humanity since their own is not in question.

Another person may need the support of a therapeutic relationship for a limited time. He shows not only the blocking and conflict already mentioned, but the confusions and anxieties that follow when one's interpersonal supports become unstable. With these persons the approach is to strengthen them in relationship until they can be taught the techniques they need to move forward on their own. (Most students belong in this category.)

It is only with the person whose support has been radically unstable—the one who begins to fit the classification of *patient*—that the therapist's *full* participation in the phenomenal field of the other may be an essential requirement. With such a person, encounter may be the one bridge to the true state of his crisis and the means whereby his mode of hypnosis can be known and resolved.

Any long-term therapy will, of course, reach that level of involvement at which the therapist works from the approach of existential phenomenology. But with college students it will be less frequent and then only for brief moments in an interview or for a few crucial interviews. Full participation and involvement remains for me, however, even in the most superficial of interviews, the possibility in the background of all that happens—the call to the "center" of the other, the call that enables him to see what he needs and does, and what he needs to do in the here and now to mobilize the health in himself.

I happen to believe that with this kind of involvement there is no need to fall back on the so-called therapist-patient game; the person senses this, gives up his "role" as patient, and comes out of hiding. Each interview can then offer possibility of touching the other, and of the therapist himself being touched and changed. And thus the person may come to an understanding of what he is. For want of a better formulation, I call this *the organismic event.*

THE ORGANISMIC EVENT

How does the therapist enable the person to meet the crisis so he takes the "walk through hell" and thus resolves the crisis for himself?

Participation in the phenomenal field of the other is one way to approach the person's verbal language and his body language. Are they the same voice? Is the message unified? Or is there a split between what the person says with his mouth and what he says with the rest of himself? This splitting, when it is present, is a factor in the total crisis situation; and if the person fails to understand what the many levels of the organism express, he may remain the proverbial house divided—he fails to make peace with himself.

What we see in divided communication is a form of conflict. While the pattern of splitting and its body language may vary from person to person and from hour to hour, they are always aimed at diminishing the person's awareness of what happens to him. They may involve many kinds of alienating maneuvers, scotomizing techniques (which entail muscular contractions) as well as various forms of conditioned behaviors, which I have called hypnotic trance states. By *hypnotic state* I intend the same situation Perls calls *the state of dreaming*, but with the additional consideration here of the dreaming state as being a form of hypnosis that is based in, and kept going by, sets of conditioned behaviors. There can be literally hundreds of forms of hypnotic dreaming, all of which are a response to *fear*, be it fear of the past, fear of the present, or fear of the future. Fear in that sense is ontologically prior to anxiety, and is the base situation out of which the so-called neurotic anxieties flow. The conditioned aspect entails the patterns of behaviors the person has evolved and learned in situations of fear, particularly in those situations that were, for him, matters of life and death. The conditioned behaviors operate largely on the levels of unawareness (unconsciousness), and are well protected by the fear against penetration and change.

One of the forms of hypnosis that can come up again and again in crisis is the "hypnosis of the spoken word." This conditioned behavior is present when the person fails to realize that his verbal language may not be empirical fact, but mere verbalism—what Perls has aptly called "the sentence game." The person creates for himself a "verbal world," which is to say a world of words and sounds in which the musical note of the organism is heard faintly, or not at all. When that is one of his hypnotic states, we need to jog his other senses, even to force him sometimes to be silent so that he can begin to hear once again the more central note of the organism.

As language can be a form of hypnosis when its limits are not appreciated, the precise use of language can be, paradoxically, one of the paths to liberation. I speak now of *naming* things and experiences by their given (existential) names. I am continually surprised how often it is that the person in therapy is unable to name his experiences precisely. A particularly poignant example of that difficulty can be the utter lack of contact with anxiety. Not only does a person on occasion not know its name, but he can be overwhelmed by its many manifestations; he seems never to have been taught its relationship to excitement. Such persons become "clutchers," always on the edge of the breakthrough but failing to make the step since they lack contact with adequate breathing. (While adequate breathing is one of the venerable techniques in the Gestalt tradition, it is for me a continual surprise how esoteric this elemental organismic event remains, even among psychotherapists.)

If the process of *naming* helps the person to understand *what* he experiences, the process of *localization* helps him to know *where* he experiences it. With localization we can become specific with the person, and he can learn to tune in to his body language in order to mobilize his support functions more adequately.

Naming and localization, however, are no more than precise techniques that lead toward the terminus in the organismic event—that moment in which the person finally allows himself to be grasped by some aspect of his total being he has heretofore been avoiding. In crisis therapy with students, that moment is often close at hand. For that reason, techniques tend to fall somewhat into the background in deference to taking hold of the observed behavior and integrating it into the ongoing organismic flow.

It might be well at this point to stress again the experimental orientation in the Gestalt way and to note specifically that it is not a method of applying techniques. The emphasis is, rather, on the *discovery* of techniques that will enable *this* person to resolve his crisis and come forward in his development. That project is always a cooperative endeavor, one in which both persons do something with each other, in which they adopt and discard hunches and techniques with splendid abandon until the moment of breakthrough and integration happens.

One of the joys of working with college students is the aptitude and pleasure with which they adopt an experimental approach to the therapy and themselves—once they know for sure that the therapist is sincere in his attempt to discover together the student's world, to find out precisely how this world is being organized, and to see what needs to be done to make it more habitable. I have found students to be amazingly creative, quick to sense what is organismically valid, and just as quick to reject what is contrived, premature, or merely verbal. In my opinion, the new discoveries that await us in the field of psychotherapy, and in the larger area of holistic psychology as well, will come from the study of students and those like them, who work through their difficulties in the moment of their living encounter with crisis.

DIALOGUE

It may be evident at this point that I no longer use such words as *patient, symptom, treatment*. Instead, there is frequent use of such terms as *person, dialogue, encounter, organismic event*. These concepts point in the direction I find myself traveling, which is toward dialogue with the person on whatever level of himself he begins to unfold.

Treatment becomes dialogue when there is a response in kind and in sympathy. The reply, even when it is not yet the full response that will be eventually there, is still a reply. The dialogue begins always in the first tentative groping of the persons toward each other in their incompleteness.

I have found that dialogue is one of the more profound solvents for hypnosis since it provides the support that was lacking in the long ago. It introduces as well the sympathetic "vibration" the person will need if he is to enter once again (but now no longer alone) the conditioned aspect of his behavior pattern, and so try out new, unconditional behaviors.

He will need to enter the conditioned state in order to contact and assimilate, insofar as he can, these conditioned pieces of himself. In so doing, he will come to realize that on those levels of himself he is a *machine*, unfree and determined, much as the white rat in the maze who is so hypnotized by his training that he jumps to the right at the sound of the buzzer. This can be a shaking experience. It is a wrench to his accustomed perception of himself as a free individual who determines who he is and what he will be. Yet, just this wrench may be necessary if he is to awake to the mechanical factors in his living and himself, namely, those levels on which he is *an object*.

The extent to which a therapist will confront the particular person with his machine-like pattern, or even whether he touches on it at all, is determined, of course, by the particular situation. This is a matter of therapeutic intuition, and does not need further discussion here since it cuts across boundaries of schools of therapy. It is seldom very easy, however, for anyone to swallow and digest the fact that he is a machine, at least not in the beginning. Therapeutically, the primary considerations seem to be how necessary the conditioned behaviors are to the person, how available he is (with support) to assimilating the fact, and how essential it is for his growth that he know. Each person is a complex network of factors for which no static rule can be laid down.

Two things at least are patent: that not only are those levels of the person most resistant to change, but they are the realm also in which the therapist himself is in his most vulnerable state; liable himself to become hypnotized, or conditioned, by the person's conditioned behavior pattern. The early analysts understood this aspect very well, and they warned against the kind of emotional plague the person can emanate when his deep unconscious (unaware) impulses and wishes are coming into view in the therapy. This is the situation where the person becomes problematical for the therapist.

I would like to discuss just one example of this, namely, the temptation *to indulge the person on the level of his pathology*—to encourage him to remain stuck at the level of his particular problem, topic, or trauma, so that attention remains centered where it is no longer merited organismically. This is a mistake for it allows (reinforces) the student then to *invoke* his state of hypnosis (his depressions, miseries, imagined hurts, etc.) and thus to continue it. He focuses on superficial or peripheral symptoms in order to avoid the confrontation with his more basic conditioned state (with himself and what he is doing).

Paying attention so as to become aware of the phenomenal situation in the relationship is quite different from the kind of sticky preoccupation and perseveration found in the indulging mode. It is, to put it in another way, the difference between entering the person's world and wallowing with him in it. In the former instance, the lawfulness and resiliency of the organic rhythm is the orienting note: we flow with what comes and goes, as it comes and goes. In the indulging mode, there is encouraging of the continued existence of a piece of conditioned behavior the organism no longer needs. It is another instance then of a substitute act, and an instance therefore of shared hypnosis—that is, when the therapist does not mobilize himself enough to interrupt it!

I have learned, to some extent, to be sensitive to the signals of the coming hypnotic trance in myself and to pay close attention to my own support so I do not fall into dread and hatred that is often found at the core of these emotional "plague spots." I have also learned that, for me at least, the fitting response is honest and loving anger (when it comes), since in that anger there is intimate involvement and a call to the person. There is then the possibility of an encounter with what is occurring and "living it out" in the here and now.

With college students, this is often enough to bring the *person* out of hiding. At that moment, somewhat shamefacedly, he *looks* at the person who refuses to "indulge him on the level of his pathology." It can be the beginning of the realization that there is a possibility open to him other than the one he has been following. The fact is, he may not have been able to imagine an alternative mode of behaving, and the possibility that there are other ways of relating himself to the world dawns on him with wonder and awe.

The person's motivation in indulging the "pathological" side of himself is his fear of tackling and facing his incompleteness. It is his unwillingness also to reenter those situations of indignity, confusion, and loneliness in which he feared his world would collapse—and he with it. He has an investment therefore in speaking *of* it, but not *to* it, and he thus presents his neurosis for treatment instead of himself. When someone else refuses to accept this statement of his case, when he can be persuaded to abandon for a time this mode of camouflage, there is the chance that contact and change can occur through dialogue.

But this requires a partner he can trust. He knows enough to stay away from such a processing when there is no one there with sympathy for him and understanding of his limitations and his capabilities. The work of crisis intervention entails the building of just that situation—namely, partnership.

CRISIS RESOLUTION

In choosing to emphasize the more strictly therapeutic factors in crisis intervention, I have ignored the management of the student's college environment. This is important since in many crisis situations with students, environmental pressure can be the key factor in the crisis, and its modification *is* therapeutic. The *community psychological approach* to crisis bases its approach on understanding the larger gestalt of *this* student in *this* community at *this* period of his development. And "being there for the student" is not just the matter of holding his hand for a couple of interviews in an office during the week; it is the matter also of intervening for him wherever necessary in his community, of helping to modify the responses of that community and its pressures. Being useful to him in the crisis thus means working with him on his attitudes, *and* manipulating those environmental factors which he cannot now manage successfully. We speak to him, and we speak to the significant others who are in relationship with him and with us.

The partnership with the person in crisis is, therefore, a partnership of the person and of all those who are involved in the crisis—be they professors, counselors, parents, therapists, etc. What makes the community approach work is continued conversation among the many "helping" persons who impinge on the student at this time. These persons need to talk to each other and to cooperate with each other in the primary intention of being useful to the person in crisis. Without this mutuality, crisis intervention would be a much more harrowing experience—and a saddening experience as well, since it then could evolve into chronic, long-term psychotherapy, with the therapist sitting helplessly by for a couple of hours a week, knowing all the while that there is little possibility of changing those "pathologic" factors in the student's environment which keep him coming to therapy and which he discusses each hour in helpless resignation.

When the therapist can help to modify the external pressures so they become less insistent, the person is then thrown back on himself, and his energies can be focused on the "internal" environment, on the structures within himself that need to be manipulated and changed. In that regard, I have found that full resolution of the crisis hinges generally on four existential situations: namely, (1) allowing oneself to be processed, (2) saying good-by, (3) forgiveness, and (4) allowing oneself to love.

Allowing oneself to be processed has been discussed at some length above, and it will be sufficient now simply to repeat that it entails the willingness to undergo the suffering of having one's conditioned behavior pattern made conscious and then changed. As far as I can tell, it is one of the core situations in the crisis. And it is necessary in the "evaluation period" to come to know as soon as possible what conditioned patterns keep the person stuck where he is. It is a mistake to assume the person understands these factors in his personality, even when he assures us he does—as he probably will once we begin to make the first tentative forays in their direction. He has, as I have said, an investment in keeping those unaware aspects of his personality "out of reach," even when the "health" in him struggles to contact and assimilate them.

The many Gestalt methods of resistance analysis and integration are of inestimable help at this point since they provide the needed precision in moving directly to the areas in which the conditioned behaviors are now being mobilized. With students, whose conflicts are often quite alive, these methods on occasion seem to be more magic than techniques. The ease with which a student can relieve himself of a psychic cramp only hastens his appreciation of the therapy. Since he is more liable to trust himself to an expert than to a fumbler, he moves forward more quickly from evaluation to actual work on himself when given precise orientation. I am inclined lately not to differentiate between *evaluating* the crisis and *working on* the crisis since the person's readiness to do something with his situation is mostly what counts. He can be ready in the first five minutes!

While techniques help to open up the areas for work, and integrative methods help to integrate the split-off behaviors in the person's conflicts, the *healing* he will need for full resolution of the crisis has to do with the three final situations I will now discuss.

Saying good-by is one of Perls's contributions. In rests in his more basic formulation of neurosis as an *unfinished situation*, namely, the failure to respond to a situation in terms of the "reality needs" of the time and the failure thus to assimilate and digest what was there. In failing to say good-by (to finish the situation), the person creates for himself a coterie of ghosts and phantoms which then remain on the fantasy levels of his living as various forms of plaguing, nagging, fear induction, etc.—and which show themselves in concomitant body language!

Forgiveness is a further example of finishing the situation, but with additional emphasis on giving up the resentments, hatreds, and other feelings which are the core of the conflict and which keep the person attached to his conditioned pattern. Many of the resistances a person erects against the processing of his conditioned state can rely on resentment for their motive power. Often, even when he sees how a piece of behavior is operating to his detriment and that he no longer needs it, he remains stuck in the behavior because he refuses to forgive whomever may have been the "culprit" in the long ago. Through clenched teeth, the sentence comes, "I'll never forgive you!"

I have found that abrasive irony and exaggeration to the point of absurdity is sometimes necessary to help "the blood to flow" once again. For the person often has become "bloodless" and cold (we call it hostility) as he has nursed, and cultivated, and invoked over the years the memory of the original indignity. It matters little that he sees, on one level of himself, the absurdity of keeping the situation unfinished. The fact is his heart has become cold, and his resentment closes the bridge to dialogue and reconciliation.

He will need to confront these facts if he is to change essentially. And he will very likely find out in the process that any of his present attempts to "overwhelm," or "fight," or "subdue" the resentment and hatred leads only to the conditioned behaviors becoming more nimble and powerful. He needs to be taught (and for this insight I am grateful to Herman Rednick) not to resist but gently to let go of his resenting. Another way of describing it is "to starve the conditioned behaviors out of existence"—what psychologists call "allowing the behavior to drop out by nonreinforcement."

As the person learns how to let go of the resentment and to forgive, he discovers that his capacity for loving comes forward at the same time.

With this he has, at last, what he needs to effectively decondition his state of hypnosis. The road ahead is then within sight and contact; it takes only a step and the crisis is finished.

Allowing oneself to love is the essential solvent of the state of hypnosis. It is the step into genuine freedom and the new beginning, since it is on the basis of loving that the mechanical factors in the personality become transparent and are eventually transcended. It is the step therefore into the liberty of the dialogue of limits, the life of community, the lived life.

The development of the loving possibilities in the person is a matter of practice and training. It is behavior that can be taught and developed, just as one can be taught to play a musical instrument, or to drive a car, or to speak Greek. But being taught how to do something involves *conversation*, in the sense that we converse with the skill we want to develop. And learning to love, to send out love to another, is also this, but something more also, since the conversation in loving is the conversation of the heart.

When we speak from the heart, we do not speak in usual terms because the speaking is then transformed, and it becomes not the *speaking out* of the everyday but the *sounding out* from the deep in oneself to the deep in the other. I have seen this in work with students: I will ask in the confused moment when the path has become obscured, "And what does your heart say to this?" And the reply sounds out, sometimes without pause or hesitation. (For when the head is doubtful, the heart often knows the way!)

It is not until the conversation reaches the heart of the crisis at hand that the speaking out becomes the sounding out to each other. When this is a shared experience from both sides, it is the genuine dialogue that Martin Buber knew—the dialogue in sympathy wherein resolution and reconciliation becomes possible.

The therapist enables the coming of dialogue in every moment of the work on the crisis when he is mindful of the difference between speaking out to the person and sounding out to him. He enables dialogue by centering himself in his heart, by mobilizing his capacity to love, no matter how diminished that capacity may be in the here and now. He works with himself and the other toward the coming of dialogue, whether the matter at hand be a technique, or a moment of waiting, or the moment of silence. Even when the appropriate response is speaking out, he holds as background for himself the possibility that in the next moment he will be changed, that he will transcend his own conditioned state and sound out to the other. This is the work of the crisis, the work of the therapy: to transform ourselves with the other, and in this sounding out to meet him and know him.

Some may view this approach as mystical. I suppose it is, insofar as we ground ourselves in the mystery we live out, a mystery we can never quite reduce to concepts and words. For each of us is spirit also while incarnated in a body, and is incomplete in himself (Marcel, 1966). We need dialogue, therefore, with the other to complement and complete ourselves in our process of creative adaptation in community. The empirical fact is this: when we send out love, when we sound out to someone with whom there is conflict, bitterness, resentment, and unfinished situations—when we sound out to that person his heart is enabled to respond.

I would not be offended if someone called this the "theological" model of psychotherapy. It is, insofar as it is a groping toward the "kingdom" that is at the center of each person and an attempt to formulate in this groping how that kingdom becomes incarnated in the shared world of the organismic event. The theological model is the model of the person's ultimate possibilities: the realm in which instinct is transformed on the basis of love, the realm in which the organism integrates itself in the world, not on the basis of substitute acts, nor with partial solutions, but in loving compassion as a free-flowing gestalt open to the world and the Self.

REFERENCES

Marcel, G. *Homo viator*. New York: Harper, 1965
Montaurier, J. *Passage through fire*. New York: Holt, Rinehart and Winston, 1966.
Perls, F. S. Hefferline, R. F., & Goodman, P. *Gestalt therapy*. New York: Julian Press, 1951. (Republished: New York: Dell, 1965.)

CHAPTER 20

GESTALT THERAPY AS AN ADJUNCT TREATMENT FOR SOME VISUAL PROBLEMS

Marilyn B. Rosanes-Berrett

There is radiance and glory in the darkness could we but see, and to see we have only to look. I beseech you to look.

Fra Giovanni

Most studies involved with visual afflictions stress anatomical and structural deviations without regard to psychological factors. However, psychosomatic medicine has shown how artificial is the dividing line between psyche and soma, and the eyes are part of the soma. The content of speech, motoric behavior, breathing processes, voice and verbal behavior, sensory awareness, are all affected by feeling states such as embarrassment, expectancy, dread, and excitement. Visual processes are no exception to the rule.

At the turn of the century, Bates, the innovator of an eye-training system in which relaxation procedures are mainly used, recognized some emotional and personality factors that seemed to relate to common visual anomalies and disturbances such as myopia, hyperopia, and strabismus. In recent years, some investigations have substantiated Bates's findings, providing evidence that psychological factors play a significant role in myopia, hyperopia, and more serious visual defects; note Van Alphen (1952, 1961), Kelley (1958), Palmer (1966), and Rosanes (1966). In his early work with "conversion hysteria" and his later work in relating anxiety to symptom-formations, Freud recognized that some forms of blindness might be caused by emotional states. However, little has been done to introduce a psychotherapeutic approach into the treatment of visual anomalies.

Bates's relaxation procedures were, of course, a combination of psychological and physical measures. But the psychology did not go deep enough. A few people today still teach relaxation drills of the Bates type to promote better eye functioning. Others offer visual training that employs various mechanical devices to encourage and develop binocular functioning. A small group, recognizing that visual-motor and space perceptions are impaired, has been developing techniques to improve these functions. Some successes are claimed by each group. But statistically significant studies are lacking, and the rate, degree, and maintenance of improvement appear to be variable. The variable results remain an enigma to the several types of practitioners engaged in visual training, because they do not pay sufficient attention to the psychological aspects of vision.

Although diagnostic and surgical procedures have improved, the recognition that vision, like other functions of the body, might become distorted and impaired because of personality difficulties is generally lacking. Deviant visual functioning and the structural malformation which develops from it are not considered in the light of the possibility that the individual is expressing a psychological disturbance through the visual system. When changed functioning persists over an extended period, anatomical changes eventually occur, as we see in people who develop extremely bad posture. If even bones can change as a result of continuous poor functioning, it is reasonable to assume that the eyes can do likewise.

When such new insights are gained or old ones understood more fully, there is often a delay in applying the new principles. The treatment of refractive errors as well as other visual problems has suffered because of the inability of orthodox practitioners to use new findings. Insights reaped in recent years from psychological studies have not yet made any appreciable inroads in the general handling of visual problems.

Through the use of hypnosis, Kelley (1958) demonstrated improved vision in myopes. He also found indications of myopia in some normally sighted people when he placed them in a stress situation. Rosanes (1966) was able to bring about improvement in myopia with suggestion and visual imagery. Young (1961) caused the development of myopia in monkeys by restricting distance vision.

Gestalt therapy is a particularly suitable treatment approach for such common visual anomalies as myopia, hyperopia, and strabismus. Its aim is to make the patient aware of how he functions in "present time." The concern is with *process*—the patient's actuality as it occurs. Through the use of the self-awareness continuum and dreams experienced in the here and now, the patient comes into touch with present, ongoing behavior; that is, he experiences or makes explicit that which is implicit and generally glossed over. With an appreciation of his own unique way of functioning, a finer sensitivity is developed, and the stage is set for discovery and growth. The patient can face the realities of his existence and so know the purpose of his visual disturbance. This therapeutic approach is a direct method of contacting parts of the personality that have been alienated and are again made to belong to one's self. When the patient can take responsibility for his experiences, needs, desires, and wishes, he can perceive how he uses his various organ systems, including the visual apparatus.

To a great extent, those with the commonest eye difficulties are unaware of how they use vision. When the patient recognizes how and when he stares, pushes, and distorts his eyes in the process of seeing, he may allow himself to experience looking differently; that is, he may look casually, effortlessly, and yet be alert and see. In myopes, the individual is prone to limit motoric expression. Rosanes (1966) notes that the type of anxiety prevalent in the myope is one that he generally does not experience; it is covert, with a decrease in motor activity. It might be said that he is afraid movements might be seen and be dangerous, and so he tends to hold back activity and thus frustrate himself. The anxiety may accompany a restriction of oxygen intake, a form of stage fright. Through the awareness continuum, the patient comes to realize what his inner communications are, and how he may interrupt them. The distorted eyes and visual mechanisms tell the story, which some call *repression*.

In psychotic states, anxiety is blown up to panic proportions, and this too can have its effect on vision. Some psychotic patients, particularly those with paranoid delusions, frequently mention that their distance vision blurs more markedly as their fright increases, and clears again as they grow calmer.

Extreme dependency needs appear to play a role in some serious visual problems, which are unknowingly used to maintain environmental supports or attention. By having extremely poor eyesight or even blindness, some persons find an excellent justification for getting help of all kinds.

The following cases illustrate the process of Gestalt therapy in the treatment of visual anomalies. All were diagnosed by an ophthalmologist or optometrist, who also checked the visual performance periodically throughout the Gestalt psychotherapy.

A twenty-one-year-old male was referred because of fluctuating myopia; that is, the ciliary muscles were spastic in various degrees at various times, and so convex lenses generally indicated for myopia were prescribed. However, the patient could not be fitted with one pair because of this continual fluctuation in the clarity of his vision. When asked to stay with feeling his eyes, he became frightened and expected punishment for desires, bodily experiences, which he dared not know. With further concentration on what the experiences were, he could come into touch with erotic sensation and an accompanying desire to masturbate. This, he believed, was a sin for which he would be punished. The first time he had had the conscious urge to masturbate, at sixteen, he was told by his priest that it was a mortal sin. At the same time, he experienced a blurring of distance vision. From then on, his visual clarity fluctuated and he experienced no erotic feelings, nor did he allow himself to masturbate. In therapy whenever he was asked to experience his eyes, the desire to masturbate arose again. This in turn brought on the frightening feeling of being punished for sinning. Nevertheless, it was only when he could allow the erotic feelings to come up that he could also experience some degree of visual clarity.

A nine-year-old child was referred when he realized that the blackboard in school was not clear, and the ophthalmologist diagnosed myopia. When the child was asked to visualize a blackboard with clear writing, he became aware that he dared not look at the board, because he felt he could not learn or understand what was demanded of him. (Later, he admitted that he did not want to learn.) He experienced himself sitting very tight, not daring to move or look in any direction. He forced himself to look and kept staring as if the blackboard were in front of him. The more he stared, the greater the blur. When asked to allow himself to look casually, he became frightened and said he could not learn; he could not please his parents; he was really a wicked child and did not want to see himself or let himself be seen. He was encouraged to stay with the anxiety he felt, which was most uncomfortable. After a while the anxiety subsided, and he could let himself look casually at the whole room. He was able to see clearly for a short period. Again he would feel wicked, and again he would experience the anxiety and the blurring out of vision. This appeared to be a repetitive pattern until he could stay with the notion of *self-imposed* wickedness. Fortunately, the pattern was of recent origin and not deeply ingrained. Eventually he could hold the clear sight.

This child was a six-year-old hyperope with reading difficulties. She was a hyperactive girl who had great difficulty sitting still more than three minutes, and was unable to concentrate on reading matter. Using the Gestalt approach to reexperiencing aspects of a dream she related, the therapist persuaded her to get in touch with so-called holes or alienations in her personality. After some initial anxiety, the child was able to recognize her need to keep watch against witches and ogres—she felt like one herself. She could not allow herself to concentrate at a close point as she might miss the danger she constantly expected. When experiencing the conflict of staying with the close point and being on guard against what might come from the distance, she realized that she could not read this way and that one eye seemed to be out in the distance while the other was at the close point. She was asked to look into the distance and to become aware of being on guard and of the conflict. By constantly staying with this child, and allowing her to look into the distance and assure herself that nothing was there to hurt, the therapist enabled her to come back and read. The hyperopia no longer appeared.

Frequently, when a patient who is not seeing well is asked to experience himself, he relates that he feels empty. The Gestalt approach encourages him to stay with the emptiness. When he allows himself to experience this emptiness fully, the hole disappears. There is a filling-up process. Through this process, the patient, then experiencing completeness, can look around both in the inner and outer environment and allow what is there to enter safely into awareness.

The language of the body has been recognized as meaningful in understanding conflicts, fears, and other emotional states. Since Gestalt therapy uses body language directly, this approach to visual problems has brought clearer understanding of the purposes of blurry, faulty, or blocked vision. When a patient speaks for the organ in distress—in this case the eye—he becomes aware of what the eye is expressing through distorted functioning and/or structure. The alienated affective expression can then be experienced. I (the eye) dare not see me or know how I feel. When I limit my sight, I deny that which is threatening and so avoid uncomfortable experiences or recognition of that which should not exist for me. To identify with the alienated feelings is to see again. This is necessary before lasting improvement of vision is possible.

The varying degrees of visual fusion and lack of fusion, in the extreme case of strabismus, are examples of the deficits in integration existing in the patient. The right eye functions independently of the left. Thus a conflict is expressed directly in the eyes again. When one eye is permitted to have a dialogue with the other, each voicing the feelings expressed through that part of the personality, the split is understood. When the patient recognizes the conflicting expressions and strife of his personality, there is closure, relief, and comfort, and the two eyes are able to work together. Oneness or wholeness is then experienced and the fusion difficulty no longer exists. In other words, binocularity (fusion) and integration of the personality go together.

There is no split between mind and body, but parts of the personality can be split off and alienated. Whatever one is not in touch with in one's personality cannot be expressed and used for growth. It is essential for the implicit to become explicit. Ordering oneself to change, however, only exaggerates the split. Genuine change occurs only when one is in touch with self. Then ears that dared not hear, eyes that dared not see, and a heart that dared not feel can come to life again and function normally.

REFERENCES

Bates, W.H. *The cure of imperfect sight by treatment without glasses.* New York: Control Fixation Pub. Co., 1920.

Kelley, C. R. *The psychological factors in myopia.* Unpublished doctoral dissertation, New School for Social Research, New York, 1958.

Palmer, R. D. Visual acuity and excitement. *Psychosomatic Medicine,* 1966, *28,* 364-374.

Perls, F. S. *Ego, hunger and aggression.* New York: Random House, 1969. (Orig. publ., London: George Allen & Unwin, 1947.)

Rosanes, Marilyn. *Psychological correlates to myopia compared to hyperopia and emmetropia.* Unpublished doctoral dissertation, Yeshiva University, New York, 1966.

Van Alphen, G. W. *On emmetropia and ametropia.* New York: S. Korger, 1961.

Van Alphen, G. W., et al. A comparative psychological investigation in myopes and emmetropes. *Proceedings of the Royal Netherlands Academy of Science, Amsterdam, Series C:55,* 1952, *5,* 689-696.

Young, F. A. The development and retention of myopia by monkeys. *American Journal of Optometry & Archives of American Academy of Optometry,* 1961, No. 292.

CHAPTER 21

AWARENESS TRAINING IN THE MENTAL HEALTH PROFESSIONS

John B. Enright

Competence in clinical work in the mental health professions requires accessibility to the flow of inner experience. The first and most subtle cue to some state in the other—anxiety, hostility, sexiness, etc.—is awareness of some similar or complementary state in oneself. This would certainly be accepted as a theoretical statement by most people in the mental health professions, but when it comes to practice or teaching, we are not always consistent. For example, we often teach students to observe external signs of affective states in their patients (for example, voice and appearance changes), neglecting to make clear that external observation is not the way things really work. If I wait until my patient's veins are bulging, his neck is red, and his voice low with fury, to say "I believe you are angry," then I and the relationship are in trouble. If I am open to my own experience, long before the state described above has been reached, I will have been aware of some at first puzzling irritation and/or fear in myself. My awareness of this will then spontaneously help shape the ensuing events in the interview and hopefully lead to some usable, conscious expression of anger by the patient rather than the extreme organismic expression described above.

Although recognition of the importance of awareness of inner experience has been increasing for some time in the mental health professions, there seems to have been a "training gap" in its practical use. For years, the importance of awareness and the ways of achieving it were taught only haphazardly and as a by-product of other teaching. Good students developed it because they had the knack and because they identified with teachers who also had it, but there was little conscious focusing on the process of awareness per se. Often, when the need for increased awareness was recognized, personal psychotherapy would be suggested. Although often fairly successful in helping the student achieve this kind of awareness, psychotherapy is expensive and gives a subtle flavor of pathology to the whole process, as though awareness were to be reserved for "problems" rather than illuminating all life and interaction. In the past few years, group therapy for trainees has become more widespread and, more recently, encounter groups and sensitivity-training groups have begun to fill this training gap satisfactorily. There is still, however, much room for experimentation and for trying many approaches. For a number of reasons, I have found the philosophy and techniques of Gestalt therapy ideal for presenting students with the concept of awareness and with a practical training situation in which to develop the techniques and attitude of awareness. The purpose of this paper is to describe the use of Gestalt therapy for this purpose and to discuss some of its advantages.

Before presenting the training situation, a brief discussion of the concept of awareness is necessary. Awareness is immediate experience developing with, and as part of, an ongoing organism-environment transaction in the present. Although it includes thinking and feeling, it is always based on current perceptions of the current situation. Awareness includes some intention and directionality of the self toward the world; in pure form, there is a momentary weakening of the self-other barrier and the "object" of awareness seems momentarily to be included in the self.

A few people seem to experience this condition more or less continuously. In them, it is nothing special, just there, flowing along with behavior. For most of us, who tend to block this state of consciousness fairly regularly, the experience of awareness is frequently accompanied by a feeling of tension release that is pleasurable even if the awareness is of a painful situation. Since the organism and the world are never exactly the same, awareness always includes a sense of discovering the unknown and of taking a chance. I am quite serious in asserting that most of us, including those of us in the mental health professions, are much of the time, to a surprising extent, not fully aware of our actual present. Much of the content of our consciousness is remembering, speculating, planning ("rehearsing" for our next interpersonal performance), or carrying on a busy inner dialogue (or monologue). More specifically, we professionals sitting with a patient may be diagnosing, "prognosing," planning our next interpretation, wondering what time it is getting to be, etc.—we are only too rarely being really open to our own experience of self and other. Those of us who are not seriously mentally ill remain sufficiently in touch with the actual environment to move through it reasonably effectively. We respond to its salient characteristics, but miss so many nuances that our experience of the world and the other is often pale and our memories of it, therefore, weak. Engaged as we are with our own phantoms, we attend only sketchily to the other. Since he then seems rather pale and incomplete, we fill him out with our own projections and react vigorously to these. The resulting encounter often gives a convincing show of life and involvement where, in fact, there is little. It is probably true that many of us in the mental health professions, through dint of effort and sense of duty, attend better to our patients than to people in the rest of our lives, but with them, too, we suffer from the inability really to listen fully and see clearly.

It is, I believe, possible to teach students in the mental health professions quite directly how to get in closer touch with the constant flow of subjective awareness that is always potentially present. It might be more accurate to say that the student comes to awareness training more to unlearn than to learn. He has already had, as a developing human being, thousands of hours of highly motivated training in awareness of self and other. Unfortunately, he has also spent thousands of hours, in home, school, peer group, and profession, learning to suppress such awareness in the name of decency, order, adjustment, and decorum. Much of what happens in an awareness training seminar simply helps him reclaim to fuller awareness what he already knows. Not that decency, order, etc. are set aside or the necessity for them denied. Rather, the need for such control is shifted from the control (or blocking) of *awareness* to the control (or modulation) of *behavior*. With broader awareness of where he is, whom he is with, and what he is doing, come more choices, more flexibility, and hence more precise appropriateness of behavior—in both a person's professional and his personal life.

The broad goals of awareness training usually make sense to trainees quite readily and can be presented conceptually in a few minutes. It remains then to demonstrate, to structure a situation in which individuals can experience the expansion of awareness directly in themselves and feel the consequences of taking this view seriously. We set out to maximize the individual's awareness of, and responsibility for, his own actual, total behavior in this place, at this time, with these people. In keeping with the concreteness and orientation of Gestalt therapy toward actual behavior rather than abstract conceptualizations, I will simply describe what I do in a typical awareness training group, recognizing that another person with another group would live these principles in his own unique and thus somewhat different way.

The group format or structure in which awareness training can be done is extremely flexible. I have conducted groups involving from four to about forty people, with students and with practitioners of most of the mental health disciplines, for anywhere from one to thirty sessions. The principles of this point of view and some experiencing of it can be quite vividly presented in one session of about an hour and a half, leaving some permanent effect on at least some of the members. Longer periods of time, of course, will have a greater effect on more people, but it is remarkable how much of the essence of this point of view can be presented quickly.

TECHNIQUES OF AWARENESS TRAINING

For a single session with a large group, I begin with a brief abstract statement of the awareness concept, then I form a small circle of six to eight volunteers in front of the larger group (in a smaller group, of course, everyone joins the circle). The starting situation is quite similar no matter how large the group, how many meetings are anticipated, or who the members are. Individuals in the group are asked to take a few minutes each, simply to begin a few sentences with "Now I am aware that—" No further instructions are offered, and feedback from other group members and the leader is minimized during the first round of this experiment. The leader will occasionally assist an individual through a long hesitation by asking, "What are you experiencing now?" or just "And now?" Direct questions to the leader or another person—for example "Is this right?" "What do you think?", etc.—are simply rephrased into the suggested format. "Now I am aware of wondering if I am doing this correctly." "Now I am aware of wanting to ask—" The first two or three times that an individual seems to run down and show signs of wishing to stop, I try to help him report this experience of running down and wishing to stop. "My mind is blank, I can't go on," becomes "Now I am aware of feeling blank and unable to go on," but after two or three such assists, I terminate with one person and go on to the next.

By the time everyone has finished one round of the experiment, most individuals are bursting with comments about their own experiences while doing the experiment or their observations of others. Comments on their own or other people's limited repertoire of phenomena are common. Frequently, individuals will report some additional experience they had, either those held back during the first round or those experienced while someone else was reporting. During this discussion, we usually touch on a number of common features; one is the phenomenon of censoring, which, of course, everyone experienced usually without reporting it. I point out that in doing the experiment, they can report awareness of the *act* (censoring) without getting into the material censored. This discussion often serves as a springboard for the general point that an *activity* (censoring, remembering, anticipating, speculating) is something other than its *content* (the memory, anticipated event, theory, etc.). This is of fundamental importance in the development of the awareness technique. An individual who, as he reports a memory, can maintain the steady background awareness "Now I am reporting a memory," is not losing touch with his current actuality and getting lost in the memory, or speculation, or whatever. To attain this separation requires considerable practice, but I want to point out and begin to practice this separation as soon as possible.

I will also usually point out, if the group has not already done so, how each individual tends to limit himself to certain domains of awareness, concentrating perhaps on muscular sensations, visceral, visual, auditory, or in the case of most professional groups, concentrating very heavily on almost purely cognitive-verbal activity. Usually most professional groups also are struck with the extent to which they structure the experiment as a *task*—as a *product* for which they will be "graded" or which can be done rightly or wrongly. Frequently, individuals in the professions also respond to the experiment as a situation in which there is something wrong with them if they can't "produce." I try to convey the recognition that there is no way *not* to do the experiment; that the awareness of feeling unable to go on is a respectable awareness, with as much validity as anything else they could produce. The feeling of searching for something to report, is itself something to report. Even at this early stage, I begin to introduce the notion that the way to hang onto a feeling and be stuck with it is not to report it, whereas to report fully any awareness clears the way for something new.

The first time the group goes through this experiment, I give as little direction as possible and discourage comments from others in the group. It is impossible to avoid some implicit setting of group standards and expectations, but in general I try to keep it as open and unstructured as possible. At the end of the first trial, then, everyone has struggled with this elusive "task" of reporting awareness and has experienced a certain amount of strain, discomfort, and awkwardness, frequently leading to some resentment against me or the task. Everyone has watched the others in the group do the experiment and has seen them obviously structure the situation in ways that make it difficult for themselves, and usually everyone has experienced the feeling of wanting to show someone else how easy it is and set them straight. Finally, everyone has had a chance to discuss and conceptualize, and of course, most students in our professions immediately feel more at ease in this kind of occupation than in the awareness experiment itself.

The next step is to begin to manipulate the person or situation to alter or expand his awareness. In whatever way he is blocking the growth and development of awareness in himself, we want him to begin to unblock. What and how we do this must grow out of each individual's attempt to perform the awareness experiment. Sometimes this next phase can develop spontaneously out of the discussion, and we can move directly from concept discussion into the awareness frame of reference. For example, if I feel I am getting into an argument with a member of the group or playing the evidence game, I may report this awareness and ask for his. If I see two people beginning to compete with each other, as occasionally happens ("My awareness is more aware than your awareness"), I may try to make this competition explicit. Frequently, after the first discussion time, I formally go back into the awareness experiment in order to introduce this second phase, usually selecting as a starter whoever in the group has shown the most interest and readiness for this kind of experience.

In this second attempt at the awareness experiment, instead of leaving it open and unstructured, and letting happen whatever happens, I begin actively to engage with each individual in some way that will help him stop blocking or limiting himself. The simplest approach to this is to begin to ask him to concentrate on the hitherto ignored facets of his behavior, to bring the "fringe" temporarily into the center of awareness. He is showing us all the time in his tensions and attention what is important to him organismically; now we ask him to bring these into awareness. Such comments as the following are typical of this approach. "Are you aware that you are smiling?" "Can you describe what you are doing with your hands?" "Can you experience how you are sitting in the chair?" "Can you hear your voice? How does it sound to you?", "What are you looking at now?", "I noticed you glanced at X—what were you aware of just then?" What happens next, of course, depends on the person. In his response, I listen for whatever seems most involving or central to him and pick up in some way on that. If he describes, for instance, that he is holding his left hand with his right, I might ask him which hand he notices more—the one holding or the one held—and then suggest he write a dialogue between the hands; what would the right hand say to the left, what would the left hand answer back. If, as he glanced at someone else in the group, he was aware of hoping to make a good impression, I might suggest to him that he say directly to this person, "I want to make a good impression on you." Whatever his awareness, I will ask him to act in some way to expand it, to include in it more of what he is doing.

Occasionally, this approach will lead to a rather sudden expansion of awareness with attendant relief and pleasure. A nurse in one group reported feeling pain in her left leg as her most vivid sensation. I asked her what she could do to increase the pain and she demonstrated that, by leaning further away from me the pain became greater. Most members of the group could immediately see the significance of this but not she. Then I asked her to play the part of her leg and asked her what the leg would say to her. Speaking as her leg, she said, "Stop putting so much pressure on me!" Still she sat there tense and expectant. I then asked if there was anyone in her current environment that she, as herself, could make that same statement to. At that point, she and the group burst into laughter, and it was simple for her to make the statement to me. (Of course, paradoxically, when she *could* make the statement to me, she no longer needed to.)

In another group, a man was talking rather hesitantly in a bored voice while looking mostly past me rather than at me. "What are you looking at?"

"The tree tops outside the window."

"Can you describe them?"

"They are waving so freely."

"What would you like to say to them?"

"Tree tops, I envy you so free out there."

"What might they say to you?"

"Do we feel sorry for you, trapped down there in that stuffy room!"

"And who is trapping you?"

At this point, the man could possibly expand his perspective, realizing that he is in the room on a totally voluntary basis and, in fact, in most ways enjoys being there. Perhaps then he could begin to experience how he produces in himself the "trapped" feeling. If he still seemed preoccupied with the image of being trapped, perhaps we might then ring him with chairs, *really* trapping him physically, and explore his experience in that situation.

More frequently, these interventions that point out other facets on which to focus awareness simply are small steps without the sudden and dramatic effects described above, but we keep working with them against the chronic narrowing and shutting out of awareness that most people engage in reflexively and routinely.

The above examples are fairly simple ones in which the point we arrived at in a few minutes was never very far from awareness. Many times, the movements or tensions that substitute for, and therefore block, awareness are far more inaccessible, often being "miniaturized" into tiny movements that are almost invisible and yet sum up and sustain a whole point of view and set of expectations about life. For example, one medical student in a group punctuated almost every remark (made in a very intense voice) with a flick of his head to the right. I had another student stand behind him and hold his head fairly tightly. After a minute or two, the head movement disappeared and the man began to flick his right wrist slightly at the end of each comment. Another student held his wrist. Soon a fairly noticeable shrug of the right shoulder appeared to replace that. At this point, I had him then exaggerate the shrug extensively, turning it into an entire body movement; within a minute or two, he was able to put this gesture into the words, "Who cares?" This was the miniaturized organismic counterpoint to his overtly expressed close interest in what I was saying.

One phenomenon I have occasionally been able to open up within one session—although it frequently takes longer—is the fundamental disturbance of awareness I call *attributing*. This is the phenomenon of directly experiencing a feeling as though it were someone else's. For example, "So-and-so is bored with the group." "I am aware they are expecting something from me." "X is mad at me." For many people this is experienced as a primitive, irreducible phenomenon, no more puzzling or unusual-seeming than the fact that if we touch an object with a stick held in the hand we actually "feel" the touch at the end of the stick, rather than in the hand. Nor is there anything "wrong" with this mode of experiencing, except when the person uses it to block another experience (either similar or complementary) which would be felt as belonging to *him* in the relationship rather than as belonging to the *other*. If, by concentrating awareness on the other's expectation, I avoid awareness of my own need to produce, I am less in touch with the whole transaction and my part in it and, therefore, less able to function optimally in it. Likewise, if I experience someone else as angry, and use this experience to mask my own anger, I am not fully in touch with the transaction and my part in it, and will eventually act inappropriately in it. These phenomena are usually lumped under the term "projection"; I find "attributing" more precisely descriptive and acceptable for these particular manifestations.

The task of awareness training when the individual reports this mode of experience is somehow to disturb or shake up the perceptual balance he has thus achieved so he will find the experience more truly his own. I remember vividly how this was done to me for the first time when, in a group I had just joined, I commented, "X looks like he is looking at the rest of us as if we're a bunch of insects under a microscope." Immediately, I was asked to look at each other group member in turn as though through a microscope and express this attitude toward him. At first, the activity seemed very forced and artificial, but I gradually felt some genuine feeling and force behind it; and by the time I had gone around the group, I was involved in expressing this feeling quite strongly. I went on at this time to discover also my fear of being an outsider in a group, and of being rejected by them. It is, interestingly, irrelevant whether or not I was correct in my attribution. As a matter of fact, X reported later that he did feel pretty much the feeling attributed to him. The demonstration of attributing and its function is sometimes more dramatic and easier if the attribution happens to be quite wrong, but it may be completely correct and still indicate a disturbance of awareness. It is rather rare that much can be done with the phenomenon of attributing in one or two meetings, but at least it can be clarified and challenged, and the individual set up for later questioning of his own use of it.

One other kind of interaction is fairly common even in the first meeting of a group. This is an individual's claiming not to hear or understand one or more of my comments or questions. I know my level of volume and intellectual clarity quite well, and if in my opinion I have not departed too much from my usual level, I will refuse to repeat or clarify when asked. Instead, I will ask, "What did you hear?" or "What did you understand?" Far more often than not, the individual can answer, repeating what I said verbatim. This is often a dramatic demonstration to the rest of the group of "denial," but more importantly, the individual himself can almost experience denial from within, can actually experience wishing not to hear even as he recognizes he has. The full exploration of the significance and function of this phenomenon for the individual can wait until later; in the beginning, it is enough simply to take a dramatic step away from manipulative dependency to responsible reliance on one's own senses. Similarly, the individual who presents himself as confused and not understanding can be brought to the point of experiencing directly his wish not to understand instead of masking this as confusion.

When some individuals in a group seem anxious or reluctant to participate, I have found it desirable to start with more structured exercises. A great variety is available from a variety of sources: psychodrama, body awareness, theater games, communication theory, etc. These can all be presented and discussed from the awareness point of view, and can serve as nonthreatening ways for group members to get involved with each other and with me. As such a group progresses and comfort increases, we can move to a more "open-ended" format in which each member's modes of blocking awareness through posture, language habits, and repetitive roles can be explored in more individualized ways. Dreams, fantasies, and outside life events can be increasingly brought in and translated as much as possible to the here-and-now frame of reference. Whether the meeting is brief or extended, structured or open ended, the aim throughout is to position people to expand their awareness of their current behavior, and to demonstrate the power of the Gestalt principles of *concrete attention to detail*, rather than abstract conceptualizing; *doing, with organismic involvement*, instead of talking about; and *accepting responsibility for one's own behavior* instead of denying, projecting, attributing, displacing, etc.

AWARENESS TRAINING VERSUS GROUP THERAPY

Obviously, a group extended over time begins to resemble group therapy in many ways. Much of what is done and said could well happen in a therapy group, and the results are frequently "therapeutic". Nonetheless, I try to avoid forming a therapy contract or structuring the group as therapy for two reasons. One is that occasionally, in some settings, a student does not feel that it is appropriate for his department to *require* therapy—a position with which I quite agree. However, I still feel that advanced students in the mental health professions must be exposed to some form of training in awareness expansion and be put under some pressure to use it. In the awareness training situation, the student is exposed to the opportunity of seeing others use the situation.

To insure that I or the group does not get overly zealous and put too much pressure on an individual, I have developed the convention that anyone can signal he wishes to stop and withdraw at any time. I may ask him what his objection is to continuing, but I will honor his request. Occasionally, it is frustrating to stop in the middle of an interesting and probably valuable interaction, but it is of overriding importance that the student retain control over his involvement. Sometimes, someone will use the signal to be coy rather than because he is genuinely anxious. It is usually amusing to watch such a person become reinvolved in the next two or three minutes after stopping, and sometimes even fight to reachieve the position he has just abandoned.

One other reason for avoiding the therapy model is that, unfortunately, the therapeutic process is commonly regarded as necessarily a sober and serious business. This tone I most heartily wish to avoid. I will often suggest that a group view the session as adult play in which we might pursue a fancy or develop a fantasy just for the hell of it, even if no serious learning purpose can be discerned at the outset. I will occasionally make faces at people or mimic and exaggerate their posture without any explanation or warning. At times, when a conversation is getting deadly serious and we are losing touch with the real situation, getting lost in speculation, I will interrupt and suggest a babble conversation in which we talk to each other without words but try to convey everything we can simply by voice tone. If someone objects to one of my suggestions (for example, that they babble, or talk to an empty chair, or stand up and assume some posture) on the grounds that it is "silly," I will instantly do something similar but sillier. I have stood on chairs, lain down on the floor, and assumed any number of bizarre postures to shake people out of their deadly serious physical and psychological postures. At times, I have short-circuited verbal arguments that were getting heated by suggesting we Indian wrestle. The attitude I attempt to convey is that, just as children learn the most important lessons in life in their most totally carefree play, so do adults often become more effective in what they are doing and enjoy it more when they can "let go" and stop trying so hard to accomplish something.

The attitude and techniques of *awareness* and some of the procedures for communicating this point of view, either in one-time demonstrations or in continuous groups, have been based on the principles of Gestalt therapy, as developed by Perls and others. This point of view is very simply that continual in-touch-ness with the flow of subjective awareness of the self-world interaction here and now is the most trustworthy source of information available to an individual. No amount of speculation or other purely cognitive activity can lead as surely to behavior that is natural and right for him in this time-place. Furthermore, a normal individual has *already fully developed* the capacity for this flow of awareness, but has also learned a variety of ways of closing off the flow. The goal of awareness training is to help him discover and thereafter modify his own particular ways of shutting out awareness. As a by-product of doing this for himself, he will learn some ways of helping others to do the same, but such "techniques" of therapy are only by-products of his own work with himself, and I have come to believe that it would be a mistake for a student to undertake awareness training primarily as a way of learning techniques to use on others.

Some of the approaches and "techniques" described here (by-products of my own search for fuller awareness) have seemed helpful to many people. The point of view developed in such training seems not to be incompatible with any theory or school of therapy and can give additional depth and breadth to almost any point of view. Awareness training can be undertaken individually with an experienced Gestalt therapist as teacher-therapist, or strictly by oneself, using the excellent program for self-teaching presented in *Gestalt Therapy* by Perls, Hefferline, and Goodman. I have found the group situation, however, to be by far the most effective setting for this kind of personal development.

CHAPTER 22

THE GESTALT
ART EXPERIENCE

Janie Rhyne

The sessions I lead are therapeutically oriented experiences in which the participants work with art materials to create paintings and sculptured forms as a means of becoming aware of themselves and their environment on a perceptual level. Although we use words to describe what we do and how we do it, the basic emphasis is on the preverbal, primitive level of immediate experiencing.

The approach is based on Perls's formulations of Gestalt therapy. My background training as an art therapist includes a self-designed academic program combining art, psychology, and anthropology, to which I have added several hundred hours of working as a participant in Gestalt therapy workshops led by various Gestalt-oriented psychotherapists.

Many people are curious about what we do in the art-experience sessions. Are we doing therapy? Are we creating art forms? Are we having fun? Are we playing games? Are we being childish? Are we acting like idiots?

My answer is that we are doing all of these. The activities or products may seem chaotic and meaningless, but they are related to the philosophy that knowing for one's self on the perceptual level is the most valid kind of knowing.

Most of the participants in the art groups function adequately in their living situations. Rather than therapy, they are seeking some added dimensions in their lives, such as increased self-awareness, enjoyment, or spontaneity.

I offer an assortment of art materials (clay, paint, glue, chalk) to an assortment of people (psychiatrists, nurses, social workers, hippies, middle-class suburbanites). I suggest that they use the experience of working with these materials to find out what they are feeling inside themselves. I also ask them to experiment with their senses and patterns of movement to find what message they want to give themselves, to trust their own inner awareness of what they want to express, so that they discover in themselves the capacity to create their own nonverbal symbolic language.

Each person recognizes and interprets the images he makes in his own way. Some beautiful art forms emerge from this process, and some fearfully ugly ones. But aesthetics is irrelevant when we are working for self-discovery, and judgments of good or bad are eliminated as irrelevant. The question asked is, "What are you finding out about yourself?"

My job is not to analyze. The participants find their own answers in images and sometimes in verbalizing their private explorations to the group and to me. I am catalyst and facilitator, responding to movements, representations, and words. Although I have learned techniques to help people to get in touch with hidden areas of themselves, my best response is intuitive. I know that the best thing I can bring to my work is a sense of relatedness between me and the individual with whom I am working. When I go with him and feel with him, good things happen for both of us. When I am alienated from myself or he from himself, nothing valid happens to either of us.

The groups I lead vary in scheduling so much that even if I wanted to, I could not work out a program or single procedure to use consistently. Some groups are with me for only one evening, some for a weekend; some spend several hours daily for a week or more, and some come together once a week for a number of months. The kinds of people who come are also varied—in their backgrounds, ages, motivations, and general orientation in living. I continue to be fascinated by the differences I see in these individuals and also by a deep communality that emerges when differences are not only accepted by the participants but are welcomed as a way for each person to realize a wider comprehension of the infinite range of variation among persons.

However, some of the groups consist of people who come together because of mutual interests and so bring a certain group identity with them. For instance, I have worked with groups of black teen-agers, young students from an experimental college, the psychiatric staff of a university hospital, inexperienced psychiatric nurses in training, etc. Naturally, each of these diverse groups has a sort of in-group personality with its own attitudes, ways of verbalizing, and modes of self-expression which influences the way I relate to it and the specific projects I propose. As much as I can, I get the sense of the group and choose the techniques I feel will be most effective for that particular constellation of people at that time.

I respond to what I feel as being important happenings among the participants and expect myself as well as each of them to be flexible in how and what we do in any session. However, I have designed a "process pattern," which I find a natural and effective sequence of ways of exploration into each person's perceptual awareness areas. The parts of the pattern develop as the process of discovery takes place. When there is time enough, I encourage people to use the art materials simply to find how and what they can express graphically instead of verbally; they discover their own vocabulary of forms and colors. Then, depending on the amount of time available, we begin the process of exploring-experiencing-expressing, with concentration on each person's sensing of himself alone. Emphasis is on the ungrammatical but essential awareness of *"This is me. I am."* In this phase, I stress concentration on personal identity unrelated to environment or others. I then propose a gradual progression of learning to include a perception of self in space, in time, in relationship to one another, in relationship with several others, and finally, in moving within the group in various environments.

In the process, I not only allow for but actively encourage times of regression and retreat into one's self. In a continuing group, the participants begin to create their own process, which develops in its own particular way. As this happens, I become less directive and act only as a catalyst and guide. Sometimes the group becomes essentially autonomous and needs me only to provide materials and suggestions for using the art experience to become more aware of what is happening. I am delighted when this takes place. I learn much from this process and feel free to become a participant myself, enlarging my own experiencing along with the others.

The eleven art experiences which follow illustrate the process I have described above. The reader is invited to make possible his own art experiences by carrying out any or all of the suggested procedures. Attempted or not, they give some indication of the kinds of experiences made possible through this approach.

SUGGESTIONS FOR DEVELOPING YOUR PERSONAL VOCABULARY OF SEEING, SOUNDING, MOVING

Have in front of you sheets of paper of varying sizes and shapes. If in a studio, have many kinds of chalks, crayons, pens, brushes, and paints that are yours to use. The studio should be large and secluded enough for you to move about and to be free to make any noises you want to.

And so, begin to find out for yourself your personal vocabulary for expressing yourself nonverbally.

The brilliantly colored chalks are coarse and dry. They fit into your fist and you can make bold lines and shapes.

The wax crayons are smaller and harder. The lines and forms you can make with them are shiny and slick, definite and clean.

The oil crayons are delicate and soft. You can blend them into rich tones that merge into one another.

The felt-tip pens contain watercolors. You can draw fluid lines and fill in clear, transparent areas.

With the paints, you can do almost anything; but they require more skill and take more time, so wait to use them until you have some knowledge of your own way of expressing yourself with form and color.

Do not decide what you are going to *try* to draw. Just go ahead and do what you feel like doing. Pick a color you like and move it around on the paper—scribble, doodle, let go of your trying. Make happy lines, tender lines, angry lines. Fill in shapes that express something you feel. Try different colors and various combinations of shapes. Recognize those that have some significance to you personally. Repeat those forms on other sheets of paper, not analyzing or even interpreting what meaning they have for you. Just be aware of how you are feeling when you make them.

You learn for yourself your own visual language; in creating your individual way of expression, you discover the messages you give yourself.

As you draw, begin making noises that seem to express the forms you are making. Don't use words—only sounds and only your own sounds, the ones that feel natural to you. Don't stop drawing; let your sounds flow with your lines. You synchronize your visual rhythms with your vocal ones. Then, stop drawing and start moving your body in whatever way you find you want to, expressing what you have drawn and the sounds you are still making. Stand up and dance; lie down and roll; sit and rock; crawl, stomp, wiggle, leap, curl up—whatever movement seems to convey to you what you are feeling. Your movements are part of your private sensory language, and the sounds you make are your own way of saying something to yourself without wordiness.

Now, you are communicating nonverbally, with sights and sounds and movements, sending and receiving messages. *You are using your personal preverbal vocabulary.*

My nonverbal language changes as I change and I discover it as I use it. To me, a bright clear red is noisy and a purplish scarlet moans quietly. Pale blue whispers; black is silent. Orange and yellow move toward me. Mauve retreats, and greens stay where they are. A line moving from the bottom of a page quickly upward has a rising inflection. If it goes off the page into space, it makes a noise like "*whoo-oo-oo-oop*"; a straight, broad band moving horizontally across a page hums quietly; a curved spiral sings its rhythm with a lilt; a lot of little dots and broken shapes chatter. A perfect circle and an unbroken sphere say something like "*om*." A thick, dark, descending line groans heavily.

These are some of my personal, subjective ways of perceiving sights, sounds, and motions all at once. When I draw or paint, I am putting some part of my sensing self into the process of discovering how I am communicating what I am aware of in myself. When I make noises, I am hearing myself sounding my feelings; when I move and become aware of how I am moving, I am experiencing myself as an instrument for expressing myself.

You have a preverbal language, too. Yours and mine are each unique to each of our personal selves; each of us has created a private vocabulary based on our individual ways of experiencing and perceiving. Ordinarily, we are not aware of using this kind of language in communicating with each other. Usually, we rely on the content of words to get across our thought to other people. We even talk to ourselves with words, either aloud or subvocally, carrying on a dialogue with ourselves. While we do this word-ing, we are not usually conscious that our silent languages are expressing how we really feel: Your handwriting indicates how you are feeling. The doodles you make are a way of saying something. The tone of your voice conveys messages beyond, and sometimes quite different from, the content of your structured sentences. Your gestures and body movements communicate your emotions.

Although each of us uses an individual silent language, we are not usually aware that we are giving and receiving communications that have nothing to do with words. But in this particular art experience, you do become aware of what you are expressing; of how you are *being* right then in the group. You show one another your drawings and listen to one another's sounds and see one another's movements. Your awareness of yourself and of others is more deeply felt and more explicit when you enhance your verbal ability to say what you think with the natural capacity to perceive and express how you *are* with your whole self.

CREATING YOUR SELF WITH CLAY

Twelve people sit on the floor in a large circle, apart but facing one another. Hold in your hands a lump of clay. Let your palms and fingers feel the clay—cool, damp, slippery—a mass of dirt and water. With your hands, arms, and shoulders, weigh the clay. Move it from one hand to the other, getting the feel of it, balancing it, rolling it around as you will. Throw it lightly upward and catch it again. With your hands, explore how you can mold the clay, changing its surface, its texture, and its form. You can press, twist, squeeze, stretch, break, gouge, fold, smooth, scratch, caress—do all of these things to the clay and be aware of what you are feeling as you do them.

With your eyes closed, staying with your own feelings, fantasize as if you are dreaming—play a game with yourself in pretending *this lump of clay is you.* You can create your self by what you do to yourself. Do what you feel like doing, and feel what you like doing. Do not try to conceive of any representation of yourself or try to form any image of yourself. Let form or formlessness emerge or not as you make a record of your movements with the clay.

As your hands move, they will shape the clay. As you touch the surface of the clay, you will texture it. Be aware of the forms and tactual qualities of the clay as you feel them in relationship to you and what you do to yourself in living. If, in this process, a form grows and you recognize it as having personal meaning to you, let the form develop as it will, and let it change as you feel right with the changing. When you feel a sense of discovery and excitement, go with this excitement and create the form that feels like you. Open your eyes and see the form you have created. Be aware of your identity with it and of how much you can accept the clay as being an expression of *you.* As you look at your clay figure, relax your eyes, letting them become receivers of your image and your perception of yourself. Beginning with your eyes, relax your whole body. Lie down on the floor in a comfortable position and let yourself go on a fantasy trip. For these minutes, imagine that there is no one in the world but you.

What are you? You are not a simple, monolithic being. You are a complex structure, with many parts making up your whole. Physically, emotionally, and spiritually you are continuously in motion within yourself. Every part of you is affected by every other part—you cannot separate your mind from your body from your soul. Your breathing affects your feeling, your thinking affects your breathing; when you feel fear, you become tense, when you're tense, you can't feel—when you don't trust your senses, you think so much you can't know anything that makes sense. All of these complex, interwoven patterns are you. You are a whole, too, functioning as a figure with the world around you as your background. You are a constellation in a galaxy. You are enough to make you dizzy. Allow yourself to be dizzy. Stop analyzing, stop thinking, and allow yourself to sense and *accept your being you as you are*—let yourself flow with yourself wherever your fantasies take you.

You may go far away and isolate yourself in your private world—wherever you are. In your own time, begin coming back into the world of here and now. Bring yourself back into the group. Open your eyes and see all the others around you. Be aware of each person in the room and receive what you can from each.

Speak to them of your experience in making your image only if you want to. Know, if you speak, that you can never, with words, describe the totality of your experience. At best, you can tell us only a condensed version. Sometimes, however, if you feel strongly about what you have done, your words, your tone of voice, perhaps your tears or laughter, may say it all. If not, and you feel frustrated at not being able to express what you experience, remember that the important thing is that you know what you are saying to yourself—that you recognize and accept as yours whatever you have done.

YOUR SELF IN YOUR ENVIRONMENT

Select from the varied sizes, shapes, and colors of papers provided, one particular piece you can imagine as representing to you as you feel in your personal environment at this moment. Choose one drawing tool: pencil, crayon, chalk, paint, or even an ink-soaked rag that you can hold in your hand.

Sit where you will not be distracted by what the others are doing or the sounds they are making. Concentrate for a few moments on the blank sheet of paper and be aware that you have chosen this particular piece to symbolize your personal environment. Is it large or small, square or rectangular, rough or smooth, light or dark? Consider your choice and what it may mean to you. Do the same with the drawing tool you selected. Take your time and give your imagination freedom to roam about in quiet awareness.

When you feel that you are using the right media and space, begin simply and slowly by making one mark on the paper and consider its placement as representing where you are in your environment right now. In a corner? In the middle? At the bottom or top? Off to one side? Then, imagine this mark on the paper to be your center, and begin to extend its size, in any way that feels like you living from your center and in relationship to the boundaries of your chosen environment.

Do you stay small and simple, or do you spread out all over the page? Is the area too large for you or do you feel confined by too little room in which to be you? How do you feel as you enlarge the shape of you in your environment? Do you stay close to your center or leave it isolated while you wander all over the page?

Stay with your awareness of how and what you are doing, and do not judge or explain, even to yourself. Just find out for yourself how you feel yourself being in your present environment. Don't try to change anything. Just *know* for yourself where you are at this time in your perception of experiencing yourself as a figure on a background.

YOUR LIFE TIME

For this experiment you will need four rolls of paper of varying widths—six inches, one foot, three feet and four feet—and each hundreds of feet in length. You could spend many hours, maybe days, unrolling that paper and drawing on it, so for this experience I'd like you to fantasize that the length of paper in each roll represents infinity.

Choose which width of paper you want to use to draw and paint on and you can cut off as much length as you have a feeling for using. Before you make your choice, however, spend some time in a form of meditation. Get comfortable, close your eyes, and let yourself be cognizant of your concept of time in relationship to you. If you can, having realized how you conceive of time intellectually and abstractly, let go of those philosophical ideas; go into your perceiving of time as you *live* it. Time in itself neither begins nor ends; perhaps time curves, goes backward or forward, repeats, or stands still. I don't know what "it" does—and I don't think you do. So for now, forget "it."

We are all aware of our lifetime. I, as a process, a continuum of awareness, know time as *my lifetime*—passing, being, going. As I live in my time, I am involved with the conciousness of past-present-future. Let yourself, in fantasy, go into these areas. Wander around in your past, present, and future, and sense the space each has in your living and being. Don't try to understand, judge, or categorize your time sense. Simply find out for yourself how you live in *your* time.

Then choose a width of paper that seems right to you to draw on, and roll off as much length as you want, cutting off that amount of time-space for you to use in representing *your* temporal-spatial self. Use any medium and combination of techniques. Start anywhere on the paper and move in any direction. Divide the space into time areas as you feel like doing—or don't divide, if that's the way you see yourself living time.

In this experience, there are no rules for you to follow in expressing how you are living in time. Find out how you are living your lifetime and that's enough for here and now.

Use your drawing as a concrete reference when you talk to the group of how you are in your lifetime.

Use your art work as a bridge, communicating to yourself and to others some awareness of yourself in your lifetime which you know on a perceptive level but which you cannot express in words.

YOUR SELF AND AN OTHER IN SPACE

Sit facing a partner and between you place a large, blank sheet of paper and a basket of fist-size chalks of many colors. You and your partner look at each other directly for a time until you feel you have made contact, that on some level you know the other. Then, look at the paper between you; be aware of its spatial dimensions and realize that the space you see belongs to both of you; for now the paper represents an environment in which you two are being together. You both draw on the one sheet at the same time, discovering, as you do, what you feel in sharing your relationship with the other within that space. Using lines, shapes, and colors, you can communicate in many ways. Using no words, you can demand space to be left alone in; you can push your partner into a corner; you can share some areas or the whole page; you can go toward or retreat from each other; you can support, cross out, cover up, cooperate with, oppose, lead, or follow your partner. Your possibilities for nonverbal interaction are limitless.

When you both feel that you have finished your graphic communicating, talk a while with each other, finding out how explicitly you gave and received your messages. Then, change partners, and repeat the process.

You are representing graphically on a simple, primitive level your perception of territoriality and how it affects and is affected by your relationship with another person.

AN OTHER WHO IS ALSO YOU

Take in your hands a large amount of clay and hold it for awhile, moving the mass with your hands, letting them express what you are feeling without trying to be explicit, even to yourself, about what your hands are doing. Close your eyes and gradually focus your awareness on some person with whom you have deep emotional ties, someone primary in your ways of responding to life. This person may be miles away; you may not have had any contact with him for years; he may be physically dead; he may, perhaps, exist for you only in your fantasy life. Choose to concentrate on someone who is so much with you on an emotional level that you are unaware, on a conscious rational basis, of what part of you is this other, and whether or not you perceive the other at all, except as a part of you.

Find out, using the clay to make explicit for yourself, how you can form an image of this other as you perceive him to be. Be aware of how much of you is *your* imagery. How much of your emotional energy is invested in this other? Do you know experientially who the other *is*, apart from you? Can you separate his "is-ness" from your own? Is this other also you? Are you making an image of a disowned part of yourself?

Explore and discover your awareness as you work with the clay. Ask yourself the questions that seem relevant to you in this area and find your own answers.

GIVING ATTENTION TO ANOTHER PERSON

Choose a partner from the group, arranging by mutual consent to be with someone you do not know very well. Maybe you are interested in this other person and curious to know him better; maybe you don't like him; maybe he seems so alien to you that you can't communicate at all. Choose and be chosen.

Each of you takes handfuls of clay and a small clay board on which to work. Sit down on the floor back to back with your partner, each of you placing your clay in front of you but not touching it for a while. Instead, touch your partner with as much of your back, shoulders, head, and arms as you two can agree on nonverbally. Do not look at each other; make contact only with your touching and your movements. Lean on each other; push backward and forward; find out how you move together and how you do not. Give your full attention to sensing the other person as you feel him to be.

At a time when you, as partners, can communicate that you have reached some kind of recognition of the other, lean forward and begin working the clay into an image representing what impressions you have received from and with your partner in making contact only in this way. When you have finished the clay image, turn and face your partner and with the two clay figures between you, talk quietly and briefly with each other of how you've described your responses in making your clay images.

Then, providing yourselves with paper and drawing tools, come back to your same partner and sit facing each other, without touching, but close enough so that you can make contact with your eyes. See each other with your eyes; discover as much as you can of the other using only your eyes as senders and receivers of messages. Maintain this nonverbal relating as long as you both want to, staying with each other until you feel you really are with each other. Then, draw a portrait of the other as you know him through his eyes. The portrait can be representational, abstract, or symbolic; whatever way you want and can do it. Again, have a brief, quiet verbal conversation without going into detailed interpretations or explanations.

Now, try knowing the other through your hands. Touch and explore your partner's hands. Move your hands together in whatever way you two find natural for you. Be aware of your own feelings and desires and resistances, at the same time concentrating your attention on what your partner is conveying to you with his hands. When you feel that you have reached a time for terminating your contact, draw a representation of your experiencing him through your hands and his exploration of you.

Using all three images as references, speak now with each other in any way you want to, using words, touching, drawing, movement, and perhaps silence. Let yourselves be with each other as you can and want to be.

If you want to, and other partners agree, come together again as a group and present each other to the group as a whole. If there is time, change partners and repeat the sequence with another, being aware of how you respond to each. Be especially aware of how much you can know another being, unique, different, separate from you and at the same time *with* you in mutual response, when you give each other your concentrated attention.

CREATING A WORLD THAT IS YOU

For this experience, you use collage and assemblage as art techniques that make it possible for you to put all sorts of materials together in some way you identify as being *yours*. You can use paper, wood, wire, leaves, stones—anything that you find and want to use, and that communicates to you, "This is my world, made by me, for me, with whatever I choose to use."

The simplest technique is paper on paper, using rubber cement or white glue to make an arrangement of different colors, forms, and areas. You can use colored papers, both opaque and semitransparent; sections cut or torn from magazines, newspapers, wallpaper books; cardboard or parts of boxes. From a two-dimensional collage, you can build into a third dimension and make an assemblage. Or, you can begin with a structure which is a free-standing sculptural form or a mobile made to hang by wire from the ceiling.

Wander around for a while, in the studio and, if possible, outside, *seeing* what is available to you and being aware of your feeling of personal identification with materials and objects. You don't have to explain to yourself or to anyone else why you want to use some and not others. Coose what you feel like using and use them in any way you have a feeling for doing.

Perhaps, you will want to show your worlds to each other and talk about them with the group as a whole. Perhaps not. The important thing is that you see your own world and recognize for yourself, "I structured this world with materials I chose; within the limits of what is possible for me, I take responsibility for creating my own personal world."

ACCEPTING AND REJECTING WHAT IS OFFERED

Neither you nor I, in actuality, can choose entirely what will be in our personal worlds; we learn experientially in the living process that we must continually accept and reject from what is being offered to us by others. Each of us creates our own individual Gestalt by assimilating that which we can make a functional part of our own structure.

The next art experience can make you aware of how you feel and what you do when you let others put upon you anything they want to.

For this session, sit in a closed circle with one sheet of paper and felt-tip pens in many colors near you. Begin a drawing on your sheet of paper, starting but not finishing a graphic description of something important to you. At a signal, pass your drawing to the person on your left, at the same time receiving from the person on your right the drawing he has begun. See what this drawing means to you and work on it as if it were yours, adding and changing it as you want to. At the signal, pass this drawing to your left and receive another from your right, and so on around the circle until the drawing you began originally comes back to you.

You may not recognize it easily. What you put on the paper has been modified by what several others have put there. Your drawing may even be obliterated by those of others. But look at it and really see what is there on the page. Be aware of how you feel in seeing the expressions of others imposed on your own.

Is there anything of you left in that composite drawing? Is there anything which is not you, but which you'd like to keep? Are there areas you'd like to obliterate? What do you want to do with this pattern that is in your hands now? Using art materials, what can you do?

Be aware of your feelings and take some action that expresses them.

MAKING A WORLD TOGETHER

Sit around a large paper circle that belongs to all of you. Place on it a pile of assorted stuff: odd shapes of colored paper, pieces of string, straw, beads, bits of wood and foam rubber.

Pretend that the circle is a space where you, as a group, can create a world, and that the materials on the circle are elements from which you can choose, to use in creating a Gestalt, a figure on and related to the background of *your* world—the world you make here and now among yourselves.

From the pile of materials on the world, choose individually what you want to use in representing *you* in the world. Remove these from the common pile and claim them as your own. When each of you has done this, make a group decision as to what you will do with the materials left on the world, which no one wants to use at the moment.

Provide scissors, crayons, and glue to work with. Use these tools and your materials to create a collage on the circle representing your interrelationships and how you are perceiving yourselves as *being* in one limited environment. Talk with each other as you work, use sounds to express your responses, move about the circumference of the world, but stay with and be active in making the world, unless you do not want to have any part in this activity. If you feel a need to withdraw, leave the room physically.

There are no rules as to what kind of world you create and how you go about it except those that evolve among you in the process of your working and being together as intensely as you can be. As you do this, be aware of your personal role in this process and your feelings of how much of what you are doing now you also do in your real-world living situation.

You are playing an imagery game that makes concrete and explicit your acceptance of yourself as an active creator of the world of process with many others—what we are each being and doing in an environment which is nothing in itself. With our capacities for awareness and our abilities for action, we make our own world out of materials available to us.

The representations we make of our perceptions of our ways of being in our world are "images" when we make them with art materials. This imagery can become a way of exploring, experiencing, and expressing what is not imagery—what is the reality of me and of you, speaking in the first person singular in the present tense.

MOVING TOGETHER

For this art experience, the most essential element is your own willingness to let go of your dignity and let happen what will.

You also need space—a big space to move in and a hard, rough surface to draw on. A tennis court is perfect; a wide sidewalk will do. Have several boxes of brilliantly colored chalks handy—the big, fat, fist-sized ones. Wear old clothes and go barefoot. When you finish, you'll be a mess so have hot water and soap somewhere nearby.

With chalk in hands, all of you start drawing on the hard-surfaced area. Move as you draw and draw as you move. Make lines and areas, and make them big and flowing. Move together and draw together. Draw on each other. Celebrate together that we can be alive together when we are each ourselves. Enjoy.

CHAPTER 23

ANGER AND
THE ROCKING CHAIR*

Janet Lederman

> I sit in my rocking chair.
> I see you.
> Children with muscles taut;
> bodies rigid;
> frowns;
> clenched fists.
> I see your anger.
> I sit in my rocking chair.
> I am open,
> flexible, moving,
> strong.
> I am comfortable and supportive.
> I can be used by you.
> I sit in my rocking chair.

You can yell at this rocking chair. You can kick it. Soon some of you will yell at me; some of you will kick me; some of you will bite me or will hit me. I will spank you. I may even wrestle with you. Then, little child, you will put up such a fight! You will fight with every bit of anger you have, and I will fight you back. Our bodies will touch. You will experience my strength. You will be in touch with my willingness to be in touch with your anger. I am not afraid of your reality. You will try to get away. I may even have to sit on you and then you will let your tears flow . . . a "bully," beginning to melt into childhood. Your taut muscles

---

*This chapter has been expanded into a book of the same title, published by McGraw-Hill, 1969. The classroom I describe is for children who could not be maintained in a "normal" classroom situation. Their ages range from six to ten years old. Each has some behavioral problem. The school, a regular elementary school, is in the heart of an urban poverty area. Most of the children are members of minority groups.

begin to relax; your sobs begin to fade. I get off. I am not holding you down any more. If you want to go, I will not stop you now. You don't run away. You are quiet and we are side by side.

"What did you do, Mark?"
"I bit you."
"What did I do when you bit me?"
"You spanked me."

I take your hand. You let me. You do not pull away. Together we walk over to the rocking chair. You sit on my lap. We talk. We hug. I pet you. You feel good to me. You are a child. I am an adult. I give you a cloth to wipe the perspiration from your face.

"What do you want to do now, Mark?"
"I don't know."

"I have an idea. See if you like it." You are very quiet now. "You could sit in the rocking chair and just rock for awhile."

We get up. You climb back into the rocking chair. You put your thumb in your mouth and you rock.

A classroom of average size.

Tables and chairs scattered about.

Tables isolated against a wall.

"Maybe you want some time alone."

Rugs on which to sit. Rugs on which to lie.

Corners in which to put your shoes.

My rocking chair.

Games, puzzles, records, building tools, building blocks,
wood,
trucks,
easels and paint.

The walls are bare when first you come.

Here is a folder.

You may decorate it if you wish.

Then, pin it on the waiting wall.

There is your name for all to see.

You exist for me.

But how do you exist for you?

You say, *"I'll beat him up; then he'll know who I am."*
Anger.

Anger.

That is real for you.

But anger is not usually acceptable in school.

You play "bully."

You play "helpless."

You say,

>   *"I won't."*
>   *"I can't."*
>   *"You can't make me."*
>   *"You're not my mama."*

Steve, you walk in an hour late.

Norma, you won't talk.

You respond to "a school."

You respond to "a schoolroom."

You respond to "a teacher."

>   *"I won't."*
>   *"I can't."*

Each of you carries your own expectation. Each of you has his own image. Each of you tries to avoid what is happening "now."

Reggie you fling open the door, stomp in, look around, go over to Steven and you hit him.

"What are you doing, Reggie?"
>   *"Nothing."*
"What did you just do to Steven?"
>   *"Steven looked at me."*
"What did *you do* to Steven?"
>   *"Steven's a baby."*
"What did you do to Steven?"
>   *"Hit him."* (You are smiling slightly.)
"Yes, now put that into a sentence starting with the word, 'I'."
>   *"I hit Steven."* (Your slight smile is now a big smile.)

I have introduced you to the "now." I am also building your awareness, Reggie. I am trying to make you aware of what *you* are doing. I am trying to make you aware of your existence. I will continue with this process, for you will not accept awareness easily.

"What are you doing now, Reggie?"

>   *"Now I am hitting Norma."*
>   *"Now I am yelling at you."*

"Now I am learning to write."

"Now I am hugging you."

Reggie, I will try to make you aware of your existence every time you write a story or paint a picture. I will try to make you aware of your existence by having you look into a mirror. And, Reggie, I have a Poloroid camera ready when you do something you thought impossible.

"What are you doing now, Reggie?"

"Sawing a piece of wood for my boat."

"Who is sawing the wood?"

"I am sawing a piece of wood for my boat."

"How are you working?"

"Quietly and not bothering anyone else."

"Who is working quietly and not bothering anyone else?"

"I am working quietly and not bothering anyone else."

"Have a piece of candy, Reggie."

Games and puzzles;

dolls and trucks scattered about the room.

Pencils on the floor . . . spilled paint.

"I want to write. I can't find a stupid pencil."

"I want to paint. I can't find a fucking brush."

"Give me a pencil."

"Find me a brush."

"Buy some new puzzles."

"Get some new trucks."

"Buy me . . ."

"Give me . . ."

"Fuck you—this is a fucking room."

"I am going to steal a ball from another room."

I am not here to "pick up" after you. I am not here to take care of the tools you use, or the games you enjoy. If I "pick up" after you, you will not experience the frustration of missing parts and broken toys. If I take care of your things, you will have no way of discovering how to care for your equipment. I will do nothing for you that you are capable of doing for yourself.

We gather at the rocking chair. There you encounter the toys, games, and equipment. You encounter the room. You explore and discover new ways of responding to school.

After repeated frustration and repeated work together, you begin to say,

> *"I'm going to clean up now."*
> *"Don't let Troy play with the games—he breaks everything."*

Children, you live in a chaotic world. Your world can expand beyond your chaos. The first step in this process is for you to touch your chaos. You must touch your chaos; you must live through your chaotic experiences in the classroom. You must not avoid these experiences. So often the superstructure of school does not permit this kind of contact. Here and now you are free; you are free to come into contact with your chaos.

> "Rearrange the room."
> Moving furniture
> Tables pushed . . . pulled.
> Chairs sliding across the room.
> Noise mounting.
> I watch.
> Random movement.
> An hour passes . . . no order, no direction.
> Random motion.
> The motion slows.
> The furniture still chaotic.
> You are walking, moving, no direction.
> No direction.
> No order.
> Soon you avoid touching the furniture.
> Soon you avoid looking at each other.
> Random contact.
> Noise.

> *"This room looks dumb."*
> *"I don't want to be in this room."*

> Silent room.
> Children, you begin to look at me.
> You are beginning to touch your immobility.
> You are beginning to be in touch with your need for help.
> I wait.

I will not respond to you until you make an explicit demand for my help.

Soon you say,

> *"I don't know what to do."*
>
> *"Where can I put this table?"*

I suggest that you put four tables in the center of the room.

You want help—you accept help.

The movement takes on direction.

In the process of doing, you discover that you have ideas of your own. As the semester continues, you learn to suggest changes periodically. You try various arrangements. You begin to get in touch with "change."

You are children, children who still need your mothers. You protect your mothers.

> *"Nobody calls my mother a name."*

Troy, you walk into the room, you look at me, and you yell,

> *"You don't do anything right, you black bitch!"*

We all gather in a circle at the rocking chair. I start talking about getting angry at the people with whom we live.

"How do some of the people you live with make you angry?"

> *"My brother tears my books."*
>
> *"My father whips me."*

Soon, Troy, you say,

> *"My mother didn't cook my hamburger enough."*

I ask you to come sit next to me. You walk over and sit down. You have a frown on your face. There is an empty chair in front of you.

"Troy, pretend your mother is sitting in that empty chair in front of you. Tell her what you are angry about. You may say anything you want to say, since she is not really here."

Troy, you begin, *"Mama, you know this meat is raw. I hate raw meat."*

"Troy, sit in the other chair and pretend to be your mother. What does she say?"

> *"I didn't know it was raw."*

"Now be Troy again."

> *"Mama, you don't do anything right!"*

"Now be your mother."

> *"I wash your clothes, I iron your shirts so you'll look good for school."*

"Now be Troy again."

"I know. But I can't eat this hamburger. I'm going to throw it away and make another one."

You continue with this dialogue. You tell your mother what you resent and also you tell her what you appreciate. Your mother is not destroyed. Next, you begin to expand your world; instead of throwing the hamburger away, you discover other "possible" solutions for the situation.

"Troy, look at the children in the room; look at me. What do you see? Is there anyone here you are angry with?"

You look around the room, you smile, you become somewhat shy. You are aware of yourself; you are aware of others. Your anger is finished. You can see us.

Troy answers, *"No, I'm not mad at anybody. Can I take the ball out at recess?"*

Patrick, you run into the room yelling,

"She took away our ball. That Mrs. Brown is a bitch. I didn't do anything."

I suggest you come up to the chair next to me; put Mrs. Brown in the empty chair, and tell her what you are angry about. When you start to play the "blaming game," I suggest you bring the situation into the "now" and have an encounter with whomever you are blaming. Depending on what you can accept, I either stop you with the awareness of both sides of the situation, or you go on to explore other possible ways of behavior that may be more appropriate to the situation.

"I won't!"

"I can't!"

"I don't want to read that dumb book!"

Books are of little value to you as they do not relate to your present world.

"I hate my fucking sister. She beat me up!"

You have just told an explicit story with words that have explicit meaning for you. I suggest that you write your story.

"I don't know how to spell the words."

I write the words on a separate piece of paper and you write them on your paper. I give you the words as you ask for them. This is also proof that I am listening to you. If you are ready, the same story can be expanded into fantasy. You may find other emotions available to you. As a result, your real world may expand.

"What would you like to do to your sister?"

"I can't do anything. She is bigger than I am."

"She is not here and this is just pretend. Tell her what you would like to do to her."

"I'd like to hit you."

"What else would you like to do?"

"I'd like to kick you."

"What else?"

"That's all, I'm finished."

Now you begin to write your story. You are full of energy. You are completing unfinished business.

You read your story back to me. You can now read it to anyone you choose. You pin your story on the wall. You put it above your name. Your emotions exist and you are acceptable. You are real and you are real to others. You have made another contact with your expanding world.

The above is a process, not a task, in which reading and writing become an integral and creative way for you to relate to your world. The process deals with *your* fears, your fantasies, your various personae, your mother, father, siblings, cousins, teachers, and neighbors and not with "Dick and Jane and the Fireman," who are nothing to you.

"I won't."

"I can't!"

"Maybe I can."

The name of this game is "Get the Middle-Class Teacher's Goat!" You wait for the room to be very quiet. You begin to sing when you see another child who you imagine will sing along with you. It is even better if there are two or three who seem to be possible joiners. You select a very special song.

"I have a girl from Culver City,
She's got meat balls on her titties.
She's got ham and eggs
Between her legs . . ."

I listen. You repeat your song.

"I like the way you boys sing. Come over to the tape recorder." We all walk over to the tape recorder. I suggest you sing your song into the tape recorder. Your eyes are getting very big.

"Oh no! You're going to take it to the principal."

"I like the way you sing. You can erase it when we are finished." You begin to giggle. You are willing to take the risk. The tape recorder

intrigues you. You begin to sing. I play the tape right back. You listen.
You laugh.

"My voice sounds funny."
"That's no good. You could hear us laughing."
"Let's do it again."

You sing again. This time there is more concern with the sound and
the rhythm. You listen again. You are beginning to like your voices. You
begin to improvise; you pick up something to drum. We have another
taping session.

"Hey, I know a better song."

You rearrange your positions for greater quality. Your rhythm is
becoming more complex. You listen again.

"Hey man, I sound good."
"Hey, we could go on TV."
"Hey, could we sing for the school?"

The game is over. Each of you has discovered another part of yourself. Another way to relate to your world. I have not fulfilled your expectations of anger, shock, and punishment. I avoided a frontal attack on
"Meatballs and titties."

"I can sing."
"I can listen to me."
"Listen to me."
"Look at me."
"I can stay in school all day."
"I can read."
"I can."
"I am."

Your world is expanding. You begin to see other rooms. They seem
available for you.

"I want to go to Miss Oshrin's room."
"Go ask Miss Oshrin if you can visit her room today."
"You ask her."
"I don't want to go to Miss Oshrin's room."
"OK. Then write me a note."
"You don't need a note from me. You go ask *her* for a note saying
it is all right for you to visit today."
"I am afraid to go ask her."

"Then stay here." I walk away.

   "I'm going to Miss Oshrin's room." Smiling, you leave the room.
You are willing to take a risk. You visit, you stay for a short while. *You*
know when you are ready to come back. You try other rooms. You come
back. You are very selective. You begin to explore more and more. I
begin to accommodate your needs less and less. You are beginning to
get in touch with boredom here in this room. You know a little about
what is available to you in other situations. Your exploration continues.
You begin to feel your strengths. You have successes. You experience
failure, you are able to accept some failure now. *You* are not a failure.
You discover more of the school world.

   "Look at the story I wrote in Miss Carney's room today."
   "I did spelling in Miss Cutler's room."
   "Mr. Cardinal says I have to read this book before I can build
a boat in his room. Help me learn to read it."

Dancing, moving.
You have fun being animals sleeping

                     finding food
                     fighting.
You have fun discovering the ways in which your body can move;
       human fingers move this way,
       paws move that way.
You have fun being snakes and lizards sliding and slipping.
You have fun being birds and making your arms into wings.
I watch you when you are tigers and listen to your roars.
I hear you pounding drums.
I see you plucking the strings of a guitar;
You use your left hand, then your right.
You use your hand, your head, your foot to make a balloon go across
       the room.
I hear your laughter as you run with your kite.
I hear you scream with delight.
Feather dusters moved by your hands to your own rhythms, inside
       and out.
You run to me and give me a hug.
I see you.
I feel you, we touch each other's worlds.

CHAPTER 24

STAFF TRAINING FOR A DAY-CARE CENTER*

Katherine Ennis and Sandra Mitchell

> *So shall we*
> *sit upon our lovely hands?*
> *Or shall we reach*
> *and touch, and speak across*
> *the long fields?*
> E.I. Van Buren

We believe that a good day-care center is alive; that it vibrates with noise, feelings, and curiosity; that it offers an opportunity for growth and learning; and that it enriches the lives of the children who attend and of the adults who care for them. Unlike a kindergarten or a nursery school, which operate for a few hours in the morning and/or afternoon, our center is open from 7:00 A.M. until 12:00 midnight, seven days a week, and each child is with us about nine hours a day. We believe that much that happens with that child during those nine hours is directly related to the growing edge of the adults who care for him and to the relationships between those adults.

About a year ago, as we looked at the relationship between ourselves and other staff members and at the way they were relating with each other and with the children, we saw much behavior that, if not actually destructive, certainly was not growth facilitating. We saw our difficulties in accepting the limitations of staff members and our reluctance in expressing anger toward them. We saw them sulking when their feelings were hurt, gossiping about each other, displacing their angry feelings into the children, and competing for the children's affection. In many instances, we were all relating with the children and with each other from

---

*The St. Joseph Infirmary Day Care Center provides care for the children of women employees of the hospital. The Center is licensed by the Georgia Department of Family and Children Services to care for fifty children during each of two hospital shifts. The children range in age from six weeks to six years. The staff is comprised of a director, a program director, twelve teachers, and a housekeeping aide.

introjected *shoulds* rather than from a realistic acceptance of ourselves or the children.

As the directors, we felt frustrated. We had tried involving the rest of the staff in program planning for the children and in decisions about equipment purchases for their rooms. We had encouraged them to take additional day-care vocational courses to increase their understanding of children's growth and development, and we had made specific reading requirements in areas where we felt they needed more knowledge. We had observed their growth in many ways, but the area which we felt was most important—that of relationships—seemed relatively unchanged.

We had to accept the fact that "learning" was not going to solve our communications problems. The clue seemed to lie in staff members' having the opportunity to experience the kind of open, honest communication that we had seen occur in Gestalt groups and in Art and Movement Workshops devoted primarily to nonverbal communications process. Our staff members have varied cultural, educational, and experiential backgrounds, and we realized that the help of a professional therapist was needed to provide opportunities to effect significant changes in our interactions as a staff. We realized also that each staff member would have to recognize a need for better communication, be willing to risk change, and understand the importance of professional help to facilitate that changing. We told them our concern about the center and the kinds of behavior we saw. We also shared with them our excitement about the growth that had occurred with us individually and in our relationship with each other as a result of our experiences with direct verbal and nonverbal communication in Gestalt workshops. We let them know of our belief that similar experiences with them might improve and clarify our relationships as a staff. We acknowledged our limitations—the relative newness of our own growth and our lack of experience in leading a group—and explained our need for professional help. We found that they shared many of our dissatisfactions, felt the need for change, and were willing to try working with a consultant. Following this meeting, we asked the hospital administration for financial assistance to help us secure the services of a psychologist for consultation. Our request for six visits was made with the understanding that the administration would pay approximately two-thirds of the consultant's fee, and that we, as a staff, would pay approximately one-third.

Our experiences with the rest of the staff in the above decision-making process had brought us all closer together. We had been honest with them about our concern for the center and about our helplessness in making any change without their involvement. We felt they had responded honestly and were willing to take some new interpersonal risks. Since we knew that it would take time to implement our request for funds, we asked ourselves how we could encourage more of the openness we had just experienced with them. The experiences we had assimilated during and as a result of the Gestalt groups we had attended provided the answer.

We shared a belief in the tenets of Gestalt therapy and the conviction that these tenets were not confined to the therapeutic encounter. We began slowly to try some of the techniques that seemed especially relevant to us. In staff meetings, in individual conferences, and in our daily encounters, we struggled to come across straight with them and encouraged them to do the same with us, with each other, and with the children. As we met with them, we tried to "stay in the here and now" and began to try the "How do you feel?" and "What's going on now?" kinds of questions instead of "What do you think?" or "Why?" We did not introduce any of the nonverbal art and movement techniques at this time because we were not sure we could handle the depth of feeling they might evoke. We continued working on our relationship with each other and took advantage of every workshop, marathon, institute, short course, and lecture that was offered to enrich our individual growth. We were striving for congruence in our own lives, and we wanted to have the kind of center that would nourish in others the capacity to experience intellectually, emotionally, and sensorially.

In the months that followed, we found that our Gestalt-oriented approach did break down some of the communications barriers we had been experiencing with the rest of the staff. They were being more honest, but they still had trouble expressing many of their feelings directly, and we, although somewhat more free, were not as honest or as spontaneous with them as we wanted to be. Frequently, we could see some of the projections and defensive maneuvers that were going on, but we did not have the knowledge or experience to help them or ourselves solve these deeper conflicts. We felt keenly our need for professional guidance and were anxious for the administrative *yes* that would make it possible.

The excitement we all felt when we finally received approval for a consultant was accompanied by a sense of relief. The therapist chosen was a clinical psychologist who was essentially existential in his therapeutic orientation. He had evolved his own style of therapy and moved comfortably between the approaches of Gestalt therapy, transactional analysis, and theme-centered therapy. He had worked with children, adults, families, and groups—and in addition, he had some experience as a consultant for a day-care center.

On the day of our first session, all of us were excited and/or scared. Our consultant began by making a "contract" with each of us for the first meeting. These contracts involved our stating one thing that we wanted from that meeting for ourselves (for example, better understanding of a co-worker, the opportunity to deal with unresolved conflicts and/or unexpressed feelings) and his agreeing to help us get it. "Getting something for ourselves" remained the theme of our first six sessions. We now had a time when we could explore the feelings that made us uncomfortable, clarify our communications, and risk new ways of relating. Our consultant gave us his support and knowledge as we struggled to express our anger, hurt, tenderness, and love. He also had the courage to shatter our fantasies and to confront us with our manipulations and projections. We discovered that growth is sometimes painful, sometimes joyful, and always rewarding.

Our sixth session was devoted to saying good-by to our experiences with each other during the past five sessions and deciding whether we would continue meeting. Saying "good-by" made us aware of how much we had gotten for ourselves. It also made us aware that we wanted more of these experiences together. We knew that we would have to submit an evaluation of these sessions to the hospital administration along with a request for additional funds if we were to continue meeting. However, we did not want to stop meeting while our request was being processed, so we decided to pay the entire fee ourselves until we received a reply from the administration or until we decided we wanted to stop.

We met three times over a period of six weeks before our request for twelve additional sessions was granted. After our request was approved, we proceeded in basically the same manner as in our initial meetings. We continued our confrontations with each other—we examined experientially our modes of relating and the defenses we used to keep from relating. There were times when a seeming lack of involvement during our meetings led us to question the value of our continuing. Simply raising the question seemed to help us reevaluate what we did want. It also made us aware that we were taking risks with each other daily that in the beginning we could take only in the safety of the sessions. Each time we questioned the value of our meetings, we decided to continue.

At approximately the same time that our consultant started coming to the center, we began leading the teachers in the art-and-movement experiences we had been reluctant to risk without the support of a therapist. These once-a-week sessions were designed to help them "lose their minds and come to their senses." They had opportunities to become more aware of their bodies by localizing sensations in the various parts and by becoming more aware of breathing, muscular tensions, and posture. Touching, lifting, and holding provided opportunities to experience interacting with each other on a bodily level. Blindfold walks allowed them to examine their ability to trust each other and to experience their other senses. The directed fantasies of creative-imagery games helped them to restore the balance between imagination and reality. They used various art media, such as clay, chalk, and paint, to explore and communicate their feelings in an unstructured manner. At the completion of each of these experiences, we encouraged them to talk about what they had been aware of during the experience and what they were aware of then.

At the time of writing, we have met with our consultant for ten of our twelve sessions, and we have continued leading the art-and-movement experiences. We have found that our verbal group encounters and the art-and-movement experiences are complementary. Used together, they have facilitated our growth as a staff more effectively than either experience would have if used alone. The following comments from the other staff members support our perceptions of the growth that is occurring:

> I feel very good about myself . . . I feel that I am human . . . I feel more alive.

> I have a great struggle in saying what's on my mind . . . I want to tell a person off so bad I cry on the inside . . . with [the consultant's] help, I have learned to deal with this much better . . . the center is now a place I am proud of . . . When I watch some of the older children that were once infants which I [cared for], I find that I am very pleased with myself.

> I had difficulty showing my true feelings with [the rest of the staff] . . . Especially angry feelings and tenderness . . . After only two of the sessions, I was beginning to express my true feelings . . . We began to work more as a team . . . [As a result of the art-and-movement sessions] I became very aware of my body and senses, and the bodies and senses of my fellow staff members. They suddenly came alive for me—three-dimensional, flesh-and-blood human beings—people with whom I could laugh, love, argue, and cry . . . I began to burst the bonds which made me a prisoner within myself . . . I have begun to find new ways of doing things.

> Children are children and not adults and that they should be treated with all the understanding and kindness that one has . . . I wish that everyone could see and feel what we are doing.

> [The consultant] has helped me to understand myself . . . I feel better about the center and about myself.

> I feel that I belong here.

> I feel his continued services will mean a great deal to the staff.

We have made gains in many other areas. As we look at the relationships in the center now, we are aware that we are all being more direct. We hear these questions: "How do you feel about that?" "What's happening?" "What do you mean?" or we hear: "That makes me mad." "If you want something from me, ask me directly. I can't read your mind." "I like you." "I appreciate your saying that to me." We are all more openly affectionate with each other and with the children. We see the teachers encouraging the children to be aware of their bodies by calling attention to their breathing, or the way they are sitting, or how their skin feels. We see them helping the children to become aware of their feelings by acknowledging their anger, hurt, loneliness, or joy. We see them encouraging the children's creativity by providing unstructured art experiences, by listening to them attentively, and by valuing them as unique individuals. We have moved somewhat closer to our goal of having a center that will nourish in the children who come and in the adults who care for them the capacity to experience and develop their intellectual, emotional, and sensory capacities.

CHAPTER 25

DECEPTION, DECISION-MAKING, AND GESTALT THERAPY *

Bruce Denner

Recent work (Denner, 1967; Levy, 1967; Rettig & Sinha, 1966) provides evidence that, with very little coaxing, the college student can be led into practicing bad faith. Of particular interest to us has been the deception involved in the failure to report a criminal breakdown in the social order. In another paper Denner (in press) explored individual differences in the relationship between cognitive-perceptual style and response to a disconcerting, unexpected event we've explored. This study found that students who report seeing relatively less autokinetic movement, and who also require relatively more tachistoscopic presentations of an ambiguous visual stimulus before identifying it, are relatively more reluctant to report that they had observed someone acting as if he had taken something from a lady's handbag. [Results of this same study provide evidence that these two classificatory variables are not highly correlated $(r = .03)$].

An understanding of this finding rests on the analysis of the autokinetic and tachistoscopic tasks. It has been argued that a subject's perception of autokinetic movement is facilitated by his willingness to report his immediate experience without regard for the distinction between real and unreal (Gardner, Holtzman, Klein, Linton, & Spence, 1959). It seems reasonable to assume that an individual who requires relatively more stimulus input before committing himself to a perceptual judgment has a relatively high need for information. Therefore we concluded that individual differences in reluctance to report a possible crime are related to need for information and preoccupation with the distinction between the real and the unreal.

Of course, interpretation of these two variables may be questioned.

---

*Reprinted with permission of the author and the American Psychological Association from the *Journal of Clinical and Consulting Psychology*, 1968, *32*, 527-531.

But the postexperimental reports of "reluctant" witnesses, especially their preoccupation with "reality" and their refusal to act because of insufficient information, suggests that the analysis is sound.

This study sought to provide more data to support the general notion that reluctant and unreluctant witnesses differ in their cognitive-perceptual orientation. Some of the categories developed within the Gestalt theory of therapy (Perls, Hefferline, & Goodman, 1951) seemed to provide a basis for understanding the predicament of a witness who must respond in a context of minimal information where events are disconcertingly unexpected. (Perls et al. discuss at length what is involved in failing to respond adequately to what is happening in one's environment. They point out that some people tend to become lost in abstractions, and hence may be peculiarly out of touch with the concrete objects and events in their world.)

Gestalt therapists demonstrate loss of contact with the environment by means of brief exercises that require examination of aspects of an individual's behavior and his world that he rarely examines closely. Assuming that these exercises (or, as called by the Gestaltists, experiments) discriminate between those who are in contact and those who are not, reluctant witnesses should respond differently than unreluctant ones. Thus, students with a low need for information and low concern for the real-unreal distinction (unreluctant witnesses) were compared with students with a relatively high need for information and high concern for the real-unreal distinction (reluctant witnesses) with regard to their performance on some modified versions of Gestalt therapy exercises. The exercises required verbal responses to questions and commands that both catch the listener by surprise and make unusual demands to report things as they are and as they might be. It was conjectured that if the reluctant witness, in contrast to the unreluctant witness, was more unresponsive to the unexpected demand to report current and/or possible experiences, then his failure should be revealed both in the temporal and semantic aspects of his verbal response.

The reluctant witness has been depicted as an individual who delays and encounters difficulty in reporting his experiences. Thus it was hypothesized that a group of individuals with a relatively high need for information and a high concern with the real-unreal distinction would reveal a pattern of longer reaction times to, and higher rates of hesitation pauses in, the Gestalt exercises. Moreover, they should also reveal their reluctance to respond in the evasiveness and digressiveness of their response. Finally, since it has been argued that the reluctant witness is in less contact with his objects—internal as well as external—the content of his report should be relatively less immediate and concrete.

METHOD

Subject Selection

A test of need for information and a test of concern with the distinction between the real and unreal (described in detail in Denner, in press) were administered to 63 undergraduates at Indiana University who participated in the study as part of their introductory course requirements.

The need-for-information task involved the tachistoscopic presentation of a string of nonsense words, namely, "A haky deebs reciled the dison tofently um flutest pav," at a presentation rate known to make detection very difficult. The subject was instructed to "look at the card and report what you see," but told nothing else about how accurate his report need be. He was permitted to see the card as many times as he chose before making his report. Hence, the number of presentations requested is a measure of his need for information. The subject's concern with the distinction between the real and unreal was tested by measuring the amount of autokinetic motion reported over a two-minute period under standard observing conditions.

From this subject pool two experimental groups ($N = 10$) were formed and invited back for a second session during which the Gestalt therapy exercises were administered. The subjects were chosen as either having low need for information and low concern for the real-unreal distinction (Group I, Unreluctant Witness, seven females and three males) or having high need for information and high concern for the real-unreal distinction (Group II, Reluctant Witness, six females and four males). The groups were categorized by the use of approximately the same cutoff points of a frequency distribution of scores on the two tasks obtained in an earlier study (Denner, in press). Group I had a mean tachistoscope score of 11.3 trials (SD = 6.2 trials) and a mean autokinetic score of 102.2 seconds (SD = 12.6 seconds); Group II had a mean tachistoscope score of 147.2 trials (SD = 21.8 trials) and autokinetic score of 44.7 seconds (SD = 25.8 seconds).

Procedure

The subjects who participated came to the laboratory on two separate occasions. During the first session, the two perceptual-judgment criteria tasks were administered; the second session was devoted to the Gestalt therapy exercises. The experimenter asked the subject to sit down in a comfortable chair on one side of a rectangular table that was partitioned in half by a piece of cardboard. When seated, experimenter and subject could not see each other. The subject could observe the cardboard and the small opening through which the experimenter could slip a 5"x 8" card.

Except for the microphone, there was nothing to be seen in the room or on the walls. The following instructions were read:

> Today I am going to ask you to answer some questions about yourself and the world you live in. The questions are written on a 5"x 8" card. When we are ready to begin, the card will be slipped through the opening in front of you. You should answer as quickly as you can but answer in your own way. Of course, right and wrong does not apply here. You are free to deal with the question any way you want to. Make your answer long or short, but be sure to tell me when you have finished. Again, respond as quickly as you can, respond naturally and freely, and please don't try to figure out what I want you to say. It is all up to you but try to answer as quickly as you can.

The entire session was tape recorded. The subject was aware that a tape was being made of the session. Before the first session he was informed that at some time during the study he might be asked questions about himself and that his response, although kept strictly confidential, would be taped. None of the subjects objected to the procedure or decided not to participate in the study.

The following set of question-commands were given one at a time to every subject.

1. Think of the opposite. What if you were a man instead of a woman or vice versa? Tell me about it.
2. Notice one of your daily habits, for example, the way you eat. Suggest some alternative ways of going about it.
3. How do your friends differ from your enemies? Tell me.
4. If you were to die at this moment, what would happen?
5. Pay attention to your body. What do you feel inside? Describe it.
6. Pay attention to a visual object, namely, this ashtray. Describe the object. What do you see?
7. Make up sentences stating what you are aware of at this moment.
8. Select some memory which is not too distant or difficult. Recall the experience out loud.

As the experimenter placed each card in front of the subject (note that for Exercise 6 an ashtray was put through the opening along with the card), he said, "Here is card number 3." In this manner one could determine from the tape which card was before the subject and how long it was before he responded. Finally, in order to randomize the order of presentation of the deck of cards, they were shuffled before every subject.

RESULTS

Two temporal aspects of the verbal response were studied, namely, reaction time and hesitation-pause time.

Reaction time for each question-command was measured by the duration of time that elapsed between the last word spoken by the experimenter (the card number) and the first word spoken by the subject. It is to be noted that the first word articulated by the subject was considered the beginning of the response—extralinguistic utterances were not considered to be legitimate beginnings of a verbal response. Analysis of variance (2 [Groups I & II] x 8 [cards] with cards within subjects), of these scores indicated a significant effect only for groups (F = 6.6; df = 1/18; $p < .01$). Inspection of the means in Table 1 reveals that Group I (10.46 seconds) responded more quickly than Group II (17.91 seconds).

TABLE 1

Comparison of Group I and Group II with Regard to the
Temporal and Semantic Aspects of Their Response to
the Gestalt Exercises

CATEGORIES	GROUP I	GROUP II
Reaction time Mean seconds	10.46	17.91*
Hesitation-pause time Mean seconds	.096	.203*
Evasiveness score (1 = least, 10 = most) Mean score	5.6	7.8**
Concreteness score Mean rank (N = 20)	15.4	5.6**

Note.—Group I = Low need for information, unconcerned about reality.
Group II = High need for information, concerned about reality.
*$p < .05$.
**$p < .01$.

Hesitation pausing was defined, to distinguish it from pausing in general, as interruptions in the flow of speech that lasted three seconds or longer. Pauses of this duration are generally considered more indicative of cognitive blocking or internal planning than of breathing pauses between words or sentences (Goldman-Eisler, 1961; Lounsbury, 1954). For each subject total response pauses of more than three seconds were noted, and their duration summed. But because total responses varied in length from question to question and from subject to subject, it was deemed necessary to divide the total pausing time by the total response time. Thus, the hesitation-pause-time score takes into account the number of hesitations and the duration of the response. Analysis of variance (2 [Groups I & II] x 8 [cards]) of these scores yielded only a significant main effect for the group ($F = 4.8$, $df = 1/18$; $p < .05$). Group I obtained a lower hesitation-pause score than Group II—.096 seconds versus .203 seconds (see Table 1).

The semantic properties of the verbal response were examined in the light of two categories: evasiveness and concreteness. (Coders judging the responses used a set of typical responses and criteria specified for each card as a standard. These can be obtained from the author.)

Evasiveness. A response was considered to be evasive if the question or command was avoided either through direct refusal to respond appropriately or through digression. To evaluate the responses, each one was printed on a 5" x 8" card and randomly presented to three coders unfamiliar with the purpose of the study. Their task was to assign a score from 1 to 9, with 1 representing a complete refusal to respond and 9 an entirely nonevasive answer.

Two questions were asked here: Were the three coders in general agreement about the evasiveness of each response? How did the two groups fare with regard to this measure? A reliability analysis provided a positive answer to the first question—average $r = .93$. Evidence pertaining to the second question was obtained by computing a 3 (Coders 1, 2, & 3) x 2 (Groups I & II) x 8 (cards) analysis of variance with cards within subjects on the scores given by the coders. Whereas no significant main effect was found for coder or cards, there was, however, a significant main effect for groups ($F = 37.9$; $df = 1/36$; $p < .01$). The mean evasiveness scores in Table 1 indicate that Group I was judged less evasive (5.6) than Group II (7.8).

Concreteness. In general, a response was considered concrete if it made reference to objects or their properties in the here-and-now. Every response was judged to be either concrete or not concrete. In order for a response to be considered concrete, two judges unacquainted with the experimental hypothesis had to agree.

The number of concrete responses was totaled for each subject (maximum number = 9), and these concreteness scores were converted into ranks. The hypothesis that Group I's verbalization would be relatively more concrete than Group II's was evaluated by calculating a Kruskal-Wallis one-way analysis of variance by ranks ($H = 70.8$; $df = 1$; $p < .001$), and the mean ranks of both groups clearly indicate that Group I (15.4) was judged more concrete than Group II (5.6).

IMPLICATIONS

The results of this study can be summarized as follows: The inclination to delay identifying a stimulus under conditions of minimal exposure (conceptualized as need for information) and the tendency to vacillate in reporting autokinetic movement (understood as concern with the distinction between the real and unreal) are related to a particular style of responding to question-commands that require a report of one's experience. This style, *reluctant witnessing*, is characterized by (*a*) a relatively long reaction time, (*b*) relatively more frequent hesitation pauses, (*c*) evasiveness, and (*d*) lack of concreteness. Although observing a nondescript object such as an ashtray or reporting an innocuous experience from the past is a far cry from witnessing a criminal act, there is an interesting similarity in the reluctant witness's response to both situations. In both he avoids reporting things as they are. But also, especially in the context of the Gestalt exercises, he demonstrates a puzzling unwillingness to entertain changes in the status quo.

The occurrence of this phenomenon is undoubtedly dependent upon a number of cognitive operations. More likely than not, the more critical operations involve information-processing, judgment, and the linguistic encoding of experience that is a necessary condition for verbal expression. Although we concede that one may be interested in the experimental question of the independent role each operation plays in producing the effect—namely, a reluctance both to report the actual and to consider radical change—we are not convinced of the utility of dividing the total response into these categories. Perhaps our strongest objection to conceptualizing the response as part processes to be studied independently is that nowhere can we see perception without judgment and judgment without language.

Our persuasion is to consider the percept, the judgment, and the verbal statement as aspects of a decision-making process (Price, 1967) and hence to consider the differences in degrees of reluctance to report descriptively about one's actual and possible experiences as differences in decision-making. That is, the reluctant witness functions as if he decided to distance himself psychologically from experience and hence to avoid representation of his direct experience through delaying tactics and lack of concreteness.

Consequently, if he is essentially out of touch with current happenings, he can hardly be expected to entertain a radically different experience, for example, being a man instead of a woman. One word of caution, though: it is perhaps easy to misconstrue what has been argued here to mean that we are positing a "decision-maker" inside the head of the witness, which decided not to look at the immediate, ongoing events. Obviously, any description of behavior that invokes a "ghost in the machine

[Ryle, 1949]" creates more problems than it solves. Surely one can ask, who makes the decisions for the little decision-maker in one's mind? It is the person—not his mind—who has made and is making decisions and these decisions are revealed to others in the person's behavior, verbal or otherwise. Nor does it seem appropriate at this time to speculate about the level of awareness at which this decision is made. The importance of the decision lies in the orientation it produces and the consequences it has for behavior.

In the purse-snatching study one consequence is clear, namely, that positive action is paralyzed. From the viewpoint of Gestalt therapy, the observer remains a reluctant witness because his verbalizing does not terminate in action toward the objects in his external environment. Rather than acting upon physical objects, he tends to move names and words around. In his effort to achieve objectivity he loses contact with "the feeling, the drama, the actual situation." It is his detachment which makes him prone to deception. To the extent that the decision-maker becomes involved in the process of decision-making rather than in the ultimate effects of his decision-making, he may deceive others through failure to act. Paradoxically, he may be deeply concerned with deception while he practices bad faith. But as his performance on the Gestalt exercises suggests, the reluctant witness hesitates to verbalize what he is immediately aware of. Therefore, rather than acting and testing the situation, the reluctant witness may tend to suppress the experience and the questions associated with it.

Finally, deception viewed from this perspective must, as others have suggested (Mowrer, 1964), play some role in the origin and maintenance of behaviors socially judged to be psychopathological. Could the repeated failure to act when direct action is called for, coupled with the suppression that one has failed, produce a condition wherein the individual is plagued with vague feelings of uneasiness called anxiety? Moreover, assuming that a reluctant witness is in this condition, would he not likely become trapped in it? Being oriented toward delay, evasiveness, and lack of concreteness, the reluctant witness may represent his situation both to himself and to others in a manner which obscures or distorts the problem. In more traditional terms, he may appear perceptually defensive or repressed. Naturally, one may want to inquire into the motivational basis for the reluctant style. But motivational questions aside, it is clear how a certain orientation toward symbolizing experience—namely, evasiveness and lack of concreteness—can produce a state of anxious conservatism in which one is out of contact with what actually has happened or is happening but is reluctant to entertain change.

REFERENCES

Denner, B. Informers and their influence on the management of illicit information. Paper presented at the meeting of the Midwestern Psychological Association, Chicago, May 1967.

Denner, B. Did a crime occur? Should I inform anyone? A study in deception. *Journal of Personality*, in press.

Gardner, R., Holzman, P., Klein, P., Linton, G., & Spence, H. Cognitive control: A study of individual consistencies in cognitive behavior. *Psychological Issues*, 1959, *1*, (4).

Goldman-Eisler, F. A comparative study of two hesitation phenomena. *Language and Speech*, 1961, *4*, 18-26.

Levy, L. Awareness, learning, and the beneficent subject as expert witness. *Journal of Personality and Social Psychology*, 1967, *6*, 365-370.

Lounsbury, F. Pausal, juncture and hesitation phenomena. In C. Osgood & T. Sebeok (Eds.), *Psycholinguistics: A survey of theory and research problems*. Bloomington: Indiana University Press, 1965.

Mowrer, O. H. *The new group therapy*. New York: Van Nostrand, 1964.

Perls, F., Hefferline, R., & Goodman, P. *Gestalt therapy*. New York: Dell, 1951.

Price, R. Signal-detection methods in personality and perception. *Psychological Bulletin*, 1966, *66*, 55-62.

Rettig, S., & Sinha, J. Bad faith and ethical risk sensitivity. *Journal of Personality*, 1966, *34*, 275-286.

Ryle, G. *The concept of mind*. New York: Barnes & Noble, 1949.

CONTRIBUTORS

ARNOLD RAY BEISSER received his M.D. degree from Stanford University School of Medicine in 1949, and his Diplomate in Psychiatry from the American Board of Psychiatry and Neurology in 1958. He is currently director of the Center for Training in Community Psychiatry for the State of California Department of Mental Hygiene, and serves as associate clinical professor in the School of Medicine, Department of Psychiatry, U.C.L.A. Dr. Beisser received training in Gestalt therapy in workshops with Frederick S. Perls and James S. Simkin. He is the author of *The Madness in Sports* (Appleton-Century-Crofts), as well as numerous other articles in psychiatry and psychotherapy.

LOIS BRIEN is assistant professor of speech and communication in the Program in Speech Pathology and Audiology at Case Western Reserve University, and is a research associate at the Cleveland Hearing and Speech Center. She received her Ph.D. degree from the State University of Iowa and was a postdoctoral fellow at Western Reserve University. Dr. Brien is a consultant programmer for an N.I.H. Division of Dental Health grant, School of Dentistry, Case Western Reserve University. She is also associated with the Gestalt Institute of Cleveland.

HENRY T. CLOSE received his B.D. degree from Fuller Theological Seminary in 1955 and his Th.M. from Columbia Theological Seminary in 1962. He is currently a chaplain supervisor at the Georgia Mental Health Institute in Atlanta and a consultant in pastoral counseling to a private psychotherapy clinic. He has served as chaplain and pastoral counselor in both general hospital and state mental hospital settings.

RUTH C. COHN was educated in Berlin, and trained as a psychoanalyst at the Zurich Psychoanalytic Institute in Switzerland, moving to the United States with the spread of Nazism in Europe. In New York, she has worked as a therapist in private practice and as a training analyst, teaching courses for the Post Graduate Center for Psychotherapy. She has been active in the American Academy of Psychotherapists, serving as an officer and on the editorial board of the journal, *Voices*. She has

310

made numerous presentations and demonstrations of her approach at regional and national meetings and workshops. Her more recent work has been in experiential and Gestalt therapy, and she has developed the interactional theme-centered workshop approach for working with groups. She is the founder and director of the Workshop for Living-Learning in New York and works intensively in the training of group leaders and therapists. Mrs. Cohn has published a number of articles on psychotherapy.

BRUCE DENNER is assistant professor of psychology at Indiana University, where he is on the staff of the Psychological Clinic as therapist and supervisor of testing and therapy. He received his Ph.D. in psychology from Clark University in 1965. Dr. Denner's current research is in strategies in interpersonal relationships, deception, and response to emergency situations.

KATHERINE ENNIS is director of St. Joseph's Day Care Center in Atlanta, Georgia. Her undergraduate training was in psychology at Georgia State College. She has participated in a number of workshops at the Institute for Psychological Services, Inc., and Adanta in Atlanta. She is a member of the Child Development Advisory Board to the Vocational Education Division of the Atlanta public school system, day-care consultant to the Parent-Child Centers of Chattoga and Whitfield counties, and teaches courses in the Child Development Program of the Atlanta Area Technical School.

JOHN BURKE ENRIGHT received his Ph.D. in psychology from the University of California, Berkeley, in 1959. He has held positions as clinical psychologist at the Langley Porter Clinic in San Francisco and as assistant professor of medical psychology in residence for the Department of Psychiatry, School of Medicine, U.C.L.A. He is currently in private practice in Corte Madera, California. Dr. Enright is a Diplomate in Clinical Psychology of the American Board of Examiners in Professional Psychology. He has worked extensively with Gestalt training groups and has been active in the programs of Synanon.

JOEN FAGAN received her Ph.D. degree in psychology from the Pennsylvania State University. She is professor of psychology and director of clinical training at Georgia State College in Atlanta and is engaged in part-time private practice of psychotherapy. Dr. Fagan is a Diplomate of the American Board of Examiners in Professional Psychology, a member of the American Academy of Psychotherapists, and a member of the board of directors of Adanta. She has worked extensively in Gestalt therapy training workshops with Frederick S. Perls, James Simkin and others. Dr. Fagan's research interests are in innovations in psychotherapy, communication and interaction in families, and awareness training.

WALTER KEMPLER received his M.D. from the University of Texas in 1947 and completed his residency in psychiatry at U.C.L.A. in 1959. He is the founder-director of the Kempler Institute for Psychotherapy with Families and is in private practice in Los Angeles. In 1964, Dr. Kempler was coleader of the Gestalt training workshop for professionals at Esalen Institute (with Frederick Perls and James Simkin). His focus of professional interest and publication is in family therapy.

ELAINE KEPNER received her Ph.D. in psychology from Case Western Reserve University. She is currently an assistant professor in the Department of Psychology and project director of the Community Mental Health Training Program, Cleveland College, Case Western Reserve University. She is a member of the executive board of the Cleveland Institute for Gestalt Therapy and a psychotherapist in private practice.

JANET LEDERMAN's undergraduate education was in art and her graduate training in education. She has had extensive teaching experience in all elementary school grades, most recently in Los Angeles in classes for emotionally disturbed and culturally deprived children. There she began developing her own techniques of utilizing principles of Gestalt therapy working with ghetto children. She has conducted workshops and training programs with teachers in Los Angeles and at Esalen Institute, and is currently working with training programs in humanistic education. Miss Lederman is an artist and author of a book on her work with children, which has recently been published (1969) by McGraw-Hill.

ABRAHAM LEVITSKY received his Ph.D. in clinical psychology from the University of Michigan and has held teaching positions at Brooklyn College, the University of Michigan, and Washington University. He has been in private practice in St. Louis, Missouri, and San Francisco, his current residence. He has led workshops in Gestalt therapy at Esalen Institute and in San Francisco, and is currently on the board of directors of the San Francisco Gestalt Institute. He has served as vice-president of the American Society of Clinical Hypnosis and is associate editor of the *American Journal of Clinical Hypnosis*.

SANDRA MITCHELL has been involved in day care and early childhood education for twelve years, eight years as a teacher, two as program director for an E.O.A. center and, for the past two years, assistant director of St. Joseph's Hospital Day Care Center. She has studied psychology and education at Georgia State College and has attended training workshops in the Atlanta area. She is currently assisting with classes in awareness training for day-care workers in the Child Development Program of the Atlanta Area Technical School and with adult education groups at the Unitarian Universalist Church.

CLAUDIO BENJAMIN NARANJO received his M.D. from the University of Chile in 1958. He completed his residency in psychiatry at the Psychiatric Clinic, University of Chile, in 1961 and received training in psychoanalysis at the Chilean Institute of Psychoanalysis. From 1962 to 1967 he was a research psychiatrist at the Medical School of the University of Chile. During that period, Dr. Naranjo was Fulbright Visiting Scholar for the Department of Social Relations, Harvard University, and a Guggenheim Fellow for study in the psychology of values. He is currently a research associate at the Institute of Personality Assessment and Research, University of California, Berkeley, and on the staff of the San Francisco Gestalt Therapy Institute. Dr. Naranjo has led Gestalt workshops at Esalen Institute in Big Sur, California, and in San Francisco.

VINCENT FRANCIS O'CONNELL received his Ph.D. in psychology from Adelphi University in 1955 and his Diploma in clinical psychology from the American Board of Examiners in Professional Psychology in 1963. Dr. O'Connell was trained in Gestalt therapy by Frederick S. Perls in Columbus, Ohio, and at the New York Institute for Gestalt Therapy. He has held the positions of chief psychologist, Columbus Psychiatric Clinic, Columbus, Ohio; coordinator of psychological training, the Psychiatric Institute, Ohio State University; and senior staff psychologist, the Guidance Center, Inc., Daytona Beach, Florida. His current position is university psychologist of the Student Health Services, University of Florida. Dr. O'Connell is editor of the American Academy of Psychotherapists' *Newsletter*.

FREDERICK S. PERLS received his M.D. from Frederich Wilhelm University in Berlin, in 1921. He was trained in psychoanalysis at the Psychoanalytic institutes of Berlin, Frankfurt, and Vienna. He served as assistant to Kurt Goldstein in his work with brain-injured soldiers. He credits his contacts with Wertheimer, Tillich, Buber, Goldstein, and other theorists in the professional and academic circles of Germany of the twenties and thirties for inspiring the early development of Gestalt therapy. Forced to flee Germany with his wife, Laura, he worked in private practice in Amsterdam and later South Africa, where he became a training psychoanalyst and established the South Africa Institute for Psychoanalysis. In 1942 he published *Ego, Hunger and Aggression*, the first statement of the application of the principles of Gestalt psychology to personality development and psychotherapy. Four years later Dr. Perls and his family moved to the United States, where he worked in private practice in New York, Miami, Los Angeles, Cleveland, and San Francisco, and was psychiatrist in residence at Esalen Institute, Big Sur, California. He has founded or helped establish institutes for Gestalt therapy in New York, Cleveland, San Francisco, and Canada. He now resides at the Gestalt Institute of Canada, Vancouver, B.C.* He is author of *Gestalt Therapy* (with Hefferline and Goodman, 1951), *Gestalt Therapy Verbatim*, and *In and Out the Garbage Pail*.

LAURA PERLS received her Ph.D. in psychology at the University of Frankfurt, Germany, studying with Wertheimer, Gelb, and Goldstein. She received training in psychoanalysis at the psychoanalytic institutes of Frankfurt, Berlin, and Amsterdam. From this rich background she contributed to her husband's work in the development of Gestalt therapy, in Johannesburg, South Africa, and later in New York, where they founded the New York Institute for Gestalt Therapy in 1952. Dr. Perls's major work has been in integrating body-awareness training with psychoanalytic, Gestalt, and existential approaches. She is currently in private practice in New York and is involved in leading workshops and the training of therapists.

ERVING POLSTER received his Ph.D. in psychology from Western Reserve University in 1950. He has taught at the University of Iowa and at the Graduate School of Theology at Oberlin College, Oberlin, Ohio. A student and practitioner of Gestalt therapy since 1953, Dr. Polster is currently chairman of the postgraduate training faculty at the Gestalt Institute of Cleveland as well as a psychotherapist in private practice.

JANIE RHYNE received her B.A. in art and psychology from Florida State University and did graduate work at Alabama Polytechnic and the University of Heidelberg in Germany, receiving an M.A. in art and cultural anthropology from Florida State University. She studied and worked as an artist in Mexico, Spain, and Canada. She has received training with Dr. Frederick S. Perls and others in the field of Gestalt

---

*Dr. Perls died in 1970, before the third printing of this book.

therapy, and at present is co-director of art activities for the San Francisco Gestalt Therapy Institute, working as an art therapist with the institute and also privately. She has led art experience groups at Cowell Hospital, the University of California, Georgia State College, San Mateo College, and other institutes.

MARILYN B. ROSANES-BERRETT received her Ph.D. in psychology from Yeshiva University. She is a pshchologist for the Children's Center, Department of Welfare, New York City, and is on the staff of therapists for the Country Place, Warren, Connecticut. Since 1949, she has been involved in extensive research in visual perception and improvement of sight. Dr. Rosanes-Berrett is a member of the New York Institute for Gestalt Therapy.

IRMA LEE SHEPHERD received her Ph. D. in psychology from Pennsylvania State University and is a Diplomate in clinical psychology. She is currently professor of psychology and director of postgraduate training at the Institute for Psychological Services, Inc., Georgia State College in Atlanta, Georgia. In addition, she is engaged in part-time private practice of psychotherapy. She is a member of the executive council of the American Academy of Psychotherapists and of the board of directors of Adanta. Dr. Shepherd has been cotherapist in Gestalt training workshops with Frederick S. Perls and James S. Simkin.

JAMES S. SIMKIN has been coleader with Frederick S. Perls of Gestalt therapy training workshops for professional psychotherapists at the Esalen Institute during the past six years. His Ph.D. in clinical psychology was awarded by the University of Michigan in 1951. His postdoctoral training in Gestalt therapy was at the New York Institute of Gestalt Therapy from 1952 to 1955. He has taught at the University of Michigan, Rutgers University, California State College at Los Angeles, and U.C.L.A. Extension. He is a Diplomate in clinical psychology of the American Board of Examiners in Professional Psychology. He has been engaged in the private practice of psychotherapy for the past fourteen years, and is the director of the Los Angeles Institute for Gestalt Therapy.

RICHARD W. WALLEN died in 1968. Before his death, he was vice-president of the Personnel Research and Development Corporation of Cleveland, Ohio, and a member of the board of directors of the Cleveland Gestalt Institute.

BIBLIOGRAPHY OF WRITINGS IN GESTALT THERAPY

BOOKS

Lederman, J. *Anger and the rocking chair: Gestalt awareness with children.* New York: McGraw-Hill, 1969.
A prose poetry account of the use of Gestalt methods with disturbed children in elementary schools.

Perls, F. S. *Ego, hunger and aggression.* London: Allen &Unwin, 1947; New York: Random House, 1969.

Perls, F.S. *Gestalt Therapy Verbatim.* Lafayette, Calif.: Real People Press, 1969.
Perls gives an explanation of his recent thinking about Gestalt therapy, followed by transcripts of therapy sessions.

Perls, F. S., Hefferline, R.F., & Goodman, P. *Gestalt therapy.* New York: Julian Press, 1951. (Republished: New York, Dell, 1965.)
The basic writings in Gestalt therapy. Both books are difficult reading but contain the main theoretical structure, rationale, and many procedures of continuing application and value.

Pursglove, P. D. (Ed.) *Recognitions in Gestalt therapy.* New York: Funk & Wagnalls, 1968.
A collection of articles of historical interest and value, including a number of selections from the writings of Paul Goodman.

Shostrom, E. L. *Man, the manipulator.* Nashville: Abingdon Press, 1967. (Republished: New York, Bantam Books, 1968.)
A popularized discussion of methods of manipulation placed in a Gestalt therapy framework, with a number of therapy vignettes.

Simkin, J. S. (Ed.) *Festschrift for Fritz Perls.* Los Angeles: Author, 1968.
A collection of mimeographed articles, anecdotes, poems, and art contributed by friends, colleagues, and students in honor of Perls's seventy-fifth birthday.

MANUSCRIPTS IN PRESS AND IN PREPARATION

Kepner, E. *A primer of Gestalt therapy.*
Naranjo, C. I. *The attitude and practice of Gestalt therapy.*
Perls, F. S. *In and out of the garbage pail.*
Manuscript of autobiographical reminiscences.
Rhyne, J. *The Gestalt art experience.*
Wolfe, E.L. *Gestalt therapy and Zen Buddhism.*
Yontef, G. A review of the practice of Gestalt therapy. Doctoral dissertation, University of Arizona.

ARTICLES

Blumenstein, S. Sense and non-sense: The new Gestalt. Unpublished manuscript, Georgia State College, 1969.
Clements, C. C. Acting out versus acting through: an interview with Frederick Perls. *Voices*, 1969, *4* (14), 66-73.
Fagan, J. Gestalt therapy. Paper presented at the Southeastern Psychological Association, Atlanta, April, 1967.
Greenwald, J. A. Structural integration and Gestalt therapy. *Bulletin of Structural Integration,* 1969, *1*, 19-20.
Greenwald, J. A. An introduction to the philosophy & techniques of Gestalt therapy. *The Bulletin of Structural Integration*, 1969, *1*(3), 9-12.
Greenwald, J. A. The art of emotional nourishment: Self-induced nourishment and toxicity. Unpublished manuscript, Beverly Hills, California, 1969.
Greenwald, J. A. The art of emotional nourishment. *Voices*, in press.
Kempler, W. Experiential family therapy. *International Journal of Group Psychotherapy,* 1965, *15*, 57-71. Also in P. D. Pursglove (Ed.) *Recognitions in Gestalt therapy.* New York: Funk & Wagnalls, 1968.
Kempler, W. The experiential therapeutic encounter. *Psychotherapy: Theory, Research & Practice,* 1967,*4*, 166-172.
Naranjo, C. I. I and thou; contributions of Gestalt therapy. *Esalen Paper,* 1967, No. 5. Also in H. A. Otto & J. Mann (Eds.), *Ways of growth: approaches to expanding awareness psychiatry for laymen.* New York: Grossman, 1968.
Naranjo, C. I. The unfolding of man. Educational Policy Research Center, Stanford Research Institute, Palo Alto, California. Research Note EPRC-6747-3, 1969.

Nevis, E. C. Beyond mental health. Paper No. 2 (mimeo.), Gestalt Institute of Cleveland.*

O'Connell, V. F. Until the world become a human event. *Voices*, 1967, *3*, 75-80.

Perls, F. S. Theory and technique of personality integration. *American Journal of Psychotherapy*, 1948, *2*, 565-586.

Perls, F. S. Morality, ego-boundary, and aggression. *Complex*, 1953, *9*, 42-51.

Perls, F. S. Gestalt therapy and human potentialities. *Esalen Paper*, 1965, No. 1. Also in H. A. Otto (Ed.), *Explorations in human potentialities*. Springfield, Ill.: Charles C. Thomas, 1966.

Perls, F. S. Workshop vs. individual therapy. *Proceedings of the 74th Annual Convention of the American Psychological Association*. New York, 1966.

Perls, F. S. Group vs. individual therapy. *ETC.*, 1967, *24*, 303-312.

Perls, F. S., Hefferline, R. F., & Goodman, P. Gestalt psychotherapy. In W. S. Sahakian, *Psychotherapy and Counseling*. N.Y.: Rand McNally, 1969.

Perls, Laura. Notes on the psychology of give and take. *Complex*, 1953, *9*, 24-30. Also in P.D. Pursglove (Ed.), *Recognitions in Gestalt therapy*. New York: Funk & Wagnalls, 1968.

Perls, Laura. Two instances of Gestalt therapy. *Case Reports in Clinical Psychology*, Kings County Hospital, Brooklyn, New York, 1956. Also in P. D. Pursglove (Ed.), *Recognitions in Gestalt therapy*. New York: Funk & Wagnalls, 1968.

Polster, E. A contemporary psychotherapy. *Psychotherapy: Theory, Research & Practice*, 1966, *3*, 1-6. Also in P. D. Pursglove (Ed.), *Recognitions in Gestalt therapy*. New York: Funk & Wagnalls, 1968.

Polster, E. Trends in Gestalt therapy. Paper presented at the Ohio Psychiatric Association, Cincinnati, February, 1967. Also in Cleveland, Gestalt Institute of Cleveland, No. 11.*

Polster, E. The integrative effect of social psychotherapy. *Proceedings of the 75th Annual Convention of the American Psychological Association*, Washington, D.C., 1967.

Rhyne, J., & Vich, M. A. Psychological growth and the use of art materials: Small group experiments with adults. *Journal of Humanistic Psychology*, 1967, *1*, 163-170. Also in Sutich, A. J., & Vich, M. A. (Eds.), *Readings in humanistic psychology*. New York: Free Press, 1969.

---

*Available at $0.75 each, from the Gestalt Institute of Cleveland, 12921 Euclid Ave., Cleveland, Ohio 44112.

Roszek, T. The future as community. *Nation*, 1968, *206* (16), 497-503.

Simkin, J. S. An introduction to the theory of Gestalt therapy. Cleveland: Gestalt Institute of Cleveland, No. 6.*

Simkin, J. S. Innovations in Gestalt therapy techniques. Unpublished manuscript, 1968.

Strupp, H. H. Therapists' evaluations of two demonstration interviews. *Psychotherapy: Theory, Research & Practice*, 1968, *5*, 137-141.

Van Dusen, W. The theory and practice of existential analysis. *American Journal of Psychotherapy*, 1957, *11*, 310-322. Also in H. M. Ruitenbeek (Ed.), *Psychoanalysis and existential philosophy*. New York: Dutton, 1962.

Van Dusen, W. Existential analytic psychotherapy. *American Journal of Psychoanalysis*, 1960, *20*, 35-40. Also in P. D. Pursglove (Ed.), *Recognitions in Gestalt therapy*. New York: Funk & Wagnalls, 1968.

Zinker, J. C. Note on the phenomenology of the loving encounter. *Explorations*, 1966, *10*, 3-8.*

Zinker, J. C., & Fink, S. L. The possibility for psychological growth in a dying person. *Journal of General Psychology*, 1966, *74*, 185-199.*

*Available at $0.75 each, from the Gestalt Institute of Cleveland, 12921 Euclid Ave., Cleveland, Ohio 44112.

TAPES AND FILMS

TAPE RECORDINGS

American Academy of Psychotherapists tapes, available from A.A.P. Tape Library (Dr. Irwin Rothman, Director), 6420 City Line Avenue, Philadelphia, Pennsylvania 19151:

Perls, F. S. *Gestalt therapy seminar* (2 hrs., 10 min.). Three excerpts from a seminar with Dr. Perls and a group of therapists and students; a discussion of the Gestalt concept of projection and its reassimilation, work with dreams, and a complete dream sequence. A.A.P. Tape Library, No. 16, $10.00.

Sagan, G. *Gestalt expressive therapy* (45 min.). A woman whose presenting problem is inability to express and/or inhibit anger moves toward expressing herself freely. A.A.P. Tape Library, No. 18, $7.50.

Simkin, J. *Individual Gestalt therapy* (35 min.); *Interview with Dr. Frederick Perls* (50 min.). On track one, Dr. Simkin emphasizes the here and now, nonverbal communications, and use of fantasy dialogues. On track two, Dr. Simkin interviews Dr. Perls, who talks about the development of Gestalt therapy. A.A.P. Tape Library, No. 31, $5.00.

Esalen recordings, available from Big Sur Recordings, P.O. Box 6633, Carmel, California 93921:

Perls, F. S. *Dream theory* and demonstration (1 hr.). Esalen Recordings, S214-1, $7.50.

Perls, F. S. *Fritz Perls* reads portions of unpublished autobiography work-in-progress (1 hr.). Esalen Recordings, S215-1, $7.50.

Perls, F. S. *Fritz's circus* (9 hrs.). Demonstrations of Gestalt therapy; a complete weekend seminar. Esalen Recordings, 306-9, $67.50.

Perls, F. S. *Dream sessions* (4 hrs.). Confrontation and self-encounter. Esalen Recordings, 407-4, $30.00.

Perls, F. S. *More dream sessions* (4 hrs.). Confrontation and self-encounter. Esalen Recordings, S307-4, $30.00.

Perls, F. S. *Gestalt therapy lectures* (4 hrs.). Talks and demonstrations with Esalen staff. Esalen Recordings, 406-4, $30.00.

FILMS

Sessions in Gestalt therapy with Frederick S. Perls, on 16mm. film, available from the Mediasync Corporation, P.O. Box 486, Del Mar, California 92014:

Grief and pseudo-grief (33 min.). "Here, two cases of what Freud called the mourning labor are illustrated. One example masks resentment while the other patient, a young Israeli woman, resolves the remainder of her mother fixation and achieves a considerable step in growing up," says Dr. Perls of this film. "In addition, the first example is important because it demonstrates the utilization of humor to mobilize emotional involvement, while the second case illustrates the need for detail in order to empty out a symptom completely." Rental, $30; purchase, $185.

The birth of a composer (24 min.). Dr. Perls describes this session as a "very lively and beautiful film that shows the transition from self-defeat to creativity. The patient's achievement of authenticity is highly moving." Rental, $15; purchase, $80.

Demon (14 min.). In *Demon*, a patient moves to Dr. Perls's famous "hot seat" and externalizes the terrifying *dybbuk* (devil) that has been imprisoned within him. "This film," says Dr. Perls, "demonstrates the exorcism of the *dybbuk* of the patient's dreams through the expression of a murderous hate against his mother." Rental, $15; purchase, $130.

The impasse (22 min.). An excursion into the death layer of a young man, providing a clear example of the third (implosive) level of Dr. Perls's neurosis theory. Here, he places special emphasis on nonverbal communication. Rental, $25; purchase, $130.

Relentless greed and obesity (16 min.). While this session bears an unusual title, it provides a striking example of the second (role-playing) layer of neurosis as defined by Dr. Perls. Rental, $15; purchase, $80.

The death of Martha (40 min.). Produced in cooperation with television station KEBS, this film is a record of a portion of Dr. Perls's work with a small group of secondary school counselors from throughout the United States. He says *The Death of Martha* "is a case of a woman who is quite out of touch with her emotions. Based on a dream and a pseudocatatonic deadness, the work is a little slow in development but is closed by a final beginning of melting." Rental, $30; purchase, $200.

The case of Mary Kay (15 min.). Also part of Dr. Perls's work with the counselors, this session shows a young woman's journey from pseudophobia to authenticity while providing a simple illustration of the therapist's "empty chair" technique. Rental, $15; purchase, $80.

The treatment of stuttering (12 min.). Although this film was produced from a videotape and its technical quality is consequently mediocre, Dr. Perls has included it in this series because "this few minutes of therapy with a long-time stutterer is a dramatic example of the movement from the implosive to the explosive layer." Rental, $15; purchase, $75.

A session with college students (50 min.). Recorded in San Francisco during a televised workshop with six college students, this film demonstrates preliminary encounters with anxiety and offers three examples of noninterpretive dream work. Rental, $30; purchase, $200.

Fritz (14 min.). An impressionistic study of Frederick S. Perls in his home at Esalen Institute, Big Sur, California. Available from Sheil-Kama Productions, P.O. Box 926, Half Moon Bay, California 94019.

Films available from Psychological Films, 205 West Twentieth Street, Santa Ana, California 92706:

Three approaches to psychotherapy. A female patient is interviewed by three different therapists.

Film No. 1, Dr. Carl Rogers (48 min.). This includes a general introduction to the series, a description of client-centered therapy, an interview by Dr. Rogers with Gloria, and a summary of the effectiveness of the interview.

Film No. 2, Dr. Frederick Perls (32 min.). Included are a description of Gestalt therapy, an interview by Dr. Perls with Gloria, and a summary of the effectiveness of the interview.

Film No. 3, Dr. Albert Ellis (37 min.). This film consists of a description of rational-emotive therapy, an interview by Dr. Ellis with Gloria, a summary of the effectiveness of the interview, and an evaluation by the patient of her experiences with all three therapists.

Rental prices: Each film separately: color, $25; black & white, $15. All three films, one showing of the series: color, $50; black & white, $30.

Purchase prices: Single film: color, $350; black & white, $200. All three films: color, $950; black & white, $550.

A session with college students (1 hr.). Dr. Frederick Perls demonstrates his method for discovering and expressing the meaning of dreams of college students. Rental, $15; purchase, $200.

In the Now (45 min.). A training film of excerpts from a 10-hour workshop conducted by Dr. James Simkin. Three different people are shown, including a dream session, a situation involving the enactment of a recent event, and a current interaction, illustrating principles and techniques of Gestalt therapy. Rental, $25 per day; purchase, $185. Available from Dr. James S. Simkin, Suite 206, 337 South Beverly Drive, Beverly Hills, California 90212.

Family Therapy Sessions (30 to 60 min.) on 16mm. film are available from Kempler Foundation Film Library, The Kempler Institute, 6233 Wilshire Boulevard, Los Angeles, California 90048. A catalogue will be sent on request.

INDEX